WHAT IF?

Robert Cowley is the founding editor of *MHQ: The Quarterly Journal of Military History* – the award-winning magazine in the United States. He has worked in book and magazine publishing, and lives in New York City.

Essays by

Alistair Horne

Geoffrey Parker

John Keegan

and others

EDITED BY ROBERT COWLEY

WHAT IF?

MILITARY HISTORIANS IMAGINE

WHAT MIGHT HAVE BEEN

PAN BOOKS

The sidebar articles were previously published in the spring
1998 issue of *MHQ: The Quarterly Journal of Military History*.
They are reprinted by permission of the authors.

Map and picture research–Michele Mancuso

First published 1999 by G. P. Putnam's Sons,
a member of Penguin Putnam Inc. New York

This edition published 2001 by Pan Books
an imprint of Pan Macmillan Ltd
Pan Macmillan, 20 New Wharf Road, London N1 9RR
Basingstoke and Oxford
Associated companies throughout the world
www.panmacmillan.com

ISBN 0 330 48724 8

798

A CIP catalogue record for this book is available from
the British Library.

Printed and bound in Great Britain by
Mackays of Chatham plc, Chatham, Kent

CONTENTS

List of Illustrations   ix

Introduction by Robert Cowley   xi

Infectious Alternatives ✦ *William H. McNeill*   1

   The Plague That Saved Jerusalem, 701 B.C.

     A GOOD NIGHT'S SLEEP CAN DO WONDERS—BARBARA N. PORTER

No Glory That Was Greece ✦ *Victor Davis Hanson*   15

   The Persians Win at Salamis, 480 B.C.

Conquest Denied ✦ *Josiah Ober*   37

   The Premature Death of Alexander the Great

Furor Teutonicus: The Teutoburg
   Forest, A.D. 9 ✦ *Lewis H. Lapham*   57

The Dark Ages Made Lighter ✦ *Barry S. Strauss*   71

   The Consequences of Two Defeats

The Death That Saved Europe   •   *Cecelia Holland*   93

    The Mongols Turn Back, 1242

If Only It Had Not Been
    Such a Wet Summer   •   *Theodore K. Rabb*   107

    The Critical Decade of the 1520s

      IF THE HOLY LEAGUE HADN'T DITHERED—PETER PIERSON

The Immolation of Hernán Cortés   •   *Ross Hassig*   121

    Tenochtitlán, June 30, 1521

The Repulse of the English Fireships   •   *Geoffrey Parker*   139

    The Spanish Armada Triumphs, August 8, 1588

Unlikely Victory   •   *Thomas Fleming*   155

    *Thirteen Ways the Americans Could Have
    Lost the Revolution*

      GEORGE WASHINGTON'S GAMBLE—IRA D. GRUBER

What the Fog Wrought   •   *David McCullough*   189

    The Revolution's Dunkirk, August 29, 1776

Ruler of the World   •   *Alistair Horne*   201

    Napoleon's Missed Opportunities

      NAPOLEON WINS AT WATERLOO—CALEB CARR

If the Lost Order Hadn't Been Lost   ❖   *James M. McPherson*   223

     Robert E. Lee Humbles the Union, 1862

A Confederate Cannae
     and Other Scenarios   ❖   *Stephen W. Sears*   239

     How the Civil War Might Have Turned Out Differently

       VIETNAM IN AMERICA, 1865—TOM WICKER

The What Ifs of 1914   ❖   *Robert Cowley*   261

     The World War That Should Never Have Been

       BISMARCK'S EMPIRE: STILLBORN—JAMES CHACE

       THANKS, BUT NO CIGAR—DAVID CLAY LARGE

       THE ARMISTICE OF DESPERATION—DENNIS E. SHOWALTER

How Hitler Could Have Won the War   ❖   *John Keegan*   295

     The Drive for the Middle East, 1941

       WHAT A TAXI DRIVER WROUGHT—WILLIAMSON MURRAY

       TRIUMPH OF THE DICTATORS—DAVID FROMKIN

Our Midway Disaster   ❖   *Theodore F. Cook, Jr.*   311

     Japan Springs a Trap, June 4, 1942

       THE CASE OF THE MISSING CARRIERS—ELIHU ROSE

D Day Fails   ❖   *Stephen E. Ambrose*   341

     Atomic Alternatives in Europe

       THE SOVIET INVASION OF JAPAN—ROBERT COWLEY

Funeral in Berlin ❖ *David Clay Large* 351

   The Cold War Turns Hot

China Without Tears ❖ *Arthur Waldron* 377

   If Chiang Kai-shek Hadn't Gambled in 1946

   A QUAGMIRE AVOIDED?—TED MORGAN

   THE END—ROBERT L. O'CONNELL

LIST OF MAPS

page

25   The Persian Empire Conquers Greece: Xerxes' Invasion, 480–479 B.C.

50   Alexander's Interrupted Journey, 334 B.C.

67   A Roman Germany, A.D. 9

83   The Mediterranean: Islamic Lake, A.D. 732

103   The Mongols Conquer Europe, 1240–1244

125   The Route of Cortés: Where the Conquest of Mexico Could Have Been Stopped, 1521

146   The Spanish Invasion of England, 1588

167   The British Victory in New York, Autumn 1777

194   Trapping George Washington: Brooklyn Heights, August 30, 1776

234   Robert E. Lee's Gettysburg Campaign, Autumn 1862

244   A Confederate Cannae, June 1862

264   The Consequence of German Victory, 1914

303   Hitler's Desert Storm, 1941

327   The Great Pacific War, 1941–1946

389   Two Chinas on the Mainland, 1950

LIST OF ILLUSTRATIONS

page

7   The Assyrian Juggernaut: Lachis, 701 B.C.

20   Savior of the West: Themistocles, 480 B.C.

40   Alexander—Without "the Great," 334 B.C.

77   Islam Checked at the Battle of Poitiers, A.D. 732

129   Cortés vs. the Aztecs: Conquest in the Balance, 1521

144   Planning the Conquest, 1586

161   Bunker Hill, 1775: Revolution's Premature End?

206   The Floating Summit, 1807

344   D Day: The Weather Factor, 1944

368   Confrontation at the Berlin Wall, 1961

INTRODUCTION

I t has been said that "what if?" (or the counterfactual, to use the vogue word in academic circles) is the historian's favorite secret question. What ifs have a genuine value that goes beyond the "idle parlor game" (the historian E. H. Carr's phrase). They can be a tool to enhance the understanding of history, to make it come alive. They can reveal, in startling detail, the essential stakes of a confrontation, as well as its potentially abiding consequences. What if the Persians had beaten the rowers of Athens at Salamis in 480 B.C.—perhaps the single most important day in the history of the West—or if the Spanish Armada had won and the Duke of Parma's army had occupied London? On the night of August 7–8, 1588, a chance of wind is all it might have taken to reverse the result of another of history's most famous naval confrontations. Or what if the Germans had beaten back the D Day landings? What if the storm that raged over Europe on June 5, 1944—the day before the Normandy invasion was scheduled—had not unexpectedly let up? Once again, weather made all the difference. Stephen E. Ambrose examines some of the consequences of a D Day failure, none of them pleasant—including the atom bombing of Germany.

History is properly the literature of what did happen; but that should not diminish the importance of the counterfactual. What ifs can lead us to question long-held assumptions. What ifs can define true turning points. They can show that small accidents or split-second decisions are as likely to have major repercussions as large ones (the so-called "first-order" counterfactual). Consider the sudden fog on the East River that allowed George Washington and his badly beaten army to escape to Manhattan after the Battle of Long Island in the summer of 1776. Without that fog, as David McCullough points out, Washington might have been trapped on Brooklyn Heights and forced to surrender. Would there have been a United States if that had happened? You can also cite the British captain's decision not to pull the trigger when he had Washington in his gunsights at the Battle of Brandywine a year later. That might have had the same result. Few events have been more dependent on what ifs than the American Revolution. We are the product of a future that might not have been.

What ifs have a further important function: They can eliminate what has been called "hindsight bias." After the Battle of Britain failed, was there any way that Hitler could have won the Second World War? For the past fifty-odd years, historians have viewed the summer of 1940 as his high-water mark. But one of our foremost military historians, John Keegan, points out in these pages that if Hitler had decided not to invade Russia, history could have turned out much differently. If, after his victory in Greece in the spring of 1941, he had decided to invade Turkey or the Near East, he could have seized the oil he so desperately needed— and taken on the Soviet Union later, with a better chance of victory. Much as we like to think otherwise, outcomes are no more certain in history than they are in our own lives. If nothing else, the diverging tracks in the undergrowth of history celebrate the infinity of human options. The road not taken belongs on the map.

This is a book about the key events of military history seen in a new light: as they might have been if certain outcomes had been different. In the tenth anniversary issue of *MHQ: The Quarterly Journal of Military History*, we asked historians this question: What do you consider the most important might-have-beens of military history? The answers we got were by turns surprising, entertaining, and occasionally frightening—but at all times plausible. (You will find some of those original scenarios reprinted here.) Frivolous counterfactuals have given the question a bad name, and we avoided speculations such as what would have happened if Hannibal had possessed an H-bomb or Napoleon, stealth bombers—problems actually posed in one of our war colleges. Plausible, then, is the key word.

As George Will wrote, "The salutary effect of *MHQ's* 'What if' exercises is a keener appreciation of the huge difference that choices and fortuities make in the destiny of nations."

This volume, with its twenty chapters, is an expansion of the original concept. The authors of these chapters are some of the same historians who wrote for that feature: Stephen E. Ambrose, William H. McNeill, Theodore K. Rabb, Alistair Horne, Geoffrey Parker, John Keegan, Victor Davis Hanson, Stephen W. Sears, Lewis H. Lapham, Thomas Fleming, David McCullough, and James M. McPherson, to name a few. The book is organized chronologically, and ranges over 2,700 years of the human record. Nothing is more suited to what if speculation than military history, where chance and accident, human failings or strengths, can make all the difference.

What if a mysterious plague had not smitten the Assyrian besiegers of Jerusalem in 701 B.C.? Would there have been a Jewish religion? Or Christianity? Talk about split-second outcomes: What if the upswing of a battle-ax had not been interrupted and a twenty-one-year-old Alexander had been killed before he became "the Great"? Or if Cortés had been captured (as he nearly was) at the siege of Tenochtitlán, today's Mexico City? It's very likely that a young United States would have had to deal with a major Native American empire on its southern borders. Consider, too, the role of accident: If, in our Civil War, the famous "Lost Order" hadn't been lost, the chances are, as James M. McPherson writes, that the Confederate states would have remained independent. But, in fact, a similar Lost Order affected the outcome of the Battle of the Marne in September 1914—and hence of World War I itself.

For historians, as the maxim goes, the dominos fall backward. In *What If?* we will attempt to make them fall forward.

—*Robert Cowley*

WHAT IF?

WILLIAM H. McNEILL

INFECTIOUS ALTERNATIVES

The Plague That Saved Jerusalem, 701 B.C.

Military events, even seemingly insignificant episodes, can have unforeseen consequences, ones that may not become apparent at the time they happen and occasionally not even for centuries. It seems appropriate to begin this book with such a moment in history, the Assyrian siege of Jerusalem, then the seat of the tiny kingdom of Judah, in 701 B.C. That siege, by Sennacherib, king of Assyria, was lifted after a large part of his army succumbed to a mysteriously lethal contagion. The Assyrians simply moved on: For the largest empire of its time, the reduction of yet another walled city was not cost effective. For those holed up inside, however, deliverance came as a heavenly sign (though its causes were probably environmental), and one that, needless to say, would have far-reaching implications. But what if disease had not intervened? What if the walls had fallen, and the usual pillage, rape, murder, and forced exile of the population had been Jerusalem's lot? What would our lives, our spiritual underpinnings be like 2,700 years later?

1

Whatever the pestilence was, it became the leveler at Jerusalem. Disease has to be counted as one of the wild cards of history, an unforeseen factor that can, in a matter of days or weeks, undo the deterministic sure thing or humble the conquering momentum. History is full of examples. There was the plague that ravaged Athens for more than a year and led to its capture and the dismantling of its empire in 404 B.C. An outbreak of dysentery weakened the Prussian force invading France in 1792 and helped to convince their leaders to turn back after losing the Battle of Valmy, thus saving the French Revolution. The ravages of typhus and dysentery are the hidden story of Napoleon's calamity in Russia. The war-vectored influenza epidemic of 1918 may not have changed immediate outcomes, but how many potential reputations did we lose to it—people who might have made a difference to their generation? Bacteria and viruses may thus redirect vast impersonal forces in human societies, and they can also become forces in their own right.

✦ *William H. McNeill, professor emeritus at the University of Chicago, won the National Book Award for his RISE OF THE WEST. Among his twenty-six other books are a survey of military history, THE PURSUIT OF POWER, PLAGUES AND PEOPLES, and, most recently, KEEPING TOGETHER IN TIME: AN ESSAY ON DANCE AND DRILL IN HUMAN HISTORY. In 1997, he received one of the most prestigious international prizes for a lifetime of distinguished scholarship, the Erasmus Award.*

What if Sennacherib, king of Assyria, had conquered Jerusalem in 701 B.C. when he led his imperial army against a coalition of Egyptian, Phoenician, Philistine, and Jewish enemies, and handily defeated them all? This, it seems to me, is the greatest might-have-been of all military history. This may be an odd thing to say about an engagement that never took place; yet Jerusalem's preservation from attack by Sennacherib's army shaped the subsequent history of the world far more profoundly than any other military action I know of.

From Sennacherib's point of view the decision not to press the siege of Jerusalem to a conclusion did not matter very much. The kingdom of Judah was only a marginal player in the Near Eastern balance of power, being poorer and weaker than Sennacherib's other foes. And the king of Judah had been well and truly punished for having dared to revolt against him. For as Sennacherib declared in an inscription on the walls of his palace at Nineveh that recorded the victories of the entire campaign, his army had occupied no fewer than forty-six walled places in the kingdom of Judah and compelled Hezekiah, king of Judah, to shut himself up in Jerusalem "like a bird in a cage."

But, unlike other rebellious rulers in the area, Hezekiah did retain his throne, and the worship of Jahweh in the Temple of Solomon continued uninterrupted. Sennacherib's victory over the kingdom of Judah was therefore incomplete, a fact whose consequences were far greater than he or anyone else at the time could possibly imagine.

Hezekiah (ruled ca. 715–687 B.C.) began his reign in a time of acute uncertainty. Seven years before he ascended the throne and became Jerusalem's thirteenth ruler of the house of David, the neighboring kingdom of Israel, comprising the larger and richer part of David's kingdom, met irretrievable disaster when an Assyrian army, commanded by Sargon II,

3

captured the capital, Samaria, and carried off thousands of survivors to distant Mesopotamia. Strangers came at Assyrian command to cultivate the emptied fields, but they left the city of Samaria a shattered ruin.

Did this mean that the God of Moses and of David, the selfsame God still worshipped in the temple that Solomon had built for him in Jerusalem, was no longer able to defend his people? Or had God punished the Israelites and their rulers for disobedience to his will as made known in sacred scriptures, continually refreshed and brought up to date by the inspired words of his prophets?

The question was urgent, and all the more portentous because, if one took the second view, the God of Moses and of David had used the mightiest ruler of the age as an instrument for punishing his people, even though the Assyrians worshipped other gods and did not even pretend to honor God's commandments. This ran counter to common sense, which held that the gods worshipped by different peoples protected their worshippers as best they could. Victory and defeat therefore registered the power of rival deities as well as the strength of merely human armies. It followed that when the Assyrians began their imperial expansion, each new victory unsettled older religious loyalties and ideas among the peoples they conquered, creating a religious vacuum in the ancient Near East that was eventually filled by the unique response that occurred among the people of Judah.

That response began to take shape when King Hezekiah embraced the view of a party of religious reformers who set out to purify the worship of Jahweh by concentrating it in the temple. Destroying "high places" in the countryside where other rituals prevailed was part of the program. So was respectful consultation with inspired prophets, among whom Isaiah, son of Amoz, was then the most prominent.

But King Hezekiah did not rely entirely on supernatural help. He also strengthened Jerusalem's walls and expanded his borders modestly before joining the alliance against Sennacherib. And when the invading Assyrians defeated the Egyptians, he hurried to come to terms with the victors and had to pay dearly for the privilege of remaining on his throne, handing over various precious materials, including three hundred talents of silver and thirty of gold, some (perhaps most) of which came from the temple in Jerusalem. But he did retain his throne; and his heirs and successors maintained the little kingdom of Judah for another century and more by paying tribute to Assyria and carefully refraining from rebellion. Nevertheless, balancing precariously between rival great powers based in Egypt and Mesopotamia did not last forever. Instead, in 586 B.C., the kingdom's autonomy collapsed when Nebuchadnezzar, king of Babylon, did what Sennacherib had threatened to do, capturing Jerusalem after a long siege and bringing the dynasty of David to an end, destroying the temple, and carrying most of the surviving inhabitants off to an exile in Babylon.

As we all know, this was not the end of Jewish history, for the exiled people of Judah did not pine away. Instead they flourished by the waters of Babylon, and reorganized their scriptures to create an unambiguously monotheistic, congregational religion, independent of place and emancipated from the rites of Solomon's destroyed temple in Jerusalem. Moreover, the revised Jewish faith, tempered in exile, subsequently gave birth to Christianity and Islam, the two most powerful religions of our age, and of course also retains its own, distinctive following around the world and especially in the contemporary state of Israel.

None of this could have come to pass if the kingdom of Judah had disappeared in 701 B.C. as the kingdom of Israel had done a mere twenty-one years earlier in 722 B.C. On that occasion, the exiles from Israel soon lost their separate identity. By accepting commonsense views about the limits of divine power, they abandoned the worship of Jahweh, who had failed to protect them, and became the "Ten Lost Tribes" of biblical history. In all probability, the people of Judah would have met the same fate if the Assyrian army had attacked and captured Jerusalem in 701 B.C. and treated its inhabitants as they had treated those of Samaria and other conquered places before. If so, Judaism would have disappeared from the face of the earth and the two daughter religions of Christianity and Islam could not possibly have come into existence. In short, our world would be profoundly different in ways we cannot really imagine.

But figuring out what actually happened before the walls of Jerusalem so long ago is quite impossible. Sennacherib's boastful inscription carved onto the walls of his palace of Nineveh is a piece of imperial propaganda rather than sober history; and the three biblical narratives that tell the story of how the Assyrians failed to take the holy city were shaped by ideas about God's miraculous intervention in public affairs that few historians accept today.

Nonetheless, the biblical stories, inaccurate or exaggerated though they may be, were what really mattered. In all subsequent generations, they shaped Jewish memories of what had happened before the walls of the city, and this memory made it plausible to believe that the God of Moses and of David was in fact omnipotent, protecting his worshippers from the mightiest monarch of the day. This episode, as interpreted by the pious party in Jerusalem, made monotheism credible as never before; and emphatic uncompromising monotheism was what fitted the Jewish religion to survive and flourish in the cosmopolitan age that the Assyrian conquests had inaugurated. After all, mere local gods were hard to believe in when every part of the ancient Near East came to depend on what distant rulers, alien armies, and other groups of strangers did, and failed to do. Only God's universal power could explain public events satisfactorily. Consequently, Jewish monotheism prospered and was able to exercise an ever-widening influence, especially through its two daughter religions, down to our own time.

Religious ceremonies tied to a single, sacred place did not suffice in such a world. But abandoning local, ancestral religion and accepting the gods of alien, imperial rulers, whose superior power had been demonstrated by success in war, was a craven, unsatisfactory response. Uniquely, the inhabitants of the small, weak, and dependent kingdom of Judah had the temerity to believe that their God, Jahweh, was the only true God,

THE ASSYRIAN JUGGERNAUT

A relief from the Assyrian captial of Ninevah shows the final assault by battering rams, left, on Lachis, in Israel's twin kingdom of Judah, 701 B.C. Captives are marched away, lower right. Sacked and burned, the city ceased to exist. It was a fate that seemed to await nearby Jerusalem and the nascent Jewish faith—without which Christianity and Islam are inconceivable.

(Photograph by Erich Lessing/Art Resource, NY)

whose power extended over all the earth so that everything that happened was in accordance with his will. The circumstances of the Assyrian withdrawal from the walls of Jerusalem in 701 B.C. confirmed this implausible belief, proving God's universal power to pious and eager believers more clearly and far more convincingly than ever before. This makes it the most fateful might-have-been of all recorded history.

The biblical version of the campaign appears three times over, in II

Kings 18–19; II Chronicles 32; and the Book of Isaiah 36–37. The three accounts agree in all the essentials and in some instances even employ the same words and phrases. Let me quote from Isaiah, according to the King James version:

> Then Rabshakeh [commander of the Assyrian army sent against Jerusalem] stood and cried in a loud voice in the Jews' language, and said, Hear ye the words of the great king, the king of Assyria, . . . Beware lest Hezekiah persuade you, saying: the Lord will deliver us. Hath any of the gods of the nations delivered his land out of the hand of the king of Assyria? Where are the gods of Hamath and Arphad? . . . have they delivered Samaria out of my hand?

[Isaiah 36:13, 18–19]

Hezekiah responded to this direct challenge to God's power by praying:

> O Lord of hosts, God of Israel, that dwelleth between the cherubims, thou art the God, even thou alone, of all the kingdoms of the earth; thou hast made heaven and earth. Incline thine ear, O Lord, . . . and hear all the words of Sennacherib, which hath sent reproach to the living God . . . Now therefore, O Lord our God, save us from his hand, that all kingdoms of the earth may know that thou art the Lord, even thou only.
>
> Then Isaiah, son of Amoz, sent unto Hezekiah, saying . . . thus saith the Lord concerning the king of Assyria, He shall not come into this city, nor shoot an arrow there, nor come before it with shields, nor cast a bank against it . . . For I will defend this city to save it for mine own sake, and for my servant David's sake.
>
> Then the angel of the Lord went forth and smote in the camp of the Assyrians a hundred and fourscore and five thousand; and when they arose early in the morning, behold, they were all dead corpses. So Sennacherib, king of Assyria, departed and went and returned and dwelt in Nineveh. And it came to pass . . . that his sons smote him with the sword . . . and Esarhaddon his son reigned in his stead."

[Isaiah 37:16–17, 20–21, 33, 35–38]

Thus, according to the Bible, God saved his people and destroyed the impious Assyrians by spreading lethal pestilence among them. Such a miraculous deliverance showed that both King Hezekiah and the prophet Isaiah were right to rely on God's power and protection. More than that: It proved God's power over the mightiest ruler of the age. Who then could doubt that the prophets and priests of Judah, who so boldly proclaimed God's universal power, were telling the truth? Who indeed?

Yet doubters remained, as the biblical account of the reign of Hezekiah's son and successor, Manasseh (ruled ca. 686–642 B.C.), makes clear. King Manasseh remained tributary to the Assyrians throughout his reign and thought it prudent to come to terms with alien gods as well, setting up "a carved image, the idol he had made, in the house of God," and allowing other heathen forms of worship that, according to the Book of the Chronicles, were "evil in the sight of the Lord." [II, 33: 2, 7]

Moreover, for those of us who are disinclined to believe in miracles, the biblical account of how Hezekiah prepared for the Assyrian attack on Jerusalem contain some tantalizing hints that suggest entirely mundane factors that may have provoked epidemic among the besieging Assyrians. It is also easy to imagine other pressing reasons why Sennacherib may have decided to refrain from besieging the strongly fortified city of Jerusalem, quite apart from epidemic losses his army may have suffered outside the walls. (Incidentally, the figure of 185,000 disease deaths must be vastly exaggerated; no ancient army came close to such a size, much less one operating in the barren environs of Jerusalem.)

What really happened therefore remains entirely unsure. But wondering about how the course of world history was affected by subsequent interpretation of the actual course of events remains enticing. For example: Did King Hezekiah save his throne by foreseeing that the Assyrian army would have difficulty finding enough water for a lengthy siege of Jerusalem? The Books of the Chronicles tells us that "when Hezekiah saw that Sennacherib was come, and that he purposed to fight against Jerusalem, he took counsel with his princes and his mighty men to stop the waters of the fountains which were without the city; and they did help him. So there was gathered much people together who stopped all the fountains and the brook that ran through the midst of the land, saying, Why should the kings of Assyria come and find much water?" [II Chronicles, 32: 2–4]

Some modern archaeologists believe that Hezekiah ordered the construction of a 600-foot tunnel that still carries water from the spring of Gihon to the pool of Siloam, just outside Jerusalem's ancient walls. Such a difficult project must have taken a long time and can scarcely be equated with the emergency effort to deny the Assyrian adequate access to water described in Chronicles. But the tunnel may well have been part of a general effort to improve the city's defenses undertaken before or after the confrontation of 701.

In any case, one may wonder whether Hezekiah's effort to "stop the fountains" around Jerusalem compelled Assyrian soldiers to drink contaminated water and thus expose themselves to widespread infections. If so, the fact that Hezekiah and his princes and mighty men foresaw how difficult it would be to find enough drinking water in Jerusalem's dry environs may have had more to do with the Assyrian retreat than the miracle recorded in the Bible

Until the reign of King Josiah (ruled 640–612 B.C.), the pious interpretation of how God had saved Jerusalem and miraculously compelled Sennacherib to withdraw competed with the commonsense view, illustrated by King Manasseh's policy of introducing heathen worship into Jerusalem as a way of supplementing Jahweh's limited jurisdiction by appealing to other, more powerful gods as well.

For centuries, Hebrew prophets had denounced such policies, declaring that Jahweh was a jealous God who demanded exclusive devotion and obedience to his will, as revealed through their inspired utterances. As literacy spread, the words of God, delivered through his prophets, and instructing the faithful what to do in public and private matters, were (at least sometimes) written down. Hence the biblical books of prophecy began to accumulate, beginning about 750 B.C. Priests of Solomon's temple, likewise, defended the exclusive rights of the God they worshipped, and priestly editors and compilers were presumably responsible for collecting and preserving the sacred texts from which the rest of the Jewish scripture was eventually compiled. Priests and prophets did not always agree, but both championed the exclusive worship of Jahweh and rejected the commonsense religious view that recognized multiple, local gods who struggled against one another just as humans did.

Decisive triumph for the champions of Jahweh came early in King Josiah's reign, when the Assyrian empire began to collapse, and the pious party persuaded Josiah, while still a boy, to repudiate all the alien cults his father Manasseh had admitted to Jerusalem. Then, while refurbishing the temple, the high priest "found a book of the law of the Lord, given to Moses." [II Chronicles, 34:14] This, the Book of Deuteronomy, became the basis for a strenuous effort to reform religious practices and bring them into conformity to God's will as newly recovered.

Thirty-six years later, when the principal successor to the Assyrian empire, King Nebuchadnezzar, destroyed the kingdom of Judah, razed the temple, and carried the Jews away to his capital at Babylon, the pious party of Jahweh had to figure out why God had allowed such a disaster to take place. But by then the idea that God did in fact govern all the world was so firmly established that abandoning Jahweh, as the Israelites had done after 722 B.C., was inconceivable. Instead, long-standing prophetic denunciations of the sins of the Jewish people made it obvious that the Babylonian exile was God's punishment for the failure of Judah's rulers and people to observe his commandments to the full. For no matter how strenuous their effort at religious reform had been, even the most pious still fell short of obeying all of God's prescriptions.

Further effort to amend their ways, discovering God's will by careful study of the sacred scripture, was the only appropriate response. Accordingly, when weekly meetings for reading and meditating upon the meaning of the sacred scriptures became customary among the exiles, Judaism assumed its enduring form. The Jewish religion ceased to be local and became an effective guide to everyday life in cosmopolitan, urban settings, fit to survive and flourish across succeeding centuries into the indefinite future.

It may seem paradoxical to argue that the vindication of Isaiah's prophecy and of Hezekiah's religious policy by Sennacherib's withdrawal was critical for the emergence of unambiguous monotheism in the little Kingdom of Judah, whereas Nebuchadnezzar's success in carrying through what Sennacharib had merely threatened, instead of discrediting that faith, had the effect of confirming Jewish monotheism, and permitted the daughter religions of Christianity and Islam to arise in later centuries. But so it was, or so it seems to me, although most historians are so much shaped by the world's subsequent religious history as to be unable or unwilling to recognize how fateful the Assyrian withdrawal in 701 B.C. turned out to be.

But, at least for me, pondering how a small company of prophets and priests in Jerusalem interpreted what happened outside the city walls in 701 B.C. and reflecting on how their views came to prevail so widely in later times are a sobering exercise of historical imagination. Never before or since has so much depended on so few, believing so wholly in their one true god, and in such bold defiance of common sense.

◆ BARBARA N. PORTER ◆

A GOOD NIGHT'S SLEEP
CAN DO WONDERS

What if King Gyges of Lydia had stayed up late worrying about the approaching Cimmerian hordes, had entirely missed the famous dream in which the god of Assyria advised him to become an Assyrian vassal, and in the morning, tired and dispirited, had failed to trounce the Cimmerians and had died at their hands on the field of battle then, instead of several years later?

If all this had happened, modern Western culture might look a little different. Lacking his dream—and dead moreover—Gyges would never have sent his ambassadors to far-off Assyria, armed with two captured Cimmerian chiefs as a friendly present, to establish the first alliance between the two nations, in about 652 B.C. Without this initial friendly contact, Gyges's surviving sons might not have succeeded later in persuading the Assyrians to prod their allies in Asia Minor to help Gyges's heirs hold on to the throne of Lydia—whence they eventually succeeded in driving the Cimmerians out of Asia Minor altogether. And they would never have founded the Lydian empire of Asia Minor, renowned for its gold and commerce, music and art.

Since most people have never heard of the Lydian empire, this might not seem to be much of a loss, but there is worse to come. With the Lydians defeated, there would have been no one to stop the Cimmerians from continuing their ferocious march toward the sea and seizing the Greek colonial cities on the coast. With the ships of those cities in their hands, the Cimmerians could easily have gone on to attack the cities of mainland Greece, which were only a short distance to the west and which were then edging toward the great cultural flowering that

13

was to make fifth century B.C. Greece the birthplace of Western culture as we know it. Instead, mainland Greece would have become the home of the Cimmerian horse nomads, Herodotus might have written treatises on horse training instead of inventing Western historical writing, and people like Euripides might have spent their days herding horses instead of writing plays.

The moral of Gyges's story would appeal to one's mother: Go to bed early and get a good night's sleep; the fate of Western civilization may depend on it.

❖ *Barbara N. Porter is an authority on the political and cultural history of the Neo-Assyrian empire.*

VICTOR DAVIS HANSON

NO GLORY THAT
WAS GREECE

The Persians Win at Salamis, 480 B.C.

There are few moments in history when so much was decided in so little time as the naval encounter between the Greeks and Persians at Salamis in 480 B.C. (Hiroshima may also qualify, but barring our nuclear extinction, the epochal returns on it are still out.) Salamis was more than just a battle. It was the supreme confrontation between East and West, in which all manner of futures were either set in motion or denied. The Persians may have taken the lead in an attempt to check the spread of Greek individualism, but the other centralized despotic powers of the eastern Mediterranean basin apparently cheered them on. The Greek words "freedom" and "citizen," Victor Davis Hanson points out, did not exist in the vocabulary of other Mediterranean cultures.

As military operations go, the one mounted by the Persian emperor Xerxes has to be ranked in terms of size, lengthy preparation, and sophisticated planning with the Spanish Armada and the D Day invasion. That operation, which culminated at Salamis, turned out to be a last chance to stamp out the irrepressible culture of the West. "Had Fortune favored numbers, we would have won the day," a messenger tells *the mother of Xerxes in Aeschylus's* The Persians. *(The Athenian playwright had himself supposedly fought at Salamis.)* "The result shows with what partial hands the gods weighed down the scale against us, and destroyed us all." *But what if that scale had been weighted at the opposite end? What if the Persians had won? It nearly happened. It should have happened. If the rowers commanded by the Athenian statesman-general Themistocles had not prevailed, would there be, some 2,500 years later, a Western civilization in the form we know it? Or would Themistocles, had he survived Salamis, have resettled the Athenian people in Italy, thus giving the ideals of freedom and citizenship a chance for a second flowering?*

❖ *Victor Davis Hanson has published nine books, including* THE WESTERN WAY OF WAR, THE OTHER GREEKS, *and* WHO KILLED HOMER? *(with John Heath). His book on the death of the family farm,* FIELDS WITHOUT DREAMS, *was voted the best nonfiction title of 1995 by the San Francisco Book Reviewers Association. Hanson teaches classics at California State University in Fresno.*

The interest of the world's history hung trembling in the balance. Oriental despotism, a world united under one lord and sovereign, on the one side, and separate states, insignificant in extent and resources, but animated by free individuality, on the other side, stood front to front in array of battle. Never in history has the superiority of spiritual power over material bulk, and that of no contemptible amount, been made so gloriously manifest.

So wrote the often apocalyptic German historian and philosopher Georg Hegel of the aftermath of Salamis. The Greeks of the time agreed. Aeschylus's play *The Persians* is the only extant Greek tragedy based on a historical event, that of the singular victory at "Divine Salamis," where the gods punished the arrogance of the Medes and rewarded the courage of a free Greece. Epigrams after the battle recorded that Hellenic sailors had "saved holy Greece" and "prevented it from seeing the day of slavery." Legend had it that on the day of the majestic Athenian-led victory, Aeschylus fought, Sophocles danced at the victory festival, and Euripides was born. For the last 2,500 years, Western civilization has celebrated the miracle of Salamis as both the very salvation of its culture and the catalyst for a subsequent literary, artistic, and philosophical explosion under the aegis of a triumphant and confident Athenian democracy. The temples on the Acropolis, Athenian tragedy and comedy, Socratic philosophy, and the genre of history itself followed the Persian Wars: Thus, not only did the victory at Salamis save Hellenism, but the spiritual exhilaration and material bounty from the Athenians' astonishing victory made these cultural breakthroughs possible.

Before Salamis most of the Greek city-states were agrarian, parochial, and isolated, intimidated by 70 million subjects of the Persian Empire to the east, and overshadowed by millions more in the Near East and Egypt. After Salamis, the ancient Greeks would never again fear any other foreign power until they met the Romans. Indeed, no Persian king would ever again set foot in Greece, and for the next 2,000 years no easterner would claim Greece as his own until the Ottoman conquest of the Balkans in the fifteenth century—an event that proved that an unchecked Eastern power most certainly would and could occupy a weakened Greece for centuries.

Before Salamis, Athens was a rather eccentric city-state whose experiment with radical democracy was in its twenty-seven-year-old infancy, and the verdict on its success still out. After the battle arose an imperial democratic culture that ruled the Aegean and gave us Aeschylus, Sophocles, the Parthenon, Pericles, and Thucydides. Before the naval fight, there was neither the consensus nor confidence that Greek arms would protect and enhance Greek interests abroad. After Salamis, for the next three and a half centuries murderous Greek-speaking armies, possessed of superior technology and bankrolled by shrewd financiers, would run wild from southern Italy to the Indus River.

If the Persian Wars marked a great divide in world history, then Salamis served as the turning point in the Persian War. And if Salamis represented a dramatic breakthrough in the fortunes of the Greek resistance to Persia, then the role of Themistocles and a few thousand Athenians explains the remarkable Hellenic victory against all odds. Hence, it really is true that what a few men did in late September 480 in the waters off the Athenian coast explains much of what we take for granted in the West today.

First, we should remember that the decade-long Persian Wars—comprising the battles of Marathon (490), Thermopylae and Artemesium (480), Salamis (480), Plataea (479) and Mycale (479)—offered the East the last real chance to check Western culture in its embryonic state, before the Greeks' radically dynamic menu of constitutional government, private property, broad-based militias, civilian control of military forces, free scientific inquiry, rationalism, and separation between political and religious authority would spread to Italy, and thus via the Roman Empire to most of northern Europe and the western Mediterranean. Indeed, the words freedom and citizen did not exist in the vocabulary of any other Mediterranean culture, which were either tribal monarchies, or theocracies. We should keep in mind in this present age of multiculturalism that Greece was a Mediterranean country in climate and agriculture only, but one entirely *anti*-Mediterranean in spirit and values compared to its surrounding neighbors.

Hegel knew, as we may have forgotten, that had Greece become the westernmost province of Persia, in time Greek family farms would have become estates for the Great King. The public buildings of the agora would have been transformed into covered shops of the bazaar, and yeomen hoplites paid shock troops alongside Xerxes' Immortals. In place of Hellenic philosophy and science, there would have been only the subsidized arts of divination and astrology, which were the appendages of imperial or religious bureaucracies and not governed by unfettered rational inquiry. In a Persian Greece, local councils would be mere puppet bodies to facilitate royal requisitions of men and money, history the official diaries and edicts of the Great King, and appointed local officials mouthpieces for the satrap ("the protector of power") and the magi.

The Greeks might later fine or exile their general, Themistocles; had the Persians dared the same with Xerxes, they would have ended up disemboweled—like the eldest son of Pythias the Lydian, who was cut in half, his torso and legs put on each side on the road for the royal army to march between. Such was the price Pythias paid when he dared request from Xerxes military exemption for one of his five sons. Despite the arguments of recent scholarship, the cities of the Persian empire were not in any fashion city-states. We would live under a much different tradition today—one where writers are under death sentences, women secluded and veiled, free speech curtailed, government in the hands of the autocrat's extended family, universities mere centers of religious zealotry, and the thought police in our living rooms and bedrooms—had Themistocles and his sailors failed.

The thousand or so Greek *poleis* that arose sometime in the eighth

SAVIOR OF THE WEST

The statesman-admiral Themistocles (shown here in this idealized bust) led the Athenian navy at Salamis. Had he lost, would he have transported citizens of Athens en masse *and Aeneas-like to Italy, there to found a new democratic city-state?*

(Alinari/Art Resource, NY)

century B.C. immediately faced an undeniable paradox: The very conditions of their success also raised the possibility of their own ruin. The isolated valleys of Greece, the general neglect from the rest of the Mediterranean world, the extreme chauvinism of highly individualistic and autonomous small Greek communities—all that had allowed the creation and growth of a free landowning citizenry like none other. Yet, there germinated no accompanying principle of national federalism or even a notion of common defense—all such encompassing ideas of government and centralized power were antithetical to the Greeks' near fanatical embrace of political independence and individuality; for crusty yeomen citizens, the very thought of federal taxes was an anathema. Today's supporters of the United Nations would find themselves without friends in ancient Greece. Indeed, even the most radical proponent of states' rights might seem too timid to the early Greeks. In terms of the Greek legacy of regional autonomy, John C. Calhoun, not Abraham Lincoln or Woodrow Wilson, was the true Greek.

By the sixth century B.C., the economic energy, political flexibility, and military audacity of these insular Greeks had nevertheless allowed them to colonize the coast of Asia Minor, the Black Sea region, southern Italy, Sicily, and parts of North Africa. In other words, a million Greeks and their unique idea of a free polis had gained influence well beyond either their natural resources or available manpower. Again, there was no accompanying imperial or even federated notion that might organize or unify such expansionary efforts; instead, roughly 1,000 bustling city-states—as Herodotus said, unified only by their values, language, and religion—pursued their own widely diverse agendas.

Other far older and more centralized powers—whether theocracies in North Africa or political autocracies in Asia—took notice. In broad strategic terms, by the early fifth century Persians, Egyptians, Phoenicians, and Carthaginians had seen enough of these intrusive and ubiquitous Greeks as shippers, traders, mercenaries, and colonists. Could not this quarreling and fractious people be overwhelmed by the sheer manpower and wealth of imperial armies *before* its insidious culture spread well beyond the Hellenic mainland and made the eastern Mediterranean a lake of their own?

Darius I and later his son Xerxes took up that challenge in the first two decades of the fifth century. After their respective defeats, there never again was a question in the ancient world about the primacy of the Western paradigm. In the decades following Salamis, relatively small numbers of Greeks—whether Athenians in Egypt, Panhellenic mercenaries hired by Persian nobles, or Alexander's Macedonian thugs—fought in Asia and North Africa for conquest and loot; never again were Hellenic armies pressed on Greek soil to battle for their freedom. After the defeat of Xerxes, when Greeks abroad faltered, either due to manpower shortages or to the sheer hubris of their undertaking, no Eastern power dared to invade their homeland. And when the Greeks succeeded overseas, which was far more often, they habitually wrecked their adversaries' culture, planted military colonies abroad, and then sent home slaves and money. Salamis established the principle that Greeks would advance, others recede, both in a material and cultural sense.

Much has been written about Rome's later great showdown with Carthage. But despite three murderous wars (264–146 B.C.), and a nightmarish sixteen-year sojourn of a megalomaniac Hannibal on Italian soil, the ultimate decision was never in doubt. By the third century B.C., the Roman manner of raising, equipping, and leading armies, the flexibility and resilience of republican government, and the growing success of Italian agriculturists, financiers, traders, and builders—all beneficiaries of past Hellenic practice ensured by the Greeks' successful emergence from the Persian Wars—made the ultimate verdict of the Punic Wars more or less foreordained. Given the size of the Roman army, the unity of republican Italy, and the relative weakness of Punic culture, the wonder is not that Carthage lost, but that it was able to fight so savagely and for so long.

In contrast to the later Romans, at Salamis the quarreling Greeks were faced with a navy three to four times larger. The Persian army on the mainland enjoyed still greater numerical superiority and was anywhere from five to ten times more numerous than the aggregate number of Greek hoplites. Persia itself could draw on manpower reserves seventy times greater than present in Greek-speaking lands and possessed coin money and bullion in its imperial vaults that would make Greek temples' treasuries seem impoverished in contrast.

Indeed, without an imperial structure, the Greek city-states were quarreling over the defense of the mainland right up to the first signs of the Persian assault. After Xerxes' descent through northern Greece in late summer 480, ostensibly more Greek *poleis* were neutral or in service to the Persians than to the Hellenic cause. And unlike Rome during the Hannibalic invasion, Athens by September 480 was not merely threatened, but already destroyed and occupied—and the population of Attica evacuated and dispersed. The situation was far worse than that which prevailed in Western Europe in mid-1940 after the Nazi victories over the European democracies.

Imagine a defeated and overrun France—without allies, Paris already destroyed, the Arc de Triomphe and Eiffel Tower in ruins, the countryside abandoned, its remaining free population in transit in small boats toward England and its North African colonies—choosing to stake its entire recovery on an outnumbered but patriotic French fleet in the harbor of Toulon. And then conceive that the French patriots and their outnumbered ships had won!—wrecking half the Nazi vessels, sending Hitler in shame to Berlin, and in a few months fashioning a heroic resistance on the occupied French mainland where its infantry went on to destroy a Nazi army many times larger and to send it back in shambles across the Rhine.

But granted that the Persian Wars marked the last chance of the other to end the nascent, though irrepressible, culture of the West, was Salamis itself the real landmark event in the Greeks' decade-long resistance to Darius and Xerxes? We can easily dispense with the first engagement at Marathon, the heroic Athenian victory fought a decade earlier. The Athenian victory there was magnificent and it prevented for the time being the burning of Athens. But Darius' invasion force of 490 on the small Attic plain northeast of Athens was not large—perhaps not much over 30,000 in all—and it had previously occupied only a few Greek islands. Darius in this probe had neither the resources nor the will to enslave Greece. At most, a Persian victory would have served as retribution for Athens's recent unsuccessful intervention on behalf of the rebelling Ionian Greeks on the coast of Asia Minor. An Athenian defeat at Marathon would have also led to a renewed indigenous tyranny under the offspring of the former tyrant Pisistratus, more sympathetic to Persia. Thus due to limited objectives and the avoidance of war with most of the other Greek city-states, a Persian victory at Marathon by itself would have sidetracked, but not ended, the Greek ascendancy.

Darius died in 486, and the task of avenging the shame of Marathon now fell to his son Xerxes. The latter was intent not on another punitive raid, but envisioned a mass invasion, one larger than any the eastern Mediterranean had yet seen. After four years of preparation, Xerxes had his troops mobilized in 480. He bridged the Hellespont into Europe and descended through northern Greece, absorbing all the city-states in his wake, unfortunate Hellenic communities that had little choice other than destruction or surrender. Whereas there is no credibility in ancient accounts that the Persian army numbered more than a million men, we should imagine that even a force of a quarter- to a half-million infantry and seamen was the largest invasion that Europe would witness until the Allied armada at D Day, June 1944. We need not agree either with ancient accounts that the Persian cavalry numbered over 80,000 horses. But it may well have been half that size, still nearly five times larger than the mounted forces Alexander would use to conquer Asia more than a century and a half later. And there were probably well over 1,200 Phoenician, Greek, and Persian ships in the Great King's naval armada.

The Greeks agreed to try to stop the onslaught at the narrow defile of Thermopylae, the last pass in Greece above the Isthmus of Corinth, where terrain offered a credible defense for outnumbered troops. At that

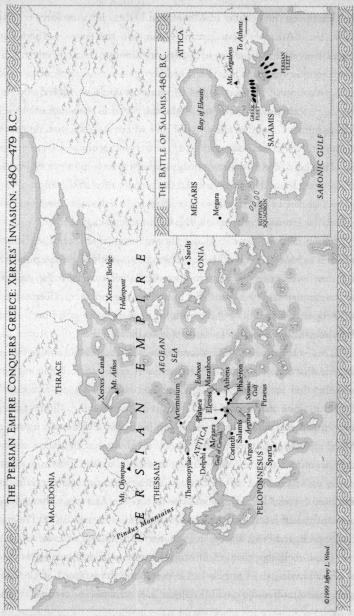

The Persian Empire Conquers Greece: Xerxes' Invasion, 480–479 B.C.

MACEDONIA

THRACE

Mt. Olympus

Xerxes Canal
Mt. Athos

Xerxes' Bridge
Hellespont

P E R S I A N   E M P I R E

THESSALY

Pindus Mountains

AEGEAN SEA

Sardis
IONIA

Thermopylae

Artemisium

Euboea
Marathon

Delphi
Plataea
ATTICA
Megara
Gulf of Corinth
Eleusis
Athens
Phaleron
Saronic Gulf
Piraeus

Corinth
Salamis
Argos
Aegina
Sparta

PELOPONNESUS

The Battle of Salamis, 480 B.C.

MEGARIS

Megara

ATTICA

Mt. Aegaleos

To Athens

Bay of Eleusis

PERSIAN FLEET

GREEK FLEET

EGYPTIAN SQUADRON

SALAMIS

SARONIC GULF

©1999 Jeffrey L. Ward

northern choke point there was less than fifty feet of passage between the cliffs and the sea. Accordingly, in August 480 the city-states sent the Greek fleet under Athenian leadership up the nearby coast to Artemisium. King Leonidas of Sparta followed by land with a token allied force of less than 7,000 hoplites. If the Persian fleet could be stalled, and the massive enemy army bottled up, all the city-states to the south might yet rally northward, join Leonidas, and so thwart the advance without much damage to the prosperous interior of central and southern Greece.

That bold Greek strategy quickly collapsed, and despite the courage of the Spartans at Thermopylae and the loss of much of the Persian fleet due to storms at Artemesium, both land and sea battles comprised together the greatest military defeat in the history of the Greek city-states. A Spartan king was now dead and his body mutilated, over 4,000 crack hoplites were killed, a large percentage of the Greek fleet was damaged, and everything north of the Isthmus at Corinth lay naked before the invader. An abandoned Athens was to be burned, and then perhaps reinhabited as a regional capital of the Persian empire—a Greek Sardis, Babylon, or Susa—to collect money for Persepolis.

Thus the battle of Salamis loomed as the next—and last—occasion to stop the Persian onslaught. Had the Greeks not fought at Salamis—or had they lost there—the consequences are easy to imagine. The Greek fleet—if it had survived or if its fractious remnants could still have been kept together—would have sailed south to the Isthmus at Corinth, where in conjunction with the remaining infantry of the Peloponnese, they would have once more tried to fashion a last-ditch defense effort similar to the failed land-sea attempt at Thermopylae and Artemisium. But now with all of northern and central Greece conquered, the Athenians and the largest Greek naval contingent eliminated, and the Persian forces jubilant from a spring and summer of constant conquest, there is no reason to doubt that a half million Persians—aided by troops from even more conquered Greek states—would not have breached the isthmus wall and poured into Corinthia and environs to the south and west. The infantry invaders would have been aided, of course, by the massive Persian fleet, which could land supplies and men where needed to the rear of the Greek defenders in Argolis and on the northern coast of the Peloponnese. In later Greek history, garrisoning the isthmus had never kept any invading force out of the Peloponnese—Epaminondas, even without naval support, proved that four times during the 360s B.C. alone.

The great battle of Plataea, fought in the spring after the Greeks' victory at Salamis, resulted in the destruction of the remaining Persian infantry in the field and marks the final expulsion of Xerxes' forces from Greece. But that landmark battle is understood only in the context of the tactical, strategic, and spiritual triumph of Salamis the September before. The Persians at Plataea fought without their king—Xerxes and some of his best Persian infantry had withdrawn to Persia after the naval defeat. There was to be no supporting Persian fleet off the coast of eastern Boeotia. And while the Greeks had bickered and fought up to the very moments before the battle at Salamis, at Plataea they were unified and confident by reason of their past naval success. Indeed, there may have been more Greeks at Plataea—70,000 hoplites and as many light-armed troops—than would ever marshal again in Greek history. Thus the Persians fought as a recently defeated force, without the numerical superiority they enjoyed at Salamis, and without their king and his enormous fleet. They could not be reinforced by sea. The Greeks, in contrast, poured en masse into the small plain of Plataea, convinced that their Persian enemies were retreating from Attica, demoralized from their defeat at Salamis, and abandoned by their political and military leadership.

The victories at Marathon and Plataea—and of course the unsuccessful Hellenic resistance at Thermopylae and Artemesium—were not in themselves the deciding battles of the decade-long Persian-Greek conflict. If Marathon delayed the hope of Persian conquest, and Plataea finished it, Salamis made it impossible. When the Persians retreated from Salamis, it was as a weakened army without its king, its fleet, and a great many of its soldiers.

Yet if Salamis was the key to the Greek victory in the Persian Wars, what accounts for the Greeks' remarkable victory there? From the fifth-century accounts in Herodotus and Aeschylus's *Persians*, together with much later second- and third-hand sources—the historian Diodorus and the biographer Plutarch being the most prominent—and topographical reconnaissance around Salamis itself, scholars can more or less reconstruct the battle with some certainty. After a tumultuous meeting of the admirals of the Panhellenic fleet, the Greeks agreed to accede to the Athenian Themistocles' plan to pit their much smaller fleet—a little over 350 ships against somewhere between 600 and 1,000 Persian vessels—in the narrow straits between the island of Salamis and the Greek mainland west of Athens. The Persians had occupied all of nearby Attica and patrolled as far south as Megara, a few hundred yards opposite the northwest tip of Salamis. In contrast, the Athenian populace was dispersed, with men of military age at Salamis, the elderly, women, and children sent to the more distant island of Aegina and the coast of Argolis to the southwest.

Besides the need to reclaim his homeland, Themistocles' more critical plan was to precipitate an immediate fight while the Greeks still had some remnant notion of Panhellenic defense and his own country was in enemy hands for only a few weeks. Themistocles argued that within the confined space of the Salamis narrows, the Persians both would lack room to maneuver and could not employ the full extent of their fleet—allowing the outnumbered though heavier Greek ships to nullify their enemy's vast numerical superiority. In such confined waters, the less-experienced Greek sailors had little worry about being outflanked and surrounded by skilled crews in sleek triremes, and so could sail out to battle, ship to ship, in massed order, seeking to ram their own stouter vessels against the first ranks of the lighter Persian, Ionian, and Phoenician fleet. Any Persians or their allies who survived could be speared by Greek hoplites posted on nearby small islands, while the disabled Greek ships and their crews could find refuge on Salamis proper.

The sea battle was fought all day—most likely sometime between

September 20 and 30, 480 B.C.—and by nightfall the Persians had lost half their ships and the fleet was scattered. The key to the Greek success was to nullify Persian numbers and superior seamanship; this was done brilliantly both before and during the battle. Misled into thinking the Greeks were withdrawing to the northwest through the channel between Megara and Salamis, the Persians committed what would turn out to be two blunders: First, they detached a large portion of their armada to safeguard the exit, thus drawing off valuable ships from the scene of the battle itself. Second, Xerxes ordered his forces, while it was still night, to sail up the channel between Salamis and the Attic mainland—ensuring that his crews received no sleep or food, while nullifying their numerical superiority in the confined waters. Our ancient accounts are in conflict over the details of the fighting, but it seems most likely that about 350 Greek triremes set out in two lines, each ranging about two miles long across the channel, intent on ramming the three opposing lines of Persian ships, which were in disorder and at this point perhaps only enjoyed a two-to-one numerical advantage. Herodotus, Aeschylus, and later sources say little about the actual collision, but the Greeks, desperate to ensure the safety of their families on Salamis and to the west in the Peloponnese, used their heavier ships to repeatedly ram Xerxes' fleet, until his various national contingents began to break off and flee the melee. Although they still outnumbered the Greek fleet, the Persians' morale was shattered and within a few days, Xerxes sailed home to the Hellespont, accompanied by an infantry guard of 60,000, leaving behind his surrogate Mardonius with a large army to continue the struggle on land the next spring. Such are the barest outlines of the battle of Salamis.

On at least two critical occasions, the leadership of Themistocles ensured that the battle was fought at Salamis and that it was won there. Quite literally, had he not been present or had he advised different measures, the Greeks either would not have engaged the Persians or they would have been defeated. Very shortly afterward the Persian Wars would have been lost, and the culture of the West would have died in its infancy after little more than two centuries. Other than Themistocles, there was no other Greek leader able or willing to marshal the Hellenic forces by sea in defense of Athens.

First, the decision to fight the Persians at sea seems to have been Themistocles' own. Earlier he had convinced his countrymen that the Delphic oracle's prophecy of salvation through the "wooden wall" meant the new Athenian fleet off the coast, especially the mention of "Divine Salamis" in Apollo's last two lines of the hexameter verse. Thus the Athenians had evacuated Attica and their capital at Athens, and fled by sea on Themistocles' initiative—a wise move since die-hard conservative hoplite infantrymen would have preferred to commit to a glorious last stand in the Athenian plain. And we should remember that the Athenian fleet of some 250 ships was recently constructed and in excellent shape—and entirely due to the persistence of Themistocles' statesmanship two years earlier. In a heated and polarizing debate, he had previously convinced the Athenian assembly not to dole out the returns from their newly opened Attic silver mines at Laurium to individual citizens, but rather to use that income to build ships and train seamen to protect the new democracy from either Greek or Persian attack. His prescient efforts in 482 had ensured that the Athenians now had a newly constructed armada right off its shores.

After the battered Greek flotilla limped down the coast from Artemesium, Herodotus relates that Eurybiades, the Spartan commander of the reconstituted Greek combined fleet, put the decision of where to fight to a council of Greek admirals. We should believe Herodotus' account that the non-Athenian Greeks quickly urged a withdrawal to bases to the south in Argolis, where they could fashion a defense at the nearby Isthmus of Corinth: "Since Attica was already lost, the majority of the views that were given came to the same conclusion, that is to sail to the isthmus and fight for the Peloponnese." That way, the Greeks felt, if defeated, they might still find refuge in their own harbors.

At that point in his narrative, Herodotus makes the Athenian Mnesiphilus despair of such a decision: "Then everyone will go back to their own city, and neither Eurybiades nor any other will be able to hold them together, but the fleet will be scattered abroad and Greece shall perish through its own stupidity." Like the failed Ionian revolt a decade earlier, the mainland Greeks, Mnesiphilus knew, would also disperse after a crushing defeat, all boasting of further resistance as they privately sought accommodation with the Persians.

But once rebuffed, Themistocles immediately called a second meeting and convinced Eurybiades to marshal the Greeks at Salamis and fight where the narrow channels between the mainland would favor the defenders, where victory meant the salvation of the displaced Athenian people, and where the Peloponnesians could defend their homeland while the enemy was still distant. Themistocles added that the Greeks could ill afford to give up any more Greek territory—the islands in the Saronic Gulf and the Megarid were now defenseless. Indeed, the Persians were building a mole to Salamis itself, over which they planned to march in order to capture the exiled Athenians holed up on the island.

It would be utter insanity, Themistocles added, to fight in the open seas off Corinth where the Greeks' slower ships and smaller numbers ensured that they would be enveloped and outmaneuvered. Finally, now in open council, he threatened to take the Athenian fleet out of battle altogether and transport his people en masse over to Italy to refound the city, should the Greeks sail away and abandon Salamis. To this last-ditch effort and threats, the Greek admirals reluctantly gave in. The decision in mid-September was made to stay put and wait for the enemy. But would the Persian ships come into the narrow straits, or simply wait off the occupied Attic coast for the nearby moored Greek ships to feud and disband?

Themistocles' second great feat was to lure the invaders' vessels into the narrows. Herodotus reports the story that Themistocles sent his slave Sicinnus across the channel at night to the Persian camp with a planted story: Themistocles and his Athenians wished a Persian victory, Sicinnus reported to the enemy. He added that the Greeks were squabbling and

31

about to flee from Salamis for the isthmus. Xerxes' last chance to trap them would be to sail immediately in the morning between Attica and Salamis and catch the Greek ships unprepared and unorganized. Indeed, the Athenians and others might switch sides and join the Persians once they entered the straits.

Classical scholars still argue over the authenticity of Herodotus's story of a Themistoclean ruse. While the tale appears melodramatic and puts the decision to deploy over a 1,000 ships on the rumor of a single slave, there is no reason to doubt either Themistocles' guile or the Persians' gullibility. After all, the Persians a few weeks earlier had won at Thermopylae solely through the betrayal of Ephialtes, a Greek traitor, who showed them a route around the pass. Very early the next morning, after the successful nocturnal mission of Sicinnus, the Persians were convinced by the ruse and began rowing into the narrows and the Greek trap. From the descriptions of Herodotus and Aeschylus, the Persians ships were stacked and confused in the narrow bay off Salamis and were unable to use either their numbers or swiftness to penetrate or outflank the Greeks, who methodically rammed them with their heavier vessels. Themistocles fought bravely in his own clearly marked ship, while Xerxes watched the debacle in safety from his throne atop nearby Mount Aegaleus.

By any fair measure, Themistocles seems mostly responsible for the Greek victory. The existence of a large Athenian fleet was critical to the Greek cause and its creation was his legacy. Other than at Salamis, there were no other naval theaters between Athens and the southern Peloponnese that so favored the smaller and slower Greek fleet. Once invaded, Themistocles persuaded his countrymen to put their faith in ships, not hoplites, had them evacuate Attica, and then convinced the Greek admiralty to risk an all-out engagement in Athenian waters, which alone offered the chance for victory. Whatever the actual circumstances of the Persians' costly decision to fight according to Greek wishes, contemporaries at least believed that Themistocles had fooled Xerxes into committing his forces immediately into the narrows. And finally, at the key moment of the engagement Themistocles led the Athenian contingent, aided by favorable tides, to cut into the enemy flank and rout the Persian fleet. In short, the key to the salvation of the West was the Persian defeat by the Greeks, which required a victory at Salamis, which in turn could not have occurred without the repeated efforts—all against opposition— of a single Athenian statesman. Had he wavered, had he been killed, or had he lacked the moral and intellectual force to press home his arguments, it is likely that Greece would have become a satrapy of Persia.

There is a postscript to Salamis that is too often forgotten. The Greek victory may have saved the West by ensuring that Hellenism would not be extinguished after a mere two centuries of polis culture. But just as importantly, the victory was a catalyst for the entire Athenian democratic renaissance. As Aristotle saw more than a century and a half later in his *Politics,* what had been a rather ordinary Greek polis, in the midst of a recent experiment of allowing the native-born poor to vote, would now suddenly inherit the cultural leadership of Greece.

Because Salamis was a victory of "the naval crowd," in the next century the influence of Athenian landless oarsmen would only increase, as they demanded greater political representation commensurate with their prowess on the all-important seas. The newly empowered Athenian citizenry refashioned Athenian democracy, which would soon build the Parthenon, subsidize the tragedians, send its triremes throughout the Aegean, exterminate the Melians, and execute Socrates. Marathon had created the myth of Athenian infantry; Salamis, the far greater victory, had just superseded it. Imperialists like Pericles, Cleon, and Alcibiades, not the descendants of the veterans of Marathon, were the key players on the horizon.

No wonder crotchety Plato in his *Laws* argued that while Marathon had started the string of Greek successes and Plataea had finished it, Salamis "made the Greeks worse as people." More than a century after the battle, Plato saw Salamis as a critical juncture in the entire evolution of early Western culture. Before Salamis, Greek city-states embraced an entire array of quite necessary hierarchies—property qualifications to vote, wars fought exclusively by those landowners meeting the infantry census, and a general absence of taxes, navies, and imperialism. Those protocols defined freedom and equality in terms of a minority of the population who had ample capital, education, and land. Before Salamis, the essence of the polis was not equality for all, but the search for moral virtue for all, guided by a consensus of properly qualified and gifted men.

Plato, Aristotle, and most other Greek thinkers from Thucydides to Xenophon were not mere elitists. Rather, they saw the inherent dangers in the license and affluence that accrued from radically democratic government, state entitlement, free expression, and market capitalism. Without innate checks and balances, in this more restrictive view, the polis would turn out a highly individualistic, but self-absorbed citizen with no interest in communal sacrifices or moral virtue. Better, the conservatives felt, that government should hinge on the majority votes of only those educated and informed citizens with some financial solvency. War—like Marathon and Plataea—should be for the defense of real property, on land, and require martial courage, not mere technology or numerical superiority. Citizens should own their own farms, provide their own weapons, and be responsible for their own economic security—not seek wage labor, public employment, or government entitlement. The oarsmen of Salamis changed all that in an afternoon.

With the Aegean wide open after the retreat of the Persian fleet at Salamis, and Athens now at the vanguard of the Greek resistance, radical democracy and its refutation of the old polis were at hand. The philosophers may have hated Salamis, but Salamis had saved Greece, and so the poor under the leadership of Themistocles had not ruined, but reinvented, Greece.

A new, more dynamic, exciting, and in some sense reckless West would emerge under the leadership of the boisterous Athenian *demos*. What later philosophers such as Hegel, Nietzsche, and Spengler would deplore about Western culture—its rampant equality, uniform sameness, and interest in crass material bounty—in some sense started at Salamis, an unfortunate "accident," Aristotle said, but one that nevertheless shifted forever the emphasis of Western civilization toward more egalitarian democracy and a more capitalistic economy. Whatever we may think of the great strengths of, or dangers, in present-day Western culture—consumer democracy increasingly set free, rights ever more expanded, the responsibilities of the citizenry further excused—that mobile and dynamic tradition is also due to Themistocles' September victory off Salamis.

In late September 480, Themistocles and his poor Athenians not only saved Greece and embryonic Western civilization from the Persians, but also redefined the West as something more egalitarian, restless—and volatile—that would evolve into a society that we more or less recognize today.

JOSIAH OBER

CONQUEST DENIED

The Premature Death of Alexander the Great

he historian Arnold Toynbee once put forward a counterfactual speculation that has gained a certain fame. What would have happened if, instead of dying at thirty-two, Alexander the Great had made it to old age? Toynbee saw Alexander conquering China and dispatching naval expeditions that would circumnavigate Africa. Aramaic or Greek would become our lingua franca and Buddhism our universal religion. An extra quarter century of life would have given Alexander the chance to achieve his dream of One World, becoming in the process a kind of benevolent advance man for a United Nations, ancient style.

Josiah Ober, the chairman of the Department of Classics at Princeton, has come up with an alternative scenario for Alexander the Great, and one darker than Toynbee's: What if Alexander had died at the beginning of his career, before he had the opportunity of adding "the Great" to his name? That nearly happened at the Battle of the Granicus River in 334 B.C., and Alexander's literal brush with death reminds us how often the interval of a millisecond or a heartbeat can alter the course of history. The conquests of the young Macedonian king would never have been realized, the Per-

sian Empire would have survived unchallenged, and the brilliant Hellenistic period, that cultural seedbed of the West, would have been stillborn. Suppose, however, that Alexander had outlasted his bout with an unnamed fever in 323 B.C.? Given his appetite for conquest and for terror as a political weapon, Ober feels, he might only have filled another two decades of life with fresh occasions for "opportunistic predation." The culture of the known world, and Hellenism in particular, might have been the worse for Alexander's reprieve.

❖ *Ober is the author of* THE ANATOMY OF ERROR: ANCIENT MILITARY DISASTERS AND THEIR LESSONS FOR MODERN STRATEGISTS *(with Barry S. Strauss) and, most recently,* THE ATHENIAN REVOLUTION *and* POLITICAL DISSENT IN DEMOCRATIC ATHENS.

At the Battle of the Granicus River in northwestern Anatolia, during the first major military engagement of Alexander the Great's invasion of the Persian Empire, young King Alexander came very close to death. At the Granicus, the Macedonians and their Greek allies encountered local Anatolian cavalry and Greek mercenary infantry under the joint command of Persian regional governors (satraps). The enemy was massed in a defensive formation on the opposite bank of the river. The river was fordable, but the banks were steep and Alexander's senior lieutenants counseled caution. After all, the king was barely twenty-two years old and presumably still had much to learn. A serious setback early in the campaign could end the invasion before it had properly begun. Ignoring their sensible advice, Alexander mounted his great charger, Bucephalus ("Oxhead"). Highly conspicuous in a white-plumed helmet, the king led his Macedonian shock cavalry in an audacious charge across the river and up the opposite bank. The Persian-led forces fell back before the Macedonian's charge, and he penetrated deep into their ranks. This was probably exactly what the Persian tacticians had planned for from the beginning. Due to the startling success of his charge, Alexander, accompanied only by a small advance force, was momentarily cut off from the main body of the Macedonian army.

At this critical moment in the battle, young Alexander was surrounded by enemies, including one Spithridates, an ax-wielding Persian noble who managed to deal the Macedonian king a heavy blow to the head. Alexander's helmet was severely damaged. The king was disoriented, unable to defend himself. A second strike would certainly kill him. And with the young king would die the hopes of the entire expedition and Macedonian imperial aspirations. In the next few seconds the future

ALEXANDER THE GREAT

A helmetless Alexander the Great, riding Bucephalus, ancient history's most famous horse, leads a charge on fleeing Persians. How different would our world be if he had died in battle—as he nearly did? This mosaic, uncovered in Pompeii, was based on a Greek painting, probably completed in Alexander's lifetime.

(Alinari/Art Resouce, NY)

of the Persian empire and the entire course of Western history would be decided. Did Alexander's life flash before him as he awaited imminent extinction? How had he come to arrive at this place, at this untoward fate? How could so much have come to depend on a single blow?

❖ ❖ ❖

Alexander was born in Macedon (the northeastern region of modern Greece) in 356 B.C., the first and only son of King Philip II of Macedon and Olympias of Epirus (modern Albania). Philip had seized control of

Macedon just three years prior to his son's birth, following the death in battle of his royal brother, Amyntas III. Prior to Philip's accession, Macedon had been a relative backwater—a semi-Hellenized border zone pressured on the north and west by aggressive Danubian tribes and to the east by imperial Persia. When not confronting system-level tribal or imperial threats, Macedon's rulers were consistently outmaneuvered diplomatically by the highly civilized Greek city-states to the south. Internally, Macedon was dominated by semi-independent warlords who followed the lead of the weak central government only when it pleased them. Yet by instituting a dramatic reorganization of the Macedonian armed forces, technological innovations (for example, the extra-long thrusting spear known as the *sarissa* and hair-spring powered catapult artillery), economic restructuring, and astute diplomacy, Philip had changed all that—seemingly overnight. By the time Alexander was ten years old, Macedon was the most powerful state on the Greek peninsula. The Danubian tribes had been first bought off, then humbled militarily. Some of the Greek city-states bordering Macedon had been destroyed: The sack of Olynthus in 348 had shocked the rest of the Greek world. Many other Greek cities were forced into unequal alliances. Even proud and powerful Athens had eventually seen the wisdom of making a peace treaty, after suffering a series of humiliating military and diplomatic setbacks at Philip's hands.

Meanwhile, Alexander was being groomed to help govern the kingdom and, eventually, assume the throne. He was well trained: His tutor in intellectual and cultural matters was the philosopher Aristotle; his mentor in military and diplomatic affairs was his own father, probably the best military mind of his generation. And in the corridors of the royal palace at Pella, Alexander learned the murkier arts of intrigue. The Macedonian court was beset by rumor and factions. The counterpoint was the hard-drinking parties favored by the Macedonian elite, all-night events that featured blunt speech and, sometimes, sudden violence. Alexander and his father had come close to blows on at least one of these drunken occasions.

In Alexander's twentieth year, Philip II was cut down by an assassin. The killer, a Macedonian named Pausanias, was in turn butchered by Philip's bodyguards as he ran for his horse. Although Pausanias may well have held a personal grudge against his king, there was suspicion that he had not acted alone. One obvious candidate for the mastermind behind the killing was Darius III, the Great King of Persia—in the mid-fourth century a mighty empire that stretched from the Aegean coast of Turkey, to Egypt in the south, and east as far as modern Pakistan. In the years before the assassination, Philip had been making open preparations for a Persian expedition; a few months prior to his death his lieutenants had established a beachhead on Persian-held territory in northwestern Anatolia. "Cutting the head from the dangerous snake" was a well-known Persian modus operandi and (at least according to later historians) Alexander himself publicly blamed Darius for Philip's death. But Darius was not the only suspect; other fingers pointed at a jealous wife— Olympias—and even at the ambitious young prince himself.

In any event, Alexander's first order of business after his father's death was the establishment of himself as undisputed king: The Macedonian rules for succession were vague and untidy, in fact any member of the royal family who could command a strong following had a chance at gaining the throne; Alexander proceeded to establish his claim with characteristic dispatch and equally characteristic ruthlessness. Potential internal rivals were eliminated, the restive Danubians crushed in a massive raid deep into their home territory. Immediately thereafter a hastily pulled together anti-Macedonian coalition of Greek city-states was smashed by Alexander's lightning march south. In the aftermath of Alexander's victory, the great and ancient Greek city of Thebes was destroyed as an example to others who might doubt the new king's resolve.

Alexander had proved himself his father's son and worthy of the throne, but his treasury was seriously depleted. He had no choice but to follow through with the planned invasion of the western provinces of the Persian empire. The prospect of war booty fired the imagination of his

Macedonian troops. The restive southern Greeks were brought on board by the prospect of revenge for long-past, but never-forgotten, Persian atrocities during the Greco-Persian wars of the early fifth century B.C. Crossing at the Hellespont, Alexander had sacrificed at Troy to the shades of Homeric Greek heroes, and then proceeded south, toward the Granicus, where he met his first significant opposition. Now, with Spithridates's ax arcing down toward Alexander's shattered helmet for the second time, it appeared as if the glorious expedition would end before it had begun.

Yet the deadly blow never landed. Just as Spithridates prepared to finish off his opponent, one of Alexander's personal bodyguard "companions," Cleitus (nicknamed "the Black"), appeared at his king's side and speared the Persian axman dead. Alexander quickly rallied, and the wild charge that might have ended in disaster spurred on his troops. Most of the Persian forces crumbled; a stubborn body of Greek mercenaries was eventually cut down. Alexander was spectacularly victorious at the Granicus—losing only 34 men and reportedly killing over 20,000 of the enemy. Spoils from the battle were sent back to Greece to be displayed in places of honor. Alexander was now on his way, and it seemed nothing could stop him. In the course of the next decade, Alexander and his Macedonians repeatedly demonstrated their capacity to overcome tremendous obstacles. They went on to conquer the entire Persian empire, and more. Alexander's conquest of the Persian empire is among the most remarkable—and most terrifyingly sanguinary and efficient—military campaigns of all time. By 324 B.C. Alexander had laid the foundations for a successor empire that might have included both the entirety of the old Persian holdings, penisular Greece, and various outlying areas as well. He established an imperial capital at Mesopotamian Babylon and began to lay plans for internal administration—and further military expeditions. Yet Alexander did not long outlive his great campaign of conquest. He died of disease (perhaps malaria) complicated by the effects of hard living (multiple serious wounds, heavy drinking) in June of 323 B.C. at the age of thirty-two, ten years after the Granicus.

The would-be unified empire never came about; in the course of two generations of savage warfare Alexander's generals and their lieutenants and sons divided amongst themselves the vast territories they had helped to conquer. Some distant northern and eastern provinces fell away from Macedonian rule—control of northwestern India was formally ceded to the aspiring native dynast Chandragupta Maurya (founder of the great Mauryan empire) in exchange for 300 war elephants. But vast regions remained: Within a generation of Alexander's death, Egypt, most of Anatolia, Syria-Palestine, and much of western Asia (as well as the Macedonian homeland and contiguous regions in Europe) were being ruled by relatively stable Macedonian dynasties. And because the Macedonian elite eagerly adopted Greek culture, this extensive region was incorporated into a Greek sphere of political and cultural influence. Dozens of major and minor Greek cities were established by Alexander and his successors: Egyptian Alexandria, Macedonian Thessalonika, Anatolian Pergamum, and Syrian Antioch are only a few of the most famous. The Greek language quickly became the common vernacular for a large part of the civilized world—and the dominant language of trade, diplomacy, and literary culture.

The brilliant Hellenistic civilization that arose in the generations following the death of Alexander not only enlarged exponentially the geographic range of Greek culture, it provided a historical bridge between the classical Greek culture of the sixth to fourth centuries B.C. and the coming age of imperial Rome. Hellenistic scholars at the famous library in Egyptian Alexandria preserved and codified the best of earlier Greek literature, while Hellenistic historians did the same for the memory of Greek accomplishments in the political and miltiary spheres. Philosophical speculation—especially the relatively individual-centered Stoicism and Epicureanism flourished among the educated elites. Local experiments in religious practice and thought were granted the possibility of a vast audience, due to the prevalence of a common language and a general attitude of religious tolerance among the ruling elites.

There were remarkable demographic shifts as people gravitated toward new opportunities: Greeks and Macedonians—in high demand as soldiers and administrators—to be sure, but also Jews, Phoenicians, and other peoples of the Near East who established enclaves in the new and burgeoning Greek cities; meanwhile older cities (including Jerusalem) were made over in a new cosmopolitan and increasingly Hellenic image. This Hellenistic (or "Greek-oriented") world was similar to the classical era in its political focus on semi-independent city-states and its highly developed urban culture. It was different from the classical era in that "Greekness" was now defined as much by cultural affinity as by ethnic heritage—individual Syrians, Egyptians, Bactrians in central Asia, along with people from many other ethnic backgrounds living in regions controlled by descendants of Alexander's generals became increasingly Greek in their language, education, literary, and athletic tastes—even while remaining quite un-Greek in their religious practices. The Hellenistic world was the milieu in which Judaism came to the attention of the Greeks and achieved some of its distinctive "modern" forms. It was the context in which Jesus of Nazareth preached his new message and in which Christianity grew up as a religion. It was, in short, Hellenistic Greek culture that was inherited by the Romans, and subsequently preserved for rediscovery in the European Renaissance and Enlightenment. And so, it is not too much to say that to the extent that modern Western culture is defined by a "Greco-Roman-Judaic-Christian" inheritance, it is a product of the world that grew up in the wake of Alexander's conquests.

❖   ❖   ❖

Alexander's seemingly premature death at the age of thirty-two stimulated one of the best known historians of the twentieth century, Arnold Toynbee, to develop an elaborate and romantic "counterfactual history," which has become a classic of the genre. Postulating a sudden recovery from his debilitating fever, Toynbee imagined a long productive life for Alexander in which conquest and exploration were nicely balanced by thoughtful administrative arrangements and a generous social policy that saw all residents of the great empire as worthy of basic human dignity. In Toynbee's optimistic counterfactual scenario, Alexander and his unbroken line of successors promoted both culture and technology, leading to the early discovery of (for example) steam power. Consequently, the great empire was invincible; Rome never became a serious threat. With the discovery of the Western Hemisphere by Alexandrian explorers, the empire eventually becomes a genuine world-state. It is ruled by a benevolent monarchy; in Toynbee's counterfactual present, Alexander's direct lineal descendent still sits secure on his throne, his subjects enjoy peace and prosperity, and all really is right with the world.

Toynbee's counterfactual was heavily influenced by the cheerful portrait painted by his contemporary, W. W. Tarn, an eloquent and domineering historian who had depicted the historical Alexander as a cosmopolitan, thoughtful, and far-sighted proto-Stoic. Tarn's Alexander engaged in warfare only as a means to a higher end—Tarn envisioned that end as a broad-based "brotherhood of man" (centered on a policy of intermarriage between Greek- and Persian-speaking groups) that would flourish beneath the benevolent imperial aegis. Yet more recent commentators (notably E. Badian and A. B. Bosworth) have emphasized a much darker side of Alexander's character. They focus on the brutality of the means by which Alexander's tenure of power and the Macedonian conquest of Persia were effected, and they assert that there was no grand vision of a higher or humanitarian end. Under this revisionist theory, Alexander cared much for slaughter and little for imperial management. Under his direct leadership the Macedonians proved to be remarkably good at wholesale butchery of less militarily competent peoples—but they contributed little in the way of culture. This alternative view of Alexander allows the development of a grim alternative to Toynbee's "Alexander survives" counterfactual. We might posit that if Alexander really had lived for another thirty years, there would have been much more widespread destruction of existing Asian cultures and disastrous impoverishment in the process of the sapping of local resources to finance a never-ending cycle of opportunistic predation that offered little but misery in its wake. And so we might posit that the Hellenistic world (and its modern legacy) might never have come about if its progenitor had lived much longer.

Yet, realistically speaking, Alexander did not die young. People in antiquity could not expect to live nearly as long as do modern people in developed countries: Disease and risks of battle tended to end their lives much earlier than we would regard as "normal life expectancy." So it is hardly remarkable that Alexander expired before turning gray—a man who repeatedly exposed himself to extraordinary physical risks on the battlefield and suffered several appalling wounds, who had many personal enemies, who indulged in frequent bouts of binge drinking, and who spent most of his life outdoors, traveling thousands of miles in an era before the development of modern sanitation or medicine in areas with diverse and unfamiliar disease pools. Rather the wonder is that Alexander lived to the "ripe old age" of thirty-two. The explanation for his relative longevity in the face of the many risks he took and the stresses he inflicted on his body can be put down to some combination of remarkable personal vigor and equally remarkable luck. And so, in terms of really plausible counterfactual history, it seems more sensible to ask ourselves, not, "What if Alexander had lived to be sixty-five?" but, "What if Alexander had died in his early twenties?" To make it more specific: What if Alexander had been just a bit less lucky at the Battle of the Granicus? What if Cleitus had been a heartbeat too late with his spear?

There is good reason to suppose that, although Alexander was very lucky indeed to ride away from the Granicus with his head intact, it was not just luck that placed Spithridates just an ax-length from the Macedonian commander early in the battle. The Persians certainly knew just where Alexander was riding among the Macedonian cavalry. The king's white-plumed helmet was a clear marker, as indeed it was intended to be, for the Macedonians. And the Persian commanders had ample reason to suppose that Alexander would lead the charge personally. The place of an ancient Greek general was typically at the front of the line, rather than in the rear echelons. Moreover, young Alexander, at the outset of an audacious expedition against a mighty opponent, had a special need to cement a reputation for personal bravery and charismatic leadership. When the Macedonian charge came, Alexander could be expected to be at its head.

If the Persian generals took any account of recent history, they had very good reason to fear well-led Greek invaders—and equally good reason to supppose that if its commander were killed, the Macedonian expedition as a whole would quickly founder. Two generations past, in 401 B.C., Cyrus II, a highly talented and consequently overambitious younger brother of the reigning Persian king, had led an army of some 13,000 Greek mercenaries against his royal elder sibling. At the battle of Cunaxa, near Babylon (in modern Iraq), the disciplined Greek hoplites trounced their opponents. But at a moment at which his victory seemed quite possible, Cyrus had led a spirited cavalry charge that smashed deep into the opposing ranks. Much too deep, as it turned out. Lacking Alexander's fortune, Cyrus was cut down as soon as he became isolated from his main force. With the military commander and pretender to the throne dead, the expedition immediately lost its purpose and its impetus. About 10,000 Greek surivors managed to fight their way out of the heart of the Empire in an epic retreat immortalized in Xenophon's autobiographical *Anabasis* ("The March Up-Country"). The success of the hoplite force at Cunaxa and the subsequent march of the 10,000 clearly demonstrated, to Greeks and Persians alike, the military potential of Greek soldiers when led against Asian forces: Persian kings of the fourth century B.C. took the point and regularly hired Greek mercenaries. But the political threat to the Persian empire had died with Cyrus II, and that lesson was not lost on his countrymen, either. Whether Cyrus's unhappy fate was due to his opponents' tactical planning or his own rashness, it provided a model for how to deal with a young, ambitious would-be conqueror at the head of a genuinely dangerous army: Lure him out and away from his main force and then cut him down at leisure. With its head amputated (given Spithridates' weapon of choice, the metaphor is particulary apt), the serpent would necessarily die. And so, what if the simple and sensible

Persian plan of "isolate and eliminate the commander" had worked at the Granicus—as it so nearly did? If Alexander had died at age twenty-two, instead of ten years later after having conquered the Persian empire, human history would have been very different indeed.

❖   ❖   ❖

With the second blow of the ax, Alexander's skull was cleaved; he died instantly. Cleitus arrived in time to dispatch his foe, and a fierce battle over the body of the fallen king ensued. The Macedonians eventually prevailed and drove back the enemy forces, but they took many casualties and the main body of the Persian forces withdrew largely intact. Moreover, King Darius III, the young, energetic, and battle-proven Persian monarch, was even now raising a huge force: Madeconian victories against Darius's local governors would be meaningless as soon as the royal army arrived in western Anatolia. Meanwhile, Darius's admirals were preparing to carry the conflict back into Greece. With no great success to report, and with the news of Alexander's death impossible to contain for long, the Macedonian expeditionary force was faced with the prospect of a major Greek uprising. With the Macedonian throne vacant; the Greeks would play the familiar game of supporting this pretender or that—and the future of every member of the Macedonian elite was bound up in the outcome of the ensuing struggle. The Macedonian war council following Granicus was brief and to the point: There was no sense in continuing the campaign, every reason to beat a quick retreat, taking whatever plunder could be grabbed up quickly on the way home. As Macedon devolved into civil war, the brief Macedonian golden age sparked by Philip's organizational genius came to an end: The next several generations closely recapitulated earlier Macedonian history, a series of weak kings in thrall variously to Greeks, Danubians, Persians, and their own strong-willed nobles.

Persia, on the other hand, entered a long period of relative peace and prosperity. Darius proved diplomatically adept and allowed the semi-Hellenized western satraps to deal with the Greeks on their own terms.

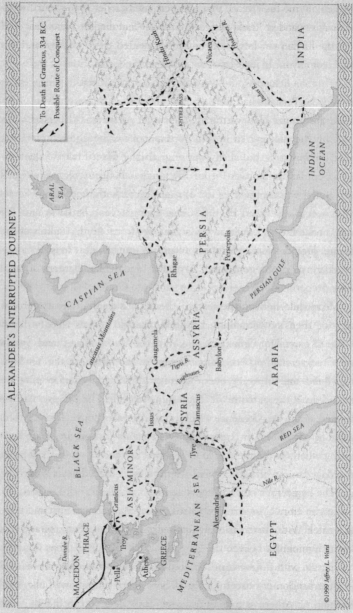

ALEXANDER'S INTERRUPTED JOURNEY

To Death at Granicus, 334 B.C.
Possible Route of Conquest

©1999 Jeffrey L. Ward

The general modus vivendi that had pertained earlier in the fourth century was expanded: Trade between Greece, Anatolia, the Near East, and even the further reaches of the empire expanded; there was less and less reason for anyone in Greece to imagine that the Greek cities of the western Anatolian littoral would welcome "liberation" from the Persian master, and the Persians had long ago lost interest in military adventurism among the bronze-clad warriors to their west. Although the Persian kings stuck by the old and successful Persian policy of religious toleration (which helped to avoid costly uprisings among the pockets of the Empire's population that were especially touchy about matters of religious purity), the worship of the God of Light and the Truth, Ahuru-Mazda, and a cosmology based on his eternal struggle with darkness and the forces of the Lie continued to spread among the multiethnic elites of the Empire, providing some level of cultural continuity that helped to undergird Persia's conservative military policy and efficient system of taxation.

Meanwhile, in mainland Greece, the big winner was the city-state of Athens. Athens's two traditional rivals, Sparta and Thebes, were both out of the picture: Thebes had been eliminated by Alexander and Sparta never recovered from a crushing defeat at the hands of the Thebans in 371 B.C. and the subsequent liberation of Sparta's serf population in nearby Messenia. With Macedon in a state of near collapse, Athens was once again the dominant military power on mainland Greece: The Athenian navy was now larger than it had been at the height of the Periclean "golden age" in the mid-fifth century. But the Athenians saw little advantage to imperialistic adventurism on the mainland or toward the east. The democratic city had proved capable of flourishing economically without an empire, focusing on its role as an international port and trading center. With Athenian warships patrolling the Aegean, piracy was kept to a minimum. Given the generally good relations Athens was able to maintain with the western satraps of Persia, the conditions were ideal for an expansion of peaceful trade in both luxury items and bulk commodities. As Athenian trading interests expanded, so too did the tendency for the expansive tendency of Athenian democracy to include non-natives and it became increasingly common for successful resident foreigners in Athens to be granted citizenship. Always a cultural mecca, Athens now became the unquestioned center of Greek intellectual and cultural life—there were relatively few Greek philosophers, poets, scientists, or artists who willingly lived elsewhere. As the citizen body and state revenues from harbor taxes grew in tandem, so too did the capacity for Athens to extend its influence into new zones.

The western Mediterranean beckoned: Italy, Sicily, southern Gaul, Spain, and North Africa were all quite well known to the mainland Greeks, and the Athenians had attempted the conquest of Sicily back in the late fifth century. But there was a real problem: The imperial Phoenician city-state of Carthage (located on the North African coast near modern Tunis) had long regarded overseas trade in the western Mediterranean as an exclusive Carthaginian monopoly, and the Carthaginians had backed up this policy with a strong naval presence. Tension between Carthaginian and Athenian traders eventually flared into open conflict between the two great sea powers. In the long and debilitating war that followed, neither side managed to gain a clear advantage. Both sides had large citizen populations from which to recruit rowers and marines; both had large war chests and so each side was able to augment its citizen levies with mercenary forces. Tens of thousands of men were lost in massive sea battles, and even more drowned when sudden Mediterranean storms caught fleets of oared warships too far from protective harbors.

The theater of war expanded: Other mainland Greek states, and especially the Greek cities of Sicily and southern Italy, were inevitably drawn into the fray, on one side or the other. As Athens and Carthage poured more and more of their resources into the bitter and futile war, other non-Greek states moved in to pick up the trade: Phoenicians in the east, and eventually Latin speakers from central Italy in the west. As the conflict droned on, new traders took over the routes and new trade goods from inner Asia, Egypt, and Europe came available; the popularity of

Hellenic cultural icons, for example, in architecture, decorated vases, and literature, tended to fade in the western provinces of the Persian empire. And Greek culture had never really caught on in most of the West.

With Carthage and the western Greek cities weakened by warfare, the big winner in the western Mediterranean was Rome. Only a mid-range regional power at the time of Alexander's death on the Granicus, Rome grew in strength by creating a coherent central-Italian defensive league; the influence of the league spread rapidly and Rome eventually entered the Atheno-Carthage conflict, ostensibly on the Carthaginian side. The result was the rapid absorption of all of Italy, then Sicily, and eventually a much-reduced Carthage into a rapidly growing Roman con-federation that had by now become a genuine empire. A temporary truce with Athens and the mainland Greeks proved ephemeral: The Romans soon found an excuse to launch an invasion of Greece. With Athens weakened by two generations of unceasing conflict, the Roman victory was assured. But Athenian stubbornness in refusing to surrender after a lengthy siege tried Roman patience. When the walls of the city were fi-nally breached, the Roman soldiers ran amok. The massacre was general and the city burned. Along with the extermination of Athens was lost the bulk of Greece's intellectual and cultural treasures: Only tattered rem-nants of Greek tragedy, comedy, philosophy, and science survived the sack. The Greek world never regained its cultural or economic vibrance; the surviving city-states were strictly controlled by the vigilant Romans. Most Romans had developed no taste for Greek culture and despised what little they knew. "Greek studies" eventually became a very minor area of the larger world of Roman antiquarian research, of interest to a few scholars with especially arcane and esoteric tastes.

The conquest of Greece brought the Romans into direct confronta-tion with the Persians. Yet a generation of skirmishes between the two great empires proved indecisive: Although Rome took over Egypt and so completed its conquest of North Africa, the Romans found that they did not have the manpower simultaneously to pacify their vast holdings in the west and at the same time to engage in a really effective large-scale war with Persia. For their part, the Persians had long ago given up thoughts of westward expansion; holding onto central Asia was enough of a challenge. Moreover, in the course of protracted diplomatic exchanges, the ruling elites of two great powers found that Persian and Roman aristocrats had much in common. Both cultures had immense respect for tradition and authority. Both were highly patriarchal, oriented toward duty and ancestors. The Romans found Ahuru-Mazda worship much to their liking—the starkly dualistic vision of a cosmos divided between forces of good and evil fit their worldview and they found it quite easy to integrate Ahuru-Mazda into the religious mishmash they had interited from the Etruscans. The Persians, for their part, found that adopting some aspects of Roman military organization helped them consolidate their hold on their eastern provinces. There was a fair amount of intermarriage between Roman and Persian noble families; and in time the two cultures became harder and harder to tell apart.

This is the world as we might have known it, divided into the relatively stable bipolar structure that has, from time to time, seemed self-evidently the appropriate and indeed inevitable fate of mankind. Under this international regime, the peoples of the world, almost infinitely diverse in their cultures and their beliefs, simply remained so—there was (for better or for worse) no hegemonic "master culture" or "central canon" to unite them. This means that there would have been no Renaissance, no Enlightenment, no "modernity." The very concept of "the Western World" as exemplifying a set of more or less clearly articulated (if always contested and imperfectly realized) cultural, political, and ethical ideals would never have arisen.

There would perhaps have been occasional outbreaks of religious enthusiasm, but these would have remained local matters, never to transcend the provincial level. For indeed by what means could they become generalized? While Latin in the West and Aramaic in the East would prove workable adminstrative languages, they were not hospitable linguistic environments for transcultural exchanges. Traders inevitably would have learned a few languages, but most people would continue to speak their own local language and nothing but, live by local laws, worship their local deities, tell their local stories, and think their local ideas. Their contact with whichever of the great empires they happened to inhabit would be limited to paying taxes and occasional military service. The peculiarities of diverse cultures might be of interest to the state-supported scholars who would make it their business to collect and categorize knowledge about the world; but these would remain few and would be supported by the governments of the two empires only because abstruse knowledge sometimes comes in handy in dealing with problems of tax collection or keeping order.

❖ ❖ ❖

And so, if Cleitus had stumbled as he hastened to save his king, we would inhabit a world very different from our own in terms of geopolitics, religion, and culture. I have suggested that it would be a world in which the values characteristic of the Greek city-states were lost in favor of a fusion of Roman and Persian ideals. The stark dualism of Ahuru-Mazda worship became the dominant religious tradition. A profound reverence for ritual, tradition, ancestors, and social hierarchy—rather than Greek reverence for freedom, political equality, and the dignity of the person— defined the ethical values of a small "cosmopolitan" elite that would rule over a diverse mosaic of cultures. And this could take place because there was no long and brilliant "Hellenistic Period"—and so no integration of a wider world into a Greek cultural/linguistic sphere.

Without the challenge of strong Greek cultural influence and subsequent Roman mismanagement in Judea, Judaism would have remained a localized phenomenon. The Persians were quite sensitive to local religious concerns; under continued Persian rule there would have been no great Maccabee uprising, no Greek Septuagint, no violent Roman destruction of the Second Temple, no great Jewish diaspora. Likewise, Jesus of Nazareth (had he not chosen to stick to carpentry) would remain a local religious figure. The New Testament (whatever form it took) would never have been composed in "universal" Greek and so would not have found a broad audience. Without the wide diffusion of Jewish and Christian texts, the cultural domain in which Mohammed grew up would have been radically altered; if a new religion emerged within the Arabian peninsula it would take a form quite different from that of classical Islam and it seems highly unlikely that it would have generated the remarkable cultural and military energies we associate with the great Jihad. Indeed, the very concept of "culture" would have a very different meaning; culture would remain overwhelmingly local rather than developing viable aspirations to universality.

Ironically, the values of our own world, which I have suggested is a result of Alexander's good luck at the Granicus, would not have pleased Cleitus the Black. As a staunch Macedonian conservative who despised innovation, Cleitus would be more likely to approve of the counterfactual Romano-Persian regime described above. But Cleitus did not live to see the world his spear thrust made: Seven years after saving his king at Granicus, he was speared to death by Alexander in a drunken quarrel over the cultural future of the nascent empire. Their quarrel, even more ironically, was (as it turned out) over contrasting counterfactual scenarios: Cleitus believed that Macedonians should stick by their traditions and should have nothing to do with the customs of the people they conquered; he dreamed of a world in which the victorious Macedonians would be culturally unaffected by their military success. Alexander, seeking to unify his empire and to gain the manpower needed for future conquests, was eager to adopt Persian court ritual and to train Persian soldiers to fight side by side with his Macedonian veterans. But neither Cleitus's Macedonia-first conservatism nor Alexander's hope for a unitary empire and unending imperial expansionism had much to do with the real new world that came into being upon Alexander's very timely death in Babylon, at age thirty-two, in June of 323 B.C.

LEWIS H. LAPHAM

FUROR TEUTONICUS: THE TEUTOBURG FOREST, A.D. 9

The first century A.D. saw the Roman Empire near its height. Its capital, Rome, was not just the center, but the envy, of the known world. In the words of the classicist Edith Hamilton, the Emperor Augustus (63 B.C.–A.D. 14) had "found Rome a city of bricks and left her a city of marble." The newest target for imperial expansion was the wilderness region beyond the Rhine known as Germany. Then in A.D. 9, twenty-two years into pacifying, civilizing, and homogenizing— its traditional modus operandi for barbarian lands—Rome suffered a reverse there from which it never recovered. In the Teutoburg Forest, tribesmen led by a chieftain named Arminius surprised and annihilated three Roman legions—15,000 men plus camp followers. Arminius had the heads of his victims nailed to trees: It provided a telling psychological message that was not lost on Rome. Violence became its own reward. The empire retreated behind the Rhine and, except for occasional forays, left Germany alone.

Almost two millennia later, we have to wonder what kind of imprint a Romanized Germany would have left on history. What if Germany had not remained for centuries a frontier, one of Europe's last—with a frontier mentality, in its darker manifestations especially, that the descendants of Arminius—or Hermann, as he was later called—have never completely surrendered? What if Arminius had not become a kind of Shanelike figure but just another co-opted local prince? What if the Roman Empire, with its temples, amphitheaters, and system of law, had extended to the Vistula? Would we have ever considered the dire prospect of a "German Question"?

❖   Lewis H. Lapham deals with some of those possibilities in the following essay. Lapham is the editor of Harper's magazine and the winner of the National Magazine Award for his essays, which have been likened to those of H. L. Mencken and Montaigne. He is the author of eight books, including two just published, THE AGONY OF MAMMON and LAPHAM'S RULES OF INFLUENCE. He is a well-known lecturer and television host.

> You may not be interested in war, but war is interested in you.
>
> —*Leon Trotsky*

During the first decade of the era not yet revealed as Christian, the Emperor Caesar Augustus was more concerned with military dispatches from Mainz than with reports of miracles at Bethlehem. He had ruled as princeps for nearly thirty years, dictating an end both to the Roman republic and a century of civil war, and at all points of the imperial compass his augurs observed auspicious omens— tranquility in Egypt, peace in Africa and Spain, the Parthians quiescent, vineyards in Aquitaine, gymnasia in Cyzicus and no cloud of rebellion anywhere on the blue horizon of the Mediterranean world.

Except, of course, in Germany. Augustus wasn't familiar with the song of Seigfried or the insignia of the thousand-year Reich, but as an army commander in the wilderness east of the Rhine he had come up against the Germanic tribes known to his legions as the Furor Teutonicus, a horde of superstitious barbarians, invariably hostile and usually drunk, worshippers of horses and moonlight, keeping their primitive calendar by counting nights instead of days, roaming like wolves through fog and snow.

Augustus assumed that eventually it would occur to one of their chieftains to turn the wagons south, and he had it in mind to prevent that accident by extending the frontier of the empire as far north as the Elbe River, possibly as far east as the Vistula and the Baltic Sea, the force of arms followed by a show of aqueducts and apple trees and the Goths reduced, as Julius Caesar had reduced the Gauls west and south of the

Rhine, to a harmless rabble of submissive colonies, "well supplied with luxuries and accustomed to defeat."

The policy was optimistic but not implausible. The Roman power in the first Century A.D. brooked neither rival nor contradiction, and its magistrates were in the habit of issuing writs of omnipotence in the name of a monarchy comprehending, in Edward Gibbon's phrase, "the fairest part of the earth and the most civilized portion of mankind," the obedient provinces, "united by laws and adorned by arts," the roads running in straight lines from the Atlantic Ocean to the Euphrates, the frontiers defended by "the spirit of a people incapable of fear and impatient of repose." If Augustus had managed to accomplish his German project, giving it the weight of milestones as well as colors on a map, the course of European history over the next 2,000 years might have taken a very different set of turns—the Roman empire preserved from ruin, Christ dying intestate on an unremembered cross, the nonappearance of the English language, neither the need nor the occasion for a Protestant reformation, Frederick the Great a circus dwarf, and Kaiser Wilhelm seized by an infatuation with stamps or water beetles instead of a passion for cavalry boots.

The Romans began the work of German pacification in 13 B.C., the year that Tiberius, the emperor's heir and stepson, brought his legions across the Alps into Austria, lower Wirtemberg, and the Tyrol. A temple to Jupiter appeared at Cologne, and soon afterward the construction of naval fortifications at the mouths of the rivers opening the German wilderness to an approach from the North Sea. The more prominent barbarians received the favor of Roman citizenship, their intransigence tempered by the music of flutes, their suspicions relieved by gifts of silk and gold. Their sons acquired an acquaintance with the Latin language, learning to fasten their cloaks with jewels instead of thorns, and for twenty years the lines of Roman settlement edged eastward into the Westphalian forest.

But in A.D. 6, the barbarians in the province Illyricum, the modern-day Balkans, rose in murderous revolt, and Tiberius was sent from Trier to punish their presumption. The brutal lesson in civility lasted three years, and while it was in progress Augustus assigned the continuing education of the Germanic tribes to Publius Quinctilius Varus. The plan was sound, but Augustus entrusted it to the wrong Roman. A soft and complacent man, Varus at the age of fifty-five owed the favor of his promotion to his marriage with the emperor's grandniece. He had served as proconsul in Africa and legate in Syria, but his knowledge of military strategy derived from the gossip of his subordinates, and his character was that of a palace functionary—dissembling, avaricious, indolent, and vain.

As "Governor of Germany across the Rhine," Varus assumed command of the empire's three most formidable legions, and he arrived from Italy with the opinion that his army was invincible and the barbarians broken to the harness of Roman law. Neither supposition proved correct, but Varus, of whom it was later said, "Fate blindfolded the eyes of his mind," didn't take much interest in facts he found disagreeable or inconvenient. He conceived his task as administrative and relied on his belief that Augustus, his wife's fond and careful uncle, wouldn't have sent him to Germany unless the work was easy. Choosing to regard Germanic tribes as easily acquired slaves rather than as laboriously recruited allies, he forced upon them a heavy burden of taxation in the belief that they would come to love him as a wise father.

Among the barbarians serving as officers on his staff, Varus bestowed the greater part of his trust and affection on Arminius, a prince of the Cherusci who had campaigned with Tiberius in Illyricum and appreciated the poetry of Horace. The contemporary historian Velleius describes Arminius as a fiercely handsome man in his late twenties, "brave in action and alert in mind, possessing an intelligence quite beyond the ordinary barbarian." He also possessed a talent for duplicity well beyond the intelligence of Varus, who thought of him as his most devoted flatterer. Arminius took the trouble to profess his admiration for all things Roman, meanwhile making the preliminary arrangements for a literal-minded performance (no orchestra, no costumes, nothing operatic) of Götterdämmerung.

The chance presented itself in the autumn of A.D. 9. Several days before Varus moved his three legions—15,000 infantry in company with 10,000 women, children, auxiliaries, slaves, and pack animals—for their summer encampment near Minden to winter quarters further west, apparently somewhere near the modern town of Haltern. Arminius disclosed the line of march to those of the Cherusci, who shared his resentment of the empire. The malcontents recruited like-minded allies among the Chatti and Bructeri, and halfway between the two military strong points, in the thickly wooded ravines of the Teutoburg Forest, a mob of screaming barbarians fell upon the Roman column.

The historians still argue about the exact whereabouts of the ensuing massacre, and over the last several hundred years they have deployed the meager literary and archeological remains—old manuscripts, gold and silver coins found buried in peat moss, shards of Roman armor, the local place names of Knochenbahn (Bone Lane) and Mordkessel (The Kettle of Death)—to suggest as many as 700 theories about the likely point of attack. Some historians place Varus's column among the upper tributaries of the Ems River, others place it nearer the rivers Lippe or Weser, but all the authorities agree that the Romans died like penned cattle. The difficulty of the terrain (a narrow causeway between steep embankments, the wet ground "treacherous and slippery around the roots and logs," overturned wagons, bewildered children, horses dying in the mud) prevented the legions from bringing to bear their superior weapons and tactics. Trained to fight in the open field, they carried heavy javelins and the short Spanish sword with which they were accustomed to cutting down their enemies in the manner of farmers reaping wheat. But in the German forest they were caught in a tangle of trees, encumbered by a baggage train strung out over a distance of nine miles, unable to form their cohorts into disciplined lines. The barbarians began the attack at dusk, hurling their spears from the rock outcroppings higher up on the hillsides, and during three days and three nights of leisurely slaughter in a cold and steady rain, they annihilated the entire Roman army. Varus committed suicide. So did every other officer who knew that it was the practice of the Cherusci to nail their vanquished but still living enemies to the trunks of sacred oak trees.

Arminius sent Varus's head to Maroboduus, a barbarian king in Bohemia on whom he wished to make a favorable impression, and Maroboduus, for diplomatic reasons of his own, forwarded the head to Rome. Dio Cassius reports the effect as memorable, Augustus so shocked by the utter destruction of so fine an army that he "rent his garments and was in great affliction," and Gibbon remarks on the emperor's consternation with his familiar irony, ". . . Augustus did not receive the melancholy news with all the temper and firmness that might have been expected from his character."

The fear of barbarian invasion drifted through the city with rumors of strange and terrifying portent—the summit of the Alps was said to have fallen into a lake of fire, the temple of Mars struck by a thunderbolt, many comets and blazing meteors seen in the northern sky, the statue of Victory, which had been placed at a crossroads pointing the way toward Germany, inexplicably turned in the opposite direction, pointing the way into Italy. Suetonious speaks of the emperor dedicating extravagant games to Jupiter Best and Greatest on condition that the Germans failed to appear on the Palatine and Capitoline Hills. Augustus declared the day of Varus's death a day of national mourning; for many months he refused to cut his hair or trim his beard, and from time to time until the end of his life, at the age of seventy-seven in A.D. 14, he was to be seen wandering through the rooms of his palace, beating his head against a wall and crying out, in a voice the historians describe as thin and old, "Quinctilius Varus, give me back my legions."

Mocked by the defeat in the Teutoburg Forest, Augustus abandoned the project of civilizing the German wilderness, and in the will that he left to his successor, Tiberius, he bequeathed the virtue of prudence—"Be satisfied with the status quo and suppress completely any desire to increase the empire to greater size." By and large, Tiberius heeded the advice, but in A.D. 15 he allowed his nephew, Germanicus, to undertake a revengeful campaign against the Cherusci. Germanicus burned crops and pagan temples, murdered large numbers of barbarians (many of them women and children, quite a few of them in their sleep) and in a dark wood between the Lippe and Ems Rivers, his army came across the remnants of their former companions-in-arms, a scene that Tacitus describes in the *Annals* as one "that lived up to its horrible associations . . . whitening bones, scattered where men had fled, heaped up where they had stood and fought back. Fragments of spears and of horses' limbs lay there, also human heads, fastened to tree trunks." Germanicus's army recovered two of the three golden eagles lost with the legions of Varus, but it didn't manage to defeat Arminius in a decisive battle, and on its recall to Rome in A.D.16, Tiberius adopted the policy of settling the empire's northern boundary along the angle formed by the Danube and the upper Rhine.

❖ ❖ ❖

The Roman withdrawal left the Furor Teutonicus unmolested by amphitheaters and well-supplied with spears and drinking songs. The barbarian clans knew Arminius by the name of Hermann, and they proclaimed him first a hero and then a legend. Their enthusiasm was approved by Tacitus, who refers to Arminius as "unmistakably the liberator of Germany. Challenger of Rome—not in its infancy, like kings and commanders before him, but at the height of its power . . . to this day the tribes sing of him." It didn't matter that Arminius failed in his attempt to unite the northern tribes in the cause of German independence; nor did it matter that in A.D. 21, at the age of thirty-eight, he was assassinated by his own clansmen, who objected to his proclaiming himself a king. His mistakes were forgiven because he had defied the majesty and cynicism of Rome, not only in the Teutoburg Forest but also in pitched battles against legions under the command of both Germanicus and Tiberius, and the memory of him was consecrated in the blood of his enemies.

Tacitus wrote his histories during the reign of Trajan, and his disappointment in the character of the emperors subsequent to Augustus inclined him to present the imagined virtues of the noble savage (loyal, freedom-loving, chaste) as moral counterpoint to the certain viciousness of Caligula and the proven decadence of Nero and Domitian—"No one in Germany finds vice amusing, or calls it 'up-to-date' to seduce and be seduced." Elaborating the theme in the *Germania*, Tacitus praises the Saxon tribes for their self-sufficiency, for having attained "that hardest-of-results, the not needing so much as a wish," and in recognition of their strength and courage he gives voice to the hope that they "ever retain, if not love for us, at least hatred for each other; for while the destinies of empire hurry us on, fortune can give no greater boon than discord among our foes."

The German inheritors of the tale adorned it through successive generations with the heavy ornament of Teutonic myth. During the third and fourth centuries A.D. the name and triumph of Arminius served as a metaphor for the valor of the barbarians crowding south upon the decay of Rome. The eighth century associated the old story with the glory of Charlemagne, the twelfth century with the conquests of Frederick Barbarossa; the chroniclers of the high Middle Ages extended the compliment of comparison to the dynasties of Hapsburg, Wittelsbach, and Holenzollern. By the end of the eighteenth century, Hermann was at one with Seigfried in the halls of Valhalla, and when the fury of early nineteenth century German romanticism descended upon the town of Detmold, the citizens voted to erect a colossal statue of Hermann on the summit of the highest mountain in the Teutoburger Wald. Nobody knew exactly where Varus had kept his appointment with doom, but Detmold was certainly somewhere in the vicinity, and the town council imagined the great hero triumphant with uplifted sword, the statue mounted on gothic columns hewn from living oak, the whole of the edifice rising to a height of nearly 2,000 feet and visible at a distance of sixty miles.

The enterprise failed for lack of funds, but what couldn't be rendered in bronze found expression in scholarship, in the work of the late nineteenth-century historians (in Britain and France as well as in Germany) advancing the several flags of European nationalism. Leopold von Ranke discovered in the prowess of Hermann an early proof of Aryan supremacy—stalwart blond people, blue-eyed and fair-skinned, resisting the advance of the mongrel races enlisted under the imperial eagles of Roman luxury and greed. Several French intellectuals traced the wonders of Newtonian science to the ancient freedoms of the German forest, and Sir Edward Creasy, prominent in Victorian England as both historian and lecturer, thought Arminius worthy of a statue in Trafalgar Square. "Had Arminius been supine or unsuccessful," said Sir Edward, in *Fifteen Decisive Battles of the World*, "this island never would have borne the name England." The book appeared to favorable reviews in 1852, and the next two generations of British and American historians (among them Teddy Roosevelt) endorsed Creasy's theory of the Roman Empire as a corruption of "debased Italians" deserving of defeat at the hands of purebred Anglo-Saxons notable for "their bravery, their fidelity to their word, their manly independence of spirit, their love of their natural free institutions, and their loathing of every pollution and meanness." Richard Wagner set the words to music, and the American pioneers carried them west against the Sioux, and the rulers of Nazi Germany fitted them to the design of Auschwitz.

❖   ❖   ❖

Begin the sequence of historical event with a different set of circumstances in a German forest in the autumn of A.D. 9 (dry weather, Varus a competent general, the rage of Arminius modified by a second reading of Virgil's *Georgics*), and Adolf Hitler might not have danced his victorious jig in a French forest in the spring of 1940. Augustus wouldn't have known how to read Luther's Bible or the flashes of Gestapo uniform (the Furor Teutonicus not having yet acquired the art of letters) but if a few words in a Gothic script appeared one afternoon on the column of a Roman peristyle, the emperor could have guessed well enough at their probable meaning. Germany-across-the-Rhine he regarded as the antithesis of civilization, a wilderness "thankless to till and dismal to behold," and although he was by no means given to a republican practice or democratic sentiment, he understood the uses of poets, the fictions of government, the glory of bees. "Wheresoever a Roman conquers," said

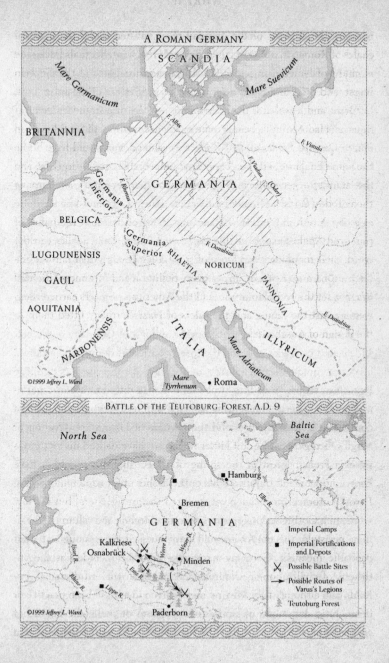

A ROMAN GERMANY

SCANDIA

Mare Germanicum

Mare Suevicum

BRITANNIA

F. Albis

F. Visula

GERMANIA

F. Viadua (Oder)

Germania
Inferior

F. Rhenus

BELGICA

Germania
Superior

RHAETIA

F. Danubius

NORICUM

LUGDUNENSIS

PANNONA

GAUL

F. Danubius

AQUITANIA

NARBONENSIS

ITALIA

ILLYRICUM

©1999 Jeffrey L. Ward

*Mare
Tyrrhenum*

• Roma

Mare Adriaticum

BATTLE OF THE TEUTOBURG FOREST, A.D. 9

North Sea

Baltic
Sea

Elbe R.

• Hamburg

• Bremen

GERMANIA

Kalkriese
Osnabrück

Werre R.

Weser R.

Ems R.

• Minden

Ijssel R.

Rhine R.

Lippe R.

Paderborn

©1999 Jeffrey L. Ward

▲ Imperial Camps

■ Imperial Fortifications
and Depots

✕ Possible Battle Sites

→ Possible Routes of
Varus's Legions

Teutoburg Forest

Seneca, "he inhabits," and if Augustus had fostered the planting of orchards as far north as Berlin, the empire thus strengthened and enlarged might have denied passage to the Mongols, admitted Moscow to the freedom of Rome, found in the aureus an early equivalent of the euro.

Nine centuries after the collapse of the Roman power, Western Europe constructed the premise of the Renaissance on the rediscovered blueprints of Latin literature—Cicero's politics, Virgil's verse forms, the histories of Tacitus and Livy, Ovid's metaphysics, Martial's epigrams. The first translations emerge in those countries that retained a memory of the empire (in Italy, England, and France, not in Germany, and nowhere east of the Vistula), but it was another 300 years before the models of classic antiquity began to be handed around among the advisors to the courts at Brandenburg and Dresden. The delay possibly accounts for the German confusion about imperialism (its nature and purpose, the distinction between diplomacy and *blitzkrieg*) that provided the twentieth century with the *causus belli* for two world wars.

Assume as antecedent that Roman conquest of Germany in the first and second centuries A.D. and the improvisation of derivative narratives no doubt could entertain a faculty of historians for the whole of a college semester. The professors might choose to set up their propositions in the manner of a board game, playing Bismark and the *ubermensch* against the drawings of Albrecht Dürer and the cantatas of Johann Sebastian Bach. No doubt they would quibble over the relative value of Schiller's lyrics and Hindenburg's artillery shells, but I suspect that the general tone of conversation would tend to prefer the solemn calm of empires to the crowd noises of the unruly provinces.

Gibbon published his history of Rome's decline and fall in 1776, the same year in which the American colonies declared themselves independent of the British crown; the tide of the Enlightenment was turning to the ebb, and within the next fifty years it was followed by a surge of revolutionary romance—in Mexico and Brazil as well as France and Germany. New definitions of freedom gave rise to the belief that even the smallest quorum of nationalist identity deserves the status of a sovereign state. The Treaty of Versailles returned the administration of Illyricum to the incompetence of the Balkan tribes, and I can imagine both Gibbon and Augustus comparing the foolishness of Woodrow Wilson to the stupidity of Publius Quinctilius Varus. A similar prejudice informs the writing of the contemporary diplomats and foreign policy analysts who mourn the absence of "transnational institutions" capable of managing the world's affairs with the sang-froid of the old Roman empire. Confronted with the chaos of unregulated capital markets—also with rogue states and renegade ideologies, with war in Africa, civil unrest in Judea, tyrants in Parthia and Leptis Minor, too much cocaine crossing the frontier near Chalcedon, too many poisons in the Mediterranean Sea—the would-be makers of a postmodern peace dream of Gibbon's "supreme magistrate, who by the progress of knowledge and flattery was gradually invested with the sublime perfections of an Eternal Parent and an Omnipotent Monarch." Augustus would have been pleased to grant them an audience.

BARRY S. STRAUSS

THE DARK AGES
MADE LIGHTER

*The Consequences of
Two Defeats*

his chapter is the story of two battles and what might have happened if their results had been reversed—as well they might have been. Both involved powers on the cusp of advance or retreat. In the first, Adrianople (A.D. 378), the Roman Empire suffered a disaster even worse than that of the Teutoburg Forest, and one that went far to send it reeling into its final decline. In the second, Poitiers (probably 732), a Frankish army turned back Muslim invaders near the Loire River at the moment when they seemed ready to spread across Europe—"The Great Land," as they called it.

Did the Roman Empire—or at least the part of it that dominated Western Europe—have to die and so give birth to the Dark Ages? Did the Dark Ages themselves (which may not have been all that dark) have to happen? As Barry S. Strauss tells us, much of the blame may fall less on Spenglerian fatigue than on the poor judgment of one man, the emperor Valens, who squandered an army in a battle that he should have avoided or delayed fighting. (Adrianople—the present Turkish city of Edirne—has the distinction of being the most fought-over city in the world, Valens's fatal reverse being one of fifteen major battles or sieges that have taken place there in just short of 1,700 years.) The Visogoths who slaughtered Valens's troops, and who also killed him, would eventually move west to capture and sack the city of Rome itself. By that time the empire was all but beyond rescue. It did not have to be that way, Strauss argues. What would a world that Rome continued to lead have been like?

The dynamism that had once belonged to the Roman Empire would pass to a new locus of power: Arabia. Less than a century after the death of the prophet Mohammed in 632, the armies of Islam had established rule as far west as Spain—the kingdom they called Al-Andalus. How important was Poitiers? Strauss comes down on the side of those historians who see it as a turning point. It certainly brought us the foremost dynasty of early medieval Europe, the Carolingians: Charlemagne was the grandson of the victor, Charles Martel. But if the battle had gone differently, so might history. As an anonymous Muslim chronicler put it: "On the plain of Tours [as the battle is sometimes called] the Arabs lost the empire of the world when almost in their grasp." It would have been an empire full of luster: These Arabs were the foremost broadcasters of enlightenment in their time.

Both Adrianople and Poitiers are cases of what might be called first-order counterfactual theory—that is, a major rewriting of history stemming from small changes. How different would our lives have been if only Valens had been more patient. If only Abd Al-Rahman, the Muslim commander at Poitiers, had survived to rally his forces.

❖ *Barry S. Strauss is professor of history and classics and the director of the peace studies program at Cornell University. His books include* FATHERS AND SONS IN ATHENS, THE ANATOMY OF ERROR: ANCIENT MILITARY DISASTERS AND THEIR LESSONS FOR MODERN STRATEGISTS *(with Josiah Ober), and* ROWING AGAINST THE CURRENT: ON LEARNING TO SCULL AT FORTY.

I n the European early Middle Ages two events took place—the fall
of the Roman Empire in the West and the Muslim tidal wave of
conquest—that might have changed everything had they turned
out differently. Had imperial Rome maintained control of Europe or had
imperial Islam restored a single, central authority there, Europe would
have been spared the chaos of the Dark Ages (ca. A.D. 500–1000). To be
sure, even chaos can yield dividends in the long run: Some would say that
the Dark Ages sowed the seeds of later Western freedom; others deny
that there was anything dark about them. Yet dark or bright, they unde-
niably lacked the order and stability that an empire brings. The fate of an
empire, be it Roman or Muslim, may have hinged on battles—battles
whose results could have gone either way.

True, the rise and fall of an empire is a long process, but the heaviest
doors pivot on small hinges, and at the battles of Adrianople (August 9,
378) and Poitiers (October 732) the hinges turned. At Adrianople, a Germanic people, the Visigoths, destroyed a Roman army and killed the emperor, thereby setting in motion a century of defeats that would finally
bring down the empire in the West. Yet it was a near-run thing. A little
patience on the part of the commander, a little rest for the men, a change
in the weather—any of these might have changed the outcome at Adrianople and ultimately saved the Roman Empire. At Poitiers, a Frankish
force defeated a Muslim army. It was a smaller engagement than Adrianople but it proved a psychological and political turning point, because
it blunted the triumphant Arab advance northward and because it propelled the efforts of the Frankish general Charles Martel to establish a dynasty. Under his grandson Charlemagne (r. 768–814), that dynasty
governed a far-flung state that laid the foundations for much of what
would follow in Europe—from kingdoms like France and Germany to lo-

cal government by royal vassals to the Christian culture of cathedral schools and decorated manuscripts. Yet had the Frankish army not killed the Muslim commander that day at Poitiers, they might have lost the battle; Europe would have lost the family that built a great Frankish state; and what might have emerged, instead, was a Muslim France or even a Muslim Europe.

Historians no longer think of early medieval Europe outside of Spain as the time and place of the Dark Ages but rather as the seedtime of European greatness. Where historians once saw a sharp break between Rome and its Germanic conquerors, they now find continuities in the "Romano-German" kingdoms; where once they perceived poverty and misery, they now see prosperous trading networks and free farm laborers; where once they saw cultural decline, they now find creativity—in Celtic manuscripts, for example, or the poetry of *Beowulf*, or the monasticism of the Benedictines. In short, many scholars no longer ask whether the Dark Ages could have been avoided because they don't believe they should have been avoided.

Yet not even the most sunny interpretation of the fifth to tenth centuries A.D. can dodge gloom altogether, not in Western Europe. Around A.D. 350, a single empire—Rome—governed much of the Near East and North Africa, as well as what is now England, France, Belgium, the Netherlands, Spain, Italy, Switzerland, and western Germany. Then violent invasions began to tear that empire apart. In the east, the Roman Empire survived as the Byzantine state for a thousand years, until the Turkish conquest of Constantinople in 1453. In the West, the last Roman emperor was dethroned in 476, a generation after the Western empire had become little more than a legal fiction. The Western empire had been tottering for years. Roman land was plundered, Roman cities were attacked—Rome itself was sacked in 410 and 455—Roman men were killed and Roman women were dragged off as war booty to marry Germanic chiefs. The central government could not stop foreigners from settling en masse on Roman lands and from eventually carving out separate kingdoms in the Roman state. The population declined enough for Pope

Gelasius (r. 492–496) to write of "Emilia, Tuscany, and the other provinces [of Italy] in which nearly not a single human existed." An exaggeration, but what really happened can be seen in the fate of the city of Rome, which may have contained one million people in the time of Christ, but by the ninth century A.D. had a population of about 25,000. By contrast, in the tenth century A.D. Córdoba, the capital of Muslim Spain, had a population of about 100,000, and Seville perhaps 60,000. In short, a single Roman Empire was replaced by smaller states, and in the process, society became more violent and less urbanized.

Europe would have been spared violence, anarchy, and misery if the Roman Empire could have survived or, once having fallen, it could have been pieced back together again. Which is why the battles of Adrianople and Poitiers are so important and so tantalizing. Each could have had a different result, if just a few changes are imagined. Let us examine each in turn.

❖ ❖ ❖

Throughout its long history, the Roman state had to face continual military challenges from the warlike peoples on its frontiers. A double threat confronted Rome in the fourth century A.D., with Persia on the rise in the east and various Germanic peoples pushing from the north. In response to frequent emergencies, the empire was divided in two, with one emperor in Constantinople and another at Rome—or rather, at Milan, the de facto Western capital because it was closer to the battle zone.

In the early fourth century A.D. the Visigoths, a Germanic people, had settled north of the Danube in Dacia (modern Romania), formerly a Roman province. About fifty years later they were invaded by other Germanic tribes, who were in turn fleeing from the Huns, a ferocious people who had ridden out of central Asia. Pushed to the point of famine, in A.D. 376, the Visigoths asked the government in Constantinople for permission to cross the Danube to seek refuge—and a permanent home—in Roman Thrace, all 200,000 or so of them, including women and children (to follow a reasonable modern estimate of numbers). It would be mass emigration of a people who gave the Romans the shivers. Yet the Eastern emperor, Valens (r. 364–378) agreed to their request.

He was no humanitarian. Valens knew that the Visigoths were dangerous warriors but he planned to co-opt them and add them to his armies, which already had a Visigothic contingent. He needed more soldiers to fight Persia. He also knew that Visigothic refugees would bring wealth with them, which his officials could skim off if not plunder outright—corruption being a depressing reality of Late Roman administration. In return, he insisted that the Visigoths lay down their arms when they crossed the Danube. The Visigoths agreed, but Valens should have known better.

No sooner did the Visigoths cross the Danube then they came into conflict with Roman officials, who outdid themselves in coming up with creative ways to fleece the refugees. The trouble was, the Visigoths fought back. In early 377 they began a revolt that defeated a Roman army and spread among other aggrieved groups such as miners and slaves. Eventually, with the help of a large cavalry contingent from their allies, they forced a Roman retreat. "The barbarians," writes the Roman historian Ammianus Marcellinus, "poured over the wide extent of Thrace like wild animals escaping from their cage."

In spring 378, the Emperor Valens prepared to counterattack with an army estimated at thirty to forty thousand men. Meanwhile, the Western emperor, Valens's nephew Gratian (r. 367–383), marched to his aid from Raetia (roughly Switzerland) where, the winter before, he had defeated other Germanic invaders. Unfortunately, Valens "rose to the level of his mediocrity," as we might say today. He had the opportunity to crush a cornered, but by no means defeated enemy; he turned it instead into disaster. Instead of waiting for Gratian's reinforcements, Valens insisted on fighting—according to critics, he did not want to share the glory of victory. In his overconfidence he gave credence to intelligence reports that the Visigoths had only 10,000 men (we don't know how many men they did have but it was far more than that). The battle would take place on

ISLAM CHECKED AT THE BATTLE OF POITIERS

Charles Martel, flourishing a battle ax, center, inspires his Christian Frankish troops to defeat the Muslim Moors at Poitiers. Had the Arabs won the battle in 732, would Islam have continued to spread across Europe?

(Carl von Steuben, 1788–1856, Battle of Poitiers. Giraudon/Art Resource, NY)

the plains near the city of Adrianople (modern Edirne, in Turkey) and it would take place immediately. It was August 9, 378.

Barbarians the Visigoths might have been, but their leader, Fritigern, had a sure instinct for the enemy's weak points, none more important than Valens himself. The emperor sent his men into battle in the broiling heat of an August afternoon in the Balkans (summer temperatures of 100 degrees Fahrenheit are common in the region) with no rest or food after an eight-mile march over rough country. The Visigoths, encamped behind a circle of wagons, were surprised by the Romans, but their men were rested and they used their opportunity well. First, they deftly sent their cavalry to turn the Roman lines and trap the legionnaires between the wagons and the Visigothic infantry. Ammianus Marcellinus describes that fateful ride: "The Gothic cavalry . . . shot forward like a bolt from on high and routed with great slaughter all that they could come to grips with in their wild career."

Then, having attacked the Romans with their cavalry first on one side and then the other, the Visigoths hit them head on with their infantry. They slaughtered the closely packed enemy troops.

It is estimated that as many as two-thirds of the Romans in the battle were killed, including thirty-five high-ranking officers. The greatest casualty was Valens himself. The catastrophe is made all the more poignant by the knowledge that it could have been avoided. Had the emperor waited for reinforcements or, failing that, had he attacked with fed and rested men the next morning, the outcome would probably have been different. Nor can we underestimate the role of accident. The Visigothic cavalry only arrived on the battlefield at the last minute; had they been detained further, there would have been no Visigothic victory. Keenly aware of their importance, Fritigern played for time by sending various negotiators to the Romans until the eleventh hour. The Roman high command might even have accepted his offer to parley, but the troops took matters into their own hands. Roman archers and cavalry disobeyed orders and began to attack the Visigoths, thereby forcing battle. So perhaps the fate of the Roman Empire lay in the hands of a nervous skirmisher.

Flush with victory, the Visigoths were now free to roam the Balkans. The loss of perhaps 20,000 to 25,000 men was big enough to imperil Rome's manpower needs. It was, said St. Ambrose of Milan on hearing the news of the battle, "The end of all humanity, the end of the world." It was, at any rate, the end of the old Roman ability to bounce back from defeat, so prominent a feature of the empire's previous history. Far from closing in for the kill, Rome allowed the enemy to settle within the boundaries of the empire, south of the Danube, in the area of modern

Bulgaria. Worse still, Rome allowed the Visigoths to keep their arms. They were, in theory, allies of Rome, but in practice they were a rival state. In the 390s, for example, the Visigoths looted Greece and the Balkans, and then, after 400, they did the same to Italy. The height of disaster came in 410, when the Visigoths, led by the wily and aggressive Alaric, took the city of Rome and sacked it for three days. It was a sign of things to come for the tottering empire.

Why did the Romans tolerate Visigothic settlement within the empire? For one thing, they needed the Visigoths as soldiers, and the Romans believed they could co-opt and tame them. Second, as Roger Collins argues, defeatism may have been at work. For many Romans, the lesson of Adrianople seems to have been that Rome could not prevail in battle against the enemy. At least, that may explain why four times between 395 and 405, in Italy and the Balkans, Roman armies fought and beat the Visigoths under Alaric, but each time they allowed them—and him—to escape and fight again. It is hard not to wonder whether Adrianople had done to Rome what the Battle of Verdun (1916) did to France—not in its military outcome, for France won at Verdun, but in its psychological outcome. The bloody battle devastated French morale for a generation and weakened military manpower badly.

Thirty years after Adrianople, Alaric and the Visigoths were in Italy. After sacking Rome, they eventually settled in Gaul and Spain. In the meantime, to save Italy, the Roman government had to withdraw troops from Britain and Gaul, which gave other Germanic tribes the opportunity to invade the empire. Britain was lost to Rome after 407, and within a generation large parts of Gaul, Spain, and North Africa were effectively independent. Now largely dependent on barbarian mercenaries to defend it, Rome had traveled far down the road to 476, when the Germans in Italy deposed the last Western Roman emperor, Romulus Augustus (r. 475–476), whose "empire" was mere fiction.

What could have been done? Arther Ferrill maintains that Rome's best hope would have been to reverse the outcome of Adrianople; that is, to win the battle, kill the Visigoths' commander, Fritigern, and two-thirds of his men. That would not have ended the security threat, because there was no shortage of barbarians ready to probe the empire's defenses and attack it, but it would have bought Rome time to regroup. It might, moreover, have generated the confidence and political will to ram through the political and military reforms needed to man the Roman army. Without such reforms, the empire would have remained weak in the long term. With Rome victorious, though, Adrianople might have proved not a Roman Verdun but a Roman defeat of the Spanish Armada, turning back the invader and inspiring assurance and reform.

What if the Roman Empire had survived? What if it had bounced back from the crisis of the years 376–476 the way it had earlier recovered from the crisis of the years 188–284? Like the Chinese Empire, the Roman state would have remained a great power dominating a huge area. With the resources of the Western empire to help it, the East Roman, or Byzantine, Empire might have defeated the Muslims in the seventh century and kept the Mediterranean a Christian lake. Beyond the Rhine and Danube, Germanic and Slavic rivals to Rome would have developed, or perhaps Rome would eventually have conquered them too. There would, of course, have been periods of disorder, inevitable invasions such as China suffered from time to time. But the empire would always have bounced back. It might have even expanded, stretching at its greatest extent from Mesopotamia to Morocco and from Britain to the Elbe, the Vistula or even—who knows?—the Dnieper.

Latin-speaking Europe, governed from a capital in Italy, would have become a more orderly and stable society than the boisterous and freedom-loving Germanic kingdoms that replaced imperial Rome. The emperor, whose office had been around seemingly forever, would have been endowed with a charisma no less potent than the "mandate of heaven" that the rulers of China enjoyed. There would have been no feudalism, no knights, no chivalry, but no Magna Carta either, no doctrine of the right of rebellion, and no parliaments.

The Roman world would have been Christian, but Christianity might not resemble what we know today. It would be Roman, of course, and Catholic—that is, universal—but the pope, if the bishop of Rome had so grand a title, would be strictly subordinate to the Defender of the Faith, that is, the emperor, just as in Eastern Orthodoxy the patriarch stayed under the Byzantine emperor's thumb. No pope could have made a Roman emperor kneel in the snow outside his door, as Pope Gregory VII did the German monarch Henry IV at Canossa in 1078. There would have been no conflict of church and state, no papal monarchy, and no Protestant Reformation. If Martin Luther ever penned his Ninety-Five Theses, he would have done so in his native Latin. They would have been delivered in executive session at a church council, and if the emperor was not amused, he would have sent Luther straight to the lions. The Romans never had much patience for dissent.

There would, of course, have been no Renaissance since, without the death of classical culture in the early Middle Ages, there would have been no need for it to be reborn. Whether Columbus would have sailed across the Atlantic from Hispania without the scientific and commercial spirit of the Renaissance to inspire him is a good question, but one thing is certain: A new Roman Empire in the Americas would have been far less dedicated to individual liberty than the English colonies turned out to be. Governed by a proconsul resident in the city of Nova Roma (New Rome, perhaps today's New Orleans), the United Provinces of America would stand as a model of the ideal proclaimed by Cicero: *otium cum dignitate:* that is, "peace with respect for rank." Merciless with their enemies but not racists, the Romans might have treated the Indians much as the Spanish did, with a mixture of brutality, missionary zeal, and a surprising willingness to intermarry.

Like the Roman Empire, the U.P.A. would be an oligarchy rather than a democracy. Truth to tell, the American founders had great respect for Rome and thought pure democracy dangerous; to some degree they modeled our government on Rome's. Yet they admired the Roman Republic and its political ferment, not the Roman Empire and its centralized monarchy. Our constitution contains a Bill of Rights; our culture is founded on a revolution in the name of liberty; our society prizes equality, although it often fails to achieve it. Were America a New Rome, it would have the same inequality of the United States today without a movement to change it; it would have a judicial system without such rights as *habeas corpus* or the guarantee against self-incrimination; it would have no reason to have abolished the profitable slave systems that grew up in the New World. New Rome would have bread and circuses but no citizens' assembly in the forum.

✦ ✦ ✦

All of this assumes that Rome could have survived the great military challenge that ripped through the Old World in the early Middle Ages—the challenge of Islam. As it turned out, the Muslim armies wreaked havoc on the surviving East Roman or Byzantine state, driving the Byzantines out of the Levant and back to their base in Anatolia and the southern Balkans. There the Byzantines were able to regroup and in places even drive back the enemy. Perhaps this is not surprising, because the Byzantines were, after all, Romans. They had inherited a thousand years of military and political skill to call on in a pinch. Had it survived, the Western Roman empire could have come to Byzantium's help, and together the two of them might have pushed Islam eastward, leaving the Mediterranean and Europe to Rome. What did happen, of course, is very different.

It was one of military history's most lightninglike accomplishments. Within a generation of the death of the prophet Muhammad in 632, the armies of Islam had conquered most of the Near East, threatening the Byzantine capital of Constantinople itself. In 711, after conquering Egypt and North Africa, Muslim armies crossed the straits of Gibraltar and attacked the Christian kingdom of Spain, which had been established by descendants of the Visigoths who beat Rome at Adrianople. The Muslims crushed the Visigoths' army and killed their king, Roderic. In less than a decade, the Muslims conquered most of the Iberian Peninsula. They called their kingdom Al-Andalus. Then, in 720, they crossed the Pyrenees Mountains to attack the region known as Septimania. Today part of

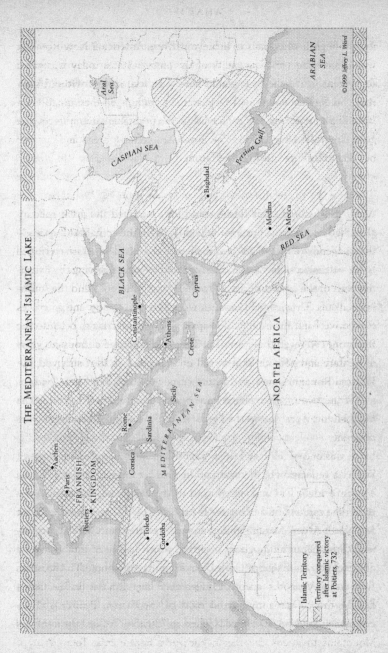

THE MEDITERRANEAN: ISLAMIC LAKE

Aral Sea

CASPIAN SEA

ARABIAN SEA

©1999 Jeffrey L. Ward

Baghdad

Persian Gulf

Medina
Mecca

RED SEA

BLACK SEA

Constantinople

Cyprus

Athens

Crete

NORTH AFRICA

Aachen

Paris

FRANKISH

KINGDOM

Poitiers

Rome

Sardinia

Corsica

Sicily

MEDITERRANEAN SEA

Toledo

Cordoba

Islamic Territory

Territory conquered after Islamic victory at Poitiers, 732

France (Languedoc), at the time it had been a Visigothic province in Gaul. Furthermore, it was the doorway into what Arab authors referred to as "the Great Land," a vague term not just for Gaul but for all of Europe. Some even envisioned their armies marching all the way to Constantinople, attacking the capital of the Eastern Roman empire by the back door, as it were.

The Muslims quickly took the city of Narbonne, an old Roman colony and an excellent strategic base. They were defeated outside Toulouse in 721, where their commander, As-Sanh ibn Malik, governor of Al-Andalus, was killed. The presence of a seasoned and disciplined officer, Abd Al-Rahman, prevented the setback from turning into a rout: He led an orderly retreat to Narbonne. Shortly afterward, the Arabs returned to the offensive, slowly expanding eastward into the Rhône valley and attacking cities from Bordeaux to Lyon. By the mid-730s, all of the major cities of the French Mediterranean coast between the Pyrenees and the Rhône were in Muslim hands. Around 730, the governorship fell to the man who had saved the day at Toulouse, Abd Al-Rahman. He was popular with the men for his largesse as well as his cool on the battlefield, but he would have his hands full with threats on both sides of the Pyrenees.

Strong central government was the exception and not the rule in the early Middle Ages. Across the Pyrenees, the "kingdom" of the Franks was more like a collection of quarreling princes. In Al-Andalus, a fault line ran between the Arab elite and the Berber tribesmen of North Africa, recent converts to Islam. The Berbers had formed the bulk of the conquering Muslim army in 711 and later years, but they complained that the Arabs took the best land and booty for themselves. By 732, the Berber leader, Munuza, had carved out a splinter kingdom in the strategic eastern Spanish high plain bordering Gaul. According to one source, Munuza made an alliance with his neighbor Duke Odo of Aquitaine. Although a Christian, Odo was a thorn in the side of his nominal overlord, the Frankish king; like Munuza, Odo aimed at his own independence. In 732, Abd Al-Rahman turned on both men. He led an expedition that captured and killed Munuza, and then he crossed the mountains and marched through Gascony and Aquitaine. We do not know the size of his army, but it was large enough to crush Odo's forces near Bordeaux, to burn and loot Christian strongholds, and to capture a large number of civilians. An estimate of 15,000 Muslim soldiers in this army, which some historians have suggested, is probably not far off the mark.

Abd Al-Rahman's men drove all the way north to Poitiers, just short of the great sanctuary of St. Martin of Tours, a kind of national shrine of the Franks, famous for its Christian piety and wealth. Tours is only a little over 200 miles from Paris.

They would go no further. Somewhere between the cities of Poitiers and Tours, perhaps at Moussais on the old Roman road, they met the army of the leader of the Franks, Charles the Pippinid. In theory only "Mayor of the Palace" (r. 714–741), a kind of prime minister, he was the *de facto* king of the Frankish kingdom, which straddled northern France and western Germany. Although he had made war on the Franks before, a desperate Odo had now sought Charles's aid.

True, the Franks were not the power they had once been under their first great king, Clovis (r. 481–511), but under the Pippinids they were on an upward trajectory. A bastard son who had to fight for power after the death of his father, Pepin II (d.714), Charles fought well—and often. Charles was a seasoned and popular warrior at the head of a victorious army when he came to Poitiers, but so was Abd Al-Rahman. It ought to have proved a dramatic showdown.

So it did, but we know frustratingly few of the details. Contemporary evidence insists that the battle took place on a Saturday in the month of October and in the year that most would date to 732, although some scholars opt for 733. The preliminaries lasted seven days, each side observing the other and, in skirmishing, looking for some advantage of terrain or timing. This would suggest that the two forces were relatively evenly matched; that is, each side had roughly 15,000 men, to make an educated guess. Although they had some cavalry, the heart of the Frankish army was the infantry, who fought closely massed and wore heavy armor, carried large wooden shields, and fought with swords, spears, and axes. The Muslims were renowned for their cavalry. Their infantry had adopted the European style of heavy armor but perhaps with mixed emotions; after all, a Bedouin curse recalled the Arabs' origins as light-armed fighers: "May you be cursed like the Frank who puts on armor because he fears death."

Finally, the great clash came. The near-contemporary continuator of the *Chronicle of Isidore* implies that the Muslims attacked: At least he emphasizes the point that the Franks held their ground—"like a wall . . . and like a firm glacial mass"—unlike other Christian armies of the day with a reputation for fleeing the battlefield. By contrast, the continuator of the *Chronicle of Fredegar* has Charles charge aggressively, "scattering them [the Muslims] like stubble before the fury of his onslaught. . . ." Fortunately, both sources agree on one point: Frankish warriors killed Abd Al-Rahman. There is reason to think that this proved decisive. True, the continuator of *Fredegar* has the Frankish victory turn into a rout, but the author worked under the patronage of Charles's brother Childebrand, so he could hardly make the Franks look less than glorious. The continuator of *Isidore* tells a more complex story: The battle continued until nightfall. The next day, the Franks approached the Muslims' tents in battle order, expecting a fight, but the enemy had withdrawn at night beneath their noses. If this account is true, then the Franks had not inflicted an obvious, crushing defeat on the Muslims. They expected that the enemy could still fight—and perhaps he could have, were he not leaderless. The Muslim army withdrew. Tours was saved.

News of the victory at Poitiers (or Tours, as the battle is sometimes called) reached as far as northern England, where the Anglo-Saxon scholar the Venerable Bede heard of it. Later generations gave Charles the surname "Martel" or "Hammer" because of his success against the Muslims. As for the Muslims, never again would their armies reach so far north in Western Europe. To the great historian Edward Gibbon, Poitiers was "an encounter which would change the history of the whole world."

In his magisterial *Decline and Fall of the Roman Empire*, Gibbon envisioned the possible consequences of Arab victory at Poitiers:

> A victorious line of march had been prolonged above a thousand miles from the rock of Gibraltar to the banks of the Loire; the repetition of an equal space would have carried the Saracens to the confines of Poland and the Highlands of Scotland: the Rhine is not more impassable than the Nile or Euphrates, and the Arabian fleet might have sailed without a naval combat into the mouth of the Thames. Perhaps the interpretation of the Koran would now be taught in the schools of Oxford, and her pulpits might demonstrate to a circumcised people the sanctity and truth of the revelation of Mahomet.

More recent scholars tend to be less sure that Poitiers made a difference. Even had Abd Al-Rahman and his men carried the day, they argue, they could not have done much more damage, since they were only a raiding party, not an occupying army. Nor could they have made the most of victory, not given the revolts about to burst forth in Spain in the 730s and 740s, revolts both on the part of Berbers and Arabs.

But if it is possible to build too much on the events of that day in 733, it is also possible to build too little. Like the Battle of Britain in 1940, Poitiers had not cut a deep crack in the invader's armor, but it had deterred him from further advance. The Muslims made Abd Al-Rahman into a martyr, but they smarted from the shame of having left booty behind for the enemy. The raid had failed: safer to stay in the fortified bases in southern Gaul. But what if the Muslims had defeated the Franks on the eighth day at Poitiers? What if the general of the Franks, Charles Martel, lay dead with many of his men? A Muslim victory might have rendered Poitiers a fishing expedition that showed that the water was well stocked and unguarded.

Even if the Muslim expedition of 732 was far from an all-out attack, it is hard to imagine it simply stopping and going home after having faced a challenge from the war leader of the Franks and having killed him. After all, the attack on Spain in 711 also began as a raid; victory whetted the appetite for conquest. No, the victorious warriors of Al-Rahman would have sacked Tours as they had sacked Poitiers, and they would have been tempted by the road to Orléans and Paris.

Meanwhile, the sons of Charles—no longer surnamed Martel—would have quarreled over the succession. No doubt one of them would have prevailed eventually, and the new leader, either Carloman or Pepin the Short, would have had to do what his father, Charles, in fact did after his victory at Poitiers: fight far-flung battles against Frisians, Burgundians, Provençals, and Muslims. That is, if he had the energy to achieve what his father would: expanding the Frankish state to the Mediterranean Sea and the Jura Mountains. But it would have been difficult, because the new leader would not be commanding men made united and confident by their victory at Poitiers, nor facing, in the Muslims, an enemy that feared the Franks: after all, the Muslims had found them wanting at Poitiers. Charles's successor accordingly might not have retaken Avignon, as Charles did in 737, nor defeated the Muslims in battle again, as Charles did, in the marshes of the river Berre in Corbières in 738. Without these victories to build on, that commander might not have driven the Muslims out of Septimania and back over the Pyrenees, as Pepin did between 752 and 759. And faced with a continued major Arab presence in southern Gaul, Pepin's successor, Charlemagne, would have lacked a free hand for his campaigns in Italy and the East—that is, if the militarily unsuccessful Pippinids had stayed in power long enough for there even to be a Charlemagne.

As for the Muslims, had they maintained their hold on their province across the Pyrenees, sooner or later they would have given in to the temptation to expand it. After all, even with the expulsion from Septimania in 759, even with Charlemagne's and his generals' campaigns across the Pyrenees in 778 and 801, the Muslims continued to raid southern France until 915. With cities like Narbonne and Avignon as bases, there would have been no need to be content with mere raids. The Muslims might have returned to the practice of sending governors of Spain to command their armies, as had been the rule before Charles's victory at

Poitiers. Berbers and Arabs might have put aside their differences in order to win booty and glory in the Great Land. Undeterred by the weakened Frankish monarchy, the conquerors might have gone from strength to strength until they crossed the English channel and planted the crescent, as Gibbon imagined, in Oxford. It would then have been emirs and imams, not dukes and bishops, who faced the challenge of invasion by Vikings in the ninth and tenth centuries. Had they been successful, the empire that had once governed Western Europe from Rome might have reemerged—as the caliphate.

What would a Muslim Western Europe—an Al-Andalus stretching from Gibraltar to Scandinavia, from Ireland to the Vistula or even beyond—have been like? Christianity would have survived, but as a protected and ever-shrinking enclave, not as the ruling faith. While continuing to practice their religion, many Christians would have become all but Arabs in their language and customs, just as happened in Muslim Spain. Many would have gone all the way and converted to Islam, as many Christians did in Spain, and more would have, if not for the steady advance of the Christian *reconquista*. No doubt the vast majority of Europeans would have become Muslims, as the vast majority of North Africans and Middle Easterners eventually did

Nor would Christianity have expanded across the globe. If Western Europeans had crossed the Atlantic in 1492 they would have done so under the banner not of the cross but the crescent. A great naval power in the Mediterranean under the Umayyad Dynasty (A.D. 632–750), a great trading power in the Indian Ocean until the advent of the Portugese, Islam is likely to have taken to the Atlantic with gusto. In the Americas they would have turned the natives into proper Europeans—that is, Muslims. Today there would only be one world religion: Islam.

In Europe, meanwhile, the Muslim elite would have made the most of its new provinces conquered after Abd Al-Rahman's victory at Poitiers. The Muslims built in Spain arguably the most civilized Western European society since the Roman Empire's heyday. In Al-Andalus, as the Arabs called their kingdom in the Iberian Peninsula, the tenth century witnessed a world of abundant agriculture and booming towns, of palaces and poetry, of art and enlightenment. Its cities put northern Europe's to shame, its traders covered wider ground, its philosophers dwarfed Westerners in their knowledge of the classical Greek heritage.

Europe would have gained much had Al-Andalus spread north of the Pyrenees. In Spain, North Africa, the Near East, indeed, wherever they went, the Muslims had the Midas touch. They encouraged prosperity through trade, agriculture, irrigation works, and city building. To be sure, not all had equal shares in prosperity. Muslim society was thoroughly hierarchical and slavery was a standard feature. In the tenth century, for example, Islamic Spanish armies and even government bureaucracies were staffed with captives from northern Spain, Germany, and above all, from the Slavic countries—our word "slave" comes from "Slav." The city of Verdun, in northern France, was Europe's greatest slave market. No doubt that market would have moved further east had the Arabs conquered Western Europe—to some outpost east of the River Elbe, maybe even to the future Berlin. In any case, Western Europe, too, would have become a slave society, and perhaps, in time, the slaves would have become the masters, coming to power in Europe as they eventually did in the Middle East.

Servile much of Islamic Europe might have been, but it would never have been coarse. When the first Arab conquerors had encountered the refinements of Persia and Byzantium it was love at first sight; no matter how far their travels took them in later years, the victorious Arabs insisted on bringing along the comforts of home. So Islamic England, France, and Germany would have been filled not just with mosques and military camps but with palaces, baths, gardens, and fountains. Tenth-century Paris might have become a second Córdoba, teeming with prosperous workshops and merchants' quarters in which every language of the Old World could have been heard; gleaming with gold-roofed, marble-columned palaces; adorned with the colors of dyes imported from India, instead of what it was—a glorified small town. Had Aachen been the seat of a caliph rather than Charlemagne's capital, it might have been adorned with light and airy mosques instead of heavy proto-romanesque churches. Nor would the improvements have been merely physical. Patrons par excellence of poetry and philosophy, the Arabs would have turned Europe into an intellectual powerhouse. Works of Plato and Aristotle would have been known by the leading minds north of the Pyrenees in the tenth instead of the twelfth century. Poets would have composed the sort of refined verses that might have pleased a courtier in Baghdad instead of the rough-hewn rhythms of *Beowulf.* No wonder that Anatole France bemoaned the outcome of Poitiers: "It was," he said, "a setback for civilization in the face of barbarism."

Yes, one is tempted to reply, but only in the short term. Islam represented the cultivated heritage of the great empires of the ancient Near East and Mediterranean, not the raw, new, and semibarbaric mores of Western Europe, under whose Germanic conquerors Roman civilization had been diluted. But in the long run the new society of the West proved more productive economically and stronger militarily than the ancient culture of Islam. Historians have no easy time explaining this paradox: why rude, Christian Europe rose to world power, beginning the Scientific and Industrial Revolutions and inventing capitalism along the way, while civilized Islam lay quiescent economically and fell to Western arms. There are no easy answers, but the most promising line of explanation may have to do with Western pluralism.

Precisely because Western Europe was barbaric it proved ungovernable; no one centralizing authority emerged. Feudal government—if that isn't a contradiction in terms—never succeeded in reining in individual knights; over the centuries, individualism became democratized and a highly prized Western value. Barons never succeeded in conquering the towns, whose merchant oligarchs pursued profit with the same aggressiveness that medieval knights made war. The Christian church never succeeded in taming the princes. As often as not, church and state were at loggerheads. Eventually, during the Reformation era, individual states opted for independence from the church. The culture that developed in Europe was, compared to Islam, decentralized, secularized, individualistic, profit-driven. It had little respect for the older civilization to the south. No wonder that it was Europe that witnessed the Renaissance, the Reformations, the origins of modern science and industrialism; no wonder that it was Europe that, for centuries, ruled the world.

The irony is that it might never have happened if not for the Dark Ages. A European caliphate after 732, like a revived Western Roman Empire after 476, might have guaranteed stability and cultural resplendence, but it would have nipped modernity in the bud. Neither caliphate nor empire would have permitted the freedom and restlessness out of which the European takeoff eventually emerged. For Europe, the Dark Ages were like a terrible medicine that almost killed the patient but ultimately rendered her stronger.

On top of all this, Europe was lucky. The years 476 and 732 would only be footnotes today if things had turned out differently in 1242. In that year, the most powerful invaders the continent had ever seen withdrew after a lightning conquest of Eastern Europe the year before. If not for the death of their king, the conquerors would have begun an unstoppable ride to the Atlantic. It is doubtful that a revived Roman Empire could have defeated them; it is all but certain that an Arab Europe could not have, given the Arab collapse before the victorious invaders in the Middle East a decade later (the capital city of Baghdad was destroyed in 1258). Those victors may have been, quite simply, the greatest set of warriors the world would ever know. They were the Mongols.

CECELIA HOLLAND

THE DEATH THAT
SAVED EUROPE

The Mongols Turn Back, 1242

The Dark Ages were pure light compared to what could have happened to Europe if, in the thirteenth century, it had been overrun by the Mongols. In 1242, Mongol conquerors had reached Eastern Europe. They had destroyed one Christian army in Poland and another in Hungary; their vanguards had reached Vienna and the Adriatic, and they were in the process of establishing the largest connected land empire in the history of the world. These horse warriors out of the central steppes of Asia, with composite bows that were far superior to European crossbows, formed the most disciplined and quick-moving fighting forces of their time. They looked, Cecelia Holland writes, "strikingly like a modern army set down in a medieval world." No one was able to stand up to them. Despisers of city dwellers, culture, and elites of any kind, they were the Khmer Rouge of their day. But if the Khmer Rouge laid waste to an entire country—Cambodia—the Mongols rampaged through an entire continent and were about to swallow another, leaving a killing-field detritus behind them. Never, probably, was the West, and the historical phenomenon it *represented, in so much danger. At the last moment, blind luck spared Europe. History may be a matter of momentum, but we can never forget that the life—or death—of a single individual can still matter.*

◆   Cecelia Holland is one of our most acclaimed and respected historical novelists, the author of more than twenty books.

I n the summer of 1241, an observer on the walls of Vienna might have caught a glimpse of strange horsemen drifting over the plains east of the city. Had the observer been well-informed, he would have known that these odd and ominous riders on their little horses were Mongols, scouts from the vast army at that moment camped only a few hundred miles away down the Danube, and the sight of them on the outskirts of his city would have frozen his blood.

Against these marauders, Vienna was almost defenseless. The Mongols had already disposed of the two most formidable armies in Eastern Europe. The decisive battles occurred within a day of each other, although widely separated in distance.

On April 9, 1241, a sizeable army of Germans, Poles, Templars, and Teutonic knights marched out of Liegnitz to attack a slightly smaller force of Mongols advancing steadily westward across northern Poland. The two armies met on the flat field of Wahlstadt. The initial charges of the heavily armored Christian knights seemed to break the Mongols, who fled. Duke Henry's men pursued, in growing disorder, straight into a perfectly laid Mongol ambush. Duke Henry's army died almost to the last man.

The Mongol army that delivered this defeat was only a diversionary force. While they were driving through Poland, the great general Sabotai and the main body of his troops forced the snowy passes of the Carpathians and descended onto the Hungarian plain. A third and smaller Mongol force circled south of the mountains through Moldavia and Transylvania to screen their flank.

Thus Sabotai was coordinating his forces across two mountain ranges and several hundred miles. One of Genghis Khan's "four hounds," or favorite generals, Sabotai was an old man in 1241, one of history's unsung military geniuses. His long and brilliant career ranged from northern China to this current campaign in Europe. His operation in Europe, in a difficult, and for him, unusual terrain, was flawless.

He and his army descended into Hungary after marching 270 miles in three days, through the snow. As the Mongols approached across the plain the Hungarian king Béla advanced from his capital, Buda, to oppose them. Sabotai backed slowly away, until he reached the bridge over the Sajo River. There the Mongols made their stand.

On April 10, one day after Liegnitz, Béla attacked this bridge and drove the Mongols back. Fortifying his camp with heavy wagons lashed together, he swiftly built a makeshift fort securing both sides of the bridge. When night fell he seemed in a commanding position.

But Sabotai's scouts had meanwhile discovered a ford downstream. During the night, the great general himself led half his army downriver and across. At dawn, Batu Khan and the rest of his army mounted a con-centrated frontal assault on the Hungarians' position. Béla swung to meet this pressure, and Sabotai attacked him from behind.

Swiftly Béla's battered troops were driven back into the wagon fort. The Mongols surrounded it, and for most of the rest of the day assaulted the Hungarians with arrows, catapults of rocks, burning tar, and even Chinese firecrackers, keeping up a constant barrage, until the embattled Christians were at the breaking point. Then suddenly a gap opened in the wall of Mongols surrounding the Hungarians. Some of Béla's exhausted and disheartened men made a dash for it. When the first few seemed to escape, the rest followed, panicking, in a wholesale rout. Attacking from either side, Sabotai and his men at their leisure destroyed the confused and demoralized mob that Béla's army had become. Only a few escaped back to Buda. One was King Béla, who did not stop running until he reached an island out in the middle of the Adriatic Sea.

With Hungary under their control and spring turning the wide plains green, the Mongols stopped. They put their herds to graze and raised their yurts on the broad flat grasslands, so much like their native steppes.

Through the summer, they rested and collected themselves for the next assault.

Western Europe awaited them, stunned and almost helpless. The Christian community was at a moment of critical weakness. The two most powerful rulers in Europe were locked in a bitter struggle for supremacy. On one side was the Holy Roman Emperor, the brilliant and brutal Frederick II, and on the other a succession of popes, determined to bring him to heel.

Preoccupied with Italy, Frederick had abandoned his German inheritance to the local nobility. Constantly at each other's throats, these lordlings showed no inclination to unite to meet the threat posed by the huge army out there on the plains of Hungary. Young King Louis IX of France, vigorous and idealistic, was gathering an army of his chivalry, but he had at best a few thousand knights. No Christian army so far had stopped the Mongols, or even slowed them down. The well-informed Viennese observer had every right to tremble for his people. The scourge of God was upon them.

❖ ❖ ❖

The impact of the Mongol conquests can hardly be overestimated, although the swift arc of their ascendancy spanned only a hundred years. Until the rise of Temujin, the remarkable man who became Genghis Khan, the name Mongol denoted only one of a number of nomadic peoples who hunted, herded, and warred over the central steppes of Asia and the Gobi Desert. Temujin changed that. He stoked up the central Mongol belief that they were born to rule the world and led his people off on a conquest that ultimately stretched from the East China Sea to the Mediterranean. His chief targets were the Chinese empires to the east of Mongolia, the Islamic states to the west and south, and the Russian cities beyond the Volga. What he did to them changed the world forever.

The wonderful chronicle *The Secret History of the Mongols* reports this conquest from the inside out, steeped in the ethos of the nomad warrior, the basis of Ghengis Khan's success. His armies were bound together by ties of sworn brotherhood and obligation, and by the powerful personality of the great khan himself. The soldiers who gathered under his standard—who took the name Mongol because that was his tribe—did so because Temujin projected such an aura of invincible will, courage, and commitment that to defy him was to defy fate. He seemed divinely ordained to rule the world. At the same time, he gave endlessly to his people. *The History* abounds with evidence of his love for them. He was the embodiment of their spirit, the living soul of the whole nation.

Toward those who were not Mongol he turned another face.

"They came, they sapped, they burnt, they slew, they plundered, and they left." In 1209, Genghis Khan and his armies attacked northern China, there learned how to storm cities, and began the long process of grinding down the world's oldest and most populous civilization. Every city fell and was destroyed. For a while the great khan contemplated depopulating the whole of northern China and converting it to pasture for his horses; he was deterred from this when an adviser pointed out that living Chinese would pay more taxes than dead ones.

In the West, steady Mongol expansion against the Turkomani peoples of central Asia brought them into contact with the flourishing states of Islam, especially Khwarezm, a land of fertile fields and fabled, thriving cities: Samarkand, Bukhara, Harat, Nishapur. In 1218, Genghis Khan invaded Khwarezm and devastated it.

Part of Genghis Khan's strategy was calculated massacre: if a city resisted his armies, once it fell to him—and they always fell—he had all the inhabitants slaughtered. The chroniclers' reports of the numbers of dead are staggering; 1,600,000 at Harat, in 1220. Rumor reached the Mongol prince Tuli that some had survived there by hiding among the piled corpses, and when he took Nishapur, some time later, he ordered the heads cut off all the bodies. At Nishapur, according to contemporaries, 1,747,000 died.

The figures are ghastly, unbelievable. What they convey is the contemporary sense of utter destruction. Even when a city surrendered, it was looted and destroyed. After Bukhara yielded, the people were ordered out of the city so that it could be sacked, the young men and women and children were carried off into slavery, the site was leveled "like a plain."

Only a few years later, the attack on Russia began. The first campaigns along the Volga won the Mongols a foothold, but the project was put on hold when Temujin died. According to Mongol custom, the great khan's eldest son received the largest portion of territory, the farthest from the center of the empire. Since by the time of Temujin's death, his eldest son, Jochi, was already dead, the inheritance fell to his grandson, Batu Khan, the founder of the Golden Horde.

In 1237, with Sabotai masterminding the campaign, Batu's Mongols attacked Russia and systematically reduced the cities there to rubble. The loss of life again was shocking; hundreds of thousands died. Then, in 1241, after a summer's fattening on the great plains of southern Russia, the Mongols turned to Eastern Europe.

❖ ❖ ❖

Why were they so unstoppable? In fact the Mongol army looks strikingly like a modern army, set down in a medieval world. Their strengths were speed and maneuverability, firepower, discipline, and an excellent officer corps.

The armies of the great Khan were organized by tens, hundreds, thousands, and tens of thousands, each segment with its officers, who were chosen not according to favor or birth but proven ability. In the Russian campaigns, although the army and the conquest belonged to Batu Khan, and a number of other members of the royal family fought in the war, everybody obeyed Sabotai, a man of relatively low birth.

This same emphasis on merit influenced the succession. Even before the great khan died, his two elder sons, Jochi and Chatagai, were enemies; if one was elected over the other, they themselves acknowledged, there would be civil war. "But Ogadai (the third brother) is a prudent man," Chatagai said; "let us elect Ogadai!" They did, and the succession passed smoothly from Genghis Khan to his third son—whom the other brothers served loyally.

Mongol life emphasized such discipline. The Mongol horseman was born into a life of war. When he wasn't fighting, he was hunting, which exercised his fighting skills. From babyhood he rode; he could travel scores of miles in a day, stop, and camp on the ground and eat a handful of meat he had brought with him and get up at dawn and go another forty miles, day after day, in snow and desert heat and wind and rain, fighting all the way. He drove three or four extra horses along with him as he rode, and could change mounts without breaking out of a gallop.

Enemy armies consistently overestimated the numbers of the Mongol forces, because for every man, there were four or five additional horses. Occasionally, the Mongols helped them along in this mistake by tying dummies onto the extra horses.

The Mongol soldier carried a double recurve bow of laminated horn, with a pull of 160 pounds, which dispatched arrows accurately up to a distance of 300 meters as fast as he could pull them out of his quiver. He wore no heavy clumsy armor, but padded leather to skid aside arrows, and silk underwear to keep wounds clean. He seldom closed with an enemy hand to hand; he died at a much lower rate than the opposition.

Above all, he obeyed orders. The battles of medieval Europe were mostly confused melees studded with individual combats; a good general was somebody who managed to get the bulk of his available forces to the battlefield before the fighting was over. Sabotai coordinated the movements of tens of thousands of men, across mountain ranges and in unknown territory, as precisely as movements on a chessboard. In battle, through a signaling system of colored banners, he could advance thousands of men at a time, send them back, turn them, and direct their charges—and when he gave orders, his men did instantly what they were told. Not for centuries would there be another army as efficient and efficacious at the gruesome business of leveling other people's societies.

Level them they did. China's population declined by more than 30 percent during the years of the Mongol conquest. Khwarezm and Persia were crisscrossed with an elaborate underground irrigation system that since antiquity had sustained a thriving culture; the Mongols destroyed them. Arabic scholars contend that the region's economy has yet to recover fully from this devastation.

The wars of the khans in Iraq and Syria went on for sixty years and reduced a vigorous civilization almost to ruins. The caliph of Baghdad, Islam's supreme authority, defied the khan, which meant he had to die. The Mongol general had the caliph tied into a leather sack and trampled to paste by horses—a sign of respect, actually, since, symbolically anyway, it avoided the shedding of his blood. The caliphate has never been restored.

The psychological impact of the invasion was incalculable. Before the Mongols swept through, the Islamic world that centered on Baghdad was intellectually vigorous, bold, adventuresome, full of poetry and science and art. They had, after all, defeated the Christians and won the long wars of the Crusades. After the invasion, the dour conservatism of the fundamentalists darkens it all.

So too with Russia. The cities were fat on their river trade, great Novgorod, Ryazan, Kiev with its golden gate, until the terrible winters of the 1230s; a dozen years later, travelers found Kiev a village of a hundred souls, huddled in a blackened boneyard. The famous Russian xenophobia is often attributed to their experiences at the hands of the Mongols.

In every conquered territory, the Mongols set up a governor and a tax collector, to continue to plunder the remaining inhabitants. Almost four hundred years later, the natives of Siberia were still paying tribute in furs that they called the *yasak*, after the *Yassa*, the Mongol law code. Once the Mongols had ridden through, no country was ever the same again.

Some intuition of this might have gone through the mind of the well-informed observer on the walls of Vienna, as he watched the Mongol horsemen in the distance and pondered the fate of Europe. The Mongols launched their campaigns in the dead of winter, so that their horses were fat and strong on summer grass. In January or February they would advance. Surely they would fall first on Vienna, just up the Danube from Hungary.

Vienna could buy some mercy by submitting at once, but that mercy was generally of a strained quality: If they suffered the same fate of Bukhara, the inhabitants would be allowed to leave the city, so that it could be plundered and destroyed, and then many of the children, women, and young men would be taken away into slavery. The rest would be scattered into the countryside, because the Mongols hated cities, and Vienna would be leveled.

By this time, the princes of Europe would be sufficiently aroused to send out another army. The well-informed observer had no reason to suspect this army would have any more success than Henry of Silesia's, or Béla of Hungary's. When that army was destroyed, Europe would lie defenseless.

The Mongols' reconnaissance was always expert and efficient. Therefore they would surely strike first for the riches of the Low Countries, overrunning Antwerp, Ghent, Bruges. Seeking pasture for their horses, they would swerve south, toward the broad meadows of middle France. On the way they would destroy Paris.

Possibly a detachment would force the passes of the Alps and descend to northern Italy, where on the plains of the Po they would again find grass to feed their horses, and cities to plunder. Some of the Italian cities might surrender, saving thereby some of their people. Cities that chose to fight would be annihilated. The Mongols would carry off everything they could lift, and burn the rest. What people remained would be in a condition of abject poverty, huddled in tiny villages. The Mongols would install governors and tax collectors, winter over on the grasslands of northern Italy and Champagne, and then, by the grace of God, they would leave.

What would remain?

Wiping out the cities of the Low Countries would erase the nascent financial center of Europe. In the thirteenth century, the vigorous wool

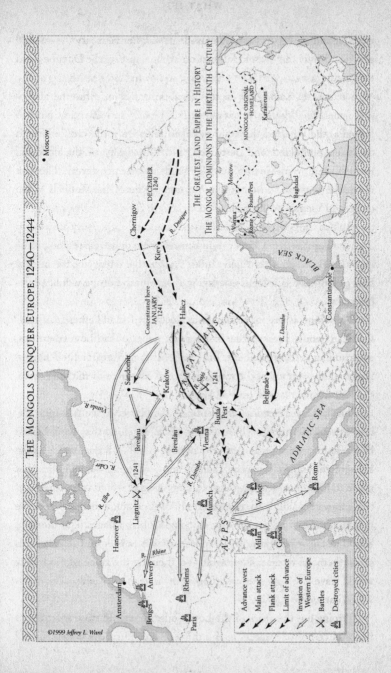

THE MONGOLS CONQUER EUROPE, 1240–1244

Moscow

Chernigov

DECEMBER 1240

Kiev

R. Dnieper

BLACK SEA

Constantinople

Concentrated here JANUARY 1241

Halicz

C A R P A T H I A N S

R. Danube

Belgrade

Sandomir

Krakow

R. Sajo

1241

Buda Pest

Vistula R.

Breslau

Breslau

Vienna

R. Oder

1241

R. Danube

ADRIATIC SEA

R. Elbe

Liegnitz

Munich

A L P S

Rome

Hanover

R. Rhine

Rheims

Venice

Milan

Genoa

Amsterdam

Antwerp

Bruges

Paris

©1999 Jeffrey L. Ward

THE GREATEST LAND EMPIRE IN HISTORY
THE MONGOL DOMINIONS IN THE THIRTEENTH CENTURY

MONGOLS ORIGINAL HOMELAND

Karakorum

Moscow

Vienna

Buda/Pest

Rome

Baghdad

Advance west	
Main attack	
Flank attack	
Limit of advance	
Invasion of Western Europe	
Battles	X
Destroyed cities	

trade centering on Antwerp and Ghent was fueling steady economic growth throughout Western Europe that would continue for three centuries; the first stock market originated somewhat later in Antwerp. The Mongol assault would pull up this developing society by the roots. Depopulated, the whole area would regress rapidly to wilderness. No one would be left to tend the windmills and dikes; the sea would come in again across Holland. The great delta of the Rhine-Meuse-Scheldt would revert to swamp. There would be no rise of capitalism or the middle class. No printing press, no humanism. No Dutch Revolt, the seedbed of the great democratic revolutions from England to America to France. No Industrial Revolution.

The destruction of Paris would be even more disastrous. Paris was the intellectual center of the High Middle Ages; at the university, the intense study of Aristotelian logic was laying the groundwork for a fundamentally new world view. The Nominalists were already insisting on the irreducible reality of the material world. A rector of the University of Paris would, a hundred years after the Mongols, develop the first theory of inertia. On these ideas would stand the great theories of Galileo, Kepler, Newton. The coming of the Mongols would leave nobody to thank them.

If the Mongols penetrated Italy, and there was nothing really to stop them, what would become of the pope? Would the Mongols tie him, too, into a sack and trample him, out of reverence for his exalted blood? The caliphate, the central authority of Islam, died with the coming of the Mongols. The papacy, surely, was in some ways more flexible, since the pope did not have to be a descendant of Saint Peter. Nonetheless, if the papacy failed, then Christendom itself would begin at once to change. Without a central authority to proclaim and enforce orthodoxy, however imperfectly, the faith would collapse into dozens of divergent sects. Without a central authority to focus opposition against, there would have been no Reformation, with its powerful new ideas about human nature.

Destroying Rome, the Mongols would destroy European society's strongest link to its antique past. Without the examples of classicism to inspire them, could there be a Dante, a Michelangelo, a Leonardo? Even if their ancestors survived the massacres, the desolation of their cities and countrysides would have reduced these people to a bleak struggle for survival with little room for poetry and art. The Mongols, in any case, would have made short shrift of Dante, with his outspoken political opinions. Leonardo, one imagines, they would have found a use for.

The well-informed observer on the walls of Vienna in 1241 could have known nothing of Leonardo, of course. He knew only that out there on the plains of Hungary waited such a terror as would level his world, steal its energies and resources, and crush its aspirations. So he watched from the walls, and girded himself, and waited for the blow to fall.

It never came. Early in 1242, the Mongol army suddenly withdrew. Thousands of miles from Vienna, a single death had saved Christendom from disaster. A single death, and the very ethos that drove the Mongol army.

The death was Ogadai's. The brilliant, humane, and drunken third son of Genghis Khan had not only kept his father's empire together but had directed its expansion. Still, the political organization of the khanate did not match its military sophistication. The Mongols remained nomad tribesmen, bound by a personal loyalty to their chiefs. When the khan died, their law required them to go in person back to their heartland to elect a new khan. On the brink of the assault on Europe, great Sabotai let the job go, and went home again.

The Mongols never returned. Their focus thereafter was on China, and in the West on Persia and the Arab states. In 1284, a Mameluke army from Egypt met a Mongol army at Ayn Jalut, in the Holy Land, and defeated them there. It was the beginning of the end. The Japanese and the Vietnamese repulsed Mongol invasions in the distant east. The tide was ebbing. The terrible ordeal was over.

In Poland, they still celebrate April 9 as a day of victory—reasoning that, however awful the defeat of Liegnitz, somehow it sapped the invaders' strength and will to continue on. Thus they cling to the illusion that the terrible sacrifice was meaningful—that they deserved to triumph. But the valor of the defenders had nothing at all to do with it. In fact it was the Mongol worldview—that same force that propelled them so furiously outward—that sucked them back home again, and so saved Europe. That, and a stroke of blind luck.

THEODORE K. RABB

IF ONLY IT HAD NOT BEEN SUCH A WET SUMMER

The Critical Decade of the 1520s

Many events conspired to make the 1520s so important. What happened during those ten years, both in Europe and the rest of the world, would permanently affect the way we now live our lives. Not for the first time in history and, as we shall see, not for the last, weather would be a major historical player. What would have happened if, in the summer of 1529, unusually heavy and persistent rains had not delayed the progress of the huge army of the Ottoman Sultan Suleyman the Magnificent in its progress toward Vienna, the main eastern outpost of Europe's dominant Habsburg dynasty? What if Suleyman's siege had not begun so late in the year? Or if he had not been forced to leave behind his mired heavy artillery, without which he could not batter down the city walls? And what would have happened if he had actually taken Vienna? An Ottoman Europe probably would not have been the result: Christian opposition ultimately would have been too powerful. More important, though, far-reaching deals would inevitably have been struck, and those who opposed the Habsburg ascendancy in the continent would have been emboldened to challenge it. One certain loser would have been Martin Luther

107

and his burgeoning but still fragile Protestant heresy. Henry VIII of England might have received papal blessing for his divorce from his Habsburg queen, and there would have been no Anglican Church—and no lost Catholic country for the Spanish to try to reconquer half a century later.

❖ *Theodore K. Rabb is professor of history at Princeton University, and the author or editor of such notable works as* THE NEW HISTORY, THE STRUGGLE FOR STABILITY IN EARLY MODERN EUROPE, CLIMATE AND HISTORY, RENAISSANCE LIVES, *and* JACOBEAN GENTLEMAN. *He was the principal historical advisor for the acclaimed and Emmy-nominated PBS television series,* RENAISSANCE.

ew decades of Western history have been as fraught with consequences as the 1520s. They began with the first recorded passage
of the Straits of Magellan, under the leadership of the captain
who gave the Straits their name; and, in the same year, a revolt in Spain
and a Danish bloodbath in Stockholm that helped shape the political future of both Iberia and Scandinavia. Just a few months later, in April
1521, Luther defied the Habsburg Holy Roman Emperor Charles V at
the Diet of Worms, setting the stage for a permanent split in the Roman
church. And before the decade ended, eight years later, a peasant uprising in Germany had unleashed new levels of virulent social repression;
Sweden had become an independent kingdom; Cortés had conquered
Mexico; the Turks had overrun Hungary and reached the walls of Vienna;
Henry VIII had intensified his quest for a divorce, which was to transform
English politics and society; and Charles V's troops had stormed through
Italy in a campaign that climaxed in one of the most devastating cultural
catastrophes of European history, the sack of Rome.

Depending on their interests and viewpoints, therefore, historians
have at various times settled on this decade as the moment of crucial
transformation in the emergence of modern times: the beginning of the
Reformation; the first major conquest in Europe's overseas expansion;
the start of a new intensity in the struggle between Islam and the West; a
turning point in the consolidation of the secular state; the end of the Italian Renaissance. And in most cases, these decisive shifts could easily have
taken different forms or moved in different directions, if only one or two
contingencies had changed.

Luther's fragile revolt, for example, was little more than three years
old when he came to Worms. His early ideas had been put forward in
three short tracts published the previous year, but without his leadership

and further writings, the fragmentary eruptions of support that had appeared by 1521 might well have petered out. There were German princes, it was true, who were genuinely moved by Luther's message, and others who had political or economic reasons to resist the will of their overlord, the Emperor Charles V, who sought to suppress the heresy following the confrontation at Worms. But when Luther vanished from sight just a few days after his appearance before Charles, it was widely assumed that he had been removed from the scene, not by his friends (as was the case) but by his enemies.

The artist Albrecht Dürer, though he was never to leave the Roman church, reacted to Luther's disappearance with a lament that echoed the fears of many:

> Is he still alive, or have they murdered him? If we have lost this man, who has written more clearly than anyone else, send us another who will show us how to live a Christian life. O God, if Luther is dead, who will explain the Gospel to us?

If Dürer's foreboding had come true, there is a good chance the Reformation would have been snuffed out, as had Jan Hus's similar protest in Bohemia a century before. For within three years, a peasant revolt claiming inspiration from Luther swept through southern and western Germany. Had the reformer not survived to condemn the peasants and reassure the princes that religious change was not an excuse for social upheaval, there is little doubt that Germany's rulers would have taken fright, rushed to reconcile with the emperor, and removed the critical support that enabled Luther to succeed.

That Cortés's vastly outnumbered incursion into Mexico, or Magellan's perilous expedition around Cape Horn, could also have come easily to grief scarcely needs arguing. Spain would probably have persisted in seeking an American empire, but one can question whether it would have been conquered so quickly and so cheaply. And it is worth remembering that, if progress had been slower overseas, it might have been overtaken in the 1530s by Charles V's mounting determination to overcome his Muslim foes in the Mediterranean. As he revised Spain's priorities, he would have regarded Algeria as a more important target of expansionist aims and resources than the wilds of a new continent. It could well have been in North Africa rather than Peru, therefore, that Pizarro and other adventurers would have sought their fame.

And that other major event of the decade, the sack of Rome, was equally beset by happenstance. As Charles V's troops, having defeated their main enemy, France, moved across a seemingly helpless Italy, none of their commanders had any designs on Rome. Indeed, the emperor was to be furious when he heard of the assault on the holy city. Charles's magisterial biographer, Karl Brandi, noted over half a century ago how much that terrible event owed to sheer ill fortune:

> Now and again in history long-forgotten decisions and long-suppressed emotions, under the direction of some invisible impulse, generate elemental forces which, like gigantic and slowly rolling dice, work out their horrible and destructive course, guided by chance alone.

Thus it was with the sack of Rome, which was inflicted on the city by an army out of control, driven by a frenzy of hunger, lack of pay, and a generalized hatred of the papacy and all its works. The result was a destruction of life, art, and treasure of awesome proportions, not to mention a flight of talent that affected Roman culture for a generation (while at the same time giving Venice, a safe refuge, an unprecedented infusion of new ideas and creativity). Yet all of this, too, could have been avoided, not only by better supply and firmer command in the imperial army, but also if either of two accidents had turned out differently the previous year.

Charles V's army had crossed the Alps under the command of Georg Frundsberg in 1526. Essential to their advance was a good supply of heavy artillery, which they had been unable to carry over the mountains, and for which their best source in Italy was Ercole d'Este, Duke of Ferrara. The Estes were a perpetual thorn in the papacy's side, particularly now, when a Medici from the rival city of Florence, Clement VII, sat on the papal throne. To forestall any deal between Ferrara and the emperor,

Clement decided to send a bribe to Ercole, but he moved too slowly and his offer arrived after the transaction had been completed. Had the pope's payment not been delayed, the artillery might never have been delivered.

The second accident occurred in November 1526, when the one really effective soldier in the Medici family, a young man named Giovanni della Bande Nere—who bore an uncanny resemblance to the later conqueror of Italy, Napoleon—was accidentally wounded by a cannonball from one of the Ferrarese guns in a small skirmish with Frundberg's troops. He died soon thereafter, thus removing the last military commander who stood between the imperial army and Rome.

Nor did this succession of misfortunes have serious consequences merely for the holy city and its medieval and Renaissance wonders. For in the very month of the sack, May 1527, nearly a thousand miles away, the queen of England, Catherine of Aragon, was being told by her husband, Henry VIII, that he wanted a divorce. Thus began "the king's great matter"—his quest for a new wife who could provide him with a male heir, a demand that at first seemed straightforward. After all, Henry had married his brother's widow; there were good biblical grounds for annulling such a marriage; and popes usually obliged the crowned heads of Europe. But this pope was now under the control of Catherine's nephew, Charles V, and so the permission was not forthcoming. Within a few quick years Henry solved the problem by having himself proclaimed head of an independent Anglican church; the Reformation gained a crucial and redoubtable ally; and English society and institutions were transformed beyond recall.

Of all the near misses and "what ifs" of the 1520s, however, none is as pregnant with possibilities as the aftermath of the Battle of Mohács in Hungary in 1526. For here we can speculate on consequences that encompass not merely one but a number of the great changes of the time: not only the Italian Renaissance and the Lutheran and Anglican Reformations, but also the clash between Christendom and Islam, and the heritage in Germany and Spain of the greatest political figure of the age, Charles V.

The victory won by the Ottoman Sultan Suleyman the Magnificent at Mohács on August 29, 1526, was unquestionably one of the decisive military engagements of world history. It was nearly three-quarters of a century since the conquest of Constantinople, but now the Turks were on the move again. Sweeping through the Balkans, Suleyman had captured the powerful citadel at Belgrade in 1521, and five years later, after turning aside to conquer the hostile island of Rhodes from the crusading order of the Knights Hospitaler of St. John, he was ready to advance further into Europe. At Mohács he encountered and destroyed the flower of the kingdom of Hungary, the last Christian power capable of resisting the Muslims in the Balkans. The slaughter that followed was ghastly. Not only did the king, two archbishops, five bishops, and the bulk of the aristocratic leadership of Hungary perish, but some 30,000 troops on the losing side either died on the field or were killed by a victor who took no prisoners. Suleyman's exultation on behalf of his faith as well as his regime leaps from the pages of his announcement of victory:

> Thanks to the Most High! The banners of Islam have been victorious, and the enemies of the doctrine of the Lord of Mankind have been driven from their country and overwhelmed. Thus God's grace has granted my glorious armies a triumph, such as was never equaled by any illustrious Sultan, all-powerful Khan, or even by the companions of the Prophet. What was left of the nation of impious men has been extirpated. Praise be to God, the Master of the World!

The Turks were masters of the Balkans. But the question remained: What next?

Suleyman's answer in 1526, as it had been in 1521 after the capture of Belgrade, was to take his crack troops, the Janissaries, back to Constantinople to regroup. Not for three years did he venture forth again, to probe further up the Danube into Austria, and to besiege Vienna. By then Charles V's brother Ferdinand (already the dominant figure in the Habsburgs' Austrian and Bohemian domains) had established his claim to what remained of the crown of Hungary against his rival, John Zapolya of Transylvania, and Zapolya in response had turned to Suleyman for help. Aware that the Habsburgs were his chief antagonists in central Europe, the sultan agreed to help the Transylvanian gain the crown on the condition that he pay tribute and owe allegiance to the Ottomans. With that agreed, Suleyman at long last marched from Constantinople on May 10, 1529, at the head of an enormous army of perhaps 75,000 men.

It was now that contingency intervened. The summer of 1529 happened to be one of the wettest of the decade. In the laconic judgment of Suleyman's biographer, Roger Bigelow Merriman, the rains "were this year so continuous and torrential that they seriously affected the outcome of the campaign." If we change "seriously affected" to "determined" we will come closer to the truth. Because of the rains, Suleyman was forced to abandon, on the way, his hard-to-move heavy artillery, which had been a crucial asset in earlier sieges. Moreover, the adverse conditions prevented his troops from marching at their normal speed; they covered ground so slowly that nearly five months passed before they reached the gates of their target, Vienna. Not until September 30 (virtually the end of the campaigning season) was Suleyman ready to send his bedraggled and weary troops into the attack, and by then he also had to contend with another consequence of the delay: the Viennese had had the time to reinforce their position. Over the summer they had been able nearly to double the size of the defending garrison, which now held some 23,000 men, 8,000 of whom had reached the city only three days before the Turks arrived. The sultan's assaults proved futile, and by mid-October he had decided to withdraw—only, so he later claimed, because Ferdinand had run away, and there would be no glory in capturing the city without his adversary.

But let us suppose it had not been such a terribly wet summer—or, to rely on human rather than meteorological happenstance, suppose that Suleyman had pressed ahead more promptly, in the much drier summer of 1527 that followed the battle of Mohács. In 1532 he showed that he was fully capable of overrunning the Habsburg territory when, despite another very wet summer, he laid waste to the Austrian province of Styria—though he did avoid Vienna, which by now was massively defended by what Merriman calls "possibly the very largest [army] that Western Europe had ever been able to collect." What might the outcomes have been if the incursion had begun in 1527 (rather than 1529 or 1532), when the conditions were right and the Habsburgs were far less prepared?

One has to assume, first, that Suleyman would almost certainly have captured Vienna. And, secondly, that he would soon have found allies in the West. As titular rulers of all Germany, and effective rulers not only of Austria, Bohemia, and the Netherlands, but also of large stretches of Italy and all of Spain, the Habsburgs were feared and resented by almost every other leader in Europe. They might now stand on the front line against the Muslims, but that did not mean their fellow Christians stood with them, for their power often seemed far more threatening than Islam. Indeed, in the very year of Mohács, the papacy, France, and many of the Italian states formed the League of Cognac to try to sweep the Habsburgs out of Italy. The campaign that led to the sack of Rome was to be Charles V's reply, but he could never have mounted that campaign if Suleyman had threatened his flank from Vienna. Indeed, there is a good chance that the participants in the League of Cognac, emboldened by the emperor's troubles, would have made a pact with Suleyman and thus have been able to end, almost before it began, a Habsburg ascendancy in Italy that was to last nearly a century and a half. After all, the Venetians had already signed a commercial treaty with the sultan in 1521, and the French were to ally with him in the 1530s. Although the pope would have had to stay aloof, the other Italian princes would have had no more compunction about joining with the infidel against the hated Habsburg in 1527 than did the Venetians or the French in these years.

With Charles distracted by Suleyman in the north, those Italian states that were his allies would soon have succumbed to the League of

Cognac. And the consequences for European culture would have been enormous, for not only the treasures of Rome but the city's entire artistic culture would have been spared the sack of 1527. Investigating the effects of that terrible event over a decade later, the art historian and painter Giorgio Vasari recounted in painful detail the grim experience of the distinguished artists whose lives had been shattered. Some had been killed; many had been assaulted, ruined, or forced into menial occupations; others had fled; and all had in one way or another been deeply affected. "One need only understand," wrote Vasari, "that violence makes delicate souls lose sight of their primary objective and regress." Indeed, one of the victims, Sebastiano del Piombo, wrote: "I don't seem to be the same Sebastiano I was before the sack; I can never again return to that frame of mind."

Even a heartwarming story recounted by Vasari—and there were not many of them—had no happy ending. As he tells it, the great Mannerist painter Parmigianino was unable to complete his *St. Jerome*

> because of the catastrophic sack of Rome in 1527. This not only caused a halt in the arts, but for many artists the loss of their lives as well. It would have taken little for Francesco [Parmigianino] to lose his too, for when the sack began, he was so immersed in his work that despite the eruption of soldiers into the houses, and Germans already inside his own, with all the noise they made, he continued to work. Bursting in on him, and seeing him at work, they were so amazed by the painting that, evidently men of breeding, they let him go on . . . But when these soldiers left, Francesco was a hair's breadth from disaster.

Eventually, Parmigianino escaped and returned to his native Parma. Whether or not Vasari was echoing a similar story from antiquity—of an artist, interrupted during a siege of Rhodes, who told the soldiers he assumed they had come to make war on Rhodes, not on art—the message was unmistakable.

Nor was this merely the exaggeration of contemporaries. The chief modern historian of the sack, André Chastel, has described Roman art as

116

traumatized for a generation, though he acknowledged that those who fled could enrich the culture of other cities, notably Venice, the prime refuge for the persecuted. And it is also worth noting that there would have been one other momentous result had Charles's troops been kept out of Italy. The emperor would not have controlled the papacy; Clement would doubtless have granted Henry VIII his divorce; and England might well have remained a Catholic nation indefinitely.

That likelihood would surely have been strengthened by the effect on Germany of Suleyman's presence in Vienna. A quick look at the map will suggest the implications of the capture of the Austrian capital for the future of Central Europe, especially if one imagines the sultan continuing westward along the Danube to the rich cities of Passau, Regensburg, and Augsburg, ravaging the terrified dukedom of Bavaria, and so forth. Either some of the princes in his path would have made deals with him—keeping their positions if they paid tribute and allegiance to Constantinople, as Zapolya had done in Hungary—or they would finally have been forced to rally around Charles V. Not that the second option would have seemed inevitable, even in the face of invasion. There had been civil warfare in western Germany in the early 1520s and a huge peasant uprising in the mid-1520s, and the emperor's pleas for unity and help against the Turk had little effect. Typical was the behavior of one gathering of princes, summoned to discuss the Turkish advance through the Balkans. Before agreeing to provide support, they decided they needed a fact-finding mission; delaying even this action, they did not finally vote to dispatch a delegation to Hungary until the day before the battle of Mohács.

Whether making deals with Suleyman or joining together to protect their lands, however, the princes of Germany would almost certainly have realized by the late 1520s that they could no longer afford the divisive presence of religious dissent. To link up with the devout Charles V they would probably have agreed to end their support for Luther, and most would have realized anyway that a united front required the suppression of the animosities caused by the Reformation. Bereft of essential protectors, and with Charles seeking to placate the papacy, Luther would have been isolated and his following would have dwindled, though the reformer himself might have found a protector in the north, far from the Danube. New movements to reform the church would undoubtedly have arisen, and Luther's impact might have been postponed rather than eradicated; but the religious complexion of Europe at midcentury would have been radically altered, with immense consequences for all her states.

One in particular catches the eye. If both England and the Netherlands had remained Catholic, and the Habsburgs had given up their Italian ambitions to concentrate on their German and Spanish territories, the struggles of the second half of the sixteenth century would have taken very different forms. With religious antagonisms subdued, Spain would not have aroused such enmity elsewhere in Christian Europe, and she would have been able to develop her empire in the New World largely free of the hatreds that eventually propelled her challengers. Today, as a result, all Americans, both North and South, would have spoken Spanish. If only it had not been such a wet summer . . .

♦ PETER PIERSON ♦

IF THE HOLY LEAGUE HADN'T DITHERED

What if twenty-year-old King Charles IX of France had followed his heart and answered the summons of Pope Pius V to join the Holy League against the Turks in 1570? Instead he accepted the cautions of Queen-Mother Catherine de' Medici, and listened to Admiral Coligny's urging that he take advantage of Spain's distraction to make gains for France—and, as Coligny hoped, the Protestant cause. Following the league's great victory at Lepanto on October 7, 1571, in which its armada crushed the Turkish fleet, Philip II of Spain fretted about French designs and kept his half brother Don John of Austria, the league's commander, in port well into 1572. The Turks rebuilt their fleet and crushed Christian rebellions in Greece. Coligny's Huguenots invaded Philip II's Netherlands, to commence the costly two-front war that would compel Philip to downgrade the Mediterranean. By the time Don John mobilized the Holy League's entire force, the 1572 campaigning season was nearly over, and he achieved nothing. Though Coligny perished in the St. Bartholomew's Day Massacre on August 24, France persisted in a foreign policy hostile to Philip. That is what did happen.

Had the league struck early in 1572, as Don John planned, with its ranks enlarged by the chivalry of France, then Greece and the Balkans may have been restored to the rest of European civilization. Instead, the Balkans would remain largely under Ottoman Turkish rule well into the nineteenth century. Frequent revolts by Balkan Christians led to ever crueler repression by the Turks and local people who converted to Islam. The resultant divisions and animosities in Balkan society still plague the world.

♦ *Peter Pierson is professor of history at Santa Clara University.*

ROSS HASSIG

THE IMMOLATION OF HERNÁN CORTÉS

Tenochtitlán, June 30, 1521

O ne of the central episodes of the 1520s was, of course, the taking of the Aztec capital of Tenochtitlán—today's Mexico City—by the Spanish conquistador Hernan Cortés. The question most asked is how so few men could topple an entire kingdom. One answer is that the Spanish force, perhaps 900 men in all, was joined by nearly 100,000 Indian allies, all eager to destroy their hated Aztec oppressors. Disease has never been a respecter of historical odds. Smallpox, which the Spanish brought with them, killed off 40 percent of the population of Mexico in a year, including one Aztec king. But Cortés, who was undoubtedly a remarkable soldier and a born opportunist, was also extraordinarily lucky. As Ross Hassig points out, "There are no shortage of plausible turning points for the Conquest." Several times the Spanish could have been stopped or annihilated in battle. Like Alexander the Great, Cortés himself missed death only because of the intervention of one of his men—who was killed as he managed to save his leader. Had Cortés been captured, he would have been sacrificed soon after, and the conquest would have crumbled. Once again we are reminded of the heavy-handed role of time and chance.

The question that is almost never asked is: What would have happened if Cortés had been killed or if his expedition had failed? Would the Spanish, as Theodore K. Rabb suggested in the previous chapter, have turned their acquisitive instincts elsewhere—North Africa, for instance? Would another attempt at conquest have been more successful? Would Christianity have been able to make inroads, even if the soldiers of Spain could not? What about the practice of human sacrifice? What sort of nation would have evolved from the Aztec Kingdom? And down the road, what effect would a large and totally Native American nation have had on the growth of the United States?

◆ Ross Hassig is professor of anthropology at the University of Oklahoma and one of the foremost authorities on the Aztecs. Among his many books are MEXICO AND THE SPANISH CONQUEST, WAR AND SOCIETY IN ANCIENT MESOAMERICA, and AZTEC WARFARE: IMPERIAL EXPANSION AND POLITICAL CONTROL.

ortés and his men leapt across the breach in the causeway to pursue the fleeing Aztecs, only to see them turn and attack. Drawn into the trap, Cortés and sixty-eight other Spaniards were captured and dragged off, leaving scores of others dead on the road. Ten captives were killed immediately and their severed heads were thrown back over the front lines, sowing consternation among the disheartened Spaniards. The remaining fifty-eight were taken to the towering Great Temple, which could plainly be seen from the Spaniards' camps, made to dance before the statue of the Aztec god of war, Huitzilopochtli, and then, one by one, they were sacrificed. Their hearts were torn out and their faces and hands flayed so they could be tanned and sent among the wavering towns as a warning. Cortés escaped this fate only through the intervention of Cristóbal de Olea, who sprang to his defense, killed the four Aztecs who were dragging him off, and freed his leader at the cost of his own life. The very conquest of Mexico hung on this single act.

The final military event in the conquest of Mexico was the Aztec surrender on August 13, 1521, after the Spaniards broke through the last defenses and fought their way into the Aztec capital of Tenochtitlán. The city lay in ruins and, for four days, the Spaniards' Indian allies continued to attack the defeated Aztecs, looting the houses and killing thousands. But the events of the Spanish conquest did not have to unfold as they did. There were many points when decisive actions by various individuals, misadventure, or poor decisions could have drastically altered the outcome of the conquest as we know it.

Mesoamerica was discovered by Francisco Hernández de Córdoba, who landed in Yucatan in 1517, where he clashed with the Maya and was ultimately repulsed with devastating losses. This expedition was followed by a second in 1518, under Juan de Grijalva, who also clashed with the Maya but who sailed beyond Yucatan and up the gulf coast to central Veracruz, where he encountered the Aztecs. Even before Grijalva's return, Governor Velázquez of Cuba authorized a third expedition under Hernán Cortés, but when he later tried to relieve him, Cortés abruptly set sail and reached Yucatan in early 1519 with as many as 450 men. If Governor Velázquez had succeeded in removing Cortés from command before the expedition's departure, the conquest would have been still-born.

But having slipped out of Velázquez's grasp, Cortés followed the route of the first two expeditions until he reached Grijalva's anchorage on the central Veracruz coast. There, Cortés was greeted by Aztec officials bearing food and gifts, but when the Spaniards refused to accede to Aztec requests to move their camp, the emissaries left. Had the Aztecs met the Spaniards with massive force, again the conquest would have been aborted or forestalled. But they did not, and once they abandoned the Spaniards on the coast, the local tribe, called the Totonacs, established contact and eventually allied with them. The Totonac king could do this because the Aztec empire relied on conquest or intimidation to subdue opponents, and left the local rulers in place. No imperial offices or officeholders were imposed to hold the system together, so this system was also vulnerable to shifts in the local power balance that could quickly and easily alter allegiances. The Spanish arrival was such a change and the Totonacs seized on it.

Having achieved the goals of exploration, contact, and trade, as authorized by Governor Velázquez, many of Cortés's men wanted to return to Cuba. Had they left, Cortés would have had too few men to continue and, once again, the conquest would have failed. However, Cortés founded the town of Villa Rica de la Vera Cruz a few miles north of present-day Veracruz, appointed a city council under the claimed authority of King Charles V of Spain, which then declared that Velázquez's authority had lapsed, and elected Cortés as captain directly under the king; he was now free from the governor's constraints. To gain royal support,

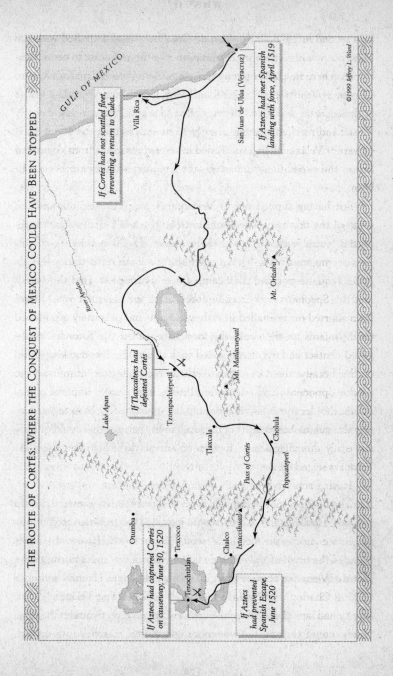

THE ROUTE OF CORTÉS: WHERE THE CONQUEST OF MEXICO COULD HAVE BEEN STOPPED

GULF OF MEXICO

Villa Rica

San Juan de Ulúa (Veracruz)

If Cortés had not scuttled fleet, preventing a return to Cuba.

If Aztecs had met Spanish landing with force, April 1519

River Antigua

Mt. Orizaba

If Tlaxcaltecs had defeated Cortés

Tzompachtepetl

Mt. Matlacueyatl

Lake Apan

Tlaxcala

Cholula

Pass of Cortés

Popocatepetl

Ixtaccihuatl

Otumba

Texcoco

Chalco

Tenochtitlan

If Aztecs had captured Cortés on causeway, June 30, 1520

If Aztecs had prevented Spanish Escape, June 1520

©1999 Jeffrey L. Ward

Cortés dispatched a ship to Spain with all the gold they had gathered thus far as a gift to the king. To keep his men from deserting, he scuttled the ten remaining ships, giving his men little option but to follow him. Leaving 60 to 150 men in the fort at Vera Cruz, Cortés marched inland with 300 Spanish soldiers, 40 to 50 Totonacs, and 200 porters.

En route to Tenochtitlán, the Spaniards neared the province of Tlax-callan (Tlaxcala), where they advanced to capture a small party of armed Indians. But they were drawn into an ambush and were saved only by their superior firepower. Attacked repeatedly in the days that followed, the Spaniards suffered many wounded; their supplies were running low. Recognizing that he faced an overwhelming hostile force, Cortés sent re-peated peace entreaties to the Tlaxcaltecs. The two sides eventually forged an alliance. The Tlaxcaltecs could have defeated the Spaniards, and had they continued the battle, as their commander wanted, Cortés's adventure would have ended. But the Tlaxcaltecs had their own reasons for allying with the Spaniards. They had been engaged in a long-term war with the Aztecs and, completely encircled and cut off, their defeat was only a matter of time. The coming of the Spanish offered them an un-foreseen way to win. A major tactic in Mesoamerican battles was to breach the opposing lines and turn the enemies' flanks, which was very difficult to do. But Spanish cannons, the matchlock muskets called har-quebuses, crossbows, and horsemen could disrupt enemy lines and, though the Spaniards were too few to exploit these breaches, the Tlax-caltecs were not. Spanish arms greatly multiplied the effectiveness of the Tlaxcaltec army.

The Spaniards stayed in Tlaxcallan for seventeen days before march-ing to the province of Cholollan (Cholula). Though welcomed by the Chololtecs, Cortés claimed he learned of a plot to attack him with Aztec help: He assembled the nobles in the main courtyard and massacred them. His reason does not ring true. Cholollan had recently switched their allegiance from Tlaxcallan to the Aztecs, so a Spanish attack was a way to resolve a political problem. A new king was chosen and Cholollan re-allied with Tlaxcallan. Two weeks later, Cortés marched into the Valley of Mexico and reached Tenochtitlán on November 8. He was greeted by Moteuczoma (Montezuma) and housed in the palace of his deceased father, Axayacatl, who had been the king from 1468 to 1481.

An enormous island-city of at least 200,000, Tenochtitlán was connected to the mainland by three major causeways that could be quickly severed. Recognizing the precariousness of his position, Cortés seized Moteuczoma within a week of his arrival, held him captive, and ruled through him for the next eight months.

When Governor Velázquez learned of Cortés's perfidy, he dispatched Pánfilo de Narváez with a fleet of nineteen ships and over eight hundred soldiers to Vera Cruz to capture him. But on learning of his arrival, Cortés marched to the coast with 266 men in late May and, aided by duplicity and judicious bribery, defeated Narváez.

Meanwhile, Pedro de Alvarado, who had been left in Tenochtitlán with eighty soldiers, claimed he had learned of an Aztec plot to attack them, placed artillery at the four entrances of the walled courtyard of the Great Temple, and then massacred an estimated eight to ten thousand unarmed Aztec nobles trapped inside. Word of the massacre spread throughout the city, the populace attacked, killed seven Spaniards, wounded many others, and besieged them in their quarters. When Cortés learned of the uprising, he began the return march with a force now numbering over 1,300 Spaniards and 2,000 Tlaxcaltecs, and reached Tenochtitlán on June 24.

Once he was inside the city, the Aztecs raised the causeway bridges and the Spaniards were apparently trapped. With their supplies dwindling and unable to fight or negotiate their way out, Cortés took Moteuczoma onto the roof to order his people to stop the attack, but to no avail, and the king was ultimately killed, either by stones thrown from the Indian throng or by his Spanish captors.

Cortés ordered portable wooden spans built to bridge the gaps in the causeways and, during a heavy rainstorm just before midnight on June 30, the Spaniards began their escape. They were quickly discovered, and only a third of the force got away. Cortés reached Tlaxcallan, but not until he had lost over 865 Spaniards and more than a thousand Tlaxcaltecs. Had the Aztecs assailed the fleeing Spaniards immediately and continuously, few if any would have survived. The 440 surviving Spaniards rested for three weeks and then, in early August, marched again and conquered nearby Aztec tributary cities.

The Indians now faced a new, nonmilitary threat. Smallpox arrived with Narváez's expedition and swept though central Mexico, killing some 40 percent of the population of Mexico in a year, including Moteuczoma's successor, King Cuitlahua, who ruled for only eighty days. Because the epidemic devastated both the Aztecs and their Indian opponents, depopulation does not, of itself, account for the conquest. But it did produce political disruption: The death of Cuitlahua meant that with the accession of his successor, Cuauhtemoc, the Aztecs had three kings in less than six months.

The first time Cortés entered Tenochtitlán, he had been trapped inside; now he sought to reverse that situation and ordered the construction of thirteen brigantines in Tlaxcallan, using the rigging salvaged from the ships he sank at Vera Cruz. There was an intermittent influx of arrivals from the coast throughout the conquest, and Cortés's forces had grown to 40 horsemen and 550 Spanish foot soldiers. Accompanied by 10,000 Tlaxcaltec soldiers, Cortés began his return march to the Valley of Mexico.

But Cortés's first major victory there was political. Since 1515, Tetzcoco, the second most important city of the empire, had been politically divided over who should succeed to the throne. Cacama took the throne with strong Aztec support, but another contender, Ixtlilxochitl, fought a civil war, conquered the area north of Tetzcoco, which he then ruled in an uneasy accommodation with Tenochtitlán. When Cortés entered the valley, Ixtlilxochitl seized the opportunity to ally with him, and the reigning king of Tetzcoco fled. Ixtlilxochitl's support gave the Spaniards a strong foothold for their attack and provided a secure logistical base. Cortés won the allegiance of disaffected cities in the valley and fought a series of battles with the Aztecs. But since Tenochtitlán was supplied by

guzmā. mchvacā.

CORTÉS VS. THE AZTECS: CONQUEST IN THE BALANCE

The Spanish conquistador Hernán Cortés (in dark clothes, left) and Indian allies meet, and best, Aztec warriors. Had his attempt to conquer Mexico failed, an enduring Native American kingdom might one day have collided with an expanding United States.

(Corbis/Bettman)

canoe, Cortés had to control the lake. When the timbers being cut in Tlaxcallan reached Tetzcoco around the first of February, the Spaniards began assembling the brigantines. On April 28, 1521, Cortés launched his ships—each over forty feet long, with twelve oarsmen, twelve crossbowmen or harquebusiers, a captain, and an artilleryman for its bow-mounted cannon. Supported by thousands of Indian canoes, they barricaded Tenochtitlán and cut off its flow of food and water.

The Spaniards now numbered just over 900, and those not on the brigantines were divided into three armies of fewer than 200 Spaniards

129

each and "supported" by 20,000 to 30,000 Indian troops each. On May 22, Pedro de Alvarado led one army to Tlacopan, while Cristóbal de Olid marched to Coyohuacan, and Gonzalo de Sandoval went to Ixtlapalapan. Cutting off three of the major routes into Tenochtitlán, the Spaniards attacked along the causeways, whose narrowness allowed them to concentrate their firepower. The Aztecs responded by building barricades and assaulting the Spaniards on both sides from canoes. But Cortés then breached the causeways, sailed his ships through, and drove off the enemy canoes. In response, the Aztecs limited the ships' movements by planting sharpened stakes in the lake floor to impale them.

There is no shortage of plausible turning points for the conquest and the examples are far from exhausted by those already suggested. But the likeliest such point, involving the fewest alterations in historical events, took place on June 30, 1521. The Spaniards and their Indian allies had been assaulting the causeways that linked Tenochtitlán to the shore for more than a month. The battles were back-and-forth struggles during which the Aztecs built barricades, removed bridge spans, and destroyed portions of the causeway, both to delay the Spanish advance and as tactical ploys. When the Spaniards crossed these breaches, the Aztecs often redoubled their efforts and trapped them when they could neither easily retreat nor be reinforced. To avoid this, Cortés ordered that no breaches were to be crossed until they had been filled. But, on June 30, when the Aztec defenses seemed to crumble in the heat of battle, the Spaniards crossed an unfilled breech on the Tlacopan causeway. Their ploy having succeeded, the Aztecs turned, trapped the attackers against the breach, took sixty-eight Spaniards captive and killed many more. The captives were all sacrificed and, fearing a shift in the tide of war, most of Cortés's allies left. Though the Spaniards ultimately survived this reversal and their allies eventually returned, it could easily have been otherwise.

Had Cristóbal de Olea not sacrificed his own life to save Cortés, he too would have been taken and sacrificed, and the defection of his Indian allies would likely have been permanent. The Spanish leader had three lieutenants but there was no clear second in command. Moreover, the Spaniards were never completely united, even behind Cortés. Repeatedly, he threatened and cajoled them and twice ordered Spaniards hanged for plotting to desert. And now with Cortés gone, Spanish unity would have disintegrated. The conquest would have been lost. What, then, would the Spaniards have done?

Exposed on the western shore of the lake without allies, the Spaniards alone could not long hold out against the Aztec assaults. And the factionalism that seethed just below the surface could not have been suppressed without Cortés since there was no single leader of equal determination and ruthlessness. Without overwhelming Indian support, there was no hope for the Spaniards and they faced three plausible choices. They could have continued the battle, but that offered only annihilation. They could have surrendered en masse but that meant death for most, if not all, of them, though isolated individuals might have slipped away with their erstwhile allies, perhaps to be hidden until the Aztecs spent their fury. Or they could have attempted an orderly withdrawal. But to where? They had been allowed to slip away during the flight from Tenochtitlán a year earlier and the Aztecs were unlikely to permit a repeat of that mistake. Moreover, then they had an ally in Tlaxcallan—who would now have abandoned them. So their only recourse was to abandon their heavy equipment and begin a 200-mile withdrawal to the gulf coast through hostile territory, a journey most were unlikely to complete. But given their fragmented loyalties and divided command, the Spaniards would probably have fallen apart and, the weakened remainder would have been vulnerable to the inevitable Aztec counterattack. The only question was how many Spaniards would have survived. Some may have reached the gulf coast and then sailed to Cuba, but most would have died in battles en route—though a lucky few may have survived capture or have been sheltered by former allies. The conquest would be over.

What would have been the probable Spanish response to this defeat?

What the surviving Spaniards in Mexico thought is not of concern here, but the opinions of the Spaniards in the Indies and Spain is. Given the seasonal pattern of transatlantic sailings, word of Cortés's defeat would probably not have reached Spain until late summer or fall of 1522 at the earliest, with any response arriving in the Indies no sooner than the following summer. New World conquests and colonization were backed by the Crown, but it was not a governmental enterprise underwritten by a national army, so a concerted military response was unlikely. Cortés's death and the disaster that beset his men, however, would have made the repudiation of his expedition politically easy. Since Cortés had violated Governor Velázquez's orders and authorization, he had also effectively gone against the king and, in light of his failure, royal support would now be solidly behind the governor.

Awareness of Mexican civilizations, lands, and wealth was too widespread in both Spain and the Indies to be ignored. But in light of the Crown's support for Velázquez, its most likely response would be to adopt the governor's original plan for trade rather than colonization. To justify his original plans and current political position, Velázquez would probably have tried to enforce his approach rigorously and with royal backing. Some degree of quarantine would be likely, with the probable emergence of a single trading center on the coast, much as Macao served Portuguese trade interests in China and Japan in the sixteenth century. It is doubtful that the Spaniards could long be held to commerce alone and the continuation of such a trading relationship may not have survived Velázquez's death in 1524 unless some other strong patron managed to secure the Crown's approval for a monopoly. But if there was to be another attempt to conquer Mexico, it would probably be some years off: Exploration elsewhere in the Caribbean was absorbing all available men and material. And the surviving Spanish adult male population of the Indies would require time to recover from the loss of some 2,000 men in Cortés's ill-fated scheme. Moreover, the increased Spanish migration that actually followed the conquest of Mexico would probably not have materialized without increased opportunities in the New World. Thus, the

Spaniards of the Indies were distracted, politically constrained, and militarily weakened. Perhaps their energies would have been absorbed by the conquest of the Incas that began in the late 1520s, where the way had been smoothed by an Inca civil war and by the devastating spread of smallpox into the Andes from Spanish settlements in Panama. Instead of Mexico, a conquered Peru would have drawn Spanish migrants, but the riches thus seized would doubtless have tempted the Spaniards to make another bid for the wealth of Mexico.

A Spanish reconquest was probably delayed rather than deterred, but the issue of the Aztec response to their victory over the Spaniards would have remained. Would they have simply lapsed back to the status quo? Not likely. Even with an Aztec victory, Mexico would have been profoundly changed by the Spanish presence. The smallpox epidemic of 1519 to 1520 had been devastating, but the deadly typhus epidemics of 1545 to 1548 and 1576 to 1581 would not have occurred without a major Spanish presence, or at least not that soon. The Aztec political landscape was significantly altered, not in the offices themselves, but in the personalities of those who replaced leaders lost to war or disease. The political infrastructure of neighboring cities and of the empire would have continued intact, but the way many rulers had switched sides during the conquest would certainly have led to retribution.

The political future of rulers in various cities who had taken their thrones with Spanish/Tlaxcaltec support was bleak and some would now be displaced as Aztec loyalists or political opportunists took advantage of the shift in power. Cities allied with Tlaxcallan would likely have defected to the Aztec side. Meanwhile, Tlaxcaltec factionalism would probably have led to the pro-Spanish ruler being deposed; his replacement would have allied with the Aztecs in an effort to forestall their own conquest. Thereafter, other defectors would have been dealt with easily, swiftly, and terminally. The Aztecs were smaller in population and weaker than before, but politically, they were stronger, having replaced rulers of dubious loyalties.

What would this have meant for a new Spanish invasion? During the first one, Cortés exploited the poorly integrated nature of the Aztec empire and the presence of a major enemy—Tlaxcallan—to secure allies. With Tlaxcallan no longer hostile, could the Aztecs cement their alliances to eliminate the rivalries Cortés had exploited? The Aztec empire was only loosely bound together. Roads and a system of porters were better developed within it than elsewhere, both basic and exotic goods flowed among its many markets, but no rigidly enforced political hierarchy bound it together. Instead, local rulers were left in power, which meant that as soon as the Aztecs showed weakness or incompetence, they might defect. Moreover, while general Mexican cultural practices were widely shared, there was no unifying religion or ideology. Intermarriage among rulers created some cross-cutting loyalties, but these took many years to form and, in the absence of an alternative way to integrate the empire more tightly, the Aztecs could not create a solid front that would be impenetrable to the returning Spaniards.

If they could not reorganize their empire, the Aztecs nevertheless had two major options open to them—they could take the offensive or they could adopt new military weapons and tactics. Since the Spaniards had built and sailed ships in the Valley of Mexico and may well have abandoned some at Vera Cruz in their flight, it is possible that the Aztecs could have launched a counteroffensive into the Indies. Though used on the Pacific coast of South America, sails were unknown in Mexico, and the Aztecs were generally ignorant of the existence or location of the Indies. So as appealing as the image is of Aztec soldiers storming Havana, it is improbable. Alternative routes for a return attack by the Spaniards were blocked from the south by other native states that were too small and too far away to materially assist them and from the north by an inhospitable desert that offered few allies, little food, and great dangers. So an Aztec offensive stance, at best, would have meant patrolling the gulf coast and waiting for a Spanish return before trying to push them back into the sea, though this costly effort would probably have flagged as the years passed uneventfully.

But Cortés's attempt to conquer them unquestionably would have affected Aztec tactics. The primary Spanish technological introductions were horses (and mounted lancers), cannons, harquebuses, and cross-bows. As they had done during their first flight from Tenochtitlán, the Spaniards probably abandoned their cannons, but this time the Aztecs might not have destroyed them as they did earlier. Some of the other weapons likely to have fallen into Aztec hands included swords, armor, crossbows, perhaps harquebuses, and maybe even horses. But what would any of this have meant to the Aztecs? They had used captured swords—some attached to poles as scythes against horses—and a cross-bow against Cortés, so even though the Aztecs did not work iron and so could neither repair nor replicate these arms, those they recovered could easily be integrated into their own forces. After all, the Aztecs already had their own broadswords, spears, bows, and armor. Indeed, since the Indians who had allied with Cortés had been taught to make excellent copper-headed bolts, there was a potentially inexhaustible supply of am-munition for the crossbows. Cannons and harquebuses required gun-powder, and while all of the ingredients were locally available, its concoction was unknown to the Aztecs, but horses might be mastered, offering the tantalizing possibility of Aztec cavalry such as Americans later encountered on the Great Plains. And if the Spaniards actually es-tablished a trade center at Vera Cruz, bladed weapons and perhaps even firearms would have flowed into Aztec hands, whether officially sanc-tioned or not. To make the most of these arms, however, actual instruc-tion would be needed and, for that, there were probably surviving Spaniards.

Changing sides was not unprecedented. Gonzalo Guerrero, who had been shipwrecked off Yucatan in 1511, had risen to the rank of military leader among the Maya, led one of their attacks on Córdoba, and refused to rejoin the Spaniards despite Cortés's entreaty. Moreover, Spain was a newly emerging entity whose king, Charles V, though the son of the rulers of Castile and Aragon, was raised in the Netherlands and was ef-fectively a foreigner. Many Spaniards owed whatever loyalties they had to their cities or provinces rather than to "Spain" and some who participated in the conquest were Portuguese or Italian, so shifting loyalties from Cortés to Cuauhtemoc was imaginable, probable, and, in fact, indispensable if they did not wish to be sacrificed to the Aztec gods. But what could the Spaniards teach the Aztecs that they had not already learned in combat? Weapons use, certainly. For instance, Spanish swords were made of steel with both cutting edge and point and so could thrust as well as slash, whereas the Aztecs' were oak broadswords edged with obsidian blades and could be used only to slash. And perhaps the Aztecs could even make gunpowder, since the three necessary ingredients were available in the Valley of Mexico, though whether they could use explosives is questionable. But new weapons aside, battle strategies and combat practices could certainly be improved as the Aztecs learned the full capabilities and limitations of the Spanish weapons and tactics.

Most of what the captured Spaniards could teach the Aztecs was refinement. They already understood the basics. And what was important was less how it affected their battlefield tactics than the political environment. The Tlaxcaltecs initially allied with the Spaniards because they recognized that those few soldiers could serve as shock troops to punch through and disrupt opposing formations in a way their own weapons and tactics could not. It had not been the presence of the Spaniards per se that had been important, but the decisive advantage they conveyed on the Tlaxcaltec army. With the surviving Spanish arms, however, this advantage was now also held by the Aztecs.

If and when the second conquest came, the various Aztec tributaries and allies would probably have been only marginally more tightly bound to the empire than before; yet even with cannons and harquebuses, the Spaniards were no longer offered the golden opportunity they had the first time. Yes, they could still perform a shock function, but any Indian group that might consider allying with them could not fully exploit it because the Aztecs, even with a limited number of Spanish arms, could also now employ shock tactics and disrupt their formations, and coupled with vastly larger armies, an Aztec victory was ultimately assured.

So, by the time the Spaniards subjugated the peoples of the Andes, leaving them crippled with deadly disease and exploitation, and they finally turned their attention back to Mexico, in the mid to late 1530s, their opportunity had passed. The allies of a returning Spanish force would have been few, their victories ephemeral, and the lucky ones would have been pushed back into the sea—the heads of the rest would have adorned the skullracks of Tenochtitlán. Any reconquest would have to await far larger numbers, more artillery, and more horses than were available in the Indies.

Time changed the situation on both sides. While there was no pan-Mexican ideology to unify the various groups, word of the inhabitants' fate in the Indies and South America slowly made its way to Tenochtitlán and a sense of Indianness that had heretofore been absent emerged in opposition to the Spaniards and expressed itself militarily as well as politically.

Limited as the Spaniards were to more passive exploitation by trade and conversion, gold and silver still flowed into Spanish coffers made wealthy by the pillage of Peru, but Spanish innovations in tools and animals were rapidly adopted by the Aztec elite, and percolated down into the commoner ranks, establishing indigenous livestock and craft industries. Instead of becoming the center of Spanish industry, with lesser benefits falling to the Indians, these innovations were adopted by the natives, even if the nobility dominated, if not monopolized, major herding activities, but with benefits that flowed throughout their society. For instance, wool would have been quickly adopted by their thriving weaving industry, just as bronze and iron would have been added to the range of goods produced and repaired by native metalworkers. Moreover, the development of the native economy made possible by these innovations strengthened indigenous rulers and filled the vacuum into which Spanish colonists would otherwise have flowed.

Spanish intrusions would have been blunted, though not eliminated, and religious orders, obeying their missionizing imperative, would have gradually infiltrated the country ahead of potential settlers. But now, confronting a vigorous indigenous priesthood that enjoyed state support and a flourishing school system, conversion was far slower. The Spanish priests also brought literacy with the Latin alphabet to Mexico and if this spread to all classes, social turmoil would likely follow, so the indigenous elite would doubtless monopolize this knowledge to increase their political and administrative hold. But a more Christianized indigenous tradition would likely have emerged. Without the sword to force conversion, persuasion and example alone were available, resulting in some Christianization and, most likely, a cessation of human sacrifice. But continued personal religious bloodletting may have been reconceived, if not toward a monotheistic end, then toward one that blended the Christian God with one or more of the more important native gods in an elevated, if not exclusive, position above the native ones.

With the gradual emergence of a far stronger indigenous economy and the development of at least a tolerable approximation of Christianity, Mexico would have been far more difficult to conquer. Mexico could have continued as a regional power and survived the expansion of the European colonies in Central and North America, if their more limited exposure to Europeans dispersed the demographic shock of introduced diseases and they prevented Europeans from exploiting it. The nation that emerged may have been much like the Mexico of today, though perhaps limited to central Mexico, organized on strong indigenous lines, yet having undergone modern development from empire to constitutional monarchy. Had this been so, American expansion toward the West may have been halted far earlier than it was—perhaps at the Mississippi, for France, which sold the United States its rights, would have had no claim on the land to the West, and Mexico, whether freely or as the better of limited options, may have left the United States of today far smaller and bordering a nation of truly indigenous Americans.

GEOFFREY PARKER

THE REPULSE OF THE
ENGLISH FIRESHIPS

The Spanish Armada Triumphs, August 8, 1588

T*he defeat of the Spanish Armada in 1588 has come down through history as a tale of missed connections, a devastating fireship attack that broke the armada's order, a sea battle that forced the Spanish ships into the North Sea, followed by a storm-plagued passage around the British Isles. A third of the fleet and half of the men aboard would never return to Spain.*

We forget how close the Spanish king, Philip II, came to success. The man who controlled the world's first empire on which "the sun never set" was determined to get rid of England's Protestant queen, Elizabeth, and make her nation once again safe for Catholicism. He wanted to end English meddling in the Netherlands, which he ruled, and keep Elizabeth from gaining a foothold in the New World. To those ends, he sent a great armada of 130 ships, which was to rendezvous with the Duke of Parma's army, veterans of the Netherlands rebellion, and escort it to a landing in Kent. But, off Calais, an English fleet intercepted the armada first—and here the what ifs begin. What if on the night of August 7–8, 1588, the winds had blown in a different direction, keeping the English fireships and battleships away from the Armada? What if the Spanish had been able to hang on until Parma and his troopships arrived? Or if they had known that the English shot lockers were practically empty? What if Parma's army had actually made its landing in Kent? The evidence suggests that Parma's seasoned troops could have marched to London, opposed only by terrified conscripts and poorly equipped militia. Philip II might have easily achieved his objective. But as Geoffrey Parker observes, he could be his own worst problem.

❖ *Geoffrey Parker is professor of history at the Ohio State University and the author of such works as THE DUTCH REVOLT, PHILIP II, THE MILITARY REVOLUTION, THE SPANISH ARMADA (with Colin Martin), and, most recently, THE GRAND STRATEGY OF PHILIP II. He is (with Robert Cowley) the editor of THE READER'S COMPANION TO MILITARY HISTORY.*

I f some British historians had their way, August 8 would be declared a national holiday, because on that day, in the year 1588, Elizabeth Tudor's navy decisively repulsed Philip II's attempt to conquer England. The failure of the Spanish Armada laid the American continent open to invasion and colonization by northern Europeans, and thus made possible the creation of the United States.

Philip II already ruled Spain and Portugal, half of Italy, and most of the Netherlands, and the Iberian colonies around the globe—from Mexico, through Manila, Macao and Malacca, to Goa, Mozambique, and Angola—creating an empire upon which, as his apologists boasted, "the sun never set." In addition, his cousin Rudolf II of Habsburg, who had grown up at the Court of Spain, ruled Germany and Austria, while his ally the Duke of Guise, leader of the French Catholics, pledged unconditional support for Philip's plans. Only the northwest Netherlands caused problems. Rebellion against the king's authority broke out in 1572, and the provinces of Holland and Zealand had defied him ever since, despite the expenditure of vast sums of money and the efforts of his best generals and his finest troops. Their sustained ability to resist infuriated Philip and the commander of his forces in the Netherlands, his nephew Alexander Farnese, duke of Parma. Gradually they convinced themselves that only English support sustained the Dutch Revolt, and in fall 1585 Philip resolved to switch his resources from the recapture of Holland and Zealand to the conquest of England. He sought and received aid from other Catholic rulers for his plan to depose Queen Elizabeth and replace her with a sound Catholic. Tuscany provided a galleon and a grant; Mantua supplied an interest-free loan; the pope promised a huge subsidy and a plenary Indulgence for all who took part.

Meanwhile the king's National Security advisers searched for a suitable invasion plan. In the summer of 1586, Philip received an annotated map that evaluated different invasion strategies. Its author, Bernardino de Escalante, dismissed as too risky a naval assault either on northwest England (by sailing north to Scotland and then into the Irish Sea) or on Wales, and instead envisaged a joint expedition by a large fleet sailing from Lisbon, which would carry an expeditionary force to southern Ireland, while the duke of Parma led a surprise attack on Kent by veterans from the Spanish Netherlands. They would cross the channel aboard a fleet of small transports as the English navy sailed away to defend Ireland. Philip II made only one—as it transpired, fatal—change. He decreed that the fleet from Lisbon must sail to the Netherlands, rather than to Ireland, and provide an escort for Parma's veterans as they crossed to England. He felt confident that his armada would prove invincible: If Elizabeth's ships tried to prevent its journey up the channel, they would fail. Parma had only to await the fleet's arrival in order to succeed.

Philip issued precise orders on how to proceed after the troops came ashore. They must march through Kent, take London by storm (preferably with Elizabeth and her ministers still in it), and hope that the queen's enemies on the periphery of the kingdom and in Ireland would rise in rebellion to aid the invaders. If no Catholic rising took place, however, or if London held out, Parma must use his presence on English soil to force Elizabeth to make three concessions: toleration of Roman Catholic worship, an end to all English voyages to American waters, and the surrender to Spain of all Dutch towns held by English troops.

In many ways, the first phase of the operation went according to plan. On July 21, 1588, a fleet of 130 ships, the largest ever seen in north European waters, sailed under the command of the duke of Medina Sidonia to effect its rendezvous with Parma's 27,000 veterans, and their 300 troop transports assembled in the harbors of Dunkirk and Nieuwpoort. On July 29, the armada entered the channel and on August 6, with its order intact despite repeated attacks by the Royal Navy, it dropped anchor off Calais, only twenty-five miles from Dunkirk. News of the fleet's approach only reached Parma that same day, however, and although he began embarking his troops on August 7, it proved too late. That night, the English launched a fireship attack that finally disrupted the armada's formation. In a ferocious battle on August 8, Elizabeth's powerful galleons managed both to inflict severe damage on individual ships and to drive the entire enemy fleet northward, away from the rendezvous.

No sooner had the armada entered the North Sea than arguments began over where the enterprise had gone wrong. "There is nobody aboard this fleet," wrote Don Francisco de Bobadilla (senior military adviser to the duke of Medina Sidonia), "who is not now saying, 'I told you so' or 'I knew this would happen.' But it's just like trying to lock the stable door after the horse has bolted." Bobadilla therefore propounded his own explanation of the debacle. On the one hand, he admitted, "We found that many of the enemy's ships held great advantages over us in combat, both in their design and in their guns, gunners and crews, . . . so that they could do with us as they wished." On the other hand, most Spanish ships experienced an acute shortage of ammunition. "But in spite of all this," he continued, "the duke [of Medina Sidonia] managed to bring his fleet to anchor in Calais roads, just seven leagues from Dunkirk, and if, on the day that we arrived there, Parma had come out [with his forces], we should have carried out the invasion."

The first English historian who seriously considered these questions, Sir Walter Raleigh, in his *History of the World* of 1614, entirely agreed. The English, he wrote, were "of no such force as to encounter an Armie like unto that, wherewith it was intended that the prince of Parma should have landed in England." The Army of Flanders, which had been fighting the Dutch with scarcely a break since 1572, had indeed been molded into a superb fighting force. Some veterans had been on active duty for thirty years and they served under experienced and resourceful officers who had risen through the ranks. During the previous decade they had conquered the rebellious provinces of Flanders and Brabant, culminating in the capture of the port of Sluis in August 1587 in the teeth of a spirited defense by the best troops and most experienced com-

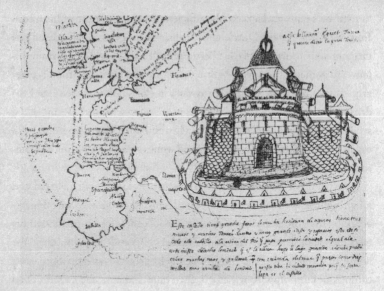

PLANNING THE CONQUEST

In July 1586, Bernardino de Escalante, a soldier-turned-priest, sat down to explain to Philip II the various ways to invade England. He had resided there thirty years before— and remembered the Tower of London ("E greet tuure," on the right) as the only important stronghold. His map therefore assessed the options of sending a fleet from Spain to sail either around Scotland and attack northeast England, or into the Irish Sea and land in Wales. Either operation seemed less dangerous than a direct assault up the channel, where, as Escalante noted, the armada would encounter "el enemigo." Events would prove him right.

(Biblioteca Nacional, Madrid, manuscript 5785/168)

manders of the Dutch and their English allies. Over the next year Parma prepared a meticulous embarkation schedule, including the precise itinerary and sequence for each unit's march from their billets to the designated ports, and even supervised two rehearsals. The fact that, when the armada arrived, almost all the 27,000 men detailed for the invasion managed to embark within thirty-six hours—no mean feat for an army in any age!—testifies to the military effectiveness of both the troops and their commanders.

144

Parma's panoply lacked only sufficient warships to protect his troops from assault by their Dutch and English enemies as they crossed the channel and a train of siege artillery. Philip II had anticipated both problems. To remedy the first deficiency, the armada included four heavily armed *galeasses*, huge oar-powered warships of shallow draft capable of driving off the Dutch ships blockading the Flemish ports. To meet the second need, the Spanish fleet carried twelve forty-pounder siege guns, together with all their accoutrements. Parma's army would thus have enjoyed full artillery support.

Very few towns and castles in southeast England could have resisted a battery from such weapons. Only solid-angled bastions, projecting beyond the main walls and protected by wide moats, could withstand heavy bombardment; and in southeast England only Upnor Castle on the River Medway, built to defend the naval dockyard at Chatham, possessed those. The larger towns of Kent (Canterbury and Rochester) still relied on their antiquated medieval walls. No defense works at all seem to have existed between Margate, the projected beachhead, and the Medway; while Upnor alone could scarcely stop the Duke of Parma and his army. Philip II had deftly selected his adversary's weakest point.

With so few physical obstacles in his path, Parma would have moved fast. When he invaded Normandy in 1592, with 22,000 men, the duke covered sixty-five miles in six days, despite tenacious opposition from a numerically superior enemy. Four years earlier, the invaders might therefore have covered the eighty miles from Margate to London in a week. Even London represented a soft target because the capital still relied on its medieval walls. They had scarcely changed since 1554, when Sir Thomas Wyatt raised a rebel army in protest against the marriage of Mary Tudor, Elizabeth's half-sister and predecessor, to Philip II. The insurgents marched through Kent, crossed the Thames at Kingston (west of the capital), advanced with impunity through Westminster, and surged down Fleet Street until they reached the city walls, where Wyatt, lacking artillery, finally lost his nerve.

Parma well knew, however, that the state of a town's physical de-

THE SPANISH INVASION OF ENGLAND, 1588

Parma's proposed route
Armada's proposed route
Armada's actual route

North Sea

ENGLAND

DUTCH REPUBLIC

Tilbury (English HQ)

London

Margate

Kingston upon Thames   Rochester   *Medway R.*   *Thames R.*

(Battle)

(Fireships)

Dunkirk (Parma's HQ)

Nieuwpoort
Gravelines

Calais

SPANISH NETHERLANDS

English Channel

©1999 *Jeffrey L. Ward*

FRANCE

fenses did not always prove decisive. Several Netherland towns with poor, outdated fortifications had escaped capture thanks to the determination of the besieged population; conversely, a few strongholds boasting modern defensive systems had fallen to the Spaniards before their time because their citizens, their garrison, or their commander succumbed to bribes. As an English officer with the Dutch army wrote on hearing of the premature surrender of yet another town to Parma: "Everybody knows that the king of Spain's golden salvoes made a bigger breach in the heart of the traitor in command than did the siege artillery." Elizabeth's troops in the Netherlands had a distinctly uninspiring record in this respect. In

1584 the English garrison of Aalst sold their town to Parma for £10,000 and in 1587 Sir William Stanley and Roland Yorke, together with over 700 English and Irish soldiers under their command, betrayed to Parma the places entrusted to their care (Deventer and a fort overlooking Zutphen), and for the most part subsequently fought for Spain against their former comrades.

Elizabeth and her advisers nevertheless set great store by the comrades of these traitors, recalling 4,000 men of the English expeditionary force in Holland to form the nucleus of the army intended to repulse the invaders. Its quartermaster general was the brother of Roland Yorke; its third-in-command, Sir Roger Williams, had fought for Philip II in the Netherlands in the 1570s. One cannot exclude the possibility that some of these men might have been prepared to sell strongholds to Parma, as their fellows had done in the Low Countries.

Elizabeth, however, had little choice. She depended on the veterans from Holland because she could call upon very few other experienced troops. The London "trained bands," who had been drilling twice weekly since March, might have put up a good fight (although some doubted it) but little could be expected from the rest of the English county militias. Few men possessed firearms, and some of those received only enough powder for three or four rounds; the militias of the southern shires proved so disorderly that their commanders feared they "will sooner kill one another than annoye the enemye"; while the queen felt obliged to maintain 6,000 soldiers along the Scottish border in case King James VI, whose mother (Mary Stuart) Elizabeth had executed the previous year, should decide to throw in his hand with the Spaniards.

All English preparations fell dangerously behind. The queen only issued orders for the southern militias to muster on July 27—as the armada approached the channel—and even then she ordered them to move toward Tilbury in Essex, separated by seventy miles and the Thames from the beachhead chosen by Philip II. A boom across the river designed to keep out enemy shipping broke at the first high tide and was never repaired; a bridge of boats designed to link the queen's forces in

Kent and Essex remained incomplete. Even at Tilbury, the linchpin of England's defenses, work only began on the fortifications on August 3, the day the armada passed the Isle of Wight. Three days later, as the fleet dropped anchor off Calais, the troops in Kent began to desert in considerable numbers. In any case, they numbered only 4000 men, a ludicrously inadequate force to throw in the path of the seasoned Spaniards, and they lacked a clear strategy. The local commander, Sir Thomas Scott, argued that his forces should spread out along the coast and "answer" the enemy "at the sea side," while the general officer commanding in the southeast, Sir John Norris, more prudently wished to withdraw all but a skeleton force inland in order to make a stand at Canterbury and there "staye the enemye from speedy passage to London or the harte of the realme."

Much of this unpreparedness and confusion stemmed from poverty and isolation. Elizabeth could raise no loans either at home (because hostilities with Spain had caused a trade recession) or abroad (because most continental bankers thought Spain would win), forcing her to delay every stage of her counterinvasion plans until the last possible moment in order to save money. On July 29, 1588, her treasurer complained that outstanding bills totaling £40,000 lay on his desk "with no probability how to get money" to pay them. "A man might wish," he concluded dourly, that "if peace cannot be had, that the enemy would not longer delay, but prove, as I trust, his evil fortune." Apart from the Dutch, England stood entirely alone.

By contrast, although on one occasion Philip II had to pawn his family jewels to raise money, he managed to provide huge sums for the Enterprise of England. The French Catholic League received 1,500,000 ducats from Spain between 1587 and 1590, and over the same period the Army of Flanders received some 21,000,000 more. The king himself claimed that he had spent 10,000,000 on the armada itself. Since about four ducats equaled one pound sterling, his total outlay on the project thus exceeded £7,000,000, at a time when Elizabeth's annual revenues hovered around £200,000. At the same time, Philip's diplomats managed either to win over or neutralize every other state in Europe. In July 1588, as the armada entered the channel, an admiring ambassador at the Court of Spain noted:

> At the moment, the Catholic King [Philip II] is safe: France cannot threaten him, and the Turks can do little; neither can the king of Scots, who is offended at Queen Elizabeth on account of the death of his mother [Mary Stuart]. The one [monarch] who could have opposed him was the king of Denmark, who has just died, and his son is young and so has other things to deal with . . . At the same time, Spain can rest assured that the Swiss cantons will not move against him; nor will they allow others to do so, since they are now his allies.

In short, he concluded, no foreign power could prevent the execution of the king's Grand Strategy for the conquest of England and the hegemony of Europe.

❖ ❖ ❖

Were these optimistic contemporary analysts correct? In *Pavane*, a novel published in 1968, Keith Roberts graphically suggested the enormous advantages that might have accrued from a complete Spanish victory.

> On a warm July evening of the year 1588, in the royal palace of Greenwich, London, a woman lay dying, an assassin's bullets lodged in abdomen and chest. Her face was lined, her teeth blackened, and death lent her no dignity; but her last breath started echoes that ran out to shake a hemisphere. For the Faery Queen, Elizabeth the First, paramount ruler of England, was no more.
>
> The rage of the English knew no bounds . . . The English Catholics, bled white by fines, still mourning the Queen of Scots, still remembering the gory Rising of the North, were faced with a fresh pogrom. Unwillingly, in self-defense, they took up arms against their countrymen as the flame lit by the Walsingham massacres ran across the land, mingling with the light of warning beacons from the sullen glare of the auto-da-fe.
>
> The news spread; to Paris, to Rome, to . . . the great ships of the ar-

mada, threshing up past the Lizard to link with Parma's army of invasion on the Flemish coast . . . The turmoil that ensued saw Philip ensconced as ruler of England; in France the followers of Guise, heartened by the victories across the channel, finally deposed the weakened House of Valois. The War of the Three Henrys ended with the Holy League triumphant, and the Church restored once more to her ancient power.

To the victor, the spoils. With the authority of the Catholic Church assured, the rising nation of Great Britain deployed her forces in the service of the popes, smashing the Protestants of the Netherlands, destroying the power of the German city-states in the long-drawn Lutheran Wars. The New Worlders of the North American continent remained under the rule of Spain; Cook planted in Australasia the cobalt flag of the [papal] throne.

❖   ❖   ❖

At first sight, this "best-case outcome" for Spain of the armada campaign does not seem too fanciful. Assassination, the constant nightmare of the childless Elizabeth's ministers, had become commonplace in early modern Europe. In France, Catholic extremists murdered not only the Protestant faction leaders Anthony of Navarre (1563) and Gaspard de Coligny (1572), but also King Henry III (1589) and his successor, Henry IV (1610.) Elizabeth survived at least twenty assassination plots: the success of any of them would have extinguished the Tudor dynasty and left a council of Regency both to direct resistance against the advance of the relentless invaders, and to find a successor.

Even without the removal of Elizabeth, whether by assassination or by capture, a Spanish occupation of Kent alone might have produced important results. Parma could have exploited his advantage to wrest concessions from a Tudor government terrified of rebellions in the north and in Ireland. Persecution of English Catholics would have ceased, allowing their numbers and confidence to increase. The overseas exploits of Sir Francis Drake and the other "seadogs" would also have ceased, leaving North America securely in Spain's sphere of influence (missionaries had already begun to advance from Florida into Virginia.) Finally, English forces would have withdrawn from the Netherlands, abandoning the Dutch to make the best settlement they could.

The Republic already contained a vociferous peace party. Although most political leaders in Holland and Zealand firmly opposed talks with Spain, some towns dissented, while the adjacent provinces that bore the brunt of the war against Spain argued strongly in favor of a settlement. According to one of Elizabeth's envoys to the Dutch: "The Common Wealth of these Provinces consisting of diverse Parts and Professions as, namely, Protestants, Puritans, Anabaptists and Spanish Hearts, which are no small number; it is most certain that dividing these in five parts, the Protestants and the Puritans do hardly contain even one part of five." And, the envoy continued, only the "Protestants and Puritans" favored a continuation of the war. Had the Enterprise of England succeeded, leaving the young republic to withstand Philip's power alone, internal pressure for a compromise would probably have become irresistible.

Without the need to maintain a costly army in the Netherlands, Spain would have been free, just as Keith Roberts fantasized, to intervene decisively elsewhere. The expulsion of the Protestants from France and the recovery for the Roman Church of many Lutheran areas of Germany, both of which occurred in the seventeenth century, would no doubt have taken place several decades earlier. The newly confident Counter-Reformation church, assisted by the power of the Habsburgs, would have virtually extirpated Protestantism from Europe. Overseas, the Spanish and Portuguese empires would have continued their expansion and steadily increased their mutual contacts, creating a unified Iberian empire whose resources would have extended the authority of Philip II and his successors all around the globe.

❖ ❖ ❖

Or would it? Counterfactual experiments in history should always include two limitations: the "minimal rewrite rule" (only small and plausible changes should be made to the actual sequence of events) and "second order counterfactuals" (after a certain time, the previous pattern may reassert itself.) In the case of Philip II, it seems reasonable to speculate that the fireships released by the Royal Navy on the night of August 7, 1588, might somehow have failed to destroy the armada's battle order—as it was, the Spaniards managed to intercept two of them and tow them out of harm's way. Medina Sidonia could then have waited for Parma and his troops, who completed their embarkation by August 8, to set forth and join him. They would then have crossed the Narrow Seas in irresistible force. Beyond that, however, the "rewrite" becomes more than "minimal."

We cannot assume that Philip II would have exploited his victory prudently. Having ruled and resided there during the 1550s (as husband of Mary Tudor), he regarded himself as both omniscient and divinely inspired where England was concerned. "I can give better information and advice on that kingdom and on its affairs and people than anyone else," he once informed the pope. This supreme confidence helps to explain why he sought to micromanage every aspect of the armada campaign, starting with the creation of a master plan that imprudently involved the junction of a fleet from Spain with an army from Flanders, separated by a thousand miles of sea, as the ineluctable preliminary to invasion. He refused to allow anyone—whether councilor, general, or admiral—to challenge the wisdom of his Grand Strategy. Instead, he urged them to "believe me as one who has complete information on the present state of affairs in all areas." Whenever obstacles threatened the venture, Philip insisted that God would provide a miracle. When, for example, a freak storm in June 1588 drove the armada back to port soon after it had set forth, and Medina Sidonia suggested that this might be a warning from the Almighty that the enterprise should be abandoned, Philip responded with naked spiritual blackmail. "If this were an unjust war," he scolded the duke, "one could indeed take this storm as a sign from Our Lord to cease offending Him. But being as just as it is, one cannot believe that He will disband it, but rather will grant it more favor than we could hope . . .

I have dedicated this enterprise to God," the king concluded briskly. "Pull yourself together, and do your part!"

Philip also rashly insisted that the armada should advance to Calais as fast as possible, without waiting for confirmation that the Army of Flanders was ready. It never seems to have occurred to him that the numerous English and Dutch warships in the channel might prevent Medina Sidonia's from sending reports of his progress, his problems, and his estimated time of arrival from reaching Parma. Instead, stinging royal rebukes awaited those aboard the fleet who counseled caution and delay.

There seems no reason to suppose that a successful Spanish invasion of southeast England would have reduced Philip's desire to meddle. Rather, he would have tried to retain total control of events, demanding that all major decisions be referred to him—a two- to three-weeks' journey away in Spain—for resolution. He would also probably have insisted that Parma should strive for total victory instead of seeking a compromise, just as he had refused to discuss a compromise settlement after every major success in the struggle against the Dutch, thus creating a stalemate that drained his resources. This, too, would have affected the continuing continental struggles. With the invasion of England bogged down, Dutch resistance would have continued and the position of the French Catholics deteriorated, straining Spain's resources yet further and pushing it toward bankruptcy. As it was, the royal treasury had to suspend all payments in 1596.

When Philip II died in 1598, at the age of seventy-one, his empire passed to his only surviving son, the nineteen-year-old Philip III. The absence of an older, more accomplished successor arose from the peculiar genetic heritage of the Spanish Habsburgs. For generation after generation, they married close relatives. Philip II's oldest son Don Carlos, arrested and imprisoned because of his dangerously unstable behavior, could boast only four grandparents instead of eight, and only six great-grand parents instead of sixteen. The gene pool inherited by his half-brother Philip (III) was scarcely better: his mother, Anna of Austria, was

Philip II's niece and cousin as well as his wife. This endogamy—or as Spain's enemies termed it, incest—arose from the desire to join territories together. Don Carlos descended from three generations of intermarriage between the ruling dynasties of Portugal and Spain. This policy, although technically successful (the kingdoms were united in 1580), literally carried within itself the seeds of its own destruction. No wonder the Spanish Habsburgs died out after only two more generations of endogamy! The conquest of England would have done nothing to improve the Habsburg gene pool; it would merely have served to create more for Philip III and his successors to lose. Second order counterfactuals suggest that, even had the armada succeeded, Spanish hegemony would not have lasted for long.

At least, however, Philip's victory in 1588 would have gone down in history as an exemplary "combined operation." Historians would have praised the selection of an ideal invasion area, the formidable planning, the immense resources, the successful diplomacy that neutralized all opposition, and the operational brilliance that (against all the odds) joined an irresistible fleet from Spain with an invincible army from the Netherlands. If, despite all its deficiencies, the duke of Parma and his veteran troops had begun their march on London on Monday August 8, 1588, then—whatever the ultimate outcome—everyone today could regard the invincible armada as Philip II's masterpiece, all Americans would now speak Spanish, and the whole world might celebrate August 8 as a national holiday.

THOMAS FLEMING

UNLIKELY VICTORY

*Thirteen Ways the Americans Could Have
Lost the Revolution*

The American Revolution is practically a laboratory of counterfactual history. There is hardly an opportunity for an alternative scenario that doesn't exist in those eight years (1775–1783). At times, as Thomas Fleming demonstrates, the unexpected seems the only real certainty. Sometimes sheer luck intervenes. A British marksman has Washington in his sights and doesn't pull the trigger. Commanders display too much or too little caution. The British make a picture-perfect landing on Manhattan Island, and then pause to wait for reinforcements while George Washington and his Continentals slip the noose. At the Battle of the Cowpens, Banastre Tarleton, like the emperor Valens at Adrianople, is too impetuous, and the Americans hold on in the South. (There are times when a short rest and a good breakfast could have changed history.) Gambles work. Washington attacks Trenton in a Christmas night snowstorm and reinvigorates the patriot cause. Good or bad choices are made under stress. Benedict Arnold disobeys orders at Saratoga, and the result is an American victory. Would the French have joined the war on our side otherwise? Animosities influence events. In a turf struggle, the British *commander in chief, Sir Henry Clinton, tells his Southern commander, Charles, Lord Cornwallis, to retreat to an obscure Virginia tobacco port called Yorktown, fortify it, and ship much of his army back north. The vagaries of weather are a given, of course, as they always have been in military operations. Take the two violent storms that sealed the fate of the British troops trapped at Yorktown in October 1781: The first prevented a rescue fleet from sailing from New York harbor and the second, a breakout attempt across the York River a few days later. How different would the outcome of the Revolution have been if the British had escaped?*

By any reasonable stretch of the imagination, Fleming reminds us, the United States should have expired at birth. We were hardly inevitable.

❖ *Thomas Fleming is the author of such historical studies as 1776: YEAR OF ILLUSIONS, biographies of Thomas Jefferson and Benjamin Franklin, THE MAN FROM MONTICELLO and THE MAN WHO DARED THE LIGHTNING, LIBERTY: THE AMERICAN REVOLUTION, and, most recently, DUEL: ALEXANDER HAMILTON, AARON BURR AND THE FUTURE OF AMERICA. He has also written numerous historical novels, including two set during the Revolutionary War, LIBERTY TAVERN and DREAMS OF GLORY. Fleming has served as chairman of the American Revolution Round Table and is the former president of the American Center of P.E.N., the international writer's organization.*

When a historian ponders the what ifs of the American Revolution, chills run up and down and around the cerebellum. There were almost too many moments when the patriot cause teetered on the brink of disaster, to be retrieved by the most unlikely accidents or coincidences or choices made by harried men in the heat of conflict. Seldom if ever was there a war with more potential for changing the course of history. Imagine the last two hundred years—or at the very least, the last hundred—without a United States of America! Picture a world in which the British Empire bestrode not only the subcontinent of India, but the entire continent of North America.

Almost as tantalizing is the society that might have arisen, with a different outcome. If the Americans had lost the war early in the struggle, they might have been permitted a modicum of self rule; there would have been few, if any hangings or confiscations. If victory had come later, when the British government and people were exasperated by long years of resistance, Americans might well have become a subject race, savagely repressed by a standing army, and ruled by an arrogant local aristocracy. The impact on Great Britain would have been almost as dire. The hardliners in the aristocracy, backed by a king who was equally narrow-minded, would have created a state that was relentlessly intolerant of democracy.

Within these extremes are other outcomes. One of the most intriguing appeared even before the war began. The child—independence—could easily have been strangled in its cradle, if some of its parents had not realized that they were performing on a stage far larger than the provincial seaport of Boston.

What if Samuel Adams had gotten his way after the Boston Massacre?

Sam Adams deserves his niche as the master agitator on the torturous path to independence. But he had a tendency to brinkmanship, demonstrated by his less than brilliant staging of the Boston Massacre. With the town occupied by two regiments of British troops, Sam thought his well-armed bullyboys from the North End of Boston could terrify the royal army into a humiliating evacuation. On the night of March 5, 1770, a well-armed 400-man mob pelted the seven-man British detachment guarding the customs house with chunks of ice and pieces of lumber. Screaming insults, they surged to within a few feet of the soldiers' guns. Sam had assured the rioters that the redcoats would never pull their triggers without a magistrate first reading the riot act, officially branding the mob as violators of the king's peace and warning them to disperse. This was something no judge in Boston dared to do, lest he get his house torn down around his ears.

Someone in the crowd struck a soldier with a club, knocking him to the ground. The man sprang to his feet and was struck by another club, thrown from a distance. He leveled his musket and pulled the trigger. Seconds later, the other members of the guard imitated him. The mob fled. As the gunsmoke cleared, five men lay dead or dying. Six more men were wounded.

Although he professed to abhor the bloodshed, Sam Adams was secretly delighted. He foresaw a trial for murder in which the soldiers would be found guilty. Rather than let them hang, the British would intervene, declaring their indifference to the verdicts of American juries. Meanwhile, Sam's propaganda machine would be denouncing the royal murderers and their London backers. It never occurred to Sam that moderates in other colonies and in England would see this denouement as proof that Boston was in the hands of an anarchistic mob, and the British might be excused for resorting to draconian measures to restore law and order.

Fortunately, one man in Boston saw this clearly—Sam's cousin, John

Adams. Although he had been active in Sam's movement, John was shocked when friends of the soldiers informed him that not a lawyer in Boston was willing to defend them, for fear of getting his windows and possibly his face smashed by Sam's sluggers. John announced he would take the soldiers' case. With masterful skill, he managed a plea of self-defense without quite revealing Sam and his friends as the perpetrators of the riot. The soldiers were acquitted and for the rest of his long life, John Adams maintained that his "disinterested action" in defending the redcoats was "one of the best pieces of service I ever rendered my country." He was unquestionably right. Moderate men in England and New York and Virginia were able to tell each other that the Bostonians were worthy of their support.

If Sam had triggered a draconian response, there might never have been a Boston Tea Party. In a town patrolled by six or seven regiments, no further riots would have been tolerated, and Sam and his lieutenants might well have been taken into custody during the peaceful three years between the Massacre and the dumping of the tea into the harbor. Instead, outsiders viewed the confrontation over a piddling but highly symbolic tax on imported tea as British arrogance and stupidity in action. The tea party was greeted with tut-tuts by the moderates but no one saw it as another demonstration of endemic Yankee lawlessness—and the moderates quickly agreed that the British government's reaction to it—closing the port of Boston and remodeling the government of Massachusetts to extract the democratic elements—was egregious overkill and a step toward tyranny. Soon Sam and John Adams were on their way to the First Continental Congress in Philadelphia.

Back in Massachusetts in early 1775, with the British 4,500-man army in Boston under a state of semisiege, confronted by swarms of well-armed minutemen whenever detachments marched into the country, Sam showed he had learned nothing from the Massacre fiasco. He proposed bringing matters to a head by launching an all-out attack on the regulars. Cooler heads prevailed, arguing that the rest of America would never support such a move—and the British would welcome it as proof that there really was a rebellion in Massachusetts, no different from the ones they had suppressed with ruthless efficiency in Ireland and Scotland.

Again, there is no doubt that the cooler men were right. When an impatient ministry pushed the British commander in Boston, Major General Thomas Gage, into action, he sent 700 men on a night march to Concord, hoping to seize the rebels' gunpowder and other war material and effectively disarm them. On Lexington Green, the marchers encountered the town's militia company. Gunfire broke out, leaving dead men on the grass. It was followed by more gunfire and bloodshed at Concord and by a running battle between the British and swarming minutemen on the road back to Boston. Sam Adams had the incident he needed to unite the Americans—and give moderate men in England grounds for attacking the government in Parliament and in the newspapers.

What if the British plan had worked at Bunker Hill?

Two months later the embryo war could have gone either way at Bunker Hill. The mythical version of this battle has the British marching stupidly up the hill to get blasted by American marksmen. In fact, the British had a sophisticated battle plan that could have ended the war if they had been able to execute it.

The field commander, Major General William Howe, intended to outflank the exposed fort on Breed's (not Bunker's) Hill by sending a column of crack light infantrymen up the beach on the shore of the Mystic River and sealing off the narrow neck of the Charlestown Peninsula, trapping the Americans like insects in a bottle. Simultaneously, the other half of the British army was to assault the weakened American lines around Cambridge, where the rebels had most of their powder and ammunition. If all went well, the Americans would be a fleeing mob by the end of the day.

Fortunately for the future of the yet unborn United States, Colonel John Stark, commander of a New Hampshire regiment and a veteran of the French and Indian War, spotted the deserted beach as a potentially fa-

BUNKER HILL: REVOLUTION'S PREMATURE END?

An early nineteenth-century engraving shows the Battle of Bunker (Breed's) Hill and a burning Charlestown, Massachusetts, on June 17, 1775. Had even one of the naval vessels in the harbor came to the aid of the British troops trying to take the hill from the other side—out of view, here—the Revolution might have been throttled that afternoon.

(Anne S. K. Brown Military Collection, Brown University Library)

tal flaw in the American position. He ordered 200 of his best men there and took personal command of them. When Howe saw this checkmate, he asked the British admiral on the Boston station to send a sloop up the Mystic River to scatter Stark's men with a few rounds of grapeshot. The admiral demurred, saying he had no charts of the river.

Howe sent his light infantrymen forward anyway, gambling that the American amateurs could not get off more than a round before the professionals were on top of them with their bayonets. It did not work that way. Stark's New Hampshire sharpshooters littered the beach with British dead and Howe was reduced to a desperate frontal assault, which cost him almost half his little army before he carried the Breed's Hill fort.

If that British admiral had the energy or the brains to chart the Mystic River, or if John Stark had failed to spot the importance of that beach, Bunker Hill would have been a very different story. Except for some sputters of resistance in Virginia and a few other colonies, the American Revolution might well have ended on June 17, 1775. Instead, the Americans were enormously emboldened by their ability to inflict crippling casualties on their foes—and the British were forced onto a humiliating defensive in a Boston ringed by hostile Yankees.

What if Washington had attacked the British army in Boston in early 1776?

A fascinating possibility preoccupied George Washington after he took command of the American army outside Boston in July of 1775. For nine months a stalemate ensued, largely caused by Washington's shortage of artillery and his inability to prevent most of his Yankee army from going home on January 1, 1776, when their enlistments expired. In March of 1776, his spies reported that numerous British ships in the harbor were taking on water and provisions, preparing to withdraw from Boston. Their destination was presumed to be New York.

By this time, Washington had acquired plenty of artillery from captured Fort Ticonderoga and his army was again a respectable size. The American commander decided to abort this enemy plan to seize New York, where they would be far more dangerous to the Revolution than they were on a cramped defensive in Boston.

Washington concocted a daring, even a hair-raising plan. First he would seize Dorchester Heights, south of the city, and emplace cannon on it. When the British attacked the position, he would send 4,000 men in forty-five bateaux, supported by 12-pound cannon on rafts, to assault Boston from the Charles River. While half the force seized Beacon Hill and similar high ground in the city, the other half would attack British fortifications on Boston Neck, opening the way for reinforcements waiting to rush overland from Roxbury. Washington was convinced that the destruction of Howe's army would cripple the British war effort and lead to an immediate peace.

At first, everything went according to plan. On the night of March 4, Washington seized Dorchester Heights and mounted cannon in a series of forts that the British would have to attack or abandon Boston. General Howe readied his army for an assault on March 5. Still an ambitious gambler, Howe planned to attack Washington's Roxbury lines with 4,000 men as the rest of his troops—about 2,200 men—advanced on Dorchester. That left only 400 redcoats guarding the side of Boston at which Washington was aiming his amphibious assault.

The stage was set for a titanic showdown. But as darkness fell on March 5, a cold, biting wind began to blow, mixing snow and hail. Soon it was a "hurrycane," in the words of one of Washington's junior officers. Howe called off his attack and Washington's plan also went into the circular files. Would it have worked? When the British evacuated Boston thirteen days later, Washington had a chance to study, at close range, the fortifications he was hoping to assault. He was awed by their strength. "The town of Boston," he admitted, "was almost impregnable." In a letter to his brother Jack, Washington called the storm a "remarkable interposition of providence."

A Washington defeat at that point in the war, while it would not necessarily have ended the conflict, would have been calamitous for his reputation. Critics in the Continental Congress and in the army were already sniping at him, fretting over his supposed timidity and indecisiveness. Would a Washington victory have ended the war, as he hoped? Probably not. The British government was in the process of shipping to America an army four times the size of the one in Boston.

What if the British had trapped Washington's army on Long Island or Manhattan?

George Washington had urged the Continental Congress to give him an army of 40,000 men, enlisted for the duration of the war. Congress believed the fantasy Sam Adams exported from Boston after Lexington and Concord: Yeoman farmers had sprung to arms to defeat British regulars. In reality, Massachusetts had an embryo army of minutemen who had been training for nine months and were five times the size of the British garrison in Boston. Washington was told to limit his army to 20,000 men, enlisted for a single year, and rely on militia—part-time soldiers who, unlike the minutemen, had little or no training. Then Congress nibbled away at Washington's army, demanding that detachments be shipped to bolster the losing war the Americans were fighting in Canada.

As a result, Washington showed up in New York with little more than 10,000 regulars—Continentals, as they were called—and summoned a horde of militia from New England, New York, New Jersey, and Pennsylvania to bolster his force. He confronted a royal army that numbered almost 30,000 men, including about 12,000 German mercenaries. At the battle of Long Island on August 27, the British, once more commanded by William Howe, devised a flanking strategy that worked. The calamitous day ended with most of Washington's army trapped in forts in Brooklyn Heights.

Two nights later, with the help of a favorable wind and a fortuitous fog, Washington stealthily withdrew his army to Manhattan. There he had two more narrow escapes. On September 15, the British landed at Kips Bay (present-day Thirty-fourth Street), routing thousands of Connecticut militia. Only excessive caution prevented the British from trapping a third of the Continental Army in lower Manhattan.

On October 18, the British landed at Pell's Point in Westchester. A fighting retreat by a 750-man Massachusetts brigade gave Washington time to get his army off Manhattan Island. By this time Washington had no illusions about the militia; most of them had gone home. While many American leaders despaired, Washington kept his head and took charge of the war. He told Congress the American army would no longer seek to end the struggle in one titanic battle. "We will *never* seek a general action," he informed the president of Congress, John Hancock. Instead, "We will protract the war." This seemingly simple change in strategy transformed the conflict into a war of attrition—precisely the kind of war the British were least prepared to fight.

If Washington and his army had been trapped in Brooklyn Heights or Manhattan, the war would have ended quickly. The stupidity of Congress's reliance on militia had become apparent to everyone. It would have been very difficult for Americans to raise another army, after the routs on Long Island and at Kips Bay. Worse, the alternative general action strategy called for replicating the Battle of Bunker Hill, an idea that obsessed most American generals. The British would never have repeated that mistake. Without Washington's new strategy, despair would have seeped through the revolutionists' ranks.

What if Washington had decided not to attack Trenton and Princeton or failed in either attempt?

Retreating across New Jersey, Washington watched the the British begin pacifying this crucial state. They circulated a proclamation, urging the civilians to swear "peaceable allegiance" to George III and receive a "protection," a guarantee that their lives and property would not be forfeited. Thousands took advantage of the offer to bail out of the apparently lost cause. The New Jersey militia, 17,000 strong on paper, evaporated. Barely 1,000 men turned out. It was a preview of how the British hoped to end the war in other colonies.

To protect the loyalists, the British stationed garrisons in various towns across the state. Washington noted they were "a good deal dispersed"—making them ripe targets for a defeat by a concentration of superior force. On Christmas night, 1776, Washington slashed across the Delaware in a driving snowstorm to capture three German regiments at Trenton. New Jersey and the rest of the almost stillborn nation became, in the words of one dismayed Briton, "liberty mad" again.

Ten days later, Washington took an even more nerve-racking gamble. He had returned to the New Jersey side of the Delaware to rally the state—and found himself confronting some 7,000 well-armed redcoats commanded by Charles, Lord Cornwallis. Wheeling around the enemy flank in a night march that was a neat riposte to Howe's maneuver on Long Island, Washington chewed up the British garrison at Princeton and retreated with booty and prisoners to high ground in Morristown. The befuddled British, fearful that he was planning to strike their main base at New Brunswick, relapsed to a timid defensive around that town, abandoning most of New Jersey to the rebels.

If Washington had hesitated to launch these two daring attacks with his ragged, barefoot army, or had failed in either attempt, the middle colonies—New York, New Jersey, Pennsylvania, Maryland, and Delaware—would have surrendered almost immediately. The South, or at least haughty Virginia, might have taken longer to subdue and the stubborn New Englanders even longer. But King George's men, skillfully appealing to moderates with the assurance that "British liberty" was a central part of the conciliation package, would have inevitably prevailed. Within a year or two at most, Americans would have been on their way to becoming replicas of the Canadians, tame, humble colonials in the triumphant British empire, without an iota of the independent spirit that has been the heart of the nation's identity.

What if General Benedict Arnold had not turned himself into Admiral Arnold on Lake Champlain?

A similar outcome could have resulted if things had gone differently in another part of the war in the fall of 1776. If Brigadier General Benedict Arnold had lacked the nautical know-how—and incredible nerve—to launch an American fleet on Lake Champlain in the late summer of 1776, the British would have wintered in Albany and been ready to launch a war of annihilation against New England in the spring of 1777.

Routed from Canada by massive British reinforcements, Arnold and the remnants of the so-called Northern Army had retreated to Fort Ticonderoga, at the foot of Lake Champlain. A more unpromising situation was hard to imagine. The British commander, Guy Carleton, was

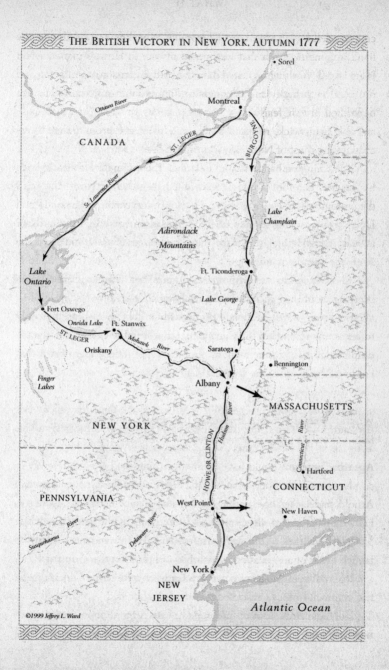

Sorel

Montreal

Ottawa River

CANADA

ST. LEGER

BURGOYNE

St. Lawrence River

Lake Champlain

Adirondack Mountains

Ft. Ticonderoga

Lake Ontario

Lake George

Fort Oswego

Oneida Lake   Ft. Stanwix

ST. LEGER

Oriskany

Mohawk River

Saratoga

Bennington

Finger Lakes

Albany

MASSACHUSETTS

NEW YORK

Hudson River

Connecticut River

Hartford

CONNECTICUT

HOWE OR CLINTON

PENNSYLVANIA

West Point

New Haven

Susquehanna River

Delaware River

New York

NEW JERSEY

Atlantic Ocean

©1999 Jeffrey L. Ward

planning to assault the so-called "Gibraltar of America" with perhaps 16,000 men and numerous Indians. To oppose him, the Americans had barely 3,500 broken, dispirited men, ravaged by smallpox and defeat.

Marching down Lake Champlain's forested 135-mile shore was out of the question. Carleton planned to come by water, backed by a fleet. Arnold decided to turn himself into an admiral and create a fleet of his own. He had made many voyages to the West Indies and Canada as a merchant and knew his way around a ship. Procuring carpenters virtually by legerdemain, he knocked together thirteen clumsy row galleys and gondolas made of green wood and crewed them with soldiers who had never been on a ship in their lives. With an insouciance that bordered on insanity, Arnold sailed this makeshift squadron up the lake and dared the British to come out and fight.

Almost too late, the impromptu admiral learned that Carleton was building a full-rigged 180-ton man-of-war, HMS *Inflexible*, which had enough firepower to annihilate his matchbox fleet all by herself. Arnold retreated down the lake to Valcour Island, where he took up a defensive position. In the British camp, numerous officers urged Carleton to advance without *Inflexible*. It was already September. In another month, snow might begin to fall. They had twenty-four gunboats, two well-armed schooners, and a huge artillery raft called the *Thunderer* afloat. But the cautious Carleton, impressed by Arnold's bravado, demurred and his army sat at the head of the lake for another four weeks while *Inflexible* was rigged and armed.

Not until October 11th, 1776, did Carleton's armada approach Arnold's fleet, anchored across the mouth of Valcour Bay. In a wild six-hour melee, the Americans took a terrific beating but held their battle line until nightfall. In the darkness, Arnold led a runaway retreat but the British caught up to him over the following three days and destroyed all but five of his ships. Ticonderoga was Carleton's for the taking. He had a five-to-one advantage in men and guns.

The American garrison pretended to be eager to fight, hurling cannon balls and curses at British scouting parties. Carleton, remembering

Bunker Hill, ruled out a frontal assault and decided it was too late in the year to begin a siege. As the British retreated to Canada for the winter, one of Carleton's officers groaned: "If we could have begun our expedition four weeks earlier." It had taken exactly four weeks for Carleton to launch *Inflexible*. Admiral Arnold and his green fleet had broken the momentum of the British counterattack from the North.

If Carleton had captured Ticonderoga in the fall of 1776 and routed or captured the Northern Army, there would have been nothing to prevent him from seizing Albany before the snow fell. In the ensuing spring he would have been able to smash into New England wherever he chose, much as Sherman ravaged the South from its exposed western flank in the Civil War. Even before he marched, Carleton would have converted Albany into a center of loyalist resistance to the Continental Congress. The Canadian commander was a far more astute conciliator than the Howes. He paroled all the prisoners he had captured in Canada and sent them home well fed and forgiven. Loyalism was strong in Northern New York, as the five-year-long bloody battles of the so-called "border warfare" would soon attest.

What if Benedict Arnold had obeyed orders at Saratoga?

A year later, it did not look as if General/Admiral Arnold's Valcour Bay heroics meant much. General John Burgoyne had replaced Carleton as the British northern commander and in early July he sailed unopposed down Lake Champlain and captured Ticonderoga with stunning ease. The disorganized Americans had largely wasted the precious months Arnold had bought them with his driving energy and combative spirit.

To oppose Burgoyne's 9,000-man army, Congress chose Major General Horatio Gates, a former British staff officer with no battle experience worth mentioning. To bolster him on the fighting side, Washington sent him Arnold, now a major general, and huge pugnacious Colonel Daniel Morgan of Virginia with his corps of riflemen. Constructing elaborate fortifications on Bemis Heights, some twenty-eight miles north of Albany, Gates hunkered down to await Burgoyne's attack. He seemed to think he could reenact Bunker Hill in the forest.

Burgoyne had no intention of cooperating with him. He had gone to immense trouble to drag some forty-two heavy guns through the woods from Ticonderoga. His plan of attack called for a flanking movement that would enable him to position these guns on high ground and hammer Gates's fortifications—and army—to pieces. Arnold saw the danger and after a ferocious argument convinced the timid Gates to let him fight the British in the woods. The result was a tremendous battle in and around cleared ground known as Freeman's Farm, in which Arnold and his men inflicted heavy casualties on the British and forced them to retreat.

Three weeks later, on October 7, Burgoyne attacked again. Now his motive was desperation. His men were on half rations; sickness and defeatism were multiplying. In a move that combined jealousy and stupidity, General Howe had abandoned him. Instead of fighting Washington in New Jersey, from which forced marches could have brought him to Burgoyne's aid, Howe had sailed south from New York to attack Philadelphia from the head of the Chesapeake. Capturing the American capital seemed to Howe a far better way to end the war than Burgoyne's plan to subdue New York and split the New England states from the rest of the American confederacy. As the British commander in chief, with an army three times the size of Burgoyne's, Howe also had no enthusiasm for letting Gentleman Johnny become the man who won the war. This otherwise incomprehensible decision is a good example of how often history turns on grudges and antagonisms between men in power.

On the American side, the sneaky Gates had infuriated Arnold by giving him no credit for his exploits in the first battle of Freeman's Farm. After an exchange of insults, Gates had relieved Arnold of command and confined him to his tent. But when the second battle began, Arnold disobeyed orders and rode to the sound of the guns. Once more his presence on the battlefield was electrifying. At the climax of the struggle, he led a frontal assault that captured a key British redoubt as a bullet shattered his leg. Gates finally emerged from his tent and ordered the redoubt held "at all hazards." Its cannon commanded the British camp.

The following night, the British tried to retreat. But swarming militia cut them off and Burgoyne surrendered his army to Gates on October 17, 1777, an event of earthshaking importance in both the military and diplomatic history of the Revolution. In France, Louis XVI's advisors decided the Americans could win the war and began backing them with desperately needed money and guns. England declared war on their ancient enemy and the conflict spread to the West Indies, Africa, and India.

If Arnold had gone along with Gates at the first battle of Saratoga, Burgoyne, a far more aggressive general than Carleton, would almost certainly have destroyed Gates's army and seized control of the Hudson River Valley. If Howe had stayed in New York and then advanced up the Hudson to meet Burgoyne, Gates's destruction would have been guaranteed with or without Arnold's heroics. A halfhearted last-minute attempt to rescue Burgoyne by a 4,000-man detachment from the New York garrison threw the Americans into near panic, even though it came to nothing.

Without Benedict Arnold at Valcour Bay and Saratoga, the war might well have ended in 1777. Without the feud between Burgoyne and Howe, it might have ended no later than 1778. By this time, the denouement would not have been so conciliatory. Many British and loyalists were calling 1777 "the year of the hangman." America's future as a dominion of England was veering from the benign fate of loyal Canada to the tragedy of rebellious Ireland. This trend would acquire ever-more vengeful momentum as the war dragged on.

What if Captain Ferguson had pulled the trigger?

Meanwhile, George Washington was fighting and losing the battles of Brandywine and Germantown in defense of the American capital, Philadelphia. As the first of these clashes developed there was a moment when the twitch of a finger on the trigger of a rifle might have changed American history forever. Washington was reconnoitering the countryside, trying to decide where to position his army to stop Howe's advance from the head of the Chesapeake. As he rode through a patch of woods near Brandywine Creek, he encountered Captain Patrick Ferguson of the British Army.

Ferguson was the inventor of the first breech-loading rifle, and he had one of those deadly weapons in his hands. It could spew out six bullets a minute and was far more accurate than the musket that was the standard gun in both armies. With no idea he had come face to face with Washington, Ferguson called on the horseman and his escort, a brightly uniformed hussar officer, to surrender. The officer shouted a warning and Washington wheeled his horse and galloped away. Ferguson took aim, then lowered his gun. He could not bring himself to shoot an unarmed enemy in the back. He was also more than a little impressed by the man's cool indifference to sudden death.

If Washington had been killed in the fall of 1777, the American war effort would have been more than a little demoralized. By now it was becoming apparent to many people that the tall Virginian was the linchpin of the struggle, the man who combined an ability to inspire loyalty in the Continental Army with a steadfast commitment to the ideals of the Revolution. On the eve of Trenton, Congress had given Washington dictatorial powers to deal with the situation—and he had humbly returned this Cromwellian authority to the politicians six months later. The probability of finding another Washington was more than remote—it was almost certainly impossible.

What if Gates had replaced Washington as commander in chief?

A few months after Washington's narrow escape from Captain Ferguson, the American commander confronted a conspiracy inside the army and Congress to depose him in favor of Major General Horatio Gates, the victor at Saratoga. If the plot had succeeded, the results would have been, if anything, more disastrous than an outcome wreaked by Ferguson's bullet.

Horatio Gates was a cunning egotist who allowed aides and friends to puff him into a competitor for the top command. After all, Washington had lost two crucial battles and the British had captured Philadelphia. The American army was now starving at Valley Forge. It was at least superficially plausible to call for new leadership.

One of the pointmen in the conspiracy was an Irish-born volunteer from the French Army, General Thomas Conway, whose name has become affixed to the plot. In fact, the "Conway Cabal" was a New England conspiracy, run from Congress by Sam Adams (once more demonstrating bad political judgment) with some background encouragement from Cousin John, who intensely resented Washington's soaring popularity. Conway was a loudmouth whom the real plotters manipulated. It soon became apparent that the cabal lacked a serious following in the army or in Congress. But for a few months, Washington's headquarters was in frequent turmoil, responding to it.

If the cabal had succeeded and Gates had become the American commander in chief, the Revolution would have almost certainly ended in a whimper. In no way could the short fussy Englishman, called "Granny" by his troops, have replaced Washington as an inspiring figure. Worse, in 1780, when Gates led an army into the South to repel a British invasion that had already captured Charlestown and most of South Carolina, he met a catastrophic defeat at Camden. On the fastest horse he could find, Horatio did not stop retreating until he was 160 miles from the battlefield.

A frantic Congress, its Continental dollars degenerating into wastepaper, the Southern states about to be overrun, might well have turned to a general with a reputation as a fighter: Benedict Arnold. By this time, however, the disgruntled hero of Saratoga was deep in correspondence with the British high command about how to best betray the American cause. Imagine his delight if he had been made commander in chief of the Continental Army! He would have been able to fulfill the ambition he hinted at when he signed some of his early letters to the British "General Monk." The pen name suggests Arnold saw himself as a reincarnation of General George Monk (or Monck), who switched sides in 1660 after the death of Oliver Cromwell and backed the restoration of the Stuart monarchy. No doubt Arnold was thinking of the wealth and titles that a grateful Charles II heaped on Monck.

Even without this gift from Congress, Arnold's plotting came close to unraveling the Revolution. His plan to surrender the key fortress of West Point to the British in the fall of 1780 went awry only because the chief of British intelligence, Major John André, was captured by some wandering American militiamen while returning to British-held New York with the plans for the fortress in his boot. A seizure of West Point would have given the British their long-sought control of the Hudson River, enabling them to isolate New England from the rest of the colonies. Such a blow, coming in a year when the American Army had been shaken by a serious mutiny in its winter quarters, the South was being overrun by British and loyalist armies, and the depreciation of the Continental dollar had reached the nadir of total collapse, could well have been the *coup de grace* that the British sensed was within reach.

What if the British had destroyed the French expeditionary force within days of its arrival?

Another moment when the war hung in the balance was rescued by George Washington's talent for espionage. With some help from a Long Island–born cavalryman, Major Benjamin Tallmadge, Washington was his own intelligence chief. He operated several networks inside New York. One of these, known as the Culper ring, smuggled him alarming news in July of 1780. The British were putting 6,000 men aboard ships for a preemptive strike at the French expeditionary force that had just landed at Newport, Rhode Island.

Nothing would have more certainly ended the war than the destruction of this 5,500-man army. Rampant inflation and war weariness were eroding the Continental Army's morale. Recruiting new men was becoming impossible because of the worthless currency. Thus far, the French alliance had been a series of bitter disappointments for the allies. A 1778 attempt to capture British-held Newport ended in a fiasco. A 1779 assault on Savannah was repulsed with severe losses. A devastating defeat such as the British hoped to inflict would have knocked a discouraged France out of the war.

Washington could not outmarch the British fleet in a race to Newport. He fell back on his spymaster's role. A double agent approached a British outpost with a packet of papers, which he claimed to have found on the road. It contained detailed plans for a massive American attack on New York. The British transports and their escorting men of war were already heading down Long Island Sound for the open sea. Signal fires were lit at strategic points on the shore (Long Island was in British hands) and the fleet hauled into Huntington Bay to receive the "captured" American war plans, rushed there by hard-riding horsemen. The dismayed British abandoned the descent on Newport and rushed back to New York, where they hunkered down in their numerous forts for an attack that never came. By the time the British realized Washington had gulled them, the French had fortified Newport, making a successful assault impossible.

The failure to knock the French out of the war forced the British to maintain a serious army in New York, complicating their new strategy, to conquer the South.

What if Daniel Morgan had lost at Cowpens?

While a stalemate prevailed in the North, the South continued to slide into British control. Georgia had returned to royal allegiance in 1779. The capitulation of Charleston in the spring of 1780, with its 5,000-man garrison, more than balanced Burgoyne's surrender at Saratoga. After the Camden rout, the Southern Continental Army dwindled to some 800 half-starved men. The new commander, Major General Nathanael

Greene, tried to persuade guerilla leaders such as Thomas Sumter to operate under his control, with no success.

Greene saw that the British would snuff out these pickup bands one by one. Under burly, aggressive Lieutenant Colonel Banastre Tarleton, the royal army had perfected a quick strike force, the British Legion, a mix of cavalry and infantry, that could travel as much as seventy miles a day, often catching the guerillas in their camps. The tough policy of requiring men to serve in the royal militia or have their crops and houses burned was also proving brutally effective. By the end of 1780, South Carolina's resistance was at the vanishing point. The British were discussing a quick conquest of North Carolina and an assault on Virginia.

In a gesture that was half strategic and half despairing, Greene ordered Daniel Morgan, now a brigadier general, to take 600 regulars and the remnants of the American cavalry, about 70 men under Lieutenant Colonel William Washington (George's second cousin) and march into western South Carolina in an attempt to rally the prostrate state. The British commander, Lord Cornwallis, dispatched Tarleton and his British Legion to finish off Morgan's feeble foray.

There seemed little doubt that the redheaded cavalryman would do the job. Scooping up reinforcements en route, Tarleton headed for Morgan at his usual pace, ignoring the cold December rain that turned the roads to gumbo. The Old Wagoner, as the muscular, six-foot-two Morgan was called, saw no alternative but headlong retreat. Barely 300 militia had responded to his pleas. As Morgan approached the Broad River, Tarleton's scouts were only about five miles behind him. The Broad was in flood and Morgan realized he might lose half his little army if he tried to cross it.

Nearby was a patch of rolling lightly wooded ground called The Cowpens, where local farmers used to winter cattle. Morgan decided to make a stand in this deserted pasture. A last desperate exhortation persuaded another 150 militia to join him. The big Virginian drew up a battle plan that made maximum use of these temporary soldiers, without

depending on them too much. He positioned the amateurs in two echelons well forward of his Continentals. They were told to give him "two
fires" and then they could run for their lives—which was what they
would do anyway.

About 150 yards behind the second line, Morgan took personal command of his Continentals on a low ridge. Behind them, sheltered by the
rise, he held William Washington and his cavalry in reserve. Morgan spent
the night going from campfire to campfire, explaining his battle plan to
every man—assuring them that if they did their jobs, the Old Wagoner
would crack his whip over "Benny" Tarleton in the morning.

Tarleton arrived on the battlefield at dawn on January 17, 1781, after an all-night march. Without giving his tired men a chance to pause
even for breakfast, he ordered them into line of battle and advanced.
That was his first blunder. His second was ignoring the way the militia
marksmen emptied the saddles of his flanking cavalry and cut down a ru-
inous number of his officers at the head of their companies.

The militia raced for the rear, giving Tarleton the impression the battle was as good as won. But he soon collided with the Continentals, who
poured volley after volley into his ranks. The British commander threw in
his reserve, the 71st Highlanders, to outflank them. To meet this threat,
the Americans ordered their flank companies to fall back and face the
Scots, a standard battlefield maneuver known as "refusing" one's flank. In
the confusion, the whole American line began to retreat and Tarleton,
thinking a rout was imminent, ordered a bayonet charge. Cheering fero-
ciously, the redcoated line surged forward.

But Morgan was still in command of the situation. He got a message
from William Washington, now out on the British right flank: "They are
coming on like a mob. Give them one fire and I'll charge them." Morgan
shouted the order to the Continentals, who turned, fired from the hip
and charged the onrushing British with the bayonet. Simultaneously, the
cavalry hit them in the rear, slashing men with their fearsome sabres.

The British, exhausted and with many companies leaderless, panicked. Some threw down their guns and surrendered; others ran. In five minutes the battle was over. Morgan had won a victory that destroyed Tarleton's army and dramatically reversed the tide of the war in the South. If Tarleton's frontal assault had succeeded, there is little doubt that North and South Carolina would have followed Georgia into royal government. Virginia, which was showing ominous signs of war weariness, was equally vulnerable, and Maryland, too, would have been sucked into this defeatist vortex. With the virtually bankrupt French government already sending out feelers for a peace conference, the British might have ended the war in possession of the entire South. In a few years they would have undoubtedly launched a renewed assault on the precariously independent Northern colonies from this base.

What if Washington had refused to march to Virginia to trap the British at Yorktown—or the British had escaped after the siege began?

After fighting a costly battle against a revived Continental Army at Guilford Court House in North Carolina, the British Southern commander, Charles, Lord Cornwallis, retreated to the coast and decided to discard the state-by-state strategy the Royal Army had been following. Only if wealthy, populous Virginia was reduced would the South surrender. Marching north and taking command of troops raiding the Virginia coast, the earl found no resistance worth mentioning from a tiny American army under Marquis de Lafayette.

But Cornwallis met a great deal more opposition from the British commander in chief, Sir Henry Clinton, who felt the earl had invaded his bailiwick and was in danger of losing the lower South to the resurgent Nathaniel Greene. An exchange of acrimonious letters let Cornwallis know who was running the war—and he glumly retreated to a small tobacco port, Yorktown, at the tip of the peninsula of the same name, with orders to fortify it and ship most of his army to Clinton in New York.

The earl nastily informed Clinton he would have to keep the entire army of 7,500 men to build the required fortifications. So the war spiraled to the late summer of 1781, still stalemated in the North and only slightly less deadlocked in the South. More and more, it was obvious that whoever struck the next blow—a victory on the level of Saratoga or Charleston—would win by a knockout.

Outside New York City, George Washington and the Comte de Rochambeau, the commander of the French expeditionary force, conferred about where to strike this blow. Washington wanted to attack New York. But his army, even with French reinforcements, was too weak. The French commander argued for a march south to try to trap Cornwallis at Yorktown. Washington dismissed it as a waste of time and energy as long as the British Navy controlled the American coast. They would rescue Cornwallis before the Allied army could force him to capitulate.

Rochambeau informed Washington that the French West Indies fleet had orders to sail north to escape the hurricane season. Why not tell them to head for the Chesapeake—while they did likewise with their soldiers? Washington reluctantly assented, although he still thought the British Navy would rout the French fleet, as they had so often in the past. He also worried that a substantial number of his unpaid war-weary soldiers would desert rather than make the march.

If Washington had refused to march to Yorktown, the French would probably have given up on him. The Revolution looked moribund. The Continental dollar was so worthless, it took, Washington gloomily noted, "a wagonload of money to buy a wagonload of hay." Recruiting officers reported zero interest in army service. The French were ready to withdraw their expeditionary force and throw in the diplomatic equivalent of the towel.

Instead, Washington marched south and a series of miracles occurred. Desertions were few, thanks to a hasty infusion of hard money from the French army's military chest, and the French fleet arrived just in time to trap Cornwallis at Yorktown. The British fleet sallied from New York to rescue the earl and his men. On September 5, in the little known

Battle of the Chesapeake Capes, the Royal Navy, commanded by a third-rate admiral named Thomas Graves, did everything wrong and the French did a few things right. The badly battered British limped back to New York and Cornwallis remained trapped on the tip of the Yorktown peninsula, a prime target for Allied siege guns.

If Graves had won the sea fight off the capes and rescued Cornwallis, American disillusion with the French would have been little short of overwhelming. The discouraged Continental Congress might have told their diplomats to get the best deal they could manage from the British in the looming peace negotiations. The Americans might have been forced to surrender large chunks of New York and most of the South. The British would also have probably claimed the trans-Appalachian west, where their Indian allies were waging a sanguinary war. The American alliance with France would have collapsed, exposing the infant republic to a world in which England remained the dominant power.

In New York, a frantic Sir Henry Clinton proposed to Admiral Graves a rescue plan that called for putting most of the army on navy ships and fighting their way into the Chesapeake to join Cornwallis. Together they would launch an all-out attack on Washington and Rochambeau that would decide the war. Alas for Sir Henry, Admiral Graves had no stomach for such a venture. He insisted he had to repair his damaged ships first. This led to a series of excuses and delays that dragged on for weeks.

On October 13, the fleet was supposed to sail—when a tremendous thunderstorm swept over New York harbor. Terrific gusts of wind snapped the anchor cable on one of the ships of the line, smashing her into another ship and damaging both of them. Once again Admiral Graves decided he could not leave until the damage was repaired. It was not the first nor would it be the last time that weather played a crucial role in the struggle for independence.

By October 15, French and American artillery had pounded Cornwallis's defenses to a shambles. Picked troops had captured two key redoubts, which enabled them to enfilade his lines. The moment approached when the Allies would launch a decisive frontal assault. A desperate Cornwallis decided on a daring getaway plan. Across the York River in Gloucester was a British outpost. Only about 750 French troops and some Virginia militia were stationed on its perimeter, largely to prevent foraging. Perhaps remembering Washington's escape from Brooklyn Heights, Cornwallis decided to ferry most of his army across the river on the night of October 16 and break out of the Gloucester lines at dawn. By forced marches, they would head north to the mouth of the Delaware, where they could easily contact British headquarters in New York.

As the Allied guns continued their relentless pounding, Cornwallis relieved the British light infantry in the front lines and marched them to the water's edge. There they boarded sixteen heavy flatboats manned by sailors of the Royal Navy. They were joined by the elite Foot Guards and the better part of the equally elite Royal Welch Fusiliers. It took at least two hours to make the trip back and forth across the broad river. Around midnight the boats returned and a second contingent embarked.

About ten minutes later a tremendous storm broke over the river. Within five minutes, there was a full gale blowing, as violent, from the descriptions in various diaries, as the storm that had damaged the British fleet in New York. Shivering in the bitter wind, soaked to the skin, the exhausted soldiers and sailors returned to the Yorktown shore. Not until two A.M. did the wind moderate. It was much too late to get the rest of the army across the river. Glumly, Cornwallis ordered the guards and the light infantry to return. About 7 A.M. on October 17, the earl, his second in command, Brigadier Charles O'Hara, and their staffs went to the forward trenches and morosely studied the sweep and scope of the allied bombardment. The commander of the artillery informed them that there were only 100 mortar shells left. The sick and wounded multiplied by the hour.

Cornwallis asked his officers what he should do. Fight to the last man? Every officer told him that he owed it to his men to surrender. They had done all that was expected of them, and more. Silently, Cornwallis nodded his assent. He turned to an aide and dictated a historic letter.

> Sir, I propose a cessation of hostilities for twenty-four hours, and that two officers may be appointed by each side . . . to settle terms for the surrender of the posts at York and Gloucester.

Not a few military authorities think Cornwallis's getaway might have succeeded, if it were not for that storm. Without the previous storm in New York harbor, Sir Henry Clinton might have embarrassed Admiral Graves into sailing on October 13. That would have gotten him to the Chesapeake before Cornwallis signed the articles of surrender on October 19. Either alternative would have created the possibility of a far different outcome. A Cornwallis getaway would have left the French and Americans frustrated and hopeless, facing a stalemated war they no longer had the money or the will to fight. American independence—or a large chunk of it—might have been traded away in the peace conference. A Clinton invasion of the Chesapeake would have triggered a stupendous naval and land battle that might well have ended in a British victory—enabling them to impose the harshest imaginable peace on the exhausted Americans and shattered French. Instead the Allies had landed the knockout blow.

What if George Washington had failed to stop the Newburgh Conspiracy?

As the war wound down to random clashes between small units in the South and West and along the northern border of New York, the American Revolution confronted one last crisis that might have made the long struggle all but meaningless. Once more the cause was rescued by that man for all seasons, George Washington.

As 1783 began, word arrived from Europe that Benjamin Franklin and the other American negotiators in Paris had signed a triumphant peace, recognizing the independence of the United States and extending American sovereignty to the east bank of the Mississippi. All that was needed now was a peace treaty between France and England. But this good news did not produce diapasons of joy inside the Continental Army.

On the contrary, this glimpse of peace just over the horizon aroused in the officer corps a surge of sullen fury. Congress had not paid them for years. In 1780, they had been promised half-pay for life. Now Congress no longer needed them and was reportedly going to welch on this agreement. Antagonism between the lawmakers and "the gentlemen of the blade," as some hostile New England congressmen called the officers, was not new. The officers decided to settle matters while they still had guns in their hands.

The officers dispatched a delegation to Congress led by Major General Alexander McDougall of New York. Choosing McDougall as a spokesman was a statement in itself. In the early 1770s, this abrasive demagogic New Yorker had been second only to Sam Adams as an agitator. The officers wanted an advance on their back pay, a solemn commitment to pay the balance eventually, and negotiation to settle the promise of half pay for life either by a lump sum payment or full pay for a number of years.

When McDougall met with James Madison, Alexander Hamilton, and other congressmen on January 13, 1783, Madison thought his language was "very high colored." Another member of the military delegation, Colonel John Brooks, warned that a disappointment would throw the army into "extremities." On February 13, Alexander Hamilton, who had retired from the army after Yorktown, wrote Washington an urgent letter, warning him that the situation was close to exploding.

Hamilton's letter arrived just in time. A dangerous conspiracy was simmering between officers at Newburgh and the army delegation in Philadelphia. Among the leaders was Major John Armstrong, aide to Washington's old enemy, Major General Horatio Gates. From Philadelphia, Armstrong wrote Gates that if the troops had someone like "Mad Anthony [Wayne] at their head," instead of Washington, "I know not where they would stop," especially if they "could be taught to think like politicians."

Soon Armstrong and another Gates man, Pennsylvanian Colonel Walter Stewart, began circulating anonymous "addresses" in the camp at Newburgh, calling on the army not to disband "until they had obtained justice." Next came another anonymous letter, urging the officers to meet and resolve to do something about a country that "tramples on your rights, disdains your cries, and insults your distresses."

Forewarned by Hamilton's letter, Washington's reaction to these Newburgh addresses was immediate and fierce. He condemned the unauthorized meeting and announced his determination to "arrest on the spot the foot that [is] wavering on a tremendous precipice." The dawn of peace had made him acutely aware that they were setting precedents for a new country. If the army got away with bullying Congress, it would cause America endless tragedies in the future.

On March 13, 1783, Washington convened a formal meeting with the officers in a large building in the Newburgh camp called The Temple. It was used as a church on Sundays and as a dance hall on other occasions. The commander in chief gave a passionate speech, pleading with the men, "as you value your own sacred honor," to ignore the anonymous letters calling for a march on Congress. He urged them to look with "utmost horror and detestation" on any man who "wishes, under any specious pretenses, to overturn the liberties of our country."

The men listened, but their faces remained hard. They were still angry. Washington closed with a plea that the officers conduct themselves so that their posterity would say, "Had this day been wanting, the world had never seen the last stage of perfection to which human nature is capable of attaining." Still, the resistance in the room remained almost palpable.

Washington drew from his pocket a letter from Congressman Joseph Jones of Virginia, assuring him that Congress was trying to respond to the army's complaints. After a moment's hesitation, he pulled out a pair of glasses. Only his aides had seen him wearing them for the previous several months. "Gentlemen," he said. "You will permit me to put on my spectacles, for I have not only grown gray but almost blind in your service."

A wave of emotion swept through the officers. More effectively than all Washington's exhortations, this simple statement of fact demolished almost every man in the hall. Many wept openly. Washington read the congressman's letter and departed, leaving the men to make their decision without him. They voted their thanks to the commander in chief, repudiated the anonymous letters, and expressed their confidence in Congress.

Washington's report on the Newburgh meeting reached Congress just in time to prevent the lawmakers from declaring war on the army. James Madison noted in his journal that the dispatch dispelled "the cloud which seemed to have been gathering." Congressman Eliphalet Dyer of Connecticut proposed that they offer the soldiers a deal—commutation in the form of five years pay in securities redeemable when the U.S. government achieved solvency. The officers accepted and the worst crisis yet in the brief history of American liberty was over.

Washington's use of the word "precipice" in describing the Newburgh confrontation was not an exaggeration. If he had failed to change the army's mind, the Revolution could have unravelled. The army might have marched on Congress to dictate terms at the point of a gun. The states, especially the large ones such as Virginia and Massachusetts, would almost certainly have refused to approve such a deal. If the army had attempted to force their compliance, civil war would have erupted. The shaky American confederation might have collapsed and the British, still with a fleet and army in New York, would have been irresistibly tempted to get back in the game. It is hard to imagine any of the states returning to the empire but some with strong loyalist minorities, such as New Jersey and New York, might have formed defensive alliances with the British to protect themselves against the rampaging Continentals. Such a foot in the door would have proved ultimately fatal to American independence.

＊ ＊ ＊

Many years later, George Washington reportedly corresponded with Charles Thomson, the secretary of the Continental Congress, about writing their memoirs. Thomson had been present at virtually every session of the Congress, from its inception in 1774 to its dissolution in 1788. Between them the two men probably knew more secrets than the entire Congress and the Continental Army combined. They decided that memoirs were a bad idea. It would be too disillusioning if the American people discovered how often the Glorious Cause came close to disaster. They jointly agreed that the real secret of America's final victory in the eight-year struggle could be summed up in two words: Divine Providence.

GEORGE WASHINGTON'S GAMBLE

By late December of 1776, the British had driven George Washington's dwindling and demoralized forces out of Manhattan and across New Jersey. The enlistments of all save 1,400 of Washington's men were due to expire by the end of the year. Nearly all were suffering from shortages of food, clothing, blankets, and tents while thousands of ordinary citizens in New Jersey were accepting British offers of pardon. The Continental Congress, anticipating the loss of Philadelphia, had withdrawn to Baltimore. It was, as Thomas Paine said, a time to "try men's souls."

If at that moment Washington's desperate attacks on the British outposts at Trenton and Princeton had failed, and if the British had destroyed his army, the rebellion might well have collapsed. Indeed, had Congress in those circumstances been tempted to seek a negotiated peace, they would have found the British offering surprisingly attractive terms (a proposal for replacing Parliamentary taxation with limited colonial contributions for imperial defense). Such terms in such circumstances might have appealed to many Americans.

But if stakes were high at Trenton and Princeton, it should still be asked whether Washington was in danger of losing his desperate gamble. Perhaps not at Trenton, where he had the advantages of surprise, superior numbers, and well-coordinated attacks, and where he gained a complete victory over a Hessian garrison besotted from celebrating Christmas. His successful attack on the British at Princeton little more than a week later—on a larger and better-prepared enemy—could much more easily have gone disastrously wrong. Had Washington been detected during his long night's march around Lord Cornwallis's flank, had the garrison at Princeton been united when the Americans arrived, or had that garrison been able to hold out longer, Cornwallis might have arrived to overwhelm Washington's exhausted men. And had those men been crushed at Princeton, Washington's reputation, the remainder of American forces, and the rebellion might have collapsed in all too rapid succession.

❖ *Ira D. Gruber is professor of history at Rice University.*

DAVID McCULLOUGH

WHAT THE FOG WROUGHT

The Revolution's Dunkirk, August 29, 1776

F or all that can be said for a deterministic view of history—for the inevitability of what T. S. Elliot called "vast impersonal forces"—chance and
luck (two related but altogether different phenomena) also play a part. How
else to explain the events of mid-August 1776, when, badly beaten at the Battle of
Long Island (Brooklyn, actually), George Washington and his small army faced what
seemed to be certain annihilation by a larger British army, one of the world's best. As
David McCullough points out, nothing less than the independence of the United
States was at stake. But the whims of weather were beyond prediction then, as they often still are. Perhaps in this case the most you can say about inevitability is that Washington almost always had the knack of seizing the right moment.

❖ David McCullough is one of the most deservedly popular historians of our time.
His TRUMAN won the National Book Award and Pulitzer for biography; THE PATH
BETWEEN THE SEAS, his account of the building of the Panama Canal, also won the
National Book Award for History. His other books include THE JOHNSTOWN FLOOD,

THE GREAT BRIDGE, and MORNINGS ON HORSEBACK. Millions know him as the host, and often the narrator, of television shows like THE AMERICAN EXPERIENCE. The past president of the Society of American Historians, McCullough has also won the Francis Parkman Prize and the Los Angeles Times Book Award. He is at present at work on a biography of John and Abigail Adams.

T he day of the trial, which will in some measure decide the fate of America, is near at hand," wrote General George Washington in mid-August 1776 from his headquarters in New York.

The Declaration of Independence had been signed in Philadelphia only days before, on August 8—not July 4, as commonly believed—and for six weeks an enormous British expeditionary force, the largest ever sent to dispense with a distant foe, had been arriving in lower New York Harbor.

The first British sails had been sighted at the end of June, a great fleet looking, as one man said, like "all London afloat." It was a spectacle such as had never been seen in American waters. And the ships had kept coming all summer. On August 13, Washington reported an "augmentation" of ninety-six ships on a single day. The day after, another twenty dropped anchor, making a total of more than 400, counting ten ships-of-the-time, twenty frigates, and several hundred transports. Fully thirty-two thousand well-equipped British and hired German troops, some of the best in the world, had landed without opposition on Staten Island—an enemy force, that is, greater than the whole population of Philadelphia, the largest city in the newly proclaimed United States of America.

The defense of New York was considered essential by Congress, largely for political reasons, but also by General Washington, who welcomed the chance for a climactic battle—a "day of trial," as he said. Yet he had scarcely 20,000 troops and no naval force, not one fighting ship or proper transport. His was an army of volunteers, raw recruits, poorly armed, poorly supplied. The men had no tents—to cite one glaring deficiency—and few were equipped with bayonets, the weapon employed by the British with such terrifying effectiveness. As a surgeon with Washington's army wrote, "In point of numbers, or discipline, experience in war . . . the enemy possessed the most decided advantage; beside the importance of assistance afforded by a powerful fleet."

Among the considerable number of the men who were too sick to fight was Washington's ablest field commander, Nathaniel Greene. Few American officers were experienced in large-scale warfare. Washington himself until now had never led an army in the field. The battle to come was to be his first as a commander.

With no way of knowing where the British might strike, Washington had chosen to split his troops, keeping half on the island of Manhattan, while the rest crossed the East River to Long Island, to dig in on the high bluffs on the river known as Brooklyn Heights—all this carried out in disregard of the old cardinal rule of never dividing an army in the face of a superior foe. When, on August 22, the British began ferrying troops across the Narrows to land further south on Long Island, about eight miles from the little village of Brooklyn, Washington responded by sending still more of his army across the East River, which, it should be noted, is not really a river at all, but a tidal strait, a mile-wide arm of the sea with especially strong currents.

"I have no doubt but a little time will produce some important events," Washington wrote in classic understatement to the president of Congress, John Hancock.

In fact, it was a situation made for an American catastrophe. With at most 12,000 troops on Long Island, Washington faced an army of perhaps 20,000. Should there be no stopping such a force, he and his amateur soldiers would have to retreat with the river to their backs. Which is just what happened.

The furious battle of Long Island was fought several miles inland from Brooklyn Heights on Tuesday, August 27, 1776. The British, under General William Howe, outflanked, out-fought, and routed the Americans in little time. The British officers under Howe included James Grant, Henry Clinton, Lords Cornwallis and Percy, and all performed expertly. As John Adams was to conclude succinctly, "In general, our generals were outgeneralled."

Astride a big gray horse, watching from a hillside, Washington is supposed to have said in anguish, "Good God! What brave fellows I must this day lose!" By later estimates, his losses were higher than he knew; more than 1,400 killed, wounded, or captured. Two of his generals had been taken captive. Many of his best officers were killed or missing. British use of the bayonet had been savage and on men who had surrendered as well, as one British officer proudly recorded, explaining, "You know all stratagems are lawful in war, especially against such vile enemies of the King and country." Washington and his exhausted men fell back to the fortifications on the Heights, waiting as night fell for a final British assault, the river to the rear.

And right there and then the American cause hung in the balance. The British, as Washington seems not to have realized—or allowed himself to think—had him in a perfect trap. They had only to move a few warships into the East River and all escape would be sealed. Indeed, but for the caprices of weather, the outcome would have been altogether different.

What actually happened was extraordinary. What so obviously could have happened, and with the most far-reaching consequences, is not hard to picture.

To be sure, the individual makeup of the two commanders played a part. On the day following the battle, influenced no doubt by his experience of the year before at Bunker Hill, General Howe chose not to follow up his victory by storming the American lines on Brooklyn Heights. He saw no reason to lose any more of his army than absolutely necessary, nor any cause to hurry. William Howe almost never saw cause for hurry, but in this case with reason—he had, after all, Washington right where he wanted him.

For his part, Washington appears to have given no thought to a withdrawal, the only sensible recourse. All his instincts were to fight. On

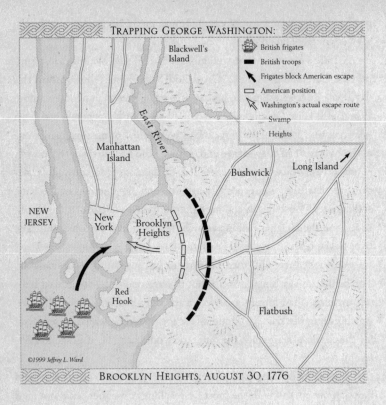

TRAPPING GEORGE WASHINGTON:

British frigates
British troops
Frigates block American escape
American position
Washington's actual escape route
Swamp
Heights

Blackwell's Island

East River

Manhattan Island

Bushwick

Long Island

NEW JERSEY

New York

Brooklyn Heights

Red Hook

Flatbush

©1999 Jeffrey L. Ward

BROOKLYN HEIGHTS, AUGUST 30, 1776

Wednesday, August 28, and again on Thursday, August 29, his food supplies nearly gone, his time clearly running out, he ordered that still more reinforcements be rowed over from New York, a decision that seems almost incomprehensible.

His men, for all their bravery and devotion to him, were worn out, hungry, and dispirited. And it had begun to rain. On August 29, the temperature dropped sharply and the rain came in torrents on the unsheltered army. During the afternoon, according to a diary kept by a local Brooklyn pastor, "Such heavy rain fell again as can hardly be remembered." Muskets and powder were soaked. In some places men stood in flooded trenches in water up to their waists. Expecting the enemy to attack at any moment, they had to keep a constant watch. Many had not slept for days. A New York man who saw them after it was all over said he never in his life saw such wretched, exhausted-looking human beings.

Washington's presence along the lines and his concern for the men were felt day and night. Seldom was he out of the saddle. On both August 28 and August 29, he appears to have had no rest at all.

But in their misery was their salvation. The driving rain and cold were part of a fitful, at times violent, nor'easter that had been blowing off and on for better than a week, and for all the punishment it inflicted, the wind had kept the British ships from coming upriver with the tide. For the new nation, it was an ill wind that blew great good, so long as it held.

Meantime, as the British historian Sir George Otto Trevelyan would write, "Nine thousand [or more] disheartened soldiers, the last hope of their country, were penned up, with the sea behind them and a triumphant enemy in front, shelterless and famished on a square mile of open ground swept by fierce and cold northeasterly gale . . ."

In a letter to John Hancock written at four o'clock in the morning, August 29, the crucial day, Washington reported only on the severity of the weather and the lack of tents that Congress had failed to supply, but said nothing of a retreat. He had seen five British ships attempt to come up the river and fail; and so he appears to have been banking on no change in the wind. Possibly he believed, too, that obstructions in the harbor—hulks sunk as hazards—had truly blocked the passage of all but small craft, a notion that was to prove quite wrong. In any event, having been outflanked on land, he stood perilously close to being outflanked by water.

The decision that so obviously had to be made came only later in the day, after it was learned that the British, under the cover of dark, were advancing by "regular approaches"—working through the night, throwing up entrenchments nearer and nearer the American lines—and after Washington at last accepted the likelihood of the British fleet at his back. Importantly, as he himself was to emphasize, the decision came on "the advice of my general officers."

According to one first-hand observer, it was General Thomas Mifflin, a self-assured thirty-two-year-old "fighting Quaker" from Philadelphia, who was the most emphatic. Mifflin, who had come over from New York with the last reinforcements only the day before, had been the one who, on his night rounds, discovered that the British were digging their way forward. Immediate retreat was imperative, the only remaining choice, he told Washington. Lest anyone question his character for making such a proposal, Mifflin asked that he be put in command of the rear guard, by far the most dangerous of assignments in a retreat.

With the rain still pounding down, Washington and his generals gathered for a council of war in the Brooklyn Heights summer home of Philip Livingston, a signer of the Declaration of Independence, who was in Philadelphia attending Congress. The time was early afternoon. The purpose of the meeting, as stated in the official minutes, was "whether under all circumstances it would not be eligible to leave Long Island." Two of the reasons given for an affirmative resolution were that the northeast wind might shift and that the consoling thought of obstructions in the harbor was now considered erroneous.

So it was decided. Preparations were set immediately in motion. An order from Washington went over to New York to collect every boat "from Hellgate on the [Long Island] Sound to Spuyten Duyvil Creek [on the Hudson] that could be kept afloat and that had either sails or oars, and have them all in the east harbor of the city by dark."

It was said the boats were needed to transport the sick and bring still greater reinforcements over to Brooklyn. Officers on the Heights, meanwhile, were to be ready to "parade their men with their arms, accoutrements and knapsacks at 7 o'clock at the head of their encampments and there wait for orders."

In all, it was a straightaway lie by Washington, intended to keep the truth from the men until the last moment—and thereby reduce the chance of panic—and hopefully to deceive the British—and the innumerable British spies in New York—once the roundup of boats was under way.

Most of the troops took the order to mean they were to go on the attack. A young captain of Pennsylvania volunteers, Alexander Graydon, would recall men taking time to write their wills. He, however, sensed something else was afoot. "It suddenly flashed upon my mind that a retreat was the object, and that the order . . . was but a cover to the real design." Yet who was to say? None of the other officers who listened to his theory dared believe it. Never in years to come could he recall the long wait without thinking of the chorus in Shakespeare's *Henry V*, describing the "weary and all-watched night" before Agincourt.

The first boats began crossing as soon as it turned dark. How it was all managed is almost beyond imagination. Every conceivable kind of small craft was employed, manned by Massachusetts men—soldiers from the ranks but sailors and fisherman by trade—from Marblehead and Salem, under the command of General John Glover and Colonel Israel Hutchinson. It can be said that the fate of the American army was in their hands. How readily the night could turn disastrous on the water, no less than on land, was more apparent to them than to anyone.

Everything was to be carried across—men, stores, horses, cannon. Every possible precaution had to be taken to keep silent—oars and wagon wheels were muffled with rags; orders were passed on in whispers. Every boat that pushed off, every crossing, was a race against time, and in black night and rain.

At one point, all seemed lost. Sometime near nine, the northeast wind picked up at ebb tide. The wind and current were more than sail could cope with, even in expert hands, and there were too few rowboats to carry everyone across before daylight. But in another hour or so, the wind mercifully fell off and shifted southwest, becoming the most favorable wind possible; and so the exodus resumed, all boats in service.

It went on hour after hour almost without a hitch. If ever fortune favored the brave, it was that night on the East River. Washington, who had proven considerably less than impressive in his first battle command, handled this, his first great retreat, with a steadiness and dispatch that were masterful. As untrained and inexperienced as his men may have been, however wet and miserable, they more than rose to the occasion. They stood for hours waiting their turns, then when told, moved off as silent ghosts, heading down the slopes to the river in pitch darkness, to the Brooklyn ferry landing, which was about where the Brooklyn Bridge now stands.

As the night progressed, and one regiment after another was withdrawn, the front lines grew perilously thin, to the point where there was almost no one left to stop an attack, should the enemy discover what was happening. It was the rear guard under Mifflin that had to stay to the last, keeping campfires burning and making sufficient noise to maintain the illusion of the full army in position.

The one hitch happened about two in the morning, when somehow Mifflin received orders to withdraw, only to learn on the way to the landing that it had been a dreadful mistake and that he and his men must return at once to their posts. "This was a trying business to young soldiers," one of them later wrote. "It was nevertheless complied with." They were back on the line before their absence was detected.

Another officer, Colonel Benjamin Tallmadge would recall, "As the dawn of the next day approached, those of us who remained in the trenches became very anxious for our own safety . . ."

Troops in substantial numbers had still to be evacuated and at the rate things were going, it appeared day would dawn before everyone was safely removed. But again "the elements" interceded, this time in the form of pea-soup fog.

It was called "a peculiar providential occurrence," "manifestly providential," "very favorable to the design," "an unusual fog," "a friendly fog," "an American fog." "So very dense was the atmosphere," remembered Benjamin Tallmadge, "that I could scarcely discern a man at six yards' distance." And as daylight came, the fog held, covering the entire operation no less than had the night.

Tallmadge would recall that when the rear guard at last received word to pull out, and "we very joyfully bid those trenches adieu," the fog was still "as dense as ever."

When we reached Brooklyn ferry, the boats had not returned from their last trip, but they very soon appeared and took the whole regiment over to New York; and I think saw General Washington on the ferry stairs when I stepped into one of the last boats . . .

When the fog lifted at about seven o'clock, the British saw to their astonishment that the Americans had vanished.

Amazingly, the entire force, at least 9,000 troops, possibly more, plus baggage, provisions, horses, field guns, everything but five heavy cannon that were too deep in the mud to budge, had been transported over the river in a single night with a makeshift emergency armada assembled in a matter of hours. Not a life was lost. It is not even known that anyone was injured. And as Tallmadge remembered, Washington, risking capture, had stayed until the last boat pushed off. As it was, the only Americans captured by the British were three who stayed behind to plunder.

The "day of trial" that Washington had foreseen deciding the fate of America had turned out to be a night of trial, and one that did truly decide the fate of America as much as any battle.

It was the Dunkirk of the American Revolution—by daring amphibious rescue a beleaguered army had been saved to fight another day—and tributes to Washington would come from all quarters, from those in the ranks, from officers, delegates in Congress, and from military observers and historians then and later. A British officer of the time called the retreat "particularly glorious." A latter-day scholar would write that, "A more skillful operation of this kind was never conducted."

But what a very close call it had been. How readily it could have all gone wrong—had there been no northeast wind to hold the British fleet in check through the day the Battle of Long Island was fought, not to say the days immediately afterward. Or had the wind not turned southwest the night of August 29. Or had there been no fortuitous fog as a final safeguard when day broke.

What the effect would have been had British naval forces come into play off Brooklyn Heights was to be vividly demonstrated just weeks later, when, with favorable wind and tide, five warships, including the *Renown* with fifty guns, sailed up the East River as far as Kips Bay and from 200 yards offshore, commenced a thunderous point-blank bombardment of American defenses on Manhattan. "So terrible and so incessant a roar of guns few even in the army and navy had ever heard before," wrote a British naval officer. Earthworks and entrenchments were destroyed in an instant, blasted to dust, while American troops fled in terror.

Had such overwhelming power been brought to bear at Brooklyn, the trap would have been closed tight. Washington and half the Continental Army would have been in the bag, captured, and the American Revolution all but finished. Without Washington there almost certainly would have been no revolution, as events were to show time and again. As the historian Trevelyan would write, "When once the wind changed and leading British frigates had . . . taken Brooklyn in the rear, the independence of the United States would have been indefinitely postponed."

Significantly, the same circumstances as at Brooklyn were to pertain again five years later, in 1783, except that the sides were switched, when American and French armies under Washington and Rochambeau had the British trapped at Yorktown, a French fleet at their back, sealing off any possible escape and leaving the British commander, Cornwallis, and more than 7,000 men no choice but to surrender.

"Oh God! It is all over!" Lord North, the British prime minister, is said to have exclaimed on hearing the news from Yorktown. It is what might well have been heard in the halls of Congress or any number of places the summer of 1776 had there been no fateful wind and fog at Brooklyn.

ALISTAIR HORNE

RULER OF THE WORLD

Napoleon's Missed Opportunities

Even if you have to admit that Napoleon was the dominant personality of the nineteenth century, there remains something more than faintly unappetizing about the man. He is the consummate come-lately, who did not hesitate to sacrifice a generation of Europeans in the pursuit of personal glory. The lives of overreachers are ready-made for counterfactual speculation, and Napoleon's more than most: We would not see his like again until Hitler. He was a man who did not know when to stop, and who can say what destination he might have taken if he had.

In this chapter, the British historian Alistair Horne examines some of the tantalizing might-have-beens of Napoleon's career. Could he have brought off an invasion of England in 1805? Was he right in selling the Louisiana Territory to the infant United States? In the campaign that led up to his most famous victory, Austerlitz, how close did the Great Gambler come to defeat in Central Europe? And what would have been the result? (Curiously, it might have forestalled a united Germany and a century of trouble.) What if Napoleon had decided not to invade Russia but had driven through Turkey and the Near East instead—*Alexander the Great's route of conquest*—to threaten British India? What if the Duke of Wellington had taken command of the British Army in North America that was offered him? He might have won the War of 1812 for England but he would have been absent from Waterloo: That may have made all the difference. Can we say what Europe—and, indeed, the world—would have been like if Napoleon had realized his "miracle" at Waterloo?

❖ *Alistair Horne is the author of two books about Napoleon—*NAPOLEON: MASTER OF EUROPE 1805–1807 *and* HOW FAR FROM AUSTERLITZ? *He has written such noteworthy studies as* THE FALL OF PARIS: THE SIEGE AND THE COMMUNE 1870–1871, THE PRICE OF GLORY: VERDUN 1916, TO LOSE A BATTLE: FRANCE 1940, *and* A SAVAGE WAR OF PEACE: ALGERIA 1954–1962. *He has been awarded both the British CBE and the French Legion d'Honneur for his historical works, and is Doctor of Literature at Cambridge University.*

Over Napoleon's extraordinary career, which lasted some twenty years, there were various times when history might have turned out differently: There were options that either he or his opponents could have taken up and moments when, had he made alternative choices, Napoleon might have remained on top to the end. What, for example, would have happened had he won at Waterloo? And what might the world have looked like today in the event of a definitive Napoleonic victory?

Napoleon was, as the historian George Rudé has written, "a man of action and rapid decision, yet a poet and dreamer of world conquest; a supreme political realist, yet a vulgar adventurer who gambled for high stakes." He had the good fortune to come on the scene in a period of revolutionary exhaustion, and it is hardly surprising that the dominant personality of his time would control the future of Europe—and the world—for so long.

The Directory, which succeeded Robespierre's Terror of 1792 to 1794, was a weak and divided government—perhaps a bit like Gorbachev and Yeltsin coming after the years of Stalinism—and 1799 could possibly have been a year of hope and reconciliation for the warring nations of Europe, at war since the Revolution had submerged France. But four years earlier, a twenty-six-year-old one-star general had made his name by the "Whiff of Grapeshot," which quelled the Paris mob. While still under thirty, Napoleon Bonaparte had won his first great military victories in Italy, between 1796 and 1797, and with the "Brumaire" coup on November 9, 1799, he found himself the de facto ruler of France; shortly afterward a national plebiscite confirmed his supremacy by making him consul for life. His rise to power in fact wrecked any prospect of an early settlement with England, especially after he persuaded the Directory to send him on his ill-fated expedition to Egypt. Up until 1803, the French perceived Napoleon as a peacemaker, but afterward saw him as a conqueror and the founder of a new empire. In the years until things visibly began to go wrong, they happily went along (indeed, much as the Germans had during the years of Hitler's easy conquests).

The brief Peace of Amiens (in the words of Winston Churchill, "the tourist season was short!") in 1801 offered statesmanship an early opportunity for a negotiated settlement. But neither Pitt's Britain, smarting from her reverses and determined not to lose Malta, nor Napoleon—proven supreme on land even though the Royal Navy had thwarted him everywhere at sea—were ready for it. No compromise peace was possible so long as an implacable Pitt faced a Napoleon unvanquished on land.

During the Peace, Napoleon busied himself internally with his first social and legislative reforms for France, but his thoughts were on further external conquests. Abroad, he pulled off the supreme coup of selling the Louisiana Territory to the young United States, thereby ensuring that she would at least remain benevolently neutral in the global conflict with England, if not an ally. Of course, here he could have clung on to these vast former territories of Imperial Spain; but this would almost certainly have brought him into conflict with the Americans—an enemy neither he nor Pitt wanted.

This fact of life had been proven over the course of the costly wrestling for the colonial islands of the Caribbean, stretching back into the *Ancien Régime*. (In the eighteenth century, it should be noted, these islands were considered to be by far the most valuable real estate in the New World.) Over the twenty-two years that the wars with France lasted, nearly half of Britain's total death toll had died in Pitt's campaigns in the West Indies, most of the casualties falling to the deadly yellow fever. In 1802 an expedition sent by Napoleon to reconquer the sugar-rich island of Santo Domingo (now Haiti) was decimated by the disease, with the commander, General Leclerc (the husband of Napoleon's sister Pauline), himself succumbing to it. Only three thousand of the original 34,000 sent there returned; nevertheless, Napoleon's restless eyes repeatedly turned to those lost jewels in the Caribbean. But, with the sale of the Louisiana Territory and the failure of the Santo Domingo operation, his options in the New World were effectively terminated—to the huge relief of Washington.

Equally, post-revolutionary France did not have the naval strength to maintain a presence in the New World. Such an endeavor would have made the Napoleonic navy a ready prey to the British. Thus this was never a viable option. Indeed, at almost every turn in Napoleon's career one sees possible options seriously conditioned by his naval inferiority vis-à-vis Britain. Wracked by mutinies, with most of its officers drawn from the purged upper classes, its ships decaying, the French Navy never recovered and was never to recover from the Revolution. In 1798, while Napoleon won on land in Egypt, offshore a young Nelson had annihilated his ships; three years later the lesson was repeated at Copenhagen. Despite this, in July 1803, Napoleon announced the creation of a "National Flotilla," with the express purpose of invading Britain. Historians continue to argue as to whether he ever really intended to; but the evidence seems to be that, like Hitler, he would have done it if he could.

Also as with Hitler, had he been able to land substantial forces, the defenders, with then vastly inferior numbers, would have been swamped. Already in 1797, an abortive attempt had been made to invade Ireland, but it was disrupted by storms. The following year, encouraged by France, Ireland exploded in a violent revolt. This was crushed, and so was a French landing two months later. Thus, as an option for Napoleon, attractive as it might seem on paper, Ireland proved no more than a blind cul-de-sac—at least so long as the Royal Navy commanded the sea approaches to England. Back in the reign of hated King John in the early thirteenth century, a French ruler invited by dissident barons had briefly held sway at Westminster; but the following year an upsurge of patriotism had led to the complete annihilation of the French fleet in the Battle of Calais. Without seeming to make too chauvinist a point, ever since then France—though often mighty on land—has seldom prospered at sea in conflict with Britain.

THE FLOATING SUMMIT, 1807

On a raft in the middle of the River Nieman in East Prussia, Napoleon (center right) meets with Tsar Alexander of Russia to divide Europe. Had his career of military conquest ended there, in June 1807, Napoleon might have established himself as the permanent master of the continent.

(Anne S. K. Brown Military Collection, Brown University Library)

Napoleon, nevertheless, set to building a vast fleet of over a thousand invasion barges. But, flat-bottomed and keelless, although ideal for landing on British beaches and estuaries, they swamped in anything but the lightest of seas, and the French suffered terrible loss of life in trial exercises. Britons took the threat seriously, but the then "Ruler of the Queen's Navee," Admiral "Jarvie" St. Vincent, was right when he declared: "I don't say the French can't come. I say they can't come by sea!" Napoleon had himself admitted after the Egyptian Campaign that, "If it had not been for the English I should have been emperor of the East, but wherever there is water to float a ship, we are sure to find [them] in our way." Although Pitt had no army worth the name at the time, it was British gold financing the continental foes of Napoleon and her fleet that repeatedly blocked Napoleon's ambitions.

By the reopening of hostilities in 1804, Nelson had fifty-five ships-of-the-line to France's forty-two, of which only thirteen were ready for active service. But, in the summer of 1805, Napoleon played his most daring card with the ruse of sending Admiral Villeneuve and his rickety fleet on a 14,000-mile voyage of deception to draw off Nelson to the West Indies—just long enough for the French Channel fleet to gain sufficient time for achieving local supremacy. With his habitual optimism, Napoleon reckoned that twenty-four hours would be enough. "We are ready and embarked," he told his admirals. Through the summer of 1805, Pitt's England, like Churchill's of the summer of 1940, waited with baited breath for the threatened invasion. On the cliffs of Boulogne, in August, Napoleon cursed the "foul wind," and his admirals. Both failed him. The right twenty-four hours never came. Once more, like Hitler, Napoleon cut his losses and marched eastward. By the end of August, a vast *Grande Armée* 200,000 strong was heading toward Austria, to meet a combined Austrian and Russian threat mustering there.

Britain was safe. But could "Invasion 1805" have worked? Was it ever a serious option? To Napoleon the arch-gambler, ever profligate with the lives of his troops, it may have seemed a risk worth taking. But at best, given the overall superiority of the Royal Navy in seamanship, ships, and commanders, it would have been a gamble with the dice heavily loaded against him—in an element that he and his marshals, so invincible on land, never understood, and would never understand. To quote the famous words of America's Admiral Mahan about Nelson's victory at Trafalgar two months later: "Those distant, storm-beaten ships, upon which the Grand Army never looked, stood between it and the dominion of the world."

The truth of that remark would pursue Napoleon all the way to St. Helena.

After some incredibly rapid marches and brilliant maneuvering across Europe, on December 2, 1805, Napoleon won his greatest victory of all at Austerlitz. Deep in the heart of Europe, in what is now the Czech Republic, with only 73,000 men and 139 guns, he pulverized the joint Austrian and Russian forces of 85,000 men and nearly twice the number of cannon. Napoleon planned superbly and knew exactly what he was doing, both at Austerlitz and earlier at Ulm. Yet, here too, in the middle of hostile territory, the risks were immense; the what ifs proliferate.

If the slow-moving Russian steamroller had reached Austria's General Mack before he was encircled at Ulm . . .

If the Prussians had entered the war in time to attack Napoleon's long-extended flanks . . .

If Russia's General Kutuzov had refused battle at Austerlitz (as he was to do with such success in Russia in 1812) . . .

Finally, if Napoleon had conducted at Austerlitz as untidy a battle as he was to fight against the much more outclassed Prussians at Jena the following year . . .

Here, particularly, in tactical terms, it seems to me that there was an option for history to have taken a different course, for events to have gone decisively against the gambler. At one moment in the Battle of Austerlitz the issue looked closely in the balance. All depended on the speed of Napoleon's top general, Davout, marching at all haste up from Vienna. But suppose, instead of Davout, the vain, incompetent, and slow-moving "Belle-Jambe" Bernadotte had been placed in that position? Bernadotte, whose deplorable conduct was to come so close to wrecking the victory at Jena in 1806, and whom Napoleon actually ordered off the field of Wagram in disgrace in 1809?

Defeated, his *Grande Armée* wiped out in the center of Europe a thousand kilometers from Paris, himself probably a captive, it is difficult to see how Napoleon could have survived failure at Austerlitz. Meanwhile, two months earlier, in October, Nelson had inflicted on him the decisive defeat of his career at the other end of Europe. From Trafalgar onward this failure to gain freedom of action on the high seas was to limit his every maneuver and option—a factor that it is impossible to overstate.

There is yet another what if option that would have followed from a French defeat at Austerlitz. The peace that was to come after Waterloo, and lasting a century, would not then have been a *Pax Britannica*. Won by feat of Russian and Austrian arms under Kutuzov, it would have been their peace, in fact Tsar Alexander's, to dictate. With such an outcome in 1805, the Habsburg Empire, ramshackle though it was, would have emerged strengthened; Russia, characteristically, would have retired behind her frontiers, possibly expanding southward at the expense of Ottoman Turkey. The big difference would have been in the development of Prussia. Not challenged by war, it would have found no motive for uniting the German states under its mantle and would have remained an insignificant entity, unlikely to threaten the peace of Europe in later generations. The European *status quo ante* of the eighteenth century would effectively have been restored.

As already mentioned, the Battle of Jena-Auerstädt (against the Prussians) the following year was a much less tidy affair; so too were the bloody battles—the last round against the Russians—of Eylau and Friedland. But by then the dice were heavily cast on Napoleon's side; success generates success, victory procreates victory. If anything, on the wider spectrum of history, Napoleon's triumphs of 1805 to 1807 were just too complete—the humiliation of his continental enemies—Austria, Russia, and Prussia—too great for them to lie down complacently without thoughts of revenge. If he had not won so resoundingly on Austerlitz's Pratzen Heights, might there have been no Waterloo ten years later? By 1807, Napoleon's best hopes for the future now lay, not on the battlefield, but in diplomacy—notably in the skilled hands of that Henry Kissinger of his times, Charles-Maurice de Talleyrand-Périgord, the self-defrocked former bishop, who was now his minister of foreign affairs.

Certainly it can be argued that, had Napoleon's head not become so swollen by such a run of apparently endless victories, Talleyrand might now have had an easier time. But, as Prussia's victory over France in 1871 was to prove, excessively successful generals do not make the best negotiators of peace. On June 19, 1807, Murat's cavalry reached the River Niemen, the Russian frontier over 1,000 miles from Paris. There the French were met by Tsar Alexander's envoys, sent to beg for an armistice.

The following week the two potentates met on board a raft hastily assembled in the middle of the river—to settle the future of the continent. As Napoleon stood on that raft, only thirty-seven, he was truly Master of Europe; but to his undoing, perhaps, he also saw himself, in the contemporary phrase of Tom Wolfe, "Master of the Universe." From Gibraltar to the Vistula and beyond, he now ruled either directly or through vassals who were his creations. "He dominated all Europe," wrote Winston Churchill:

> The Emperor of Austria was a cowed and obsequious satellite. The King of Prussia and his handsome queen were beggars, and almost captives in his train. Napoleon's brothers reigned as kings at The Hague, at Naples, and in Westphalia . . .

Before Austerlitz, Napoleon had been an object of fear; after Tilsit, he held Europe spellbound with terror. His conquests over the past ten years surely rivaled those of Alexander the Great; but where Alexander had simply marched across great spaces of defenseless Persia or India, massacring helpless populations who offered small challenge, Napoleon had marched a thousand miles across a hostile Europe, conquering great nations and powerful armies as he went. However, the parallel grows alarming: Alexander had aimed at nothing less than reaching the "End of the World." He was incapable of stopping. If only he had stopped at Persepolis. But India ruined him, the deserts of Persia killed him.

Could Napoleon now stop? Aboard the raft on the Niemen he had the option. It was his best chance to halt and consolidate his achievements. Perhaps he could have been satisfied merely with being king of Italy, uniting its disunited states; as a Corsican he was, after all, more akin to the Italians than the French, while Milan—with its statues and avenues named after Napoleon—still always strikes the visitor as being one of the few conquered cities where his name remains hallowed.

Or he could have devoted his vast energies entirely to the reconstruction of France, and the glorification of Paris: "If I were the master of France," he declared in 1798, "I would like to make Paris not only the most beautiful city in the world, the most beautiful that ever existed, but also the most beautiful that could ever exist."

And, later, regretfully: "I wanted Paris to become a city of two, three, or four million inhabitants, that is, something wonderful, powerful, and never experienced before our time . . . If the heavens had granted me another twenty years and some leisure, you would have looked in vain for the old Paris."

But few of his grandiose building projects were ever completed, and this dream of turning Paris into a gigantic monument to the fame and greatness of his rule was to be forever denied to him by military ambition.

Thus Tilsit turned out to be his last option before the tide turned irrevocably against him. The next time he ventured on to the River Niemen, just five years later, he would be on the road to his first great defeat, and the beginning of his eclipse.

The wily but astute Talleyrand comprehended the danger, saw the option now facing his chief. Talleyrand profoundly disapproved of the humiliating terms Napoleon had insisted on exacting on his defeated opponents. The terms imposed on the proud Prussians—heavy reparations and dismemberment of all their territories west of the Elbe—were particularly draconian. They would prove unacceptable and the stimulus for the national regeneration that would help defeat France from 1813 onward. Far more lethal, the all-powerful Prussia emerging from the German unification in the teeth of Napoleon's onslaught would lay the foundations for the catastrophes to overtake France at the hands of heirs of the unforgiving Prussians—in 1870, 1914, and 1940.

As far as Austria was concerned, Talleyrand had hoped that generous terms after Austerlitz would have made Austria a bulwark against Russia and ensured a balance of power in Eastern Europe. (The unfortunate Russo-Austrian alliance of 1805 had been, after all, both unnatural and unhistoric.) But she, too, was left, like Prussia, prostrate and dreaming of revenge.

At Tilsit, Russia became, nominally, Napoleon's ally. But she, too, had been humiliated, and she chafed at the creation of a Polish state, the Grand Duchy of Warsaw, set up by Napoleon on what Russia historically considered to be a Russian satellite, and on her very borders—reacting to it much as Yeltsin would greet the move eastward of NATO in the 1990s. It was therefore a thoroughly artificial new friendship, based on ephemeral self-interest and continuing hostility to Britain. To this end, Napoleon pushed a reluctant tsar into his "Continental System," the counterblockade that was aimed at strangling Britain.

None of this was what Talleyrand had striven for: Above all he wanted an end to the fifteen years of war that had been impoverishing France since the Revolution. He saw Tilsit, which left France no real friends in Europe, as perpetuating that war. He was right. In frustration and disgust, Talleyrand now defected, in effect offering his services to the tsar. It was an act of questionable treachery—which Talleyrand himself dismissed as "a matter of dates"—in an endeavor to bring down his master before he brought down France. Meanwhile, in Paris, news of Tilsit was welcomed with rather more pageantry and festivity than reality.

What could Napoleon, in fact, have achieved at Tilsit, had he followed the advice of Talleyrand? Through persuasion and diplomacy rather than military coercion, he could have imposed the uniformity of the admirable administrative aspects of the Napoleonic system across Europe. Such uniformity would, in the course of time, have probably effected a stranglehold on markets essential to British prosperity more effectively than the universally unpopular rigidity of his "Continental System"—which was to hurt his continental partners more than Britain.

In strategic terms, he might well have wooed the tsar to support him in a drive through Turkey and the Near East, to threaten the very roots of British power in India. It was, after all, not many years since France had been a power on the subcontinent. This was a dream often in the back of Napoleon's mind, ever since the abortive Egyptian Campaign of 1798, and here he would almost certainly have found sympathy in Russia, her ambitions in Central Asia being constantly at odds with Britain's. By moving chiefly overland he would have neutralized the ubiquitous menace of the Royal Navy. In the Near East he would have encountered no serious opposition; quite possibly, he would have found a role for Islam to play within the empire—provided it toed the line, politically, like other religions.

Yet one needs recall the fate of the legions of Alexander the Great. The terrible deserts of Persia and Baluchistan destroyed them, and distance coupled with disease might have done the same for Napoleon—as indeed the wastes of Russia did. Flying in the face of British seapower, his dangerously extended lines of communication were bound to be vulnerable at one point or another—perhaps at the Bosphorus, or to an expeditionary force judiciously landed in the Levant. Then, too, for how long would the Turkish warriors of the Ottoman Empire prove malleable allies, or vanquishable foes?

What this all might have meant for the Jews of Palestine invites speculation. In France, Napoleon had expressed serious (and, by the standards of the day, advanced) desires for a liberal-minded emancipation of French Jewry. At the bitter Siege of Acre in 1797 (where he had been partly frustrated by the Royal Navy), he had issued a proclamation declaring solemnly that Jewry had "the right to a political existence as much as any other nation," which was never to be forgotten. If Napoleon had had his way in the Middle East, might it have led to the realization of Jewish aspirations in Palestine over a century before the creation of the state of Israel? On the other hand, one has to recall what a gulf there was to lie between Napoleon's promises to the Poles and their fulfillment. Napoleon was impatient at having to honor undertakings once their geopolitical value had passed.

At Tilsit, however, Napoleon exchewed all these options—and the defection of Talleyrand marked a major turning point in his fortunes. As he was himself to confess in exile on St. Helena, Tilsit was perhaps his finest hour.

Attempts to seal up holes in his "Continental System" led Napoleon, within months of Tilsit, to commit his greatest strategic error to date. Portugal, Britain's oldest ally, remained her last foothold on the continent. Napoleon determined to expunge it; but in marching through Spain he created a problem for himself that was both intolerable and insoluble. This took the form of a guerrilla war that was almost impossible to win. The intractable Spanish irregulars were backed by an originally small expeditionary force of 9,000 men commanded by Sir Arthur Wellesley (later to become the Duke of Wellington). In Napoleon's self-inflicted wound that came to be known as the "Spanish Ulcer," Britain now had her "Second Front." By the end of 1809, no less than 270,000 of Napoleon's best troops were committed to the Peninsular War—or three-fifths of his total forces. This automatically, and fundamentally, altered his relations with Russia. From Tsar Alexander having been the defeated client at Tilsit, within a year it was Napoleon who was now asking for favors—notably that Russia keep Austria on a leash.

Meanwhile, Austria was energetically rearming to avenge Austerlitz.

Could Napoleon have played it differently in the Iberian Peninsula? Of course. He could simply have kept out of Spain, sealing her borders at the Pyrenees and leaving the proud and nationalist Spaniards to deal with any British adventure there. (They were, after all, still resentful of Nelson's destruction of their fleet, too, at Trafalgar. They were as likely to turn on a British invader interrupting their Iberian slumbers as they did on the French.) The trouble was that Napoleon never knew when to stop. Meanwhile, at home increasing hardship, discontent, and sinking morale meant that, in the time-honored manner of dictators, he felt he had to distract the populace by seeking ever-fresh draughts of *la Gloire*.

In the summer of 1809, Napoleon found himself at war with a resuscitated Austria. At Wagram, on the outskirts of Vienna and not far from Austerlitz, he won his last victory—though largely through dependency on foreign levies from the Saxons and Italians, hardly reliable in adversity. Unlike Austerlitz, Wagram could neither be termed a decisive or definitive victory. Austria would soon be rearming once more. The shadows were drawing in, the opposing generals were learning.

With each succeeding year, the Royal Navy's blockade of European ports extended and perfected itself, tightening the grip. There were repeated domestic economic crises in France in 1806, 1810, and 1811: Napoleon should have read the warnings. In 1810 over 80 percent of British wheat imports had slipped through Napoleon's fingers, some even coming from France herself; while, to keep the *Grand Armée* supplied with greatcoats and boots, his own quartermasters had to covertly run the British blockade. By that same year, only 3 out of 400 of Hamburg's sugar factories remained in business. But it was Russia that was most hurt and angered by the blockade; by the summer of 1811, ships in Russian ports included 150 British vessels flying the American flag. Such defiance of his System was intolerable to Napoleon, and the war clouds gathered—with a bread crisis in January 1812 providing him with an extra motivation for marching East.

The year 1811, however, was also one of the most dangerous for Britain, when a bad harvest coincided with economic crisis. Then, in 1812, a heaven-sent opportunity seemed to fall into Napoleon's lap. In June, the U.S. Congress declared war on Britain. What was to be one of the silliest (and, from the British point of view at least), most unwanted conflicts history has to offer was a direct consequence of British arbitrary measures stemming from the blockade of Napoleon's Europe. Here was an opening for Napoleon of a different order; but by the time he might have taken advantage of it, he was embroiled in Russia, defeated, and reeling back on France.

What if Napoleon had had his eyes focused on the West in 1812, instead of the East; What if he could have thought in diplomatic instead of purely military terms; What if he had still had Talleyrand at his side. Talleyrand had actually lived in the U.S. for two years—in Philadelphia, during the French Revolution—and therefore knew a little about American motivations? Because of his failure to command the seas, once again, there was little Napoleon could have done militarily to lend support to the Americans. But a Talleyrand would have lent diplomatic and moral support to fan the very real resentment against the arrogance on the high seas of the former colonial power, Britain. The game was certainly worthwhile. Let us consider one possible result. In November 1814, the Duke of Wellington was invited to take over Britain's armies in North America. Disapproving strongly of the war, he refused—as he might not have done if Napoleon had been meddling on the American side. His decision was fortunate for Britain. The fighting against those former colonies ended in a draw a few weeks later. But: if Wellington had taken a different view, or if the American war effort had been more wholehearted, sufficing seriously to threaten Canada, and Quebec especially, then Wellington could well have been three thousand miles away when Napoleon launched his supreme bid against the Allies in June 1815.

Of course, there is a possibility that Wellington might have inflicted a decisive defeat on the Americans. Would the British then have been tempted to retake substantial parts of their former colonies, as reparations? To reverse 1775? The hypothesis is hardly likely: With no desire to become re-embroiled in the New World, Britain was lukewarm in prosecution of the War of 1812. Her main priority was Napoleon.

As it was, some of Wellington's badly needed regiments at Waterloo were only just reaching Belgium from across the Atlantic on the very eve of that battle. The consequences of Wellington's own absence would have been readily calculable—and what a sublime opportunity for Napoleon!

But by November 1814, the sand had all but run out for him. Failing to do the one thing that might have turned the scales against the tsar, liberating the Russian peasants from serfdom, Napoleon had marched to destruction to Moscow and back. Out of 600,000 troops that crossed the Niemen in June of 1812, only a broken 93,000 straggled home. The limits of his empire returned to what it had had been before Tilsit. Meanwhile, at his rear Wellington was grinding relentlessly through Spain toward the frontiers of France itself.

Option: Napoleon should never have left the war in Spain at his rear—just as Hitler in 1941 foolishly attacked Stalin leaving Britain still undefeated. Better still he should not have been in Spain at all; secondly, he should never have moved into Russia. The following year, 1813, came the Battle of the Nations, with a resurrected Prussia, Austria, and Russia coalescing in the greatest concentration of force seen in the whole of the Napoleonic Wars to corner and defeat the *Grand Armée* decisively at Leipzig.

The crushing defeats of 1814, on France's own soil, followed. Yet even then it was not too late for Napoleon to have stopped: The Allied terms on offer, generous by the standards of the day, would at least have preserved the historic and geographical integrity of France. But Napoleon chose to fight on, brilliantly, vainly awaiting his "Star" to produce a miracle. But no miracle came and he abdicated in April 1814. He went into his first imposed exile on Elba, an island near Corsica. Then, after ten months he slipped away, landed in the south of France, and marched north to Paris in the resurgence of the "Hundred Days." He seemed to have his miracle at last.

We arrive on the field of Waterloo, June 1815. In the oft-quoted words of the Iron Duke, it was indeed "the nearest-run thing you ever saw"—even with Wellington there. But without him at the helm—away in Canada, as might have been possible—Blücher, his stalwart Prussian ally, would almost certainly not have made his famous eccentric move to support his allies and—with equal certainty, Waterloo would have been lost.

On the other hand, such a victory would not have ensured Napoleon's ultimate triumph. There were vast fresh forces of Russians, Austrians, and Germans already moving toward France. A second battle, or perhaps several battles, would probably have followed Waterloo. But even if the ultimate engagement had ended in the likely defeat of Napoleon, with Britain out of the war, it would have been a *continental* and not a *British* victory. What followed would have, therefore, been a peace dominated by Metternich's Central European powers—by Russia,

Austria, and Prussia instead of Great Britain. The century ahead, would, inevitably have been a very different one. Would the victors, on past form, have fallen out, creating a period of uncertainty instead of the century of stability that Waterloo bequeathed the world? Or could they between them have cemented a different kind of "Concert of Europe"?

What about America in all this equation? Might such an alternative option have imposed on the youthful colonies an accelerated pubescence in world affairs? Suppose England had been decisively defeated in June 1815, or in the Middle East and India, or excluded successfully from Napoleon's "Continental System" at any time after Tilsit, what might this have meant for the young United States? One can predict, with some assurance, that necessity, adversity, and common interest would have brought the former colonies and a Britain shorn of her world power increasingly closer together—as was to happen in 1940.

The trouble with all these various options, these hypotheses, these what ifs, is that all hang subject to Napoleon's character. A greater and better man might have admitted, as Cassius said about Caesar in Shakespeare's *Julius Caesar,* "The fault, dear Brutus, is not in our stars, but in ourselves . . ."

Napoleon, however, could never bring himself to admit that any of his reverses were his own fault. Someone else was always to blame. Or, to quote Shakespeare again, like Hamlet he could count himself ". . . a king of infinite space, were it not that I have bad dreams."

The "bad dreams" that plagued Napoleon were the fantasies of endless military conquest. Like most conquerors before and after him he never knew when—or how—to stop. Wellington understood only too well: A conqueror was like a cannonball, he once observed; it must go on. This was what caused Talleyrand to despair and defect to the tsar. As I have suggested, Tilsit was the last best hope Napoleon had of attaching his name to an enduring peace; but it was his character that prevented him from reaching up and grabbing the opportunity. And, even so, how long would the defeated and humiliated nations of Eastern Europe—

Prussia, Austria, and Russia—have allowed him to enjoy it unchallenged? It is a question that cannot be answered.

Ninety years ago, a budding young British historian (later to become one of the most famous of his generation), named George Trevelyan, won the prize for a competition in London's *Westminster Gazette* with an essay entitled "If Napoleon had won the Battle of Waterloo." As Trevelyan saw it, the instinct of an emperor, victorious at Waterloo but exhausted by endless war and overwhelmed by the cries for peace that ran down the ranks of his army, would have been to propose a pact of "unexpected clemency" to his archenemy England. The results would be: Russia out of Europe, France dominant, the Germans remaining "the quietest and most loyal of all Napoleon's subjects" (this was written seven years before 1914), and Britain isolated.

Here were overtones of a Europe perhaps not entirely remote from the dreams of a Charles de Gaulle or a modern-day Brussels technocrat.

NAPOLEON WINS AT WATERLOO

Suppose that the unfortunate Marquis de Grouchy had been able to complete the arguably unrealistic task that Napoleon assigned him on June 17, 1815, and had kept Prussia's Marshal Blücher from combining forces with England's Duke of Wellington the next day at Waterloo. In the best-case scenario for the French, Napoleon would have won that battle, and the allies would have been forced to make peace with the restored Bonapartist regime. What would that have implied for Europe and the world?

If we further imagine that Napoleon could have ceased behaving like a power-mad megalomaniac, we can entertain the thought that he would have become a reasonable player in the new congress system of diplomacy being devised by England's Viscount Castlereagh and Austria's Prince Metternich. This possibility had and has understandable attractions: If Bonaparte had been willing to become one among many players in the nineteenth-century balance of European power (which brought about the longest period of relative peace in that continent's modern history—a full hundred years) then the rise of the German empire—the event that eventually caused the destruction of the balance—would certainly have been prevented. General peace could, in such a scenario, have lasted well beyond 1914.

Unfortunately, to suppose such a result is to ignore the salient psychological compulsions that always drove the French emperor. The idea that Napoleon—an imperialist, but nonetheless a child of the French Revolution—would have been content to sit at a conference table with his former (and primarily reactionary) enemies and treat them as equals is improbable if not ludicrous. In all likelihood, he would instead have bided his time, built up his armies, and sooner or later made another play for continental domination. There is little if any evidence to suggest that Napoleon was alive to the suffering he personally brought on Europe for so many years or that he felt any responsibility for it; and so instead of delaying the calamities of 1914, Napoleon's victory at Waterloo would probably have advanced them some ninety or so years, and turned the nineteenth into just another century during which Europeans spent the better part of their time slaughtering each other at the behest of callous princes.

❖ *Caleb Carr's latest books are* THE ALIENIST *and* THE ANGEL OF DARKNESS.

JAMES M. McPHERSON

IF THE LOST ORDER HADN'T BEEN LOST

Robert E. Lee Humbles
the Union, 1862

One of the focal moments of the American Civil War, as well as a deserved staple of counterfactual history, is the finding of Robert E. Lee's Special Orders No. 191—the legendary "Lost Order." In September 1862, Lee's Confederate Army of Northern Virginia was in the process of crossing into Maryland, on his way to Pennsylvania. He had just battered Union forces at the Second Manassas; one more big victory might bring the Confederacy official British and French recognition. The Special Order, which he dispatched to his various commanders, was his strategic plan for the fall campaign. On the morning of September 13, an Indiana corporal named Barton W. Mitchell discovered in a cloverfield a bulky envelope containing three cigars and a copy of Lee's orders. The "Lost Order" was bucked up to Lee's Union opposite, General George B. McClellan. (Somewhere along the way, the cigars disappeared.) McClellan was offered a golden opportunity to divide and conquer the widely spread Confederate forces. But he frittered it away. The result was the bloodiest day of the Civil War, the Battle of Antietam—a narrow win on points for the Union but not the war-ending victory it might have been.

So much for the facts. Now for the speculation. Let us assume, as James M. McPherson does here, that the Lost Order was not lost. Lee very likely would have continued north, all but unchallenged, and military logic tells us that in the Cumberland Valley of Pennsylvania a vast battle would have taken place. Where would it have been fought? McPherson has an answer equally logical—but hardly promising for the continued existence of the United States as one nation.

❖ *McPherson is not just an expert on the Civil War but one of the finest historians writing today. He is professor of American history at Princeton University and the author of ten books, including* BATTLE CRY OF FREEDOM, *which won the Pulitzer Prize in History.*

G reat possibilities rode with the Army of Northern Virginia as it began to cross the Potomac at a ford thirty-five miles up-river from Washington on September 4, 1862. Since taking command of this army three months earlier, General Robert E. Lee had halted the momentum of Union victory that had seemed imminent in May. At that time, the Army of the Potomac had stood only five miles from Richmond, poised to capture the Confederate capital. Coming on top of a series of Northern military successes during the previous four months, which had gained control of 100,000 square miles of Confederate territory in western Virginia, Tennessee, the Mississippi Valley, and elsewhere, the fall of Richmond might well have toppled the Confederacy. But Lee launched a series of counteroffensives that turned the war around. His troops drove Union forces back from Richmond in the Seven Days' Battles (June 25–July 1) and then shifted the action to northern Virginia, where they won the battles of Cedar Mountain (August 9), Second Manassas (August 29–30), and Chantilly (September 1). Dispirited Union troops retreated to the defenses of Washington to lick their wounds.

This startling reversal caused Northern morale to plummet. "The feeling of despondency is very great," wrote a prominent New York Democrat after the Seven Days' Battles. His words were echoed by a New York Republican, who recorded in his diary "the darkest day we have seen since [First] Bull Run . . . Things look disastrous . . . I find it hard to maintain my lively faith in the triumph of the nation and the law." Reacting to this decline in Northern spirits, President Abraham Lincoln lamented privately: "It seems unreasonable that a series of successes, extending through half a year, and clearing more than a hundred thousand square miles of country, should help us so little, while a single half-defeat [the Seven Days' Battles] should hurt us so much."

225

Unreasonable or not, it was a fact. The peace wing of the Democratic Party stepped up its attacks on Lincoln's policy of trying to restore the Union by war. Branded by Republicans as disloyal "Copperheads," the Peace Democrats insisted that Northern armies could never conquer the South and that the government should seek an armistice and peace negotiations. Confederate military success in the summer of 1862 boosted the credibility of such arguments. And worse was yet to come for the Lincoln administration. Western Confederate armies, which had been defeated in every campaign and battle from January to June 1862, regrouped during July and carried out a series of cavalry raids and infantry offensives in August and September that produced a stunning reversal of momentum in that theater as well. As the Army of Northern Virginia splashed across the Potomac into Maryland, Confederate armies in Tennessee launched a two-pronged counteroffensive that not only reconquered the eastern half of that state but also moved into Kentucky, captured the capital at Frankfort, and prepared to inaugurate a Confederate governor there.

Rather than give up and negotiate a peace, however, Lincoln and the Republican Congress acted dramatically to intensify the war. Lincoln called for 300,000 more three-year volunteers. Congress passed a militia act that required the states to produce a specified number of nine-month militia and impose a draft to make up any deficiency in a state's quota. The same day (July 17), Lincoln signed a confiscation act that provided for the freeing of slaves owned by disloyal (i.e., Confederate) masters.

Southern states had seceded and gone to war to defend slavery. Slaves constituted the principal labor force in the Southern economy. Thousands of slaves built fortifications, hauled supplies, and performed fatigue labor for Confederate armies. From the outset, radical Republicans had urged a policy of emancipation to strike a blow at the heart of the rebellion and to convert the slaves' labor power and military manpower from a Confederate to a Union asset.

By the summer of 1862, Lincoln had come to agree with this position. But so far as possible, the president wanted to keep the emancipation issue under his own control. On July 22, he informed the Cabinet that he had decided to use his war powers as commander in chief to seize enemy property to issue an emancipation proclamation. Emancipation, said Lincoln, had become "a military necessity, absolutely essential to the preservation of the Union. We must free the slaves or be ourselves subdued. . . . Decisive and extensive measures must be adopted. . . . The slaves [are] undoubtedly an element of strength to those who [have] their service, and we must decide whether that element should be with us or against us." Most of the Cabinet agreed, but Secretary of State William H. Seward advised postponement of the proclamation "until you can give it to the country supported by military success." Otherwise the world might view it "as the last measure of an exhausted government, a cry for help . . . our last *shriek*, on the retreat."

This advice persuaded Lincoln to put the proclamation in a drawer to await a more favorable military situation. Unfortunately, it deteriorated further as enemy armies began their invasions of Maryland and Kentucky, two border states that seemed ripe for Confederate plucking. Northern morale continued to fall. "The nation is rapidly sinking just now," wrote a New York diarist. "Stonewall Jackson (our national bugaboo) about to invade Maryland, 40,000 strong. General advance of the rebel line threatening our hold on Missouri and Kentucky. . . . Disgust with our present government is certainly universal."

Democrats hoped to capitalize on this disgust in the upcoming congressional elections. Republicans feared the prospect. "After a year and a half of trial," wrote one, "and a pouring out of blood and treasure, and the maiming and death of thousands, we have made no sensible progress in putting down the rebellion . . . and the people are desirous of some change." The Republican majority in the House was vulnerable. Even the normal loss of seats in off-year elections might eliminate this majority. And 1862 was scarcely a normal year. With Confederate invaders in the border states, the Democrats seemed sure of gaining control of the House on their platform of an armistice and peace negotiations.

Robert E. Lee was well aware of this possibility. It was one of the factors that prompted his decision to invade Maryland despite the poor physical and logistical condition of his army after ten weeks of constant marching and fighting that had produced 35,000 Confederate casualties and thousands of stragglers. "The present posture of affairs," Lee wrote to Jefferson Davis on September 8 from his headquarters near Frederick, Maryland, "places it in [our] power . . . to propose [to the U.S. government] the recognition of our independence." Such a "proposal of peace," Lee pointed out, "would enable the people of the United States to determine at their coming elections whether they will support those who favor a prolongation of the war, or those who wish to bring it to a termination."

Lee did not mention in this letter the foreign-policy implications of his invasion. But he and Davis were aware of those as well. The much-anticipated "cotton famine" had finally begun to have a serious impact on the British and French textile industries. An end to the war would reopen foreign trade and bring a renewed flow of cotton from the South. Powerful leaders and a large part of the public in both countries sympathized with the Confederacy. The French emperor, Napoleon III, flirted with diplomatic recognition of the Confederacy, but was unwilling to take the initiative without British cooperation.

When the war had seemed to be going in the North's favor during the first half of 1862, foreign governments backed off from any overt dealings with the Confederacy. When news of the Seven Days' Battles reached Paris, however, Napoleon instructed his foreign minister to *"Demandez au gouvernement anglais s'il ne croit pas le moment venu de reconnaître le Sud."* ("Ask the English government if it does not believe the time has come to recognize the South.")

British sentiment seemed to be moving in this direction. The United States Consul in Liverpool reported that "we are in more danger of intervention than we have been at any previous period . . . They are all against us and would rejoice at our downfall." The Confederate envoy in London, James Mason, anticipated "intervention speedily in some form." The news of Second Manassas and the invasions of Maryland and Kentucky gave added impetus to the Confederate cause abroad. Britain's chancellor of the exchequer in a speech at Newcastle in October, declared, "Jefferson Davis and other leaders of the South have made an army; they are making, it appears, a navy; and they have made what is more than either; they have made a nation."

More cautious, Prime Minister Viscount Palmerston and Foreign Minister Lord John Russell nevertheless discussed a concrete proposal for Britain and France to offer to mediate an end to the war on the basis of Confederate independence—if Lee's invasion of Maryland brought another Confederate victory. Union forces "got a complete smashing" at Second Manassas, wrote Palmerston to Russell on September 14, "and it seems not all together unlikely that still greater disasters await them, and that even Washington or Baltimore may fall into the hands of the Confederates. If this should happen, would it not be time for us to consider whether in such a state of things England and France might not address the contending parties and recommend an arrangement on the basis of separation?" Russell responded three days later, concurring in the proposal for mediation "with a view to the recognition of the Independence of the Confederates." If the North refused, then "we ought ourselves to recognize the Southern States as an independent State."

The Lincoln administration was acutely sensitive to the political and diplomatic dangers posed by Lee's invasion. But the military crisis had to be dealt with first. The Union army that fought and lost Second Manassas (Second Bull Run) was an ill-matched amalgam of troops from Major General John Pope's Army of Virginia, Major General Ambrose Burnside's IX Corps transferred from North Carolina, and parts of Major General George B. McClellan's Army of the Potomac transferred from the Virginia Peninsula. There was no love lost between Pope and McClellan, who was sulking because of the withdrawal from the peninsula and who considered himself unjustly persecuted by the administration. McClellan dragged his feet about sending troops to Pope's aid, and two of his strongest corps, within hearing of the guns along Bull Run, never made it to the battlefield.

Lincoln considered McClellan's behavior "unpardonable"; a majority of the Cabinet wanted to cashier the general. But Lincoln also recognized McClellan's organizational skills and the extraordinary hold he had on the affections of his soldiers. Lincoln therefore gave McClellan command of all the Union troops in this theater, with instructions to meld them into the Army of the Potomac and go after the rebels. To Cabinet members who protested, Lincoln conceded that McClellan had "acted badly in this matter," but "he has the Army with him . . . We must use what tools we have. There is no man in the Army who can lick these troops of ours into shape half as well as he . . . If he can't fight himself, he excels in making others ready to fight."

McClellan confirmed both Lincoln's confidence and his lack of confidence. A junior officer wrote that when the men in the ranks learned of McClellan's restoration to command, "from extreme sadness we passed in a twinkling to a delirium of delight . . . Men threw their caps in the air, and danced and frolicked like schoolboys . . . The effect of this man's presence upon the Army of the Potomac . . . was electrical, and too wonderful to make it worthwhile attempting to give a reason for it." McClellan did reorganize the army and "lick it into shape" in a remarkably short time, making it "ready to fight." But then he reverted to his wonted caution, estimating enemy strength in Maryland at two or three times Lee's actual numbers and moving north at a snail's pace of six miles a day as if he were afraid of finding rebels.

McClellan clamored for reinforcements, particularly the 12,000-man garrison at Harpers Ferry. But General in Chief Henry W. Halleck refused to release these troops. That refusal created both a problem and an opportunity for Lee. The garrison threatened his line of supply through the Shenandoah Valley. So on September 9, Lee drafted Special Orders No. 191 for the dispatch of almost two-thirds of his army in three widely separated columns under the overall command of Jackson to converge on Harpers Ferry and capture it. The opportunity: a large supply of artillery, rifles, ammunition, provisions, shoes, and clothing for his ragged, shoeless, hungry troops. The problem: McClellan might get between the separated parts of his army during the three to six days it would take to carry out the operation and destroy the fragments of the Army of Northern Virginia in detail.

But two of Lee's hallmarks as a commander were his uncanny ability to judge an opponent's qualities and his willingness to take great risks. To Brigadier General John G. Walker, commander of one of the columns to converge on Harpers Ferry, Lee explained the purpose and plan of his campaign. After capturing the garrison and its supplies, the army would re-concentrate near Hagerstown. "A few days' rest will be of great service to our men," Lee said. "I hope to get shoes and clothing for the most needy. But the best of it will be that the short delay will enable us to get up our stragglers," who from exhaustion, hunger, and lack of shoes had not been able to keep up with the army. Lee believed that there were "not less than eight to ten thousand of them between here and Rapidan Station"—a fairly accurate estimate. When they rejoined the army and were resupplied, Lee intended to tear up the Baltimore and Ohio Railroad and then move to Harrisburg and destroy the Pennsylvania Railroad bridge over the Susquehanna, thus severing the Union's two east-west rail links. "After that," Lee concluded, "I can turn my attention to Philadelphia, Baltimore, or Washington, as may seem best for our interests."

Walker expressed astonishment at the breathtaking boldness of this plan, which would leave the Union army at his rear. "Are you acquainted with General McClellan?" Lee responded. "He is an able general but a very cautious one . . . His army is in a very demoralized and chaotic condition and will not be prepared for offensive operations—or he will not think it so—for three or four weeks. Before that time I hope to be on the Susquehanna."

Even as Lee was offering these observations, however, his adversary had an extraordinary stroke of luck. On September 13, two Union soldiers resting in a field near Frederick, where the Confederates had camped a few days earlier, found a copy of Lee's Special Orders No. 191 wrapped around three cigars where they had been lost by a careless

Southern officer. Recognizing their importance, the Yankee soldiers took them to their captain, who forwarded them up the chain of command until they reached McClellan. A Union staff officer vouched for the genuineness of the document, for he had known Lee's adjutant, Robert H. Chilton, in the prewar army and recognized his handwriting.

The orders gave McClellan a picture of the division of Lee's army into five parts, each at least eight or ten miles from any other while the most widely separated units were thirty miles apart with the Potomac River between them. No Civil War general ever had a better chance to destroy an enemy army in detail before it could reunite. To one of his subordinates, a jubilant McClellan declared: "Here is a paper with which if I cannot whip 'Bobbie Lee,' I will be willing to go home."

As usual, however, McClellan moved cautiously. He did drive Confederate defenders away from the South Mountain passes on September 14. But Harpers Ferry fell to Jackson on the fifteenth and Lee was able to concentrate most of the Army of Northern Virginia near Sharpsburg before McClellan was ready to attack on September 17. After an all-day battle along the ridges above Antietam Creek, Lee was compelled to retreat across the Potomac on the night of September 18. Without the discovery of the lost orders, perhaps even this limited Union victory would not have occurred.

✧ ✧ ✧

The odds against the sequence of events that led to the loss and finding and verification of these orders must have been a million to one. Much more in line with the laws of probability is something like the following scenario. Knowing that most residents of western Maryland were Unionists, Lee imposed tighter security on the army than when in friendly Virginia, to prevent penetration of his camps by any local civilians who hung around the edge and undoubtedly included several spies among their number. Lee instructed his adjutant to deliver Special Orders No. 191 directly to the relevant corps and division commanders. They were to read them in Chilton's presence and commit them to memory, after which all copies of the orders were burned except one, which Lee kept in his possession. In this way there could be no leaks.

Because of an inept defense of Harpers Ferry by its Union commander, Dixon Miles, and because of McClellan's failure to advance rapidly, the garrison surrendered 12,000 men and mountains of supplies to Jackson on September 15. Meanwhile, Jeb Stuart's cavalry performed outstanding service, bringing up stragglers and guarding the passes through the South Mountain range against the ineffectual probes of Union horsemen trying to discover the whereabouts of Lee's main force. On September 16, McClellan arrived at Frederick, which the rebels had vacated a week earlier. By then Lee had reconcentrated his army at Hagerstown. Thousands of stragglers had rejoined the ranks, and thanks to the captures at Harpers Ferry, the Army of Northern Virginia was well equipped for the first time in two months.

After a further pause for rest, while McClellan remained in the dark about Lee's location and intentions, the rebels moved north into Pennsylvania. They brushed aside local militia and the outriders of Union cavalry who finally located them. Spreading through the rich farmland of Pennsylvania's Cumberland Valley like locusts, Lee's army—now 55,000 strong—was able to feed itself better than it had in Virginia. On October 1, the van reached Carlisle. Lee sent a strong detachment of cavalry and part of Jackson's swift-marching infantry twenty miles farther to the railroad bridge at Harrisburg, which they burned on October 3. The Confederate commander also sent his Maryland scouts back into their home state to locate the Army of the Potomac. They found it near Emmitsburg, just south of the Pennsylvania border, marching northward with a determined speed that suggested McClellan finally meant to find Lee and fight him.

Those scouts also reported to Lee that they had discovered a series of hills and ridges around a town named Gettysburg where numerous roads converged, enabling an army to concentrate there quickly and fortify the

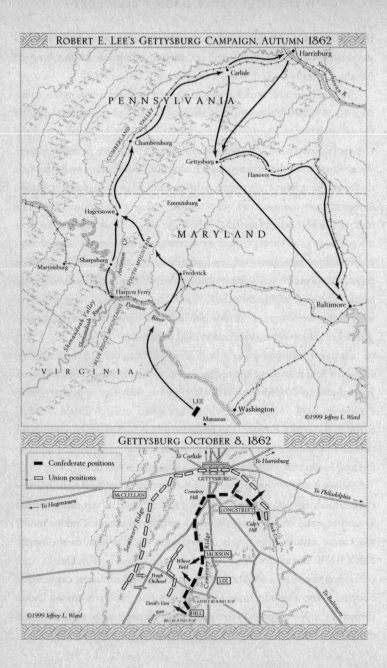

ROBERT E. LEE'S GETTYSBURG CAMPAIGN, AUTUMN 1862

Harrisburg

Susquehanna R.

Carlisle

P E N N S Y L V A N I A

CUMBERLAND VALLEY

Chambersburg

Gettysburg

Hanover

Emmitsburg

M A R Y L A N D

Hagerstown

SOUTH MOUNTAIN

Antietam Cr.

Sharpsburg

Martinsburg

Frederick

Shenandoah Valley

Shenandoah River

BLUE RIDGE MOUNTAINS

Harpers Ferry

Potomac River

Baltimore

V I R G I N I A

LEE

Washington

Manassas

©1999 Jeffrey L. Ward

GETTYSBURG OCTOBER 8, 1862

■ Confederate positions
□ Union positions

To Carlisle

To Harrisburg

GETTYSBURG

To Philadelphia

To Hagerstown

McCLELLAN

Cemetery Hill

Seminary Ridge

LONGSTREET

Culp's Hill

Rock Creek

Wheat Field

JACKSON

Peach Orchard

Cemetery Ridge

LEE

Devil's Den

LITTLE ROUND TOP

To Baltimore

Plum Run

HILL

BIG ROUND TOP

©1999 Jeffrey L. Ward

high ground. On October 4 Lee ordered his army to Gettysburg. They arrived there only hours before the enemy, and by October 6 the Army of Northern Virginia was dug in on the hills south of town.

McClellan came under enormous pressure from Washington to attack the invaders. "Destroy the rebel army," Lincoln wired him. From the Union position on Seminary Ridge, a reluctant McClellan surveyed the Confederate defenses from the Round Tops on the south along Cemetery Ridge northward to Cemetery and Culps Hills. McClellan evolved a tactical plan for a diversionary attack on the morning of October 8 against General James Longstreet's corps on the Confederate right. When Lee shifted reinforcements to that sector, the Yankees would launch their main assault through the peach orchard and wheatfield against the Confederate left center on low ground just north of Little Round Top, held by Jackson's corps. If successful, this attack would pierce a hole in the Confederate line, giving Union cavalry massed behind the center a chance to exploit the breakthrough. Napoleonic in conception, this plan had a crucial defect: It left Union flanks denuded of cavalry.

At dawn, the Union I and IX Corps carried out the diversionary attack on Cemetery and Culps Hills. Lee saw through the feint, however, and refused to shift his reserves, A. P. Hill's light division, to that sector. Longstreet held firm, so when the Union II, VI, and XII Corps attacked through the peach orchard and wheatfield, they found Jackson ready for them. Fierce fighting produced a harvest of carnage unprecedented even in this bloody war, with neither side gaining any advantage.

About 3:00 P.M., Stuart reported to Lee that the Union right was uncovered. Lee immediately ordered Hill to take his division south around Round Top and attack the Union flank in the wheatfield. Undetected by the Union cavalry, which was massed more than a mile to the north, Hill's 6,000 men burst from the woods and boulders of Devil's Den screaming the rebel yell. Many of them wore blue uniforms captured at Harpers Ferry, which increased the surprise and confusion among Union troops of the XII corps. Like a row of falling dominoes, the exhausted and decimated Union brigades collapsed. With perfect timing the rest of

Jackson's corps counterattacked, smashing the fragments of Union regiments that had rallied to resist Hill. As the fighting rolled in echelon toward the North, Longstreet's corps joined the counterattack at 4:30 P.M.

McClellan had kept his favorite V Corps in reserve. Steadied by Brigadier General George Sykes's division of regulars, they held back the yelling rebels for a brief time. But as the sun dipped below the South Mountain range, the V Corps also broke. In a desperate attempt to rally them, McClellan rode to the front. "Soldiers!" he shouted. "Stand fast! I will lead you!" As he drew his sword, a minié ball smashed into his skull and toppled him dead from his horse. Word of McClellan's death spread like lightning through the thinned and scattered ranks of Yankee units that were still fighting. The last remnants of resistance winked out. Thousands of dejected bluecoats surrendered; thousands more melted away into the dusk, every man for himself. The Army of the Potomac ceased to exist as a fighting force.

News of the Battle of Gettysburg resounded through the land and across the Atlantic. "My God! My God" exclaimed Lincoln in the White House. "What will the country say?" It said plenty, all of it bad. Peace Democrats redoubled their denunciations of the war as a wicked failure. "All are tired of this damnable tragedy," they cried. "Each hour is but sinking us deeper into bankruptcy and desolation." Even staunch patriots and Lincoln supporters like Joseph Medill, editor of the *Chicago Tribune*, gave up hope of winning the war. "An armistice is bound to come during the year '63," he wrote. "The rebs can't be conquered by the present machinery." Captain Oliver Wendell Holmes Jr. of the 20th Massachusetts, which had suffered 75 percent casualties at Gettysburg, wrote in November that "the army is tired with its hard and terrible experience. I've pretty much made up my mind that the South have achieved their independence."

In Kentucky, Union and Confederate forces had clashed in the indecisive Battle of Perryville on the same day (October 8) as the Battle of Gettysburg. Encouraged by the news from Pennsylvania, Confederate

commanders Braxton Bragg and Edmund Kirby-Smith decided to continue their Kentucky campaign. Having already occupied Lexington and
Frankfort, they began a drive toward the prize of Louisville as the Union
army under Major General Don Carlos Buell, discouraged by the reports
of McClellan's defeat and death, fell back listlessly. In Pennsylvania, after
a pause for consolidation of his supply lines, Lee began an advance
toward Baltimore. Newly emboldened pro-Confederate Marylanders
openly affirmed their allegiance. Although reserve troops manning the
formidable defenses ringing Washington dissuaded Lee from attacking
the capital, there was no Union field army capable of resisting Lee's
movements.

Hesitant to goad last-ditch resistance by attacking a major city, however, Lee paused to await the outcome of Northern congressional elections on November 4. The voters sent a loud and clear message that they
wished to end the war, even on terms of Confederate independence. Democrats won control of the next House of Representatives and the peace
wing established firm control of the party.

At almost the moment the election results became known, the
British minister to the United States, Lord Lyons, presented Secretary of
State Seward with an offer signed by the governments of Great Britain,
France, Russia, and Austria-Hungary to mediate an end to the war on the
basis of separation. "We will not admit the division of the Union at any
price," Seward responded. "There is no possible compromise." Very well,
responded Lyons. In that case Her Majesty's Government will recognize
the independence of the Confederate States of America. Other European
governments will do the same. "This is not a matter of principle or pref-
erences," Lyons told Seward, "but of fact."

Despite Seward's bluster, he was a practical statesman. He was also a
student of history. He knew that American victory at the Battle of
Saratoga in 1777 had brought French diplomatic recognition of the fledg-
ling United States, followed by French assistance and intervention that
proved crucial to the achievement of American independence. Would
history repeat itself? Would British and French recognition of the Con-

federacy be followed by military assistance and intervention—against the blockade, for example? As they pondered these questions and absorbed the results of the congressional elections, while Confederate armies stood poised for attack outside Baltimore and Louisville, Lincoln and Seward concluded that they had no choice.

On a gloomy New Year's Day 1863, a melancholy Lincoln called Republican congressional leaders and state governors to the White House. "This is not the duty I had hoped to discharge today," he told them. "Last July I decided to issue a proclamation freeing the slaves in rebel states, to take effect today," he continued sadly. "There is no chance of that now. Would *my word* free the slaves, when I cannot even enforce the Constitution in the rebel States?" Instead, "We are faced with a situation in which the whole world seems to be against us. Last summer, after McClellan was driven back from Richmond, I said that in spite of that setback, 'I expect to maintain this contest until successful, or till I die, or am conquered, or my term expires, or Congress or the country forsakes me.' Gentlemen, the people expressed their opinion in the last election. The country has forsaken us, and the next Congress will be against us. Whether or not we admit we are conquered, we must admit that we have failed to conquer the rebellion. Today I will issue a proclamation accepting the insurgents' offer of an armistice. Secretary Seward will accept the good offices of foreign powers for mediation." The president's voice choked as he concluded: "Gentlemen, the United States no longer exists as one nation, indivisible."

STEPHEN W. SEARS

A CONFEDERATE CANNAE AND OTHER SCENARIOS

How the Civil War Might Have Turned Out Differently

he what ifs of the American Civil War may be more difficult to gauge than those of our Revolution—already the times and the technology of war were more complex—but they are plentiful enough. A nation permanently divided was a real prospect during the first two years of the war, and one that certainly fueled Southern ardor for battle. If, as James M. McPherson speculates in the previous chapter, the Lost Order hadn't been lost, that might have been the inevitable outcome of Robert E. Lee's first invasion of the North. Or, as Stephen W. Sears describes in this chapter, if Robert E. Lee had pulled off a double envelopment of a large part of George B. McClellan's Union army on day six of the Seven Days' Battles in June 1862, it might well have led to the end of hostilities and negotiations for "an arrangement upon the basis of separation." But the rebellion (as the North thought of it) might just as easily have ended not long after it began. Sometimes, Sears notes, if there is any inherent logic to military operations, outcomes should have gone another way. Sometimes, too, the difference can be as slight as the path of a bullet and whether its target gets out of the way in time. As we have seen before, milliseconds can influence cen-

turies. But in other cases, an event that seems likely to bring a swing in historical direction—Sears offers by way of example the victory of McClellan over Lincoln in the presidential election of 1864—may produce the curious phenomenon of the "second order counterfactual." In other words, enormous change can in the end, merely lead us back to where we might have been all along.

❖ Stephen W. Sears is one of the foremost historians of the Civil War. His books include LANDSCAPE TURNED RED: THE BATTLE OF ANTIETAM, GEORGE B. MCCLELLAN: THE YOUNG NAPOLEON, CHANCELLORSVILLE, and, most recently, CONTROVERSIES & COMMANDERS: DISPATCHES FROM THE ARMY OF THE POTOMAC.

The Civil War—like every war—was marked by a number of pivotal moments, moments in which the balance tipped suspensefully to produce a victor or a vanquished and subsequently a crucial change in the war's direction. At these moments it was the decisions or actions of soldiers and statesmen (and in one instance here, voters) that resulted in the consequences that history records for us. But outcomes and consequences could just as easily have gone another way—sometimes, if there is any inherent logic to military operations, *should* have gone another way.

Each of the five scenarios that follow held the promise (at that moment, at least) of affecting the war profoundly or, in the case of the last one, the aftermath of the war. None of them requires a great leap of imagination to believe its premise. Without improbably distorting actual events—in the first scenario, for example, Jefferson Davis was a witness to the 1861 fighting at Bull Run—and without putting unspoken words into the mouths of the actors, then, imagine that at this handful of critical Civil War moments it turned out this way instead of that way . . .

Battle at Bull Run, or the Rebellion of '61

"You are green, it is true," Mr. Lincoln said to Irvin McDowell, commander of the newly recruited Federal army at Washington, "but they are green, also; you are all green alike." It was a remarkably prescient observation. On July 21, 1861, when McDowell's raw troops joined battle with the equally raw troops of the newly proclaimed Confederate States of America, along the banks of Bull Run west of the capital, the outcome would be decided by which of these green armies broke and ran first.

The decisive moment occurred in late afternoon. After six hours of confused maneuvering and bloody fighting, the men of both armies were nearing the limit of their endurance. The Confederates, pressed slowly but steadily back by General McDowell's flanking movement, formed a last-ditch defense on Henry House Hill. At the core of their line was a brigade of Virginians being held rigidly to their task by a flinty brigadier named Thomas J. Jackson. Charge and countercharge swept across the hilltop, but the Virginians stood fast. Then, suddenly, a Federal volley found General Jackson and he was down, struck by three bullets, his left arm mangled. He was carried to the rear and out of the battle, his moment of glory fated to be forgotten.

Without Jackson's stalwart leadership as a rallying point, his Virginians began to waver. Seeing this, the regiments on both their flanks gave way. Once again the Federals came on, and this time they would not be stopped. The center of the Confederate line broke open and fell away. Abruptly everyone was running for the rear and safety. Behind the shattered front, fearful teamsters jammed their supply wagons into the crossroads village of New Market, where shells from the U.S. batteries found them and turned the jam to pandemonium. Fear was transmuted into panic. "The larger part of the men are a confused mob, entirely demoralized," the field commander of the beaten army had to admit. "It was the opinion of all the commanders that no stand could be made . . ."

That in the end proved crucial—there was nowhere close by for the routed Confederates to take a stand, no natural barrier behind which the panicked men might be calmed and rallied. Had the battle gone the other way, had it been the raw Federals who broke and ran, they would have had the nearby Potomac and Washington's rudimentary defenses as a rallying point. As it was, for the Confederates fleeing the battlefield, the closest major defensive feature where they might attempt a stand was the Rappahannock, some twenty-five miles to the south. Hardly more than a corporal's guard would reach the river.

The Federal brigades that had done the fighting were as disorganized in victory as their foes in defeat. However, General McDowell had two divisions available in reserve to throw into the pursuit. As the flight continued through the night, exhausted, discouraged rebels by the thousands threw down their arms and surrendered to the pursuers. The most noteworthy prisoner was the president of the Confederate States. Jefferson Davis had rushed up from Richmond to witness the battle, and he was captured as he rode out into the mass of fleeing rebels to try and halt the rout.

By the second day after the battle, the ranking rebel generals, Joseph E. Johnston and P. G. T. Beauregard, had dragged what remained of their forces across the Rappahannock. On the twenty-first they had given battle at Bull Run with something over 30,000 men; hardly a quarter of that number now remained under effective command. Even though they were joined by a reserve force from Fredericksburg, just then the armed might of the Confederate States totaled barely 10,000 troops. McDowell and his legions, forming up opposite along the riverbank, were being reinforced hourly by fresh regiments from the North. No fresh regiments were forthcoming from the South.

It was only too clear to Johnston and Beauregard that within a matter of days, perhaps within a matter of hours, the enemy in overwhelming force would plunge across the Rappahannock to stamp out what remained of the rebellion's armed forces. With President Davis languishing in Old Capitol prison in Washington, the two generals took decision-making into their own hands. Neither was a revolutionary; both were traditionalists in matters of military form: When every choice promises only defeat, there is but one honorable choice. They sent to McDowell under a flag of truce to request an armistice. With a nod of approval from President Lincoln, McDowell granted it. So ended the military phase of what would come to be known as the Rebellion of '61.

Diplomacy now replaced arms. Stepping again into the limelight were Kentucky Senator John J. Crittenden and the Senate's Committee of Thirteen, who had labored fruitlessly for a compromise settlement between the Secessionists and the Unionists at the turn of the year. This time the Southerners had to play their hand without trumps. From the White House, Mr. Lincoln dictated the terms of settlement. The eleven

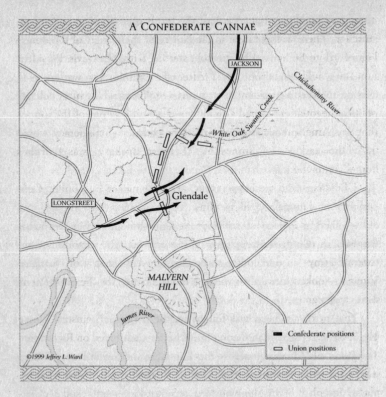

A CONFEDERATE CANNAE

JACKSON

Chickahominy River

White Oak Swamp Creek

LONGSTREET

Glendale

MALVERN HILL

James River

■ Confederate positions
☐ Union positions

©1999 Jeffrey L. Ward

states of the Confederacy must rescind their articles of secession and re-join the Union. Their armed forces must disband, and all federal property be restored. While of course slavery would not be interfered with in those states where it had been constitutionally established, its extension beyond their borders would henceforth be strictly prohibited. The Congress would enact the necessary legislation, and the Committee of Thirteen was charged with crafting a long-range plan for compensated emancipation.

With the remnant of the C.S.A. army firmly in McDowell's grip, and with the memory of the debacle at Bull Run fresh in every mind, Richmond had no choice but to accept the terms of settlement and recon-struction. There was agitation in the North for the leaders of the Rebel-lion of '61 to be hanged for treason, starting with Mr. Davis. President Lincoln would have none of it. After all, with further warfare now averted, he faced a presidential term certain to focus on the most delicate political negotiations aimed at finding a peaceful way out of the morass that was American slavery. An embittered former Confederacy would make that task all but impossible. "Let 'em up easy," was Lincoln's homely injunction.

Of course it did not happen that way. Only nicked by a bullet, Gen-eral Jackson famously held steadfast to the position on Henry House Hill—"There is Jackson standing like a stone wall!"—and in the end it was McDowell's green troops who broke and ran. The victorious Con-federate army—in due course to be christened the Army of Northern Virginia—looked forward to winning independence for the South in its next campaign.

That next campaign was fought on the Virginia Peninsula, where McDowell's replacement, George B. McClellan, advanced on Richmond. The Peninsula Campaign reached its climax in the Seven Days' Battles, which opened in the last week of June 1862. Robert E. Lee—who had re-placed Joseph E. Johnston, wounded at Seven Pines—attacked McClel-lan relentlessly, driving him back from the gates of Richmond. On June 30, at the crossroads hamlet of Glendale, Lee delivered what he intended to be the decisive blow of the campaign.

General Lee Achieves His Cannae

As Lee's biographer, Douglas Southall Freeman, would put it, General Lee "had only that one day for a Cannae . . ." It was day six of the Seven Days', and McClellan's Army of the Potomac was in rapid flight toward the James River. The routes to the river funneled through Glendale. Hot on McClellan's heels came Stonewall Jackson with four divisions. Thrust-ing in toward the flank of the retreating Yankees were three divisions under James Longstreet. Although McClellan's army was the larger of the two overall, at the Glendale chokepoint it was Lee who could bring superior force to bear against the extended enemy columns. A flank attack there by Longstreet held promise of cutting the Federal army in half; indeed, Hannibal's classic conquest at Cannae in 216 B.C.—history's watchword for a crushing military defeat—might be duplicated. Porter Alexander, that most astute of Confederate historians, said there were but a handful of moments in the Civil War when "we were within reach of military successes so great that we might have hoped to end the war with our independence. . . . This chance of June 30th '62 impresses me as the best of all."

As it happened, Lee missed this best chance by the slimmest of margins, and the Yankees escaped to fight another day. After watching Longstreet's flank assault come up just short, Lee wrote bitterly, "Could the other commands have co-operated in the action the result would have proved most disastrous to the enemy." The primary offender was Stonewall Jackson. Sunk in a state of profound lethargy that day, Jackson failed to move against the Federal rear guard, which was thus able to send strong reinforcements in the nick of time to seal off Longstreet's breakthrough.

The day might easily have taken a different course. In fact, had Jackson been his usual self on June 30, 1862, it almost certainly would have taken a different course.

❖ ❖ ❖

After three months' intensive campaigning in the Shenandoah Valley, after his dash to the Peninsula and straight into the Seven Days' fighting there, Stonewall Jackson was utterly exhausted. On day five—Sunday, June 29—with his command held inactive under Lee's orders, Jackson recognized the perilous state of his own physical and mental health. Abandoning his usual strict Sabbath evolutions, he gave orders that he was not to be disturbed and slept half the clock away. Consequently, when he faced the pivotal events at Glendale on June 30, Stonewall Jackson was refreshed and alert and eager for the test.

That morning Jackson caught up with the Yankees' rear guard, under William Franklin, at a broken bridge over the White Oak Swamp watercourse north of Glendale. Jackson's reconnoiter uncovered the considerable strength of the enemy position and set his thoughts (as usual) to a flanking movement. Enterprising subordinates found two downstream fords where infantry might cross. Jackson pounced on the opportunity. Under cover of a tremendous artillery barrage at the bridge site, he directed three brigades to cross and take Franklin's Yankees in flank and rear.

As Franklin's rear guard joined battle against this threat, Lee directed Longstreet to launch his offensive against the Federals defending the Glendale crossroads to the south. Soon the hard-pressed Glendale defenders were calling on Franklin for help. He could send them none; indeed, he even refused to return two brigades sent him "on loan" from Glendale earlier.

Longstreet smashed cleanly through the center of the extended Union line. Pushing aside the inconsequential reserves, he turned his spearhead northward, toward Franklin's embattled rear guard. When Franklin turned to meet this new threat, Jackson stormed the White Oak Swamp crossing in full force. A good half of the Federal army was cut off and engulfed by converging forces.

The Federals' plight was made all the worse by a muddled high command. Before the battle opened, General McClellan, distraught and demoralized by the turn his campaign was taking, had deserted his troops at Glendale and ridden off to join the army's advance guard on the James, well distant from the fighting. He left no one in charge, and so the defense of the "Glendale Pocket" became simply every general for himself.

"Fighting Joe" Hooker, south of the break in the line, got his division away. Phil Kearny boldly attacked and broke through the closing ring. Their two divisions, along with the four that earlier had reached Malvern

Hill on the James, now comprised the fighting strength of the Army of the Potomac. Darkness found the other five divisions trapped at Glendale and in the margins of White Oak Swamp. Lee tightened the ring during the night, and the next day, July 1, accepted the Federals' surrender. Including battle casualties, Glendale cost the Yankees 46,000 men and all their equipment. General Lee had achieved his Cannae—or at least half of it.

McClellan scrambled away to Harrison's Landing on the James with what remained of his forces. Already convinced that Lee's army was 200,000 strong (more than twice its actual count), the Young Napoleon was unstrung by the reports from Glendale. His grand campaign had ended in a Waterloo. Telling his second in command, Fitz John Porter, to surrender on the best terms possible, he sailed off in a gunboat for exile. He would not gain even that haven. Court-martialed on charges of dereliction of duty at Glendale, McClellan was convicted on the furious testimony of Generals Hooker and Kearny and cashiered.

As for General Lee, he was treated to a Romanlike triumph in Richmond. Calmly he recruited his army and re-equipped it with the rich military spoils seized from the Army of the Potomac. He knew he now faced only loud-talking General John Pope and his Army of Virginia, a patchwork assembled from the remaining Federal forces in the East. In late July, Lee set off northward. His instructions to Stonewall Jackson, leading the spearhead, were to "suppress" the braggart Pope.

The outmanned Pope did not wait to be suppressed, but fled to the defenses of Washington. Lee followed rapidly and put the city and its ragtag collection of defenders under siege. The Potomac was closed both above and below the capital, and all rail connections severed. Then, laboriously, the Confederates began to bring up the massive siege train they had seized from McClellan on the Peninsula. Watching all this from London, Prime Minister Palmerston addressed a note to his foreign secretary. The Federals had received "a very great smashing," he noted and asked, "Would it not be time for us to consider whether in such a state of things

England and France might not address the contending parties and recommend an arrangement upon the basis of separation?"

The British-French offer arrived aboard the next packet, and behind
it, the Lincoln administration knew, lay the threat of full recognition of
the Confederacy by Europe's powers. The administration realized, too,
that if it brought forces from the Western theater to try and lift the siege
of Washington—a dubious prospect at best against the brilliant Lee—the
Rebels there would march straight to the Ohio and into the heartland.
When in September General Lee sternly granted but three days to evacuate all civilians from the capital before he opened with his siege guns,
the reply was a call for a suspension of hostilities so as to negotiate "an
arrangement upon the basis of separation." Lee's Cannae had now produced everything he expected of it.

❖   ❖   ❖

The most celebrated tactical surprise of the Civil War was, of course,
Stonewall Jackson's successful flanking march and attack on Joe Hooker
at Chancellorsville. Looking back on it, Hooker was unrepentant about
his management of the battle. Jackson's movement, he wrote afterward,
"under the circumstances admitted of not a ray of probability of successful execution. Ninety-nine chances out of a hundred Genl Jackson's
corps would have been destroyed." To be sure, Hooker was hardly an un-
biased observer. Yet he had a point. General Hooker had taken specific
steps to avoid and to counter just such a surprise attack that May 2,
1863. If those orders to guard his right had been carried out as he intended them to be, how different the outcome might have been.

The Victor of Chancellorsville

On the morning of May 2, the sixth day of his campaign, Joe Hooker was
brimming with confidence. Having fixed Lee in place at Fredericksburg
with a holding force and then secretly crossed the Rappahannock up-

stream with his main body, his campaign plan showed every sign of working perfectly. He had drawn Lee out of his imposing fortifications and was threatening his flank and rear. The plan now was to force Lee to attack him in his chosen position, around the Chancellorsville crossroads.

Hooker's forces were posted in expectation of a defensive battle. His weakest corps, the Eleventh, with its less-than-stellar commander, O. O. Howard, held the right flank, farthest from the expected scene of action. To be on the safe side, however, Hooker had ordered up from the Fredericksburg front John Reynolds's First Corps, one of the best in the army, to brace Howard's position. To this point in the campaign the one serious malfunction had been in communications between the two wings of the army—couriers got lost in the woods, and the telegraphic link to the Fredericksburg front failed to work. But in this instance, for a welcome change, the link worked perfectly. Reynolds received his orders promptly, and by midafternoon on May 2 the First Corps was solidly anchoring the army's right flank.

During the morning an enemy column was sighted crossing an opening in the woods off to the south, and word of it was passed up to headquarters. Hooker was quick to warn Howard: "We have good reason to suppose that the enemy is moving to our right." Look to your exposed flank, Howard was told; mass your reserves "in order that you may be prepared for him in whatever direction he advances."

Otis Howard had only recently been promoted to command of the Eleventh Corps, and it seems that in this first action he determined to be especially conscientious about obeying orders. At the end point of his line, then, he quickly formed a long right angle facing west, throwing up log breastworks and posting his artillery. To the rear he positioned substantial reserves of men and guns. In early afternoon, as the First Corps began arriving on the scene, he made sure his line was securely tied to Reynolds's. When Howard replied to Hooker's warning, "I am taking measures to resist an attack from the west," he meant every word of it.

At 5:30 that afternoon, when Stonewall Jackson gave the word to his flanking force—"You can go forward then"—his first wave of attackers struck like an avalanche. Howard's line bent and in places even broke, but there was no surprise and no panic. Reserves, already on the alert, were moved into the gaps. Reynolds, too, absorbed the blows, and then pitched into the flank of the attackers. By the time darkness finally ended the fighting, Jackson could claim gains of only some 200 yards. When that night he was accidentally felled by a volley from his own men, he was searching in vain for some gap in the solid enemy front.

May 3, the pivotal day of the campaign, went all Joe Hooker's way. Cavalryman Jeb Stuart, who took over for the wounded Jackson, attacked repeatedly but fruitlessly in an attempt to close the huge gap between the two wings of the Confederate army. Coolly meeting these assaults, Hooker parried every blow of Stuart's and then counterattacked with two fresh corps. Stuart reeled back in defeat.

No choice remained for Lee now but to give up the fight and order a withdrawal. Taking severe losses in extricating his army from the Chancellorsville front, he fell back south toward Richmond along his railroad supply line. Hooker pursued, and the continuous fighting that spring of 1863 came to be known as the Overland Campaign—Lee stubbornly defending each river line between Fredericksburg and Richmond, Hooker patiently outflanking each line. By July, Lee and his proud Army of Northern Virginia were pinned in the trenches before Richmond. Joe Hooker, now promoted to lieutenant general, confidently managed the besieging army.

That July 1863 saw Grant's capture of Vicksburg and the opening of the Mississippi. By November, under Grant's management, the Chattanooga gateway to the Deep South was in Union hands. In the face of Hooker's steady successes in the East and Grant's in the West, Confederate morale sagged. Quickly pressing his advantage, Grant marched straight for Atlanta, took it, then cut a swath through Georgia to the coast. Spring 1864 witnessed the final campaigns. While Grant drove north through the Carolinas, at Richmond Hooker snipped off Lee's rail supply lines one by one. On April 9, 1864, at Appomattox Court House, Lee's desperate effort to escape fell short, and he surrendered to Joe

Hooker. Soon afterward, Joe Johnston surrendered to Grant in North Carolina, and the great rebellion was history.

Grant's and Hooker's partisans urged their heroes to seek the presidency in the fall. But Grant had already assured Mr. Lincoln that he would not challenge his reelection. Nor would Joe Hooker, who expressed only contempt for politics. "I will not accept if nominated and will not serve if elected," he announced loudly.

Historians of the war would rank Grant first among the Union's generals, but by consensus they credited "Fighting Joe" Hooker with conducting at Chancellorsville the most perfectly executed campaign of the entire three-year war.

❖ ❖ ❖

On August 24, 1863, President Davis telegraphed Robert E. Lee to come to Richmond from his camps on the Rappahannock to consult on grand strategy. In the East, Lee's army, despite its Gettysburg defeat, seemed able to stand off any fresh Federal threats. But in the Western theater, particularly in Tennessee, the Confederacy was in dire straits. Mr. Davis wanted Lee to send troops west from his army—and he wanted Lee himself to go West with them and take over command of the Army of Tennessee from the incompetent Braxton Bragg. As Davis put it, Lee's "presence in the western army would be worth more than the addition of a corps."

While properly deferential to the president, Lee made it clear that he was not interested in the Western command. "I did not intend to decline the service," he told Davis, "but merely to express the opinion that the duty could be better performed by the officers already in that department." At the time, Davis seems to have felt it would be a mistake to force any such change on his unwilling (and indispensable) lieutenant, and he let the matter drop. Instead, it would be Longstreet who commanded the troops sent West, and the Army of Tennessee continued its march to grim ruin under Braxton Bragg.

What if, however, Davis had adopted his commander in chief's stance and *ordered* Lee to go West, "for the good of the service"? Might the war in that theater then have taken a different course? . . .

A New General for the West

Mr. Davis, having somewhat nervously exercised his ultimate authority in the matter of this momentous command change, was wise enough to leave it up to General Lee what troops he would take West with him, and, more important, who would command the Army of Northern Virginia in his absence. Of that army's three corps commanders, James Longstreet, A. P. Hill, and Dick Ewell, only Longstreet had Lee's full confidence. Lee promptly chose him for the place.

Paradoxically, it was Longstreet who had argued long and vigorously for sending his corps from the Army of Northern Virginia to the Army of Tennessee—hoping, in the bargain, to be awarded command of the Western army himself. Now, thrust into Lee's place instead, he was insistent on having his trusted corps remain with him. Lee agreed, and rather than Longstreet's corps going West, it was the corps of Dick Ewell. Ewell's first battle as corps commander had been Gettysburg, where he had acted indecisively. Lee thought it best to take Ewell West with him and through careful supervision perhaps embolden him. Ewell had earlier performed capably enough under Stonewall Jackson's tight control; perhaps all he needed was a shorter rein.

Lee had expressed concern that the Western army's high command might not accept him as an "outsider." He need not have worried. Bragg had so alienated his lieutenants that they welcomed Lee with open arms. When he took over the command, he found immediate opportunity to employ his aggressive martial nature. Bragg's army had been maneuvered out of Chattanooga and out of Tennessee entirely, yet now the incautious Federals under William Rosecrans were ripe for a counterstroke. Bragg had planned such a stroke, but it was Lee who carried it out, at Chickamauga. On September 20, the second day of the battle, acting on a direct order from Lee, Dick Ewell's reinforcing corps from the East delivered the decisive blow. Rosecrans's Army of the Cumberland was split in half and by nightfall was retreating helter-skelter for Chattanooga.

Early the next morning, the Confederate cavalryman Nathan Bedford Forrest ranged ahead to Missionary Ridge overlooking Chattanooga and saw the chaotic situation of the fleeing Federal columns. He hurried dispatches back to headquarters: "I think they are evacuating as hard as they can go . . . I think we ought to press forward as rapidly as possible." With a single brigade of infantry, Forrest promised, he could take Chattanooga: "Every hour is worth a thousand men."

Braxton Bragg had been wont to let such shining opportunities slip away. Not Robert E. Lee. He recognized in Forrest the same sure judgment that marked Jeb Stuart in the Eastern army, and he leaped at the advice. He rushed forward every man who could carry a gun. The army would outrun its supplies, he was warned. They could resupply from captured Yankee stocks, said Lee, just as he had resupplied his Army of Northern Virginia in the Chancellorsville victory.

Over the next few days, the battered Army of the Cumberland was decimated. For one of the few times in the war, a victory in the field turned into a virtual battle of annihilation. George Thomas, whose stubborn stand at Chickamauga had been the one bright spot for the Union in that battle, stubbornly directed the retreat of the remnant of Rosecrans's army after that general was captured. Lee regained Chattanooga, and in eastern Tennessee, the now outmanned Federal force under Ambrose Burnside beat a hasty retreat. By October, Tenneessee, vital gateway to the Deep South, was once again securely in Confederate hands.

Having restored affairs in the Western theater, at least until the next campaigning season in the spring, General Lee petitioned Davis to give the Army of Tennessee to Joseph E. Johnston and to let him return to his beloved Army of Northern Virginia. Longstreet had done well enough checkmating General Meade's halfhearted moves in Virginia—the Army of the Potomac, too, had had to dispatch troops to the Western theater—but Lee considered Longstreet far too defensive-minded. Robert E. Lee still believed that Confederate independence could only be achieved in the Eastern theater, and he wanted to direct that effort. Mr. Davis could hardly refuse his most spectacularly successful general.

Alas for the Confederacy, there was only one Robert E. Lee—and also only one cautious-to-a-fault Joe Johnston. In the spring of 1864, the Union might be forced to start all over in Tennessee, but this time it was U. S. Grant who was in charge of the effort from the beginning. With his force and Sherman's, along with Thomas's tattered command reinforced to corps strength from Northern reserves, Grant reprised the brilliant maneuvering he had displayed at Vicksburg. First, he feinted the nervous Johnston right out of Chattanooga, then without pause he pressed him back relentlessly toward Atlanta. As early as September 2, 1864, Grant would telegraph President Lincoln, "Atlanta is ours, and fairly won."

Lee's command presence in the Western theater and his bright victories at Chickamauga and Chattanooga were now all for naught—gone with the wind, it would be said. In the end, all he achieved was to bring U. S. Grant to the fore, unfettered and where he was needed most.

❖ ❖ ❖

In late August 1864 the Democrats met in convention in Chicago to nominate their candidate for president. It was all but certain that General McClellan would be the nominee, and even among Republicans there were many who expected the general to be elected. One of those was Abraham Lincoln. A few days before the convention, he had his Cabinet members sign a "blind memorandum," the contents of which only he knew. He did not expect to be re-elected, he wrote, and therefore it must become the administration's duty to save the Union before the new president-elect's inauguration, "as he will have secured his election on such ground that he can not possibly save it afterwards."

The Democrats, however, proceeded to commit political suicide. At the convention, a peace-at-any-price Copperhead faction, outmaneuvering the McClellanites, seized control of the platform committee and rammed through a peace plank that termed the war a failure and called for an armistice without conditions. The general, duly nominated, found himself a war Democrat running on a peace platform. Although he repudiated the peace plank, it was a fatal handicap. The soldier vote, in particular, turned overwhelmingly against him. Sherman's capture of Atlanta made a sham of the Democrats' war-is-a-failure argument. On November 8, McClellan lost by 2.2 million to 1.8 million in the popular vote, and by 212 to 21 in the electoral college.

What if, however, the Democrats had acted sanely at Chicago? What if the majority at the convention kept control of events and wrote into the platform a strong war plank for General McClellan to run upon? Surely that would have made a difference on November 8.

Our Seventeenth President

George McClellan proved not to be as politically naive as many had thought. He understood what needed to be done to exploit the pessimism in the North and gain him the presidency. First and foremost, he had to take both New York and Pennsylvania, the two most populous states, with fully half (plus one) of the 117 electoral votes he needed for victory. The Democrats also had traditional strengths in the border states—Maryland, Delaware, Kentucky, Missouri. They were thought to have good prospects in two New England states—Connecticut and New Hampshire—and in New Jersey, McClellan's adopted state. Finally, Indiana and Illinois, with their substantial Southern constituencies, were worthwhile campaign targets. If General McClellan could capture New York and Pennsylvania, he would need but 58 more electoral votes; these "focus states" contained 79.

Sherman's capture of Atlanta, coming on the heels of McClellan's nomination, was immediately made the occasion for high celebration by war Democrats. As one party leader put it, they must be sure that McClellan people "burnt as much powder as the Republicans in celebrating the victories announced from time to time." McClellan wrote Sherman, "Your campaign will go down in history as one of the memorable ones of the world," and made sure the press got copies. The Democrats' strategy was to present General McClellan, the senior general on the active list, driven from command after his great victory at Antietam by a radicalized Republican administration, as a superbly qualified commander in chief in contrast to the bumbling civilian Lincoln. McClellan would see the war through surely and swiftly and professionally. One of his staff members told the press, "The General stated that should he be elected, he expected to be very unpopular the first year, as he should use every power possible to close the war at once, should enforce the draft strictly, and listen to no remonstrance until the rebellion was effectually quashed." That attracted much favorable notice among soldier voters.

Democratic campaigners hit hard at what they called the tyrannies of the Lincoln administration, with its trampling of such individual liberties as the habeas corpus privilege. They pointed to "abolitionist fanaticism" and social and economic chaos and costly trickeries in financing the war. It was pointed out that the Army of the Potomac, McClellan's old command, was bogged down in trench warfare under his successors, and after a bloody summer of staggering casualty lists was no closer to Richmond than McClellan had been in 1862. McClellan had opposed emancipation, but had done so privately; now both he and the platform were silent on the slavery question. Personally he was most comfortable focusing on the soldier vote, including the McClellan Legion, organized on the home front from thousands of discharged soldiers and men on sick leave and furlough.

In October, there were bellwether state elections in Ohio, Indiana, and Pennsylvania. In Ohio the notorious Copperhead Clement Vallandigham, who had attempted to disrupt the Chicago convention, was fresh in voters' minds and Republicans held the state. But Democrats scored narrow victories in Indiana and Pennsylvania; in the latter the soldier vote went decisively for the obviously still-popular onetime commander of the Army of the Potomac.

Both sides predicted a close outcome on November 8. Even Mr. Lincoln conceded New York and Pennsylvania to McClellan, although calculating a narrow six-vote electoral victory for himself. McClellan wrote ten days before the election, "All the news I hear is *very* favorable. There is every reason to be most hopeful."

The general's forecast was the more accurate of the two. On Election Day he lost in the popular vote, but won nine states in the Electoral College, 120 to 113. He gained both New York and Pennsylvania on the soldier vote, especially from Army of the Potomac loyalists. He picked up Delaware, Kentucky, and New Jersey, and had paper-thin margins in Connecticut and New Hampshire. His war stand gained him Indiana and Illinois. Election analysts pointed to the strong war plank in the Chicago platform as the decisive factor for the Democrats.

It would be nearly four months until president-elect McClellan was inaugurated, but he promptly made a point of visiting or sending strongly worded statements to Union army commanders that come March 4 the new president intended to be a vigorous, active commander in chief. In effect, he would once again be general in chief of all the armies, only this time without any superior to contradict him. So it happened. When Lee surrendered his army at Appomattox Court House on April 9, 1865, President McClellan was there at Grant's side.

By then, Abraham Lincoln was home in Springfield, Illinois, yet another in a string of one-term presidents going back to the time of Andrew Jackson. Lincoln would be remembered favorably as a president who had stood fast for the Union in 1861, and who spoke and wrote well, but in the end as a president who could not persuade the people to let him see the war through on his own terms.

Ironically, his successor, who in Lincoln's August blind memorandum was predicted to be incapable of saving the Union, saved it probably as effectively as a reelected Lincoln could have. To be sure, President McClellan faced several months of battle with the still-Republican Thirty-Eighth Congress over the process of reconstructing the Union. However, George McClellan had always done better fighting his battles with words and on paper than on battlefields, and so it would prove now.

VIETNAM IN AMERICA, 1865

Soon after dawn on Sunday, April 9, 1865, General Robert E. Lee's hungry, exhausted Army of Northern Virginia was surrounded by the overwhelming Federal forces of U. S. Grant near Appomattox, Virginia. Sitting on a log with a trusted subordinate, General Porter Alexander, Lee said he saw no way out except surrender.

Shocked, Alexander urged an alternative—that Lee order his army "to scatter in the woods and bushes . . ." to spare "the men who have fought under you for four years . . . the mortification of having you ask Grant for terms and having him reply, 'Unconditional Surrender. . . .'" Two-thirds of Lee's troops, Alexander estimated, would "scatter like rabbits and partridges," could not be caught, and could carry on the war.

That would be only about 10,000 men, Lee replied, a number "too insignificant to accomplish the least good." But suppose, he said, that "I should take your suggestion . . . The men would have no rations and would be under no discipline . . . they would have to plunder and rob . . . the country would be full of lawless bands . . . and a state of society would ensue from which it would take the country years to recover. Then the enemy's cavalry would pursue . . . and wherever they went there would be fresh rapine and destruction.

"No," the old general said. "We have now simply to look the fact in the face that the Confederacy has failed." The men should "quietly and quickly" go home, "plant crops and begin to repair the ravages of war." As for himself, "you young men might afford to go bush-whacking [but] the only proper and dignified course for me would be to surrender myself and take the consequences."

Thus did Robert E. Lee, revered for his leadership in war, make perhaps his greatest contribution—to peace. He spared the country the divisive guerrilla warfare that undoubtedly would have resulted from Alexander's despairing idea—a mean and destructive struggle that would have delayed national reconciliation for years to come.

❖ *Tom Wicker, a former columnist for the* New York Times, *is the author of several historical novels.*

ROBERT COWLEY

THE WHAT IFs OF 1914

The World War That Should Never Have Been

The conventional, and lasting, impression most of us have of World War I is the lethal stasis of the Western Front trenches. But we can now see that many questions about the kind of war it would be had been answered by the time the first trenches were dug in the fall of 1914, a time that was in fact consumed by movement and maneuver. The trenches merely ratified what the events of the first months had largely decided, pointing the century in a direction that seemed unthinkable when the year began.

Those first months of the war in 1914 reveal all manner of counterfactual outcomes. What would have happened if Great Britain had stayed out of the war? Could Germany have won? And might the world have been the better for a German victory? Could the war have ended about the time Europeans originally thought it would be over: before the leaves fell? What if the United States had never been drawn in? What would our century have been like without World War I—or with a smaller and shortened version that involved only continental powers? Most important: Did the war have to become a world war?

Even as one century ends and another begins, we are still haunted by the traumas of those years, traumas that would forever alter the balance of world power and permanently influence the way we live. What would a world without those traumas have been like? History, to paraphrase James Joyce, is a nightmare from which we are trying to awaken.

✦ *Robert Cowley, the founding editor of* MHQ: THE QUARTERLY JOURNAL OF MILITARY HISTORY *and the editor of this book, is an authority on World War I. With Geoffrey Parker, he edited* THE READER'S COMPANION TO MILITARY HISTORY.

I t was the worst of wars in the best of times. "The First World War was a tragic and unnecessary conflict," says the opening sentence of John Keegan's book on the Great War—as it was known until a greater one came along. "It was nothing less than the greatest error of modern history," says the last of Niall Ferguson's *The Pity of War.* As we approach the millennium and the end of a century of almost nonstop violence, this assessment increasingly prevails.

Could the First World War have been avoided? Could it have been confined to a scale that was not worldwide in its events and its influence? Could it have been shorter by years, with the saving of millions of lives? And could our century's saddest story have had a different ending?

To each question except, probably, the first the answer has to be yes. Some kind of outbreak was bound to happen: People then did not think in terms of extended cold wars. The nations of Europe had spent too long in dangerous opposition; the habit of diplomatic risk-taking, of violence barely suppressed that manifested itself in the arms race, was too ingrained. The conflict of nationalisms, the competition for markets and colonies, the clash of strategic agendas and hegemonic aspirations would not be denied. The war to come became an accepted part of European fantasy life; it obsessed popular literature. The question was less whether a continental civil war—which is what was shaping up—would explode, than when it would happen, what form it would take, and who would emerge on top. The basic underpinnings of European society, with its colonial extensions, would surely remain unchanged: Few doubted that victory would be worth the briefly maximum effort. And fewer still imagined that the convulsion would be so enormous and all-consuming, or would last so long and change so much. That is where error and miscalculation—often needless and repeated—came in.

THE CONSEQUENCE OF GERMAN VICTORY, 1914

North Sea

BRITAIN

Amsterdam
The Hague
Rotterdam
Arnhem

Zeebrugge
Ostend
HOLLAND

Dover
Dunkirk
GERMANY

Calais
Bruges
Antwerp
Düsseldorf

Boulogne
Ypres
Brussels
Cologne

Montreuil
Lille
BELGIUM
Maastricht

Arras
Namur
Liège

Cambrai
Coblenz

Maubeuge

FRANCE
LUXEMBOURG
Trier

Sedan

Rheims
Verdun
Saarbrücken   Speyer

Paris

Alsace-Lorraine

Toul
Nancy   Strassburg

Epinal

Mulhouse

Belfort

Territory to be annexed outright in the event
of a German victory

Future possible annexations to be obtained at
the Peace Conference

The "Tributary State" of Flanders-Wallonia, to
be under German political and economic
supervision

"Strongpoints," or fortified towns, to be under
German control

Area to come within a German Customs
Union, and to subordinate its economic life
to that of Germany

Western boundary of German strategic
control, within which the existing French
fortresses were to be dismantled

©1999 *Jeffrey L. Ward*

Based on a map in *Atlas of World War I, Second Edition* by Martin Gilbert.
©1970, 1994 by Martin Gilbert. Used by permission of Oxford University Press, Inc.

If there is a great divide in modern history, it has to be the First World War. But that historical divide did not have to be one. The war might have proved great, but it did not have to turn into a world war—as recent historians, most notably Ferguson, have begun to maintain. That metamorphosis is the key to much of what follows. If England had stayed out, or delayed its involvement, the struggle on the continent might well have been suspended by mutual agreement of the combatants toward the end of 1914—not long after the leaves fell. Germany could have won on points, as it were, maintaining a dominant position on the continent, first among nominal equals—while the decline of the British Empire might have been postponed for decades. "The American Century," which really dates from our involvement in the First World War, might also have been postponed. Would Communism have prevailed in Russia? Probably not. And if there had been no real First *World* War—the emphasis on "World" is deliberate—could there have been a Second, with its atomic conclusion? (Given humankind's prurient hanker for extreme military solutions, the Bomb, was bound to have been dropped sooner or later.)

Let us now consider several alternative scenarios, all of which might have denied these results—though no doubt bringing about others that we cannot even dream of.

England Stays Out

As the continental storm gathered in the last week of July 1914, and the major powers edged toward mobilization, the likelihood that Great Britain would go to war was slight. France, indeed, was pressuring it to make a commitment against the Central Powers. But since the defeat of Napoleon, Britain had deliberately kept itself aloof from continental involvements, and this crisis seemed no different. European entanglements would only diminish Britain's worldwide influence, power, and economic predominance.

Though Austrian Archduke Franz Ferdinand and his wife were assassinated in Sarajevo on June 28, it was not until Friday, July 24 that the

Liberal government of Herbert Asquith held its first cabinet meeting of the month specifically to discuss foreign affairs. The principal concern that day, it should be noted, was Ireland and the continuing fracas over home rule, which was perceived as the most acute threat to the Asquith government. As the tedious afternoon meeting was about to break up, the foreign minister, Sir Edward Grey, asked the ministers to stay for a few minutes. The quiet, somewhat secretive widower, whose eyesight was failing, described in his perpetually tired voice the ultimatum that Austria-Hungary had just presented to the Serbian government, the alleged conspirator in the assassinations. The ultimatum was a clear assault on Serbian sovereignty; refusal would be grounds for war. But an attack on Serbia would draw in Austria's ally, Germany, on one side, and Serbia's ally, Russia, and Russia's ally, France, on the other. The ministers listened to Grey, and then went their weekend ways.

In a letter Asquith wrote that night, he spoke of a coming "Armageddon" on the continent. "Happily," he added, "there seems to be no reason why we should be anything more than spectators." As the new week began, and military timetables for mobilization now took precedence over the qualms of continental politicians, England hung back. On July 29, a Wednesday, Austrian artillery dug in on the right bank of the Danube and began to shell the Serbian capital, Belgrade. Grey, meanwhile, gave little hint to the Germans of his intentions—which they took as confirmation that Britain would not go to war if they went ahead with their long-planned sweep through Belgium and into France. The evidence seemed to indicate that Great Britain would maintain its traditional hands-off policy. Had not the chancellor of the exchequer, David Lloyd George, told Parliament the very day that the Austrians delivered their ultimatum to Serbia that England's relations with Germany had improved so markedly that he could foresee "substantial economy in naval expenditures"? Asquith recognized that the majority of his party wanted to steer clear of the approaching conflict—and, more to the immediate point, a majority of his Cabinet. To abandon neutrality now was to risk the fall of his government. Even as late as Friday, July 31—as Austria, Russia, Turkey, and France mobilized—Asquith was still planning to make a speech at Chester on the next morning, after which he would catch a train to spend the rest of the weekend with his friend, Lord Sheffield.

Recapitulating the chronology of those next days, you can almost believe—if only for a moment—that England will not budge from the sidelines. The 947,000 young men from Great Britain and the empire will not die: The bodies will not pile up on the wire of Thiepval or sink into the mud of Passchendaele. The war will be confined to the continent; it will not become a global affair, with India, Australia, South Africa, and Canada involved. The United States, too, will stay out: Its minorities and majorities may root for one side or the other but its love/hate relationship with England will not be replaced by the alliance that has proved the most enduring strategic tryst of the century. The empire will not need us. Its strength undepleted by a war in which it played little part, it will remain the dominant presence on the globe far beyond 1945—a date that will have no special meaning in history.

But Asquith never made it to Chester for his date with Lord Sheffield and Great Britain did go to war on the evening of August 4, eleven days after Grey first broached the news of the Austrian ultimatum. The weekend still belonged to the antiwar faction. On Saturday morning, August 1, Grey had to report to the French ambassador, "We could not propose at this moment to send an expeditionary military force to the continent." He was convinced that any guarantee to France would cause the Cabinet to break up. Meanwhile, Germany began to mobilize. Financial panic swept the city. The Cabinet held crisis meetings. It seemed to be leaning toward a declaration of neutrality—which was only prevented by Grey's threat to resign. If neutrality was the government's position, he did not feel that he could support it. Over billiards, the hawkish young first lord of the admiralty, Winston Churchill, did persuade Asquith to mobilize the navy, as a protective measure: They had just learned of Germany's declaration of war against Russia. That same evening, in a mix-up, German troops marched into Luxembourg, and then retreated: The full-fledged invasion had to wait for the next day. ("A question has haunted the annals of history ever since," Barbara Tuchman writes. "What ifs might have followed if the Germans had gone east in 1914 while remaining on the defensive against France?")

Two Cabinet meetings took place that Sunday, and right until the second adjourned at 8:30 in the evening, Asquith's government seemed ready to fall. This is the possibility that tantalizes—no, agonizes—us. Four ministers offered their resignations, and if one magnetic individual among the undecideds—Lloyd George is the most likely candidate—had come forward to lead, more surely would have followed him. But Lloyd George himself wavered and instead pleaded with the resigners to hold off making their decision public.

A night's sleep, apparently, did wonders for belligerence   that, and a big assist from the Germans. On Monday morning, August 3, a bank holiday, Asquith learned of their ultimatum to Belgium, demanding the unopposed passage of the thirty-four divisions of General Alexander von Kluck's First Army. It could not have come at a worse moment. The idea that 400,000 German troops would be marching not just through a corner of Belgium but the whole country suddenly brought home the threat to England: Surely the French Channel ports of Calais and Boulogne would be menaced. And the kaiser's legions would be less than thirty miles away. Abruptly, the momentum began to swing toward war. Crowds waving small Union Jacks gathered from Trafalgar Square to the Houses of Parliament. The German ultimatum apparently came as something of a relief to the vacillating Asquith, who feared that nonintervention would cause a split in his government more intractable than intervention. The door was open for a Tory takeover—and, indeed, Churchill had already made discreet overtures to the Conservative Party. If too many members of Asquith's cabinet resigned, Churchill asked, would the opposition "be prepared to come to the rescue of the Government . . . by forming a Coalition"? (In the end only two ministers did resign.) As happened too often in those days of crisis in both England and the continent, politicians seemed more afraid of what would happen to them if they *didn't* go to war than if they did. That afternoon, in the House of Commons, Grey rose to speak for the Government. "Today," he began, "it is clear that the peace of Europe cannot be preserved . . ."

By the end of the next day, England was at war. But what would have happened if there had been wholesale resignations and the Asquith government had fallen?

Even if it had been replaced by a Coalition government that favored going to war, a delay of a week or more would have changed everything. There would have been no rearguard actions at Mons or Le Cateau, where the British Expeditionary Force (BEF) were blooded in the first encounters with a continental enemy since the Crimean War. And England might have hesitated to send the 80,000 men and 30,000 horses of its tiny army, concentrating instead on closing the sea approaches to Germany. If, on the other hand, new elections were called, the decision to go to war would have been put off until the fall. How could there have been a declaration of war *before* a general election? (Also, as it became obvious that the German wheel was not immediately menacing the channel ports, the demand for action might have been defused.)

Even without British help, the French may have been able to stop the Germans. You can debate that outcome endlessly. Their *élan* had not yet been sapped (as it would be in 1915, after the slaughters of the Artois and Champagne). And for all the general officers who were *limogés*— fired and sent back to the garrison town of Limoges—there were good commanders on the rise, men like Ferdinand Foch and Louis Félix François Franchet d'Esperey, who were more than a match for their German opposites. The French army was better than most people think, despite its cruel early setbacks. England may only have joined the war when the Germans actually did come close to taking the channel ports, later in the fall. But by that time the possibility of a deal may have surfaced, and one we shall presently consider.

Still, the outcome of the war may have been ordained that Tuesday night. Germany could probably win a continental war; it could not win a world war. But Germany would not begin to feel the weight of world involvement until later in the fall. Time, for the moment, was on its side.

Germany Wins the Marne . . . If There Is a Marne

The novelist John Bayley speaks of "the non-inevitability of events that we nevertheless know are bound to come." That was true about Great Britain's entry into the war—and it may have been even more so about the next major episode in Western Europe that summer. It's easy to view the confused series of actions, large and small, that go under the rubric "Battle of the Marne," as a clash of vast impersonal forces (and, at the start, rather equal ones), a collision of momentums. But in fact few events have so turned on command decisions, and on the frailties (more often than the strengths) of the men who made them, many of whom were in their mid- to late-sixties.

With notable exceptions, energy was in short supply among the generals of both sides. And command energy was precisely the ingredient needed for such a nonstop operational confrontation (what we used to call a campaign), whose results in those first wild days of war were often decided far behind the lines. But right up until the final days of the Marne, when forces began linking up and troops dug the first trenches, you cannot really speak of lines. Fronts were established, only to disintegrate bloodily. Combat became a struggle of perpendiculars rather than horizontals, of endless dusty marching columns probing for flanks to turn or gaps to enter—while other marchers retreated in equally long lines from the probers. There were times when opposing divisions marched parallel to one another. In the month that the Marne lasted, the two sides covered an average of 12.5 miles per day. This was not World War I as we now think of it. Generals, who rarely stayed put themselves, had all they could do to keep in touch with their own men, let alone the enemy. No one was more in the dark than the staffs of the highest commands, the German OHL and the French GQG.

If the long marches had gone as originally planned, Germany could have won. It should have won, and thus spared us many of the agonies of the next eighty-five years.

The unbroken string of German triumphs in August 1914 reminds you of the opening days of Barbarossa a generation later: Paris, whose northern outskirts were explored by cavalry patrols, could have been the chimeric Moscow. The wide enveloping movement of the Schlieffen Plan—named after its originator, Count Alfred von Schlieffen—with its weight concentrated in its right wing, swung through Belgium and hammered down to the plains of northern France: On a map, its legs, each belonging to an army, extend like those of a giant crab—a kaiser crab, as it were. The French, preoccupied with their own offensive Plan 17, a battering ram aimed at the German border—and beyond it, the Rhine and its industrial centers—were caught off guard. By the time they began to shift their forces westward, it was almost too late.

The twelve supposedly impregnable forts circling the Belgium border city of Liège were the first to fall, pounded to submission by the monster howitzers of Krupp and Skoda. Brussels fell without a struggle. Meanwhile, the French, paying little heed to the unfolding disaster, attacked from the Ardennes to Lorraine: The Battle of the Frontiers, which lasted for eleven days in the middle of August, cost them an estimated 300,000 men. When a French army finally did advance into Belgium, it was nearly overwhelmed in the Battle of Charleroi (August 22–23). Another of the Belgian fortress cities, Namur, surrendered on the twenty-third, the same day that the tiny British army, then just five divisions strong, made its vain, valiant, delaying action along the canal and the slag heaps of Mons. They managed to check the German advance in their sector by a single day. On August 24, that advance reached, and crossed, the borders of France itself, only hours behind the Schlieffen Plan's tightly mandated schedule.

It is at this point that we arrive at a historical crossroads. Suddenly, as Winston Churchill wrote in his account of the Marne, "The terrible ifs accumulate." The next nine days—August 24 to September 1—would be crucial, and they probably decided the outcome of the war. Had the German victories up to now been too easy, the scythelike sweep of their seven armies in the West too seemingly invincible?

Remember that the original plan called for the right wing to deliver the killing punch: The tip of the scythe always cuts the most hay. Legend has it that in 1913, as Schlieffen lay dying, his last words were, "Make the right wing strong!" The place of honor went to the German First Army, commanded by General von Kluck, who was the best general Germany then had in the West. While the other armies pressed southward, his assigned task was to sweep in a semicircle around Paris, to net the French in a great trap. According to the German scheme, carefully worked out and elaborated for years, a decision would be achieved by the thirty-ninth day of battle.

But Schlieffen's successor as chief of staff, Helmuth von Moltke, the nephew and namesake of the great Moltke, military mastermind of the three wars that had made Germany a nation two generations earlier, had already begun to make alterations in the plan. "Gloomy Julius," as he was called behind his wide back, never ceased worrying about the Russian threat. Long before the war started, he moved four and a half corps, 180,000 men, to the East; all came for the right-wing armies. He wondered if he had done enough. He also worried, as his predecessor had not, about a French advance into Germany. Schlieffen's notion was to let the French gobble up as much territory as they could: They would simply be caught in a sack, making their destruction that much easier. But pride dictated to Moltke that as little German soil as possible be surrendered, even for the best strategic reasons. So he strengthened his left wing, again at the expense of the right. Finally, Schlieffen's plan called for clipping through of the poodle tail of Holland around Maastricht. That would have alleviated the awkward squeezing of the two right-wing armies in Belgium at the beginning of the campaign and would have made possible a wider swing. The army of the far right—Kluck's—would have reached the channel and enveloped Lille before heading south to Paris. Strangely, Moltke the Younger had ethical qualms about violating Dutch neutrality.

Had he adhered to Schlieffen's bold amoral scheme, there would have been no "race to the sea" that followed the Marne—and, needless to say, no Ypres. The channel ports of Dunkirk, Calais, and Boulogne would have belonged to the conquerors. Though the German military did worry about the possibility of a blockade by the British navy, it discounted the ability of the British army to influence outcomes.

Those decisions weakened the German effort, but not fatally. Moltke was uncomfortable taking the kind of risks Schlieffen endorsed. Only risks, as it proved, could have won him a war. The one he did take, on August 22, was the wrong one at the wrong time. But then it did not even seem a risk when he took it—if anything, a stroke of unaccustomed brilliance and one that would forever put his stamp on the brief and glorious campaign to finish off France once and for all.

On August 14, in the opening salvo of Plan 17, the French had crossed into Lorraine, one of the provinces lost to Germany in 1871. Bands struck up the *Marseillaise* as the troops in the lead tore down the striped posts that marked the boundary. The French advanced; the Germans retreated, with only a mild show of resistance. The sack yawned invitingly. So far everything followed the Schlieffen script, a bit like a game of *Kriegspiel*.

On the nineteenth and twentieth, around the towns of Sarrebourg and Morhange, the invaders abruptly came up against prepared defenses—the trenches, barbed wire, and concealed machine-gun nests that would soon become the basic stuff of the Western Front. The Germans literally mowed down the French infantry in swathes, and then followed up with attack after attack on the reeling enemy. The French broke, streaming back to fortified positions on the ridges around Nancy—the Grand Couronné—from which they had started a week earlier. (There was momentary talk of abandoning Nancy: The French supreme commander, General Joseph Joffre, wouldn't hear of it.) Meanwhile, the Germans, initially slow in pursuit, now saw a matchless opportunity of their own.

Much of what follows took place not on the battlefield but on the telephone, and this may be the first time in history that the device assumes the role of a major counterfactual *deus ex machina*. As reports of the French debacle in Lorraine deluged the temporary OHL headquarters in the Rhine city of Coblenz, what military sugarplums danced in Moltke's head? Did it seem to him that the war in the West was as good as over? Should he exploit success to strike while French forces were on the verge of disintegration? Could he afford to lose the opportunity? A direct attack on the heights around Nancy and the fortress systems of Épinal and Toul would violate the Schlieffen scheme but the result might be another Cannae. Great pincers would squeeze the entire French line from both left and right, duplicating the model of Hannibal's legendary double envelopment of the Romans in 216 B.C. That was an August battle, too.

OHL was already discussing the idea on August 22 when a call came in from General Krafft von Dellmensingen, the chief of staff of the German Sixth Army, victors at Morhange. He was pressing for permission to finish off the French, and the sooner the better.

"Moltke hasn't decided yet," the OHL's chief of operations, a Colonel Tappen, told Krafft. "If you hold the line for five minutes I may be able to give you the orders you want."

It didn't take that long. A couple of minutes later, Tappen was back on the line with Moltke's decision: "Pursue direction Épinal."

Gone was Schlieffen's sack. Gone were the two to three corps—as many as 100,000 men—who might have reinforced the right wing when they were most needed. The rolling stock held in readiness in the Lorraine sector could have moved them west in a matter of days. Though we will never know the final casualty figures, which increasingly the German high command began to conceal, the battles around the Grand Couronné were apparently a disaster as great as Morhange had been for the French. Entrenched on steep commanding ridges, French troops hurled fire on the tight German waves as they attempted to cross the plains below. This time it was Moltke who had been drawn into a sack. And it was Joffre who, long before the battles died down on September 10, felt confident enough to remove whole divisions from the Grand Couronné and send them westward, to help tip the balance of the Marne.

But even after Moltke had made his spur-of-the-moment command to "pursue direction Épinal," a German victory was not just possible but still probable. Then, four days later, there would come another of those history-altering phone calls.

The Russians, who had mobilized with a speed that surprised OHL, had invaded East Prussia—territory that now belongs to Poland—and as German refugees swarmed back, panic began to spread. Brigadier General Erich Ludendorff, the hero of Liège, was now the chief of staff of the German Eighth Army, joining General Paul von Hindenberg; a famous military partnership was born. Already the two men felt that they had blunted the Russian thrust—and were in fact on the verge of the epic German victory of the Great War, Tannenberg.

On the night of August 26, at his headquarters in East Prussia, Ludendorff received a call from Colbenz: Once more it was Colonel Tappen on the other end. He told a surprised Ludendorff that he was sending three corps and a cavalry division as reinforcements. Ludendorff replied that they weren't needed—and besides, they could not possibly arrive soon enough to affect the battle in progress. Tappen said that Moltke was adamant, and that was that. Two nights later another call came in: The troops were on their way, but there would be only two corps plus the cavalry. To that extent wiser heads had prevailed. That meant that 80,000 more men would not be available to bolster the right wing. (As Ludendorff had predicted, the two corps arrived days after the Russians had been destroyed. Just before he died in 1916, Moltke, truly a broken man, would concede that the dispatch eastward of those two corps was his biggest mistake on the Marne.) There were now at least four corps unavailable to reinforce the most sensitive part of the operation. Add two more to that number: One corps detached from Kluck's army to guard the Belgians holed up in Antwerp and a second assigned to reduce the French fortress of Mauberge, on the Belgian border. That was a total of six corps, or upward of 250,000 men, the equivalent of an entire army.

Three telephone calls had changed everything. The first two may have thrown victory away; the third, an afterthought, at best assured stalemate. The decision in front of Nancy, which involved more men and saw a fundamental change, not just a weakening, in the Schlieffen Plan did the greatest damage to German hopes. (The Grand Couronné may be the most important overlooked battle in history.) If Moltke had not gone for a Cannae, that peculiarly German military obsession, and had reinforced the right wing instead, Kluck's First Army could have continued its hook around Paris, skirting the forts to the west and south of the city, and then turning north again in a grand knockout blow. Other than the fortress garrisons and the jury-rigged army then being assembled in Paris, there was no substantial force to dispute Kluck's progress through the countryside. Already the French government was preparing to flee to Bordeaux, and it was clear that France could not take many more reverses. The rope, stretched to the limit and beyond, threatened to snap. Would the scenario of 1870 to 1871, with its collapse and revolution, repeat itself?

Speed was essential for the Germans. The enemy must not be given a chance to recover. A victorious army can overlook fatigue—and both officers and men of Kluck's army were very tired indeed. The lean meanness of the German command was beginning to create unnecessary stress. With too few in charge forced for too long to work twenty-hour days, details were falling between the cracks. "In war as in business," the military historian Dennis E. Showalter points out, "there is a certain advantage to redundancy." Moreover, in the absence of rail lines—destroyed by the retreating French and Belgians—and reliable motor transport, supplying men with food and ammunition was a problem, and only became more so as distances increased. Communications, too, were strained. Once in French territory, army commands could not depend on the telephone. Moltke, far away in Coblenz and then, after August 29, in Luxembourg

276

City, mainly used the wireless to communicate with the Western armies—though messages were delayed by congestion at the other end (and by the time needed to decode them) or interfered with by a French station on the Eiffel Tower. Schlieffen's thirty-nine days after mobilization would come none too soon.

Let us imagine, then, that Moltke had not only managed to restrain himself after Morhange but, at the last moment had decided not to send the two corps eastward. What might have happened next? Kluck's reinforced progress continues. The forts of Verdun are surrounded—that nearly did happen at the beginning of September—and neutralized. Rheims falls—it actually was occupied briefly. And now the German center armies turn to meet Kluck's right uppercut. Moltke gets his Cannae after all. The chances are that the truly decisive battle of the war might have been fought in the Seine Valley, southeast of Paris, perhaps in the gently wooded region around Fontainebleau, so favored by generations of French artists. The scenic oils this time would have been painted by Germans.

That is the best-case scenario for the kaiser's armies in the West. Great Britain's brief contribution to the fighting would prove largely irrelevant. The war would remain a continental affair, though it would not make relations between Britain and Germany easier—especially if the Germans insisted on turning the channel ports into fortified enclaves. Meanwhile a bit more of France, including Nancy, and some of Belgium would be incorporated into the Reich. Historians like Niall Ferguson have suggested that Germany would have initiated a Central European Economics Union (which it would dominate—a bit as it has done with the EEC at the turn of the new century). France would pay huge reparations, enough to keep it underarmed and angry for another generation. Anti-Semitism, ever the bane of defeated European nations, would become a problem for it and not for Germany. There is a brighter side, though, beyond the survival of the million Frenchmen who otherwise would die in the next four years (not to mention many of the best and brightest of the other combatants). Victory in World War I hid France's backwardness. Perhaps the nation would not have been doomed to "the long nineteenth century" that only ended after another world war and a four-year-long German occupation. Perhaps the economic renaissance of that second postwar era would have been forced on it earlier.

If the Lost Map Hadn't Been Lost and If Sir John Had Taken French Leave

Could Germany still have won the battle for France at this point? Perhaps—though its options were narrowing, and increasingly the outcome depended on the actions (and reactions) of the other side. Would the French break, as they did a generation later? There were instances those days of retreat turning into panic, in which not even gun-wielding officers could stop the rush to the rear. Bands of deserters roamed the country, pillaging. A million people, a third of the population of Paris, had fled the capital, along with the government. General Joseph Gallieni, the military governor of Paris, was prepared to reduce the city to a shell if the Germans fought their way into it. He would order the dynamiting of all bridges across the Seine; not even the Eiffel Tower would be spared. The perception of catastrophe distorted the reality. That was the real danger. One more defeat might prove fatal. At the moment the French thought they were experiencing the worst, the worst was in fact over.

On August 30, Kluck made his famous decision to wheel his columns to the east of Paris. The Schlieffen Plan was all but discarded now. Kluck hoped to take by forced marches the flank of the French fleeing in front of him. He also worried about leaving a gap between his army and the German Second Army to his left, which he surely would have done if he had continued on his original course. He paid little or no heed to a new danger: General Michel-Joseph Maunoury's Sixth Army being cobbled together in Paris. The French, for their part, still assumed that Kluck's army had not changed direction. It was at this point that chance, that great leveler of historical forces, intervened.

We have now arrived at September 1, 1914, which has to be another of the counterfactual crossroads of the Marne. Late in the day, a German dispatch car ran into a French patrol in the forested country near Coucy-le-Château, an area dominated by the huge medieval castle of the Lords of Coucy. (In an act of cultural desecration, the Germans would blow it up during their retreat in 1917.) The patrol opened fire, killing everyone in the car. Among the dead was a cavalry officer who carried a saddlebag filled with food, clothing, and papers, all splashed with his blood. When French intelligence officers emptied the bag, they discovered a map. Under more bloodstains they could see numbers and pencil lines—the numbers belonging to corps in Kluck's army and the lines indicating the change of direction, to the southeast.

It was a loss that was as potentially devastating as the loss of Robert E. Lee's Special Orders No. 191 before Antietam. The French could plainly see not only where Kluck was headed but the flank that he offered them. Air reconnaissance and radio intercepts confirmed the map's revelation. When the Sixth Army did smash into that flank on September 5, it ended Kluck's hope of victory. It was all he could do to survive. The able Kluck did, by prodigies of maneuver, successfully defend the flank—but in doing so he created a worse problem for himself. We'll get to that in a moment. If the map had not been lost, Kluck might have gained a couple of precious extra days. He might have been able to reverse his advance, which had gotten dangerously far ahead of the adjacent Second Army, and his survival would not have been so precarious. The lost map of Coucy-le-Château didn't cost the Germans the war in the West. Stalemate still would have resulted, but it would have been a stalemate far more favorable to them. A Paris that was twenty-odd miles distant would be much easier to reduce and capture than one that was eighty or a hundred, as it would be when the Westen Front began to firm up as a solid line days later. That nearness would have altered German operational choices in the months to come and might have meant that they would not have remained on the defensive for so much of the war in the West. Who knows? It might have been 1870 all over again, with Paris encircled, though history tends not to repeat itself. In a world where counterfactual scenarios are forever possible, humans are also forever condemned to make new mistakes, and the future to take unpredictable turns.

Accident is one thing; intent is another. September 1 saw the resolution of another might-have-been, and one potentially more damaging to the Allied cause than the Lost Map had been to the Germans. The commander of the British Expeditionary Force, Sir John French, had apparently given in to the general panic. From the beginning, the relationship of the little field marshal with his allies had been uneasy, and Sir John— who spoke only English—was deeply suspicious of their intentions. Would his troops be thrown, willy-nilly, into a sanguinary update of Plan 17? He was a man fatally afraid of being taken advantage of and now thought only of getting his army out of harm's way, with the least damage possible to his own reputation. Joffre, eager to stabilize his line at last, had met with his British opposite on August 29 and pleaded with him to hold fast. Sir John refused. He made it clear that his army, which had lost 15,000 men in a week of fighting retreat, now needed ten days out of the line in which to rest, reequip, and wait for reinforcements. Managing to contain his rage, Joffre thanked Sir John. This not only meant that his retirement would have to continue, but that he faced the prospect of a gap opening in his line. Even entreaties by the president of France, Raymond Poincaré, to the British ambassador, and passed on to Sir John, failed to budge him. French had, in fact, told his officers to prepare for a "definite and prolonged retreat due south, passing Paris to the east and west." Moreover, he was floating an even more ominous trial balloon: withdrawal to the British base—which was then the port of Saint-Nazaire, at the mouth of the Loire. There was talk of reembarking the army for England, with the idea of landing on the continent and resuming the war later in the fall—if, that is, there still was a war.

Back in London, the British secretary of state for war, Lord Kitchener, read French's telegrams with mounting dismay. On August 31, he telegraphed back to ask whether the contemplated withdrawal wouldn't leave a gap in the Allied line, causing the French to become fatally discouraged. There was a counterfactual ring to his words. Then he persuaded the prime minister to call an urgent Cabinet meeting. Sir John could not be allowed on his own to determine a matter of national policy, the military alliance with France. At this moment, the possibility of losing the war may never have seemed closer. Late that night, Sir John's reply to Kitchener's telegram came in: "I do not see why I should be called upon . . . to run the risk of absolute disaster . . ."

Kitchener, who was standing by as French's message was decoded, made up his mind. Asquith called another hasty Cabinet gathering and Churchill ordered the firing up of a fast cruiser at Dover. Kitchener left London in the middle of the night and was in Paris by midday on September 1. He arrived at the British embassy wearing his blue field marshal's uniform—which the supersensitive French immediately took as an insult. Was Kitchener, who did not outrank him, trying to pull rank? French immediately complained about being called away from his headquarters "at so critical a time." There were others present at the meeting, but the tone of the discussion soon grew heated, and the two field marshals went into another room and presumably closed the door. Somehow, an agreement was struck: French's troops would return to the fighting line, where they would remain "conforming to the movements of the French army." French left in a huff, but Kitchener had accomplished his mission.

What if Sir John French had taken his troops out of the line and marched them to Saint-Nazaire, some 250 miles away? The notion that they would have been refitted, reinforced, and readied back in England for new service on the continent is preposterous. The chances are that British troops never would have returned—and it's hard to see how the political leaders, whoever they now were, would have dealt with a fading war spirit that, like a siren, had been recently cranked up to such a high pitch. Certainly the Asquith government could not have survived (though the empire would have profited in the long run). What would the brief ignominious role of the British have done to relations with France over the next decade or more? France may have become the loser because of it. A British withdrawal that came at the worst psychological moment—which September 1 was—might have made all the difference. How could France ever forgive Great Britain's desertion? Put it another way: Sir John's failure of nerve could have handed Germany its last chance to win the war in the West. Better that England had never become involved in the first place.

There was a sequel. Kluck, we remember, had brilliantly parried the thrust of Maunoury's Sixth Army in what came to be known as the Battle of the Ourcq. The taxis of the Marne notwithstanding—they did transport needed men from Paris—Kluck actually had the upper hand in that part of the vast Marne encounter that sprawled for five days along a 200-mile front. But to do so, he was forced to borrow the two corps that had filled the space between his First Army and Karl von Bülow's Second. He thought he could get away with it, and he nearly did. But on the last day of the Marne, the British Army, about the size of those two German corps now detraining in East Prussia, marched into the thirty-mile gap. Though it penetrated only a few miles, it had, as Winston Churchill wrote, "probed its way into the German liver." Flanks were threatened; the Germans panicked. Soon retreat spread along the entire front. The first trenches were dug. The original invasion plan called for a decision between September 6 and September 9—the thirty-sixth to the thirty-ninth day after mobilization. That happened, but not the way the Germans expected. Churchill invoked the words of the Roman emperor Caesar Augustus when he learned of the massacre of his legions in the Teutoburg Forest 1900 years earlier: "Well might the kaiser have exclaimed, 'Moltke, Moltke, give me back my legions!'"

The Brigadier and the Private

This story involves two people who never met, a British officer and a common soldier in the German army. But their lives may have touched on 1914's terminal day of crisis, October 31. In one case, history might have changed; in the other, it did.

In the weeks that followed the Marne, the opposing armies marched and fought their way northward on parallel courses, each trying without success to outflank the other. "The race to the sea" left only stalemate in its wake, as the line closed behind it. By late October, the one remaining opening, which the Allies were fast plugging, presented itself around the Belgian town of Ypres, a little more than ten miles from Dunkirk and the North Sea. Around a narrow and ever-constricting salient, there took place the year's final desperate battle.

For the Germans, a breakout at Ypres offered the prospect of the last great prizes of 1914: The channel ports of Dunkirk, Calais, and Boulogne. Their capture would not only neutralize the channel but would lengthen and otherwise inconvenience the passage of troops and materiel from England to France—if much of a British army existed after a defeat at Ypres. (Sir John French was once again seriously contemplating evacuation; but now it was Joffre who emphatically vetoed the idea.) For the second time in two months, Great Britain's contribution was at risk—though at this point the French were better able to carry on without their ally. But beyond those considerations, the bagging of the channel ports would give a tremendous boost to morale back home: The German people would have something to show for their futile and costly exertions in the West.

After twelve days in which wave after wave of German attacks broke on the thinning lines of French and British defenders, a decision seemed at hand. It happened at a place called Gheluvelt, a cluster of brick buildings on a ridge five miles to the east of Ypres. Shortly before noon on October 31, the British line here disintegrated. The defenders were outnumbered by as much as ten to one, and ill-trained but fanatically eager German reserves swept over them. A breach a mile wide opened. All it would take was for the ample reinforcements close at hand to burst through and spread out fanwise, destroying whatever remained of British cohesion. But the German troops stopped to wait for orders. None came. The early afternoon found 1,200 men, many belonging to the 16th

Bavarian Reserve Regiment, milling around the grounds of a nearby château and doing a bit of looting. But sooner or later that afternoon, the staffs would get it together, orders would go out, and those troops—and thousands more—would begin their inexorable progress forward.

Meanwhile, in a woods about a mile away, a British brigadier made a decision that quite possibly altered the course of the war. He was named Charles Fitzclarence, and he was obviously destined for greater things if a bullet hadn't permanently interrupted his career a few days later. Fitzclarence, who learned about the disaster at Gheluvelt from stragglers, rounded up the only reserves he could find, some 370 men from the 2nd Worcester Battalion, and sent them forward over a mile of undulating pasture. German artillery caught them in the open, killing or wounding more than a quarter of their number; but still they went forward. The Worcesters crashed onto the lawn of the Gheluvelt château, scattering the Bavarians. They rooted them out of hedges and fired at their receding backs. That ended the German advance. The gap to Dunkirk was plugged. Thanks to the brigadier, Great Britain would hold that day—and would stay in the war that bankrupted it.

There is a final circumstance, which no historian seems to have pointed out. Of the hundreds of Bavarians flushed out of the chateau grounds, one may have been a private from Austria, lately removed to Munich—Adolf Hitler. Two days earlier he had gone into action with the 16th Bavarian Reserve Regiment, which had taken terrible losses. Those men at the château pretty much represented what was left of its combat strength. Given Hitler's almost magnetic attraction to a fight, it's hard to think that he wasn't there. But German memoirs and regimental histories are silent on the episode. They neither seem to recognize, nor to admit, how close the Germans were to a breakthrough that day, nor do they mention the debacle at the chateau. That would hardly have suited history as propounded by the Nazis, and especially history that involved their own führer. But what if Hitler had been cut down in flight, or captured? History—the real version—would have been deprived of one of its true monsters. In this case, we hardly need to elaborate on the calamities that a single bullet might have denied.

That possibility has to be the most intriguing might-have-been of 1914.

Postscript: Falkenhayn's Despair

Immediately after the Battle of the Marne shut down, Moltke was removed—though for public relations reasons his successor, Erich von Falkenhayn, who was also the Prussian war minister, compelled him to remain at headquarters as titular chief of staff for another two humiliating months. But the new man hardly had better luck. On November 18, after the disaster of Ypres, Falkenhayn, deeply depressed, met in Berlin with the German chancellor, Theobald von Bethmann-Hollweg. He told Bethmann flatly that the war could no longer be won. He saw no way for Germany to reduce its adversaries "to such a point where we can come to a decent peace." If a negotiated settlement of some sort wasn't concluded soon, the country faced a dreary prospect: "The danger of slowly exhausting ourselves." Falkenhayn suggested overtures to Russia first, with no annexations asked. France, he was sure, would follow.

Bethmann-Hollweg turned him down. He was still convinced, he said, that Germany could, and would, win the war. Moreover, a deal with Russia and France would mean a deal with Great Britain—which, as the weeks passed, the Germans had come to regard as their real enemy, the true threat to their aspirations. Even as hostility toward England had undone Napoleon at Tilsit in 1805, so it would blind Germany in 1914. Can we extrapolate, too, a hint that Bethmann-Hollweg was afraid to face down what would surely be the blustering rage of the kaiser? Whatever his reasons, his refusal represented an irrevocable death sentence for a generation.

Soon the British Empire's legions would be arriving on the continent from the four corners of the globe. One naval battle had been fought just days before off the coast of Chile and in a few days to come, another would be fought off the Falkland Islands. In January, Turkey would briefly menace the linchpin of the British Empire, the Suez Canal—and would itself be invaded that next spring at Gallipoli. A German submarine would torpedo the liner *Luisitania*—now, there was a true accident of history—killing 128 Americans and guaranteeing the eventual entry into the war of the Great Neutral. Even as Falkenhayn made his vain pitch, the war was beginning to drag in the entire world. That day may have witnessed the last slim chance to halt its spread.

"A singular fact about modern war is that it takes charge," Bruce Catton notes. "Once begun it has to be carried to its conclusion, and carrying it there sets in motion events that may be beyond men's control. Doing what has to be done to win, men perform acts that alter the very soil in which society's roots are nourished."

Think what even a truncated war would have meant to the twentieth century. Let us say that German overtures to Russia had succeeded. Russian losses at the end of 1914, though substantial, were hardly crippling. Peace would have allowed its industrial economy, which was already showing signs of significant growth, to flourish; at the same time, some measure of democracy was taking hold. Lenin would have remained sulking in his impoverished Swiss exile: There would have been no German-arranged sealed train to carry him and his political pestilence to the Finland Station. It follows that without Lenin there would have been no Stalin, no purges, no gulags, no Cold War.

We have already considered Great Britain and France—but what of the United States? If an armistice had come at the end of 1914, our country would have remained for years what it was then: a crude, boisterous, and not always charming provincial cousin. No American boys would have crossed our Rubicon, the Atlantic. The question asked by the popular song was on the mark: "How're ya gonna keep 'em down on the farm, after they've seen Paree?" The "American Century" would have to wait, depending not on wars but on markets. The year 1918 would not have found the world's most powerful nation, Great Britain, deep in debt to us.

The long nineteenth century would surely have continued for decades, not only in France but everywhere. Europe would have retained its position of benignly condescending dominance. Take, for example, the world of letters. How much talent, barely revealed or never discovered, dissolved in the earth of all those obscenely neat Great War cemeteries? Alain-Fournier's novel *The Wanderer* or the poems of Wilfred Owen— both men gunshot victims—give us some indication of what we lost. Literary leadership was only ceded to America by the default of death. There would have been a Hemingway but no *Farewell to Arms*. "Troops went by the house and down the road and the dust they raised powdered the leaves of the trees . . ." Perhaps he would have found another way to deliver the most luminous opening paragraph of our century.

Without the events of 1914, we would have skipped a more sinister legacy, and one that has permanently scarred our lives: the brutalization that trench warfare, with its mass killings, visited on an entire generation. What men like Adolf Hitler learned in that first Holocaust, they would, as John Keegan has written, "repeat twenty years later in every corner of Europe. From their awful cult of death the continent is still recovering."

There are times when you can measure the lasting effects of a trauma only by imagining their absence.

BISMARCK'S EMPIRE: STILLBORN

"There is a dynasty on its way out," Bismarck remarked as he observed the retreat of Emperor Napoleon III after the defeat of the French army at Sedan on September 1, 1870. Less than two months later, French marshal François Achille Bazaine surrendered to the Prussians at Metz, with 6,000 officers and 173,000 men. Three months later, on January 18, 1871, the German empire was proclaimed in the Hall of Mirrors at Versailles.

The French defeat was not inevitable. The French armies were ample, and their equipment, in certain respects, was superior to that of the Prussians. The new French rifle, the chassepot, increased the number of rounds an infantryman could carry and substantially improved his range. The French also possessed the mitrailleuse, an early version of the machine gun, which carried a bundle of twenty-five barrels, each detonated by turning a handle. The French capitulation resulted very simply from poor leadership.

Holed up at Sedan and later at Metz, the famed *furia francese* was never unleashed. Even when the two German armies swept on and invested Paris under the direction of Graf Helmuth von Moltke, the French commander in the capital, with a larger force, showed himself paralyzed and allowed himself to be surrounded.

With Napoleon III nominally in command before Sedan, the French military was directionless. Had the French armies taken the offensive early, had they broken out of their fortresses, the Prussians might well have been stopped in their tracks, and the German empire, as we know it, would not have existed.

Without Bismarck's German empire, there would have been no Wilhelmine

Germany, no pursuit of power for its own sake, no French revanchism over Alsace-Lorraine, and no First World War. In which case, there would have been no Treaty of Versailles in 1919, no Second World War. Had there been no First World War, there would have been no Bolshevik Revolution, no Soviet Union, and therefore no Cold War. The course of history for the last 150 years, the horrors of the century of total war, our century, would have been irrevocably changed. Instead, an inept, posturing nephew of the greatest military commander in modern times became the unwitting destroyer of the primacy of Europe.

❖ *James Chace is the editor of the* World Journal *and professor of international relations at Bard College. He is the author of the biography,* ACHESON.

❖ DAVID CLAY LARGE ❖

THANKS, BUT NO CIGAR

One chilly November afternoon in 1889, a fur-coated crowd assembled in Berlin's Charlottenburg Race Course to enjoy a performance of Buffalo Bill's Wild West Show, which was touring Europe to great popular acclaim. Among the audience was the Reich's impetuous young ruler, Kaiser Wilhelm II, who had been on the throne for a year. Wilhelm was particularly keen to see the show's star attraction, Annie Oakley, famed throughout the world for her skills with a Colt .45.

On that day, as usual, Annie announced to the crowd that she would attempt to shoot the ashes from the cigar of some lady or gentleman in the audience. "Who shall volunteer to hold the cigar?" she asked. In fact, she expected no one from the crowd to volunteer; she had simply asked for laughs. Her long-suffering husband, Frank Butler, always stepped forward and offered himself as her human Havana-holder.

This time, however, Annie had no sooner made her announcement then Kaiser Wilhelm himself leaped out of the royal box and strutted into the arena. Annie was stunned and horrified but could not retract her dare without losing face. She paced off her usual distance while Wilhelm extracted a cigar from a gold case and lit it with a flourish. Several German policemen, suddenly realizing that this was not one of the kaiser's little jokes, tried to preempt the stunt, but were waved off by His All-Highest Majesty. Sweating profusely under her buckskin, and regretful that she had consumed more than her usual amount of whiskey the night before, Annie raised her Colt, took aim, and blew away Wilhelm's ashes.

Had the sharpshooter from Cincinnati creased the kaiser's head rather than his cigar, one of Europe's most ambitious and volatile rulers would have been removed from the scene. Germany might not have pursued its policy of aggressive Weltpolitik that culminated in war twenty-five years later.

Annie herself seemed to realize her mistake later on. After World War I began, she wrote to the kaiser asking for a second shot. He did not respond.

❖ *David Clay Large has just completed a history of the city of Berlin.*

❖ DENNIS E. SHOWALTER ❖

THE ARMISTICE OF DESPERATION

World War I is increasingly recognized as the defining event of the twentieth century, with its total wars, its genocides, its weapons of mass destruction. What might have resulted if the war had ended in a matter of weeks, as virtually all the experts predicted?

A quick decision would have had to come in the West, in 1914 the only possible theater for mass industrial war. The most plausible scenario begins with more aggressive leadership at all levels of the French and German armies. By the end of 1914, France had suffered almost a million casualties; German losses in the same period were around three-quarters of a million. These were the highest ratios of the whole war. What if generals and regimental officers had driven their men forward even more ruthlessly during the battles of the Frontier and on the Marne? What if the Germans had been even more willing to exchange lives for ground in the Ypres Salient?

This reaction fully accorded with existing doctrines of the offensive. It might have achieved some tactical victories—a more precipitate German retreat after the Marne, for example, or the capture of Ypres in a final desperate lunge. These victories, however, were unlikely to be exploited by their survivors. Attacks of this intensity instead would have depleted, perhaps exhausted, already limited ammunition reserves to a point that force more and more reliance on numbers that were vulnerable and courage that went unrequited. A 20 or 25 percent increase in casualty rates seems a reasonable immediate consequence in the battlefield environment of 1914. Administrative systems, particularly medical services, might have buckled under the strain, destabilizing the "cultures of competence" that hold armies together by regularly providing food, care, and mail. Morale in the line, at the rear, and on the home front was likely to waver, if not collapse, as losses increased exponentially with each week—to no end. Gridlock on the fighting line, revolution at home—such a sequence of events was in fact feared by prewar decision-makers. Facing its reality, the combatants might well have negotiated an armistice of desperation.

The titular "victor" is unimportant. Europe's great powers undertook World War I for negative, not positive, reasons. Even Germany's war aims in 1914 were a cobbled-together post facto shopping list. The scales of destruction and disorder accompanying a quick end to an unwanted apocalypse were likely to generate at all levels a renewed sense of Europe as a community—and a consequent sense of what it took to sustain that community. International order would be stabilized, with regional powers no longer given the kind of latitude the Balkan states enjoyed between 1911 and 1914. Germany and Russia in particular were likely to undertake domestic housecleanings. In the Second Reich, the diminished prestige of kaiser and army favored the introduction of a genuine parliamentary government. Russia, never suffering the exsanguination of 1915 to 1916, was in a position to continue its economic and political development.

As for Vladimir Lenin, in this alternate world he died an exile in Switzerland. Adolf Hitler became a familiar figure in Munich's bohemian circles. Picasso never created *Guernica*, and Albert Einstein spent a long and fruitful life as a physicist and philanthropist. It was a Europe safe for men with briefcases and potbellies, whose younger generations occasionally bemoaned its ordinariness. But while memories of the Six Months' War of 1914 to 1915 endured, older heads thanked God and the fates that they no longer lived in interesting times.

❖   *Dennis E. Showalter is professor of history at Colorado College and the president of The Society for Military History.*

JOHN KEEGAN

HOW HITLER COULD HAVE WON THE WAR

The Drive for the Middle East, 1941

A dolf Hitler may be the perfect example of how an individual with a genius for the main chance can—through determination close to madness, and more than a little luck—alter history. You can argue that if Hitler hadn't survived the First World War, someone else in a Germany ravaged by defeat, hyperinflation, and world depression, would inevitably have come forward to start the Second. In this deterministic view, people like Hitler are not causes but symptoms. But who? None of those around him had the same sort of evil charisma. The conditions he fed on may have been largely unavoidable but the Nazi revolution he created and led was not. Nor can a phenomenon so focused on one man and his whims evolve in a predictable pattern. Hitler's mind was a virtual Pandora's box of what ifs. Today we tend to forget how close he came to imposing his Triumph of the Will on much of the world: The scenario that John Keegan describes here could very well have happened. Hitler, like Napoleon, seriously contemplated a campaign through the Near East, following the route of another conqueror, Alexander the Great. In actuality, both Hitler and Napoleon came to fortunate grief in Russia. What if, in 1941, Hitler had put off *his invasion of the Soviet Union for a year and had gone for the prize that might have given him the edge against the beleaguered Allies: Middle Eastern oil?*

❖ *John Keegan, who spins the frightening possibility that follows, is one of our finest military historians, the author of such notable books as* THE FACE OF BATTLE, THE PRICE OF ADMIRALTY, *and, most recently,* THE FIRST WORLD WAR. *He is defense correspondent for the* DAILY TELEGRAPH *in London and in 1998 delivered the BBC's Reith Lectures.*

What if, in the summer of 1941, Hitler had chosen to make his major attack not into Soviet Russia but across the Eastern Mediterranean, into Syria and the Lebanon? Would he have avoided the defeat he suffered outside Moscow that winter? Might he have won a strategic position that would have brought him eventual victory?

The inducement was strong. Had he been able to solve the logistical difficulty of transferring an army from Greece to Vichy French Syria, he would then have been well placed to strike at northern Iraq, a major center of oil production, and thence at Iran, with even ampler oil reserves. The establishment of a strong military presence in northern Iran would have positioned his forces close to the Soviet Union's own oil production centers on the Caspian Sea, while a drive into Southern Iran would have given him possession of the Anglo-Iranian Oil Company's wells and vast refinery at Abadan. From eastern Iran, moreover, the route lay open toward Baluchistan, the westernmost province of British India, and thence to the Punjab and Delhi. The occupation of the Levant—Syria and Lebanon— would, in short, have placed him astride a network of strategic highways leading not only to the main centers of Middle Eastern oil supply but also to entry points giving onto the most important imperial possession of his last remaining European enemy, Britain, and also the southern provinces of his chosen ideological opponent, Stalin's Russia.

By the spring of 1941 Russia had become a strategic obsession to Hitler. After his defeat of France in 1940, he had, for a few weeks, persuaded himself that he could assure Germany's dominance of Europe by negotiating a peace with Britain. With Britain neutralized, he could have consolidated his military position and taken his time in choosing future strategic options. The defeat of the Soviet Union was foremost among them. In the aftermath of the French armistice in June, however, he did not expect to have to make an immediate call on his military resources. His appreciation of the situation was that Britain would, in a spirit of realism, accept that Nazi Germany enjoyed an unassailable superiority and consequently submit to its military dominance.

Churchill's refusal to admit realities, as seen from Berlin, and to persist in resistance, caused Hitler in July, even while he was committing the Luftwaffe to what would become known as the Battle of Britain, to reposition the ground forces of the Wehrmacht eastward, toward the new frontier of the Soviet Union as defined after its annexation of half of Poland in September 1939. At the same time, he reversed his recently taken decision to demobilize thirty-five of the infantry divisions that had fought in the Battle of France and to double the number of panzer divisions from ten to twenty. He also arranged for his war production office, during August, to select the site for a new führer headquarters in East Prussia, while in September his personal operational staff, OKW, submitted an outline plan, "Fritz" for "an offensive against the Soviet Union."

All these measures were, however, precautionary. He had certainly not yet firmly decided to attack Russia and was, indeed, still ready to negotiate an extension of the Ribbentrop-Molotov Pact of August 1939 for the further settlement of spheres of interest in Eastern Europe, as long as the terms were satisfactory to him. Molotov would come to Berlin in November to continue discussions. In the meantime, Hitler embarked on a program of diplomatic rather than military measures as a means of consolidating his power over Eastern Europe short of the Soviet border.

His instrument was the Tripartite Pact, signed between Germany, Italy, and Japan on September 27, 1940, binding any two to come to the aid of a third if it was attacked. The pact was not exclusive. Others might join and Hitler, in the autumn of 1940, decided that the uncommitted states of Central and southern Europe should. Hungary and Romania, both strongly anti-Russian and pro-German, and the puppet state of Slovakia signed, before the year was out. Pressure was then put on Bulgaria and Yugoslavia to join also, as they would the following March.

His Russian diplomacy worked less smoothly. Despite the evidence of Nazi Germany's military mastery over most of the continent and the strong suspicion that Stalin's military purges of 1937 to 1938 had gravely damaged the Red Army's fighting power, Stalin insisted upon treating Hitler as an equal throughout the complex second half of 1940. When Molotov, the Soviet foreign minister, arrived in Berlin on November 12, he proposed that the Soviet Union be allowed to annex Finland, as it already had the Baltic States, that it should guarantee Bulgaria's frontiers, despite already having taken a large slice of Bulgarian territory, that its rights of exit from the Black Sea to the Mediterranean, through the Turkish Bosphorus, should be enlarged, and that it should also be given new maritime rights in the Baltic. Hitler was outraged. When, after his departure, Molotov sent the draft of a treaty outlining Soviet requirements, Hitler order Ribbentrop to make no reply. Instead, on December 18, he signed the secret Führer Directive 21, which would become the blueprint for Operation Barbarossa, the invasion of Russia.

Between the inception of Barbarossa on June 22, 1941, and Hitler's rejection of Molotov's November proposals, many disturbing events were to intervene. To Hitler, the most irritating were those initiated by his fellow dictator, Benito Mussolini, in an attempt to establish Italy's claim to be Nazi Germany's equal as an actor on the stage of grand strategy. Mussolini had delayed his entry into the Second World War until the hard tasks in the West—the defeat of France, the expulsion of Britain from the continent—had been achieved. Mussolini had then struck easy victories. In September 1940, he invaded British Egypt from Libya. On October 28 he launched, from recently occupied Albania, an offensive into Greece, Britain's last ally on the European mainland. Both enterprises proved fiascoes. A British counteroffensive in December humiliated Italy's Libyan army, while the Greeks, outnumbered though they were, rapidly moved from defense to attack and, in a winter campaign, captured half of Albania from its Italian occupiers.

Worse was to follow. Having browbeaten the Yugoslav government of Prince Regent Paul to subscribe to the Tripartite Pact on March 25, the

Germans were confronted two days later by a patriotic military coup, which rejected the pact and made common cause with the British and Greeks, who were still united in opposition to the settlement of southern European affairs in Germany's favor. Hitler had, in February, been obliged to send troops to Italian Libya, the nucleus of the soon-to-be-famous Afrika Korps, under Erwin Rommel, to rescue the Italians from a worse defeat. He now decided to interrupt his deployment of forces for the inception of Barbarossa by instructing a subordinate operation, Marita, that would bring Yugoslavia and Greece under his complete control.

Marita was in part provoked by a British initiative. In November 1940, the Greek government, attacked by the Italians a week earlier, had accepted the deployment of R.A.F. squadrons to the Peloponnese. In March 1941, it went further. Even though it risked provoking Hitler, it agreed to welcome four British divisions, detached from the Western Desert Force in Libya, where they had recently taken part in Wavell's spectacular defeat of the Italians. The arrival of the British divisions on March 4 did indeed gall Hitler. It was also the development that encouraged the Yugoslav patriots to repudiate the Tripartite Pact, a bold but disastrous gesture. On April 6, Yugoslavia was invaded simultaneously from five directions, by the Italians from Albania, by the Hungarian army, and by German forces based in Austria, Romania, and Bulgaria. The Yugoslav army collapsed immediately, freeing the Germans and Italians to switch their troops southward into Greece.

The Greeks and their British allies sustained a longer resistance than the hapless Yugoslavs. Their defensive positions were, however, also outflanked from the start, particularly by the strong German army based in Bulgaria under the Tripartite Pact. One line after another was turned until, on April 27, the British survivors of the campaign succeeded in making their escape from southern Greek ports, leaving many prisoners and almost all their heavy equipment behind them.

Marita was another triumph for Hitler. At almost no cost, he had completed his conquest of mainland Europe, leaving only Sweden,

Switzerland, and the Iberian Peninsula outside his control or that of his allies. The Soviet Union alone remained to challenge his power. The plans for its invasion and defeat were written, however, and it only required his word to set the Wehrmacht in motion toward Moscow.

But was the road to Moscow the right direction to take? The destruction of the Soviet Union was the strategic and ideological project closest to Hitler's heart. It may be thought in retrospect, however, that a direct offensive across the Soviet frontier was not the best means of bringing the result about. In the long run, of course, the Wehrmacht would have to fight and defeat the Red Army. Military victory was, nevertheless, only one of the objects of Barbarossa. Another, almost equally as important if he were to sustain his effort and achieve the final defeat of Britain, was to secure the Soviet Union's enormous natural resources—above all its oil output. The Romanian oil wells apart, and they were insufficient to supply his needs, the supplement of oil exported from Russia under the terms of the Ribbentrop-Molotov Pact being essential, he had no source of oil directly under his control. He needed oil urgently.

Yet ample oil lay close at hand, all the closer since he had completed the conquest of Greece. Iraq, Iran, and Saudi Arabia were the world's largest providers of oil and a direct route toward their fields and refineries lay just across the eastern Mediterranean through Syria. If Turkey's neutrality were to be violated, a land route was available as well. The Levant was weakly defended. The Vichy French army in Syria and Lebanon numbered only 38,000, without modern equipment or air cover. The British army in Palestine, Egypt, and Libya numbered only seven divisions and was already locked in combat with the Afrika Korps, which buttressed a larger Italian army. Militarily, if the German-Italian forces in the Middle East were strengthened, the area was ripe for plucking. There was even the makings of a local pro-German client regime. On April 3, Rasid Ali had overthrown the pro-British government in Iraq and asked for German help. German aircraft arrived at Mosul on May 13, having staged through Syria, the Vichy French garrison feeling powerless to impede. Though Rasid Ali was swiftly overthrown by a British force operating from Transjordan—and the Vichy garrison of Syria and Lebanon defeated in a bitter three-week war in June and July—Hitler was sufficiently encouraged by the evidence of his enemies' strategic fragility in the Middle East to issue Fürher Directive 30, on May 23, outlining a project to support the "Arab Freedom Movement," in conjunction with a German-Italian offensive toward the Suez Canal. On June 11, Führer Directive 32 anticipated, among other operations, the assembly of forces in Bulgaria "sufficient to render Turkey politically amenable or overpower her resistance."

Both Directives were posited, however, on the supposition that Barbarossa would have already been launched. What if, as an alternative, the thrust into the Middle East from Bulgaria and Greece had been chosen as the principal operation for 1941? There might have been two variants.

The first would have avoided the violation of Turkish neutrality and used territory already Axis—the Italian Dodecanese islands off the Turkish coast, other Greek islands, or British Cyprus—as stepping-stones to Vichy Syria. Italian Rhodes, for example, might have been chosen as a staging point for an airborne assault on Cyprus, employing the 7th Airborne Division, in practice uselessly thrown away in the descent on Crete on May 20. Behind an airborne bridgehead in Cyprus and employing local shipping protected by German airpower, a sizable amphibious assault force could have been built up for landings in Syria and Lebanon. Once a secure foothold had been established in the French Levant, mobile columns could have raced across the desert to northern Iraq and a strong lodgment area created from which reinforcements might have begun the conquest of southern Iraq, Iran, and Saudi Arabia. The oil wealth yielded would have solved all Hitler's difficulties in maintaining his military machine. By the end of 1941, with a force of perhaps only twenty divisions, no more than he pushed toward the Russian Caucasus via the Barbarossa routes in 1942, he would have secured a position from which to threaten Stalin's oil-producing centers on the Caspian Sea, having bypassed the major geographical obstacles defending it. Barbarossa might have been

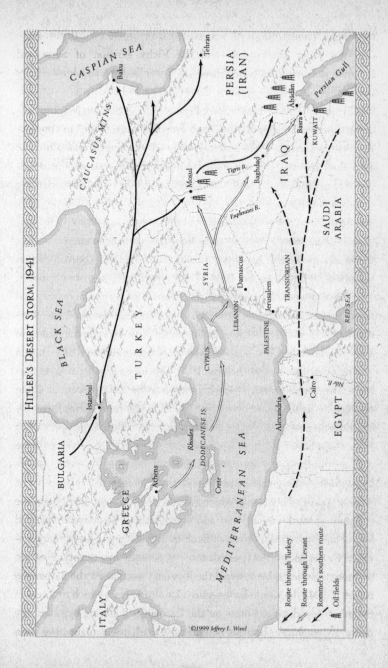

HITLER'S DESERT STORM, 1941

CASPIAN SEA
Baku
Tehran
PERSIA (IRAN)
CAUCASUS MTNS.
Persian Gulf
Abadan
Basra
KUWAIT
Mosul
Tigris R.
Baghdad
IRAQ
BLACK SEA
Euphrates R.
SAUDI ARABIA
TURKEY
SYRIA
Damascus
TRANSJORDAN
RED SEA
LEBANON
Jerusalem
Istanbul
CYPRUS
PALESTINE
BULGARIA
DODECANESE IS.
Rhodes
Alexandria
Cairo
Nile R.
Athens
Crete
EGYPT
GREECE
MEDITERRANEAN SEA
ITALY

©1999 Jeffrey L. Ward

→ Route through Turkey
⇒ Route through Levant
⇢ Rommel's southern route
卯卯 Oil fields

launched, in consequence, in 1942 in much more favorable military circumstances.

This scenario depends for its success on the assembly of sufficient shipping in the eastern Mediterranean to transport the force required. That it could have been adequately protected by airpower against British naval attack is demonstrated by the failure of the Royal Navy to sustain the landings in the Dodecanese in the autumn of 1943. What seems more problematic is the availability of maritime transports. Hitler, in Directive 32, wrote of ". . . chartering French and neutral shipping." The reality was that the British had already acquired most available vessels, forcing the Germans during the assault on Crete, for example, to depend on a fleet of wholly inadequate coastal craft to transport its ground forces. The probability is, therefore, that a strategy that depended on using island "stepping-stones" toward the Levant, attractive as it looks, would have foundered for want of shipping capacity.

A strategy that took as its starting point the violation of Turkish neutrality might, on the other hand, have worked very well. Turkey's record of neutrality during the Second World War is stoutly honorable. Wooed by the Germans, the British, and the Russians, it consistently refused to make concessions to any, despite its patent military weakness. The Turks are doughty fighters. They lacked during the Second World War, however, any sort of modern military equipment. Had Hitler decided, therefore, after the conquest of the Balkans, but before Barbarossa, to use Bulgaria and Greek Thrace as a springboard to invade European Turkey, capture Istanbul, cross the Bosphorus, and capture Anatolia, the Turkish mainland, it is difficult to see what could have stopped him. Stalin's forces, certainly, deployed as they were to defend the Soviet Union's new Eastern Europe frontier, were in no position to oppose such an initiative. The Wehrmacht, as it was to demonstrate in the Russian Steppe, was certainly capable of surmounting the difficulties of traversing the Anatolian terrain. A rapid advance to the Caucasus barrier, Russia's frontier with Turkey, would have secured the Wehrmacht's flank with the Soviet Union. From Anatolia, it could easily have irrupted into Iraq and Iran, thrust its tentacles southward into Arabia, and positioned its vanguards to envelop the Caspian Sea and menace Russian Central Asia.

Had Hitler used the Balkan victories of the spring of 1941 to align his forces for an Anatolian and Levantine victory, leading to wide conquests in Arabia and the securing of decisive positions on Russia's southern flank, it is difficult to see how a variant of Barbarossa, conceived as a pincer movement rather than a blunt frontal assault, would not have succeeded. As a by-blow, Britain's foothold in the Middle East would have been fatally undermined and its dominance of the Indian Empire dangerously threatened.

Fortunately, Hitler worked within a strategic vision limited by legalistic and ideological blindspots. Legally, he could find no quarrel with Turkey's stringently neutralist diplomacy. Ideologically, his fear and hatred of Bolshevism allowed him no freedom to choose an alternative to his desire to smash the Soviet Union by direct, frontal assault. He exulted in the great victories over Stalin in the summer and autumn of 1941 and never expressed regret, even when Russian shells were falling on his Berlin bunker in 1945, that he had set Operation Barbarossa in motion. How grateful we should be that, in the spring of 1941, he should not have chosen a more subtle and indirect strategy.

✦ WILLIAMSON MURRAY ✦

WHAT A TAXI DRIVER WROUGHT

In 1931, a taxicab driver in New York City, looking for late-night fares, was making his rounds. It was a cold, shadowy night, and as he turned north on Fifth Avenue (which then ran two ways) he discerned a figure waiting for him to pass on the almost-deserted avenue. In a hurry to find one final fare, he ignored his instinct to slow and accelerated. He hit the rather dumpy man who, perhaps looking in the wrong direction, stepped in his way.

In its obituary the next day, the *New York Times* spoke of Churchill's contributions to British politics in the Great War: his getting the fleet ready and his work at the ministry of munitions in 1918, but the obituary writer could not resist the temptation to lay the failure of the Dardanelles expedition in 1915 primarily at Churchill's door. And not surprisingly the *Times* also underlined Churchill's life as one of great political and intellectual promise—promise that he never quite fulfilled.

American historians in a beleaguered democracy at the end of the twentieth century never put the blame for the great Nazi victory in the war of 1939 to 1947 on this by now obscure event. How could one assign the troubles of a nation to a taxi accident? After all, everyone agreed that history is entirely the result of great social movements and the actions of the millions who make up humanity—certainly not the product of the actions of a few great men. But some historians still did argue that Britain's surrender in the summer of 1940 by its prime minister, Lord Halifax, was not a reasoned and sensible recognition of Britain's hopeless strategic position, and that the turning over of the Royal Navy to the Kriegsmarine had not made sense. But they could not imagine how Britain might have acquired the strategy of leadership to defeat the Nazi conquerors of Europe. And so America's armed forces again prepared to meet the Nazi forces in South America, and the wars for survival never seemed to end.

The taxi injured but did not kill Churchill—a matter of inches and milliseconds saved his life. But that's a story we already know.

❖ *Williamson Murray is Professor emeritus of history at the Ohio State University.*

✦ DAVID FROMKIN ✦

TRIUMPH OF THE DICTATORS

In the spring of 1941, Nazi Germany was poised to dominate the earth. France, the Low Countries, Norway, Denmark, Austria, Czechoslovakia, Yugoslavia, Greece, and much of Poland had been overrun by the Germans. All of Europe, save neutral Sweden and Switzerland, was in the hands of Hitler's friends and allies: dictators or monarchs who ruled fascist Italy, Vichy France, Franco's Spain, Portugal, the Balkan countries, Finland, and above all the Soviet Union.

A single German division under General Erwin Rommel, sent to rescue beleaguered Italians in Libya, drove Britain's Middle Eastern armies flying and threatened the Suez lifeline; while in Iraq a coup d'état by the pro-German Rashid Ali cut the land road to India. In Asia, Germany's ally, Japan, was coiled to strike, ready to take Southeast Asia and invade India. No need to involve the United States; by seizing the Indies, Japan could break the American embargo and obtain all the oil needed for the Axis Powers to pursue their war aims.

Hitler should have sent the bulk of his armies to serve under Rommel, who would have done what Alexander did and Bonaparte failed to do: He would have taken the Middle East and led his armies to India. There he would have linked up with the Japanese. Europe, Asia, and Africa would have belonged to the coalition of dictators and militarists.

The Nazi-Soviet-Japanese alliance commanded armed forces and resources that utterly dwarfed the military resources that the holdouts, Britain (with its empire) and the United States, could field. The English-speaking countries would have been isolated in a hostile world and would have had no realistic option but to make their peace with the enemy, retaining some autonomy for a time, perhaps, but doomed ultimately to succumb. Nazi Germany, as leader of the coalition, would have ruled the world.

Only Hitler's astonishing blunder in betraying and invading his Soviet ally kept it from happening.

❖ *David Fromkin is professor of international relations and history at Boston University*

THEODORE F. COOK, JR.

OUR MIDWAY DISASTER

Japan Springs a Trap, June 4, 1942

There is a story, no doubt apocryphal, that gamers at the Naval War College in Newport, Rhode Island, have many times replayed the 1942 Battle of Midway—but have never been able to produce an American victory. How to duplicate the luck of our dive-bombers, swooping down on the Japanese carriers at the very moments when all planes were down for refueling? Talk about the balance of a war shifting in a few moments. "Given the deadly suddenness of carrier warfare" Theodore F. Cook, Jr. has written, "How easily might it have been the U.S. Navy mourning the loss of three carriers and their splendid air crews in exchange for, perhaps, one or two Japanese flattops on June 4, 1942?"

What would have happened if the Japanese had won at Midway? With only one carrier left in the Pacific, how could we have resisted their advance? For the United States, the immediate prospects would have been bleak. The Japanese would have taken Midway Island itself. In an island-hopping plan of their own, they would have isolated Australia. And they would have initiated what they called "the Eastern Operation"—the invasion of Hawaii. How, in turn, would the United States have

311

reacted? What would our new grand strategy have been? It is hardly likely that we would have allowed the Japanese to win the war by default. Cook suggests an ingenious alternative, and one entirely fitting for the world's greatest industrial power. Timetables might have been altered but in time the pattern familiar to us would have reasserted itself—that of the "second-order counterfactual." In other words, the atomic bomb.

❖ *Theodore F. Cook, Jr. is professor of history at The William Paterson University of New Jersey. One of the foremost American authorities on Japanese military history, he is, with Haruko Taya Cook, the author of JAPAN AT WAR: AN ORAL HISTORY.*

I ncredible Victory," "The Turning Point," "Miracle at Midway," "The Battle that Doomed Japan" are among the many sobriquets used for the extraordinary events of early June 1942 that became the Battle of Midway. Admiral Chester W. Nimitz ordered a badly outnumbered American fleet, alerted by intercepts of the Japanese naval code to Admiral Yamamoto Isoroku's plans to invade Midway island in the central Pacific Ocean, to confront the aircraft carriers of Japan's Mobile Fleet, attackers of Pearl Harbor. The Americans destroyed them in a single day. Its striking power smashed, the Imperial Navy found itself suddenly forced into the strategic defensive. Allied commanders, from Ceylon to San Francisco could reasonably assume that the Japanese flood had crested. American victory at Midway secured the Allied grand strategy of seeking to defeat Germany first, and even allowed a counteroffensive against Japan to begin at Guadalcanal in August.

One month earlier, in May 1942, Admiral Yamamoto Isoroku, commander in chief of Japan's Combined Fleet, proposed an invasion of Midway Island (Operation MI) in the Central Pacific and simultaneous landings in the Aleutians far to the North at Attu and Kiska (Operation AL), as his next moves in the Pacific War. He was enraged and embarrassed by the raid, commanded by James Doolittle, made on Japan by medium-range U.S. Army bombers, launched from an aircraft carrier, that had avoided detection through the northern Pacific in April. In early May his plan to land Japanese troops at Port Moresby on the southeastern coast of New Guinea was thwarted at the Battle of the Coral Sea, even though his forces had inflicted more damage on their enemy than they suffered. Now Yamamoto pushed forward a design that would both plug the gaps in Japan's outer defenses, and, he felt certain, draw into battle and destroy the American carriers that had not been at Pearl Harbor, or knocked out at the Coral Sea. His plans were very elaborate, involving nine separate groups of ships, coordinating their movements across the vastness of the north and central Pacific.

Unfortunately for the Japanese, through the efforts of the code breakers working under the direction of Commander Joseph J. Rochefort Jr. at "Hypo," as the Pearl Harbor Navy's Combat Intelligence Unit at Pearl Harbor was known, the United States got wind of Yamamoto's impending operations. Its targets might have been anywhere, but as information streamed in, it seemed probable that Yamamoto meant to strike at Midway. Confirmation was needed. Rochefort's struggle to pry meaning out of intercepted communications coming in from all over the Pacific in the Imperial Navy's JN-25 code—only partially broken—culminated in an attempt to determine what geographic location corresponded to "AF," the objective of the future operation in an otherwise decoded message picked up in early May. It sparked debate and argument throughout Admiral Chester W. Nimitz's small circle of code-privy staff.

The story of how it was done has become the epic of the code-breakers fraternity; especially clever seems the remarkably simple ruse used to draw the Japanese into revealing the code word. Midway Island was ordered to broadcast a message on May 21, sent in the clear, that their condenser had broken down and that they would soon be short of fresh water; Pearl Harbor then sent a reply, also uncoded, that a water barge was on its way. Allied listening stations in Australia were rewarded the same day with a Japanese message dutifully reporting that "AF" was running short of water. This was decoded, translated, and flashed to Pearl immediately. It led to Nimitz's firm commitment to meet the enemy at the place—Midway—and the date—June 4—earlier intercepts had detected. He prepared a "flank attack," aiming to be waiting north of Midway Island within range of where the enemy was likely to appear, to allow his fleet, concentrated for this one operation, to get in a surprise blow on Yamamoto's fleet.

The outlines of what happened at Midway are well known. For operations aimed at Midway and the occupation of the Western Aleutians isles of Attu and Kiska, Yamamoto had 11 battleships, 8 carriers (4 of them carriers of the first rank, *Akagi*, *Kaga*, *Hiryu*, and *Soryu*, all veterans of the Pearl Harbor attack—the other two carriers in that attack were back in Japan recovering from the Battle of the Coral Sea early in May), 22 cruisers, 65 destroyers, 21 submarines, and over 700 airplanes. Nimitz was only able to send into action 3 carriers (including *Yorktown*, practically raised from the dead after the Battle of the Coral Sea by the dockyards of Pearl Harbor), 8 cruisers, 18 destroyers, and 25 submarines.

Alerted to both the objectives and timing of Yamamoto's massive operation, Nimitz, nevertheless, ordered his fleet, divided into two task forces built around aircraft carriers—Task Force 16 containing *Enterprise* and *Hornet* under Rear Admiral Raymond Spruance and Task Force 17 with *Yorktown* under Rear Admiral Frank Jack Fletcher, the latter in overall command, temporarily replacing Vice Admiral William F. Halsey, beached due to illness at this critical moment. They would be waiting for Vice Admiral Nagumo Chûichi's Mobile Force aircraft carriers when they approached Midway to bomb the island's defenses, preparatory to an invasion.

Ironically, both commanders had complete confidence in their own ability to surprise their enemy. Nimitz reinforced the Midway garrison with orders to prepare a nasty surprise for any imperial troops who sought to storm ashore, and rushed as many planes as possible—whether obsolete, oversized, or untested—to the island's airfield. He then ordered his carriers to their flanking position, designated "Point Luck." Historically, Nagumo had the more flawed appreciation of his situation. Just prior to the launch of his first strike against Midway Island, Nagumo prepared an assessment of the situation as follows that listed his premises:

1. The enemy fleet will probably come out to engage when the Midway landing operations are begun.
2. Enemy air patrols from Midway will be heavier to westward and southward, less heavy to the north and northwest.

3. The radius of enemy air patrols is estimated to be approximately 500 miles.

4. The enemy is not yet aware of our plan, and he has not yet detected our task force.

5. There is no evidence of an enemy task force in our vicinity.

6. It is therefore possible for us to attack Midway, destroy land-based planes there, and support the landing operation. We can then turn around, meet an approaching enemy task force, and destroy it.

7. Our interceptors and anti-aircraft fire can surely repulse possible counterattacks by enemy land-based air.

Hardly could he have been more wrong, and these assumptions contributed greatly to Nagumo's inability to adapt to radically different circumstances.

As it turned out, the Invasion Force, approaching from the southwest, was spotted first, on June 3, and was attacked to no effect by bombers from Midway. At first light the next day, the Japanese bombed the island, causing extensive damage, but they failed to catch the American aircraft on the ground. They were met by severe anti-aircraft fire, leading the air commander to request another strike on Midway. Nagumo, unaware American carriers were lurking near at hand—and haunted by the second-guessing that had dogged him since his supposed failure to follow up his Pearl Harbor success back in December with a crushing blow against storage facilities and depots—then authorized, at 7:15 A.M., the rearming of the aircraft kept in reserve for any American ships that might appear, for a second attack on Midway. While the crews labored to switch torpedoes and penetration bombs to weapons suited to land targets, Spruance's Task Force 16 was sighted where no enemy was expected. Despite the urging of some that he strike immediately at this dangerous and unexpected target, Nagumo ordered a second switch of armaments.

For his part, although still at extreme range, as soon as he got a fix on Nagumo's location, Spruance ordered his planes to attack. The U.S. attack was uncoordinated. The torpedo bombers, slow and vulnerable, found the enemy first, and were nearly annihilated, but they attracted most of Nagumo's fighters, and just as the Japanese commanders felt that their furious maneuvers had weathered another ineffective American attack, Spruance's dive-bombers found Nagumo's task force. Nine bombs virtually destroyed the Japanese fleet, knocking carriers *Akagi*, *Kaga*, and *Soryu* out of action, the bombers on their decks and hangers, caught before they could be launched, were consumed in the conflagration of fuel and exploding munitions that incinerated many of their crew and would lead to the loss of all three ships.

Hiryu, Nagumo's fourth carrier, escaped this attack and was able to launch planes later in the morning that found Fletcher's carrier, *Yorktown*, inflicting such serious damage that Fletcher was forced to change ships; he immediately relinquished overall command to Spruance, who ordered his now rearmed dive-bombers to strike back. They found *Hiryu* late in the afternoon, so seriously damaging the ship that she would be scuttled. Yamamoto's plans were ruined, and his last chance at revenge was lost when Spruance ordered a retirement, beyond the range of Japan's powerful surface fleet that sought a night action. Apart from a Japanese cruiser damaged in a collision, sunk by Spruance's aircraft the next day, the action was over. *Yorktown* was eventually sunk by the Japanese submarine *I-168* on June 7 as she tried to make it home. Yamamoto's grand design had ended in disaster, and the initiative had passed to the Americans.

✦ ✦ ✦

The might-have-beens of the battle have long tantalized students of the war in the Pacific. Bemoaning mechanical failures, querying small changes in the timing of events, and second-guessing command decisions in light of events known and unknown to the participants all have been common. A list of the most popular, given in Walter Lord's *Incredible Victory*, published in 1967, includes, for example: If only float plane No. 4, from the heavy cruiser *Tone* had gotten off on time, "they would have dis-

covered the U.S. fleet before rearming for that second attack on Midway;" "If only the American dive-bombers had attacked a few minutes
later, Nagumo's own strike would have been launched" (this is the famous "five minutes" claim that puts down Japan's defeat to timing); "If
only the Japanese had attacked the American carriers as soon as they
were sighted, instead of holding back until all the planes were ready." To
this list could be added: What if American dive-bomber commander
Wade McClusky had not decided to push on beyond his safe range to find
the Japanese carriers; and what if Rear Admiral Frank Jack Fletcher, his
carrier *Yorktown* sunk from under him, had not turned tactical command
over to Rear Admiral Ray Spruance, who then pressed home the attack?
These, and many other bold decisions, brave choices, and even colossal
blunders might be credited as critical in bringing about the historic victory of the American fleet at Midway, but here I look at the period preliminary to the battle that played perhaps the greatest part in America's
victory, and suggest that with a very small change, things might have
turned out very differently.

An Alternate Path? The Making of a Japanese Midway Victory

Few have doubted the importance of the battle in forging America's triumph over Japan. In the words of Admiral Chester W. Nimitz, America's
overall naval commander in the Pacific Theater and the man most credited with leading the United States Navy to victory over Japan's fleets in
the Second World War: "Midway was the crucial battle of the Pacific War,
the engagement that made everything possible." The rest, they say, is history.

But, what if in mid-May 1942, a Japanese sailor, after transcribing a
radio message he had just intercepted from Midway Island, had turned to
his superior to ask, "Why are they broadcasting this message in the clear?
Don't they care if we know that Midway is running short of water?"
What if, acting on this kernel of suspicion, the young communications officer had passed along his doubts? What if more experienced cryptogra-

phers and cipher specialists in Tokyo had not dismissed the idea that Imperial Japan's codes could be broken; what if they had considered the possibility that the Americans could possibly be playing out an intelligence gambit. They might have reasoned, "If the Americans have been able to read some of our messages and are attempting to link potential objectives with cipher designations, would not this little message be an excellent way to trick us into confirming the code word for Midway?"

What if, with a red flag raised, naval staff at Imperial General Headquarters Tokyo broadcast the now famous message of May 19, 1942, referring to "AF" being short of water not merely as a routine signal (the decryption of which today occupies an almost sacred place in the history of signals intelligence and code breaking), but as the first salvo in a Japanese intelligence offensive designed to lure the Americans to battle on terms favorable to Japan?

A simple question, heightened alertness, and suddenly what historians have often described as the decisive U.S. advantage in the close-run Battle of Midway might well have become the Japanese side's key to a great victory in the central Pacific, dramatically altering the course of the Second World War.

To rewrite the history of the Battle of Midway is to tear up one of the most cherished of American war stories, for the decisions taken during it, the sacrifices made, and the glorious results achieved have become legend. Yet, intelligence that allowed the outnumbered American carriers to ambush Nagumo Chûichi's carriers after they had bombed Midway Island could well have yielded very different results. Had Admiral Yamamoto Isoroku known, or even strongly suspected, that the Americans were privy to his plans for "Operation MI," calling for the seizure of Midway before U.S. carriers could steam up from Hawaii, he could have used his heavy numerical superiority in both carriers and aircraft to set his own trap and bring on just the decisive battle he sought.

While it is of course possible that a Yamamoto who knew his plans were known to the enemy could have abandoned his Midway operation and gone after alternative targets—perhaps Australia, Ceylon, Dutch

Harbor off Alaska, or even Fiji and Samoa (identified in Operation Plan FS favored by his opponents in the navy). But the Midway plan was a sound one, at least in the mind of the commander in chief of the Combined Fleet. To abandon his own plan, in all its elaborate elegance, seems uncharacteristic of the man. The interplay of nine different task forces maneuvering to a planned-for endgame was something Admiral Yamamoto seemed to thrill in. Indeed, he assigned himself a key part in the battle that he initially envisioned; at sea in his flagship, the super-battleship *Yamato*, just a few hundred miles behind Nagumo's carriers, he could be on the kill if Americans followed the first script he had prepared for them.

If the Americans had, in fact, gotten wind of his operations, all the better, he might well have concluded, since knowing his objective, they surely would realize that Midway could not be allowed to fall into Japanese hands. The commander of a temporarily superior fleet, from a nation that could not hope to compete over the long-haul, sought no "fleet-in-being" strategy. But in the footsteps of Japan's Admiral Tôgô Heihachirô, victor of Tsushima over the Russians in 1905, and in the spirit of Britain's Nelson, whose words rang throughout the Imperial Japanese Navy's heritage, Yamamoto could not have wished for a better opportunity than a decisive battle at the place of his own choosing.

So, instead of re-scripting Combined Fleet's grand operation and creating entirely new roles for the Americans to act out in his drama, it seems that Yamamoto, even with more than an inkling that the Americans were waiting for him, would have adjusted his operational plan at the margins rather than curb his own strategic vision of what was to follow Midway. In the minds of Yamamoto and his chief of staff, Ugaki Matome, anticipated victory there would be the opening phase of an even grander plan. Beyond lay the Hawaiian Islands and their greatest prize, Pearl Harbor, on Oahu, spoken of as "The Eastern Operation." The stakes for which Yamamoto was playing included America's Pacific Fleet base itself.

What evidence would Yamamoto have had about American deployments and intentions before the battle? The answer to that question is probably, "not much," since the Americans were so anxious to keep secret both their whereabouts and capabilities. Calculating two U.S. carriers at sea, and even adding in a third carrier, *Yorktown*, (claimed, but not confirmed, sunk at Coral Sea) or *Saratoga*, whose precise whereabouts were unknown (at the time she was steaming west from San Diego), Yamamoto could count on superiority in numbers. Yamamoto could not be certain that the United States was reacting to his plans, even if he were alerted to that possibility, but he might have had his first confirmation of America's efforts, when it became necessary for Japan to cancel "Operation K" at the end of May. This was a night reconnaissance of Pearl Harbor by long-range Kawanishi flying boats (known as "Emily" by the Allies) from Kwajalein, the second one of the war. The planes were scheduled to be refueled by submarine *I-123* at the French Frigate Shoals, several hundred miles west of Oahu, until it was found that an American seaplane tender had taken up station there on the nights of May 30 and 31. The Japanese could still have executed the reconnaissance by ordering refueling operations shifted to nearby, and equally inhospitable, Necker Island so that the flying boats could go on their way to Pearl Harbor. There they would have found no American carriers, giving Yamamoto possible corroboration that Nimitz was trying to counter his moves as Japan closed in on Midway.

In our scenario, the battle might have developed like this: Yamamoto sets his submarine picket line between Hawaii and Midway several days earlier. The subs provide early warning that the Americans are coming when one catches a glimpse of Spruance's carriers moving toward the battle area on June second. Instead of relying on a perfunctory search for an enemy he did not expect to find, Admiral Nagumo, the alert predator, has all his escorts' float planes in the air before dawn searching determinedly for the enemy; his air groups are primed on deck, ready to strike at the first opportunity. "Point Luck," the location northeast on Midway designated as the rendezvous of Task Force 16 and Task Force 17, was to become a black mark on America's map of the Pacific, for to it—and to doom—sailed virtually all of America's striking power on that ocean.

Alerted to America's readiness to meet him at the outset, most of Nagumo's immediate pre-battle assumptions about his enemy are absent. Instead of planning a two-stage operation, where he had first to reduce and then seize an enemy island base before he could move against an enemy response, Japan's Mobile Force is no longer "a hunter chasing two hares at once," as Admiral Kusaka, Nagumo's chief of staff put it, and can unleash the veteran flight leaders to seek out the enemy fleet and destroy it. Not long after dawn on June 4, a contact report comes in to Nagumo: There are the Americans—two carriers and escorts. With full concurrence of his air staff, although at extreme range, Nagumo immediately gives orders to launch against the Americans, identified as *Enterprise* and *Hornet*. Balanced attack groups of Val bombers and Kate torpedo bombers, flown by magnificent air crews, and escorted all the way to their targets by half of Nagumo's Zero fighters, bear down on Spruance. The Japanese carriers, ready for an American counterattack, spot their fighters on deck, as the armoires prepare Nagumo's planes for a second strike.

Fortune does not always favor the large battalions, and good luck may not entirely desert the Americans; a report locating Nagumo's force from a Midway-based PBY Catalina flying boat comes in just as Task Force 16's radar picks up what may be incoming Japanese planes. Spruance, himself expecting and seeking contact, launches his own strike at this target. Ray Spruance has made a split-second decision under pressure. His radar gives him the chance to get his planes into the air rather than see them caught on his carrier's decks as the enemy arrives, but the position of the enemy fleet is beyond the round-trip range of many American aircraft; he will attempt to close the distance on their return trip, he tells them, knowing that many will have no chance to make it back. The fighters of TF-16's Combat Air Patrol, those not sent as escorts on the attack, meet the incoming enemy courageously, but they are knocked aside as Japanese Zeroes engage them aggressively, downing many, using their superior maneuverability to screen the Americans from the slower bombers. Few of the attacking bombers are turned aside before they reach the frantically turning American flattops. Within ten minutes, despite the desperate efforts of every antiaircraft gunner in the fleet, torpedoes have rammed home on both beams of *Hornet*, while *Enterprise* is ablaze from several huge holes on her flight deck. TF-16 is out of action; losses among the attackers are moderate. Heroic attacks and frantic actions still lie ahead, but this Midway battle would have already taken on the tones of an American disaster.

Even as Ray Spruance is transferring his flag from *Enterprise* while her captain tries desperately to save his ship, the planes of TF-16 are intercepted by a swarm of Japanese fighters as they approach Nagumo's carrier force. With great courage, most attempt to press home their attacks, but the slow-moving torpedo bombers are slaughtered; the dive-bombers are picked up by more Zeroes, waiting for them on high, which pursue them down their less-than-perfect bombing paths with murderous persistence; all this occurs while the ships of Nagumo's force are thowing up a curtain of ack-ack, maneuvering skillfully to avoid their attackers. As at Coral Sea, American bombers inflict severe damage on a Japanese carrier, let us say *Kaga*—the largest and most likely to attract the few attackers that can release their ordinance on target—but they are unable to finish her off. With their own mother ships devastated, these pilots will not get a second chance.

The curtain rises on the second phase of the battle soon thereafter. Fletcher in *Yorktown*, core of TF-17, learns of the sighting of Japanese carriers and wants to join the action, but he is not yet close enough to participate. His planes ready to go, and making flank speed to the west, he then gets the terrible news from Spruance of his ships' condition. It is no knock on Jack Fletcher to suggest that at this moment he would have been deeply divided on the course of action expected of him. The battle orders under which he is operating were ambivalent in such a situation.

American after-action reports will look askance at Nimitz's May 27, 1942, orders to Fletcher and Spruance that they were to, "inflict maximum damage on enemy by employing strong attrition tactics," striking from the northeast of the anticipated Japanese approach. Before they departed Pearl Harbor, Nimitz had also urged that they "be governed by the principle of calculated risk" and avoid attacking a superior force unless there was a good chance of inflicting greater damage. Viewed in the wake of a decisive defeat, do these orders not seem hopelessly contradictory, tying the hands of subordinate commanders? The enemy was known to be superior before the battle. Where is the "attrition" in retreat? Nimitz would seem to have left himself few options if his "flanking maneuver" were to prove a chimera, since with all of America's forces northeast of Midway Island, he was in no position to strike at the Japanese Midway Invasion Force steaming up from the southwest. If America's carriers were beaten, would not that leave Midway's reinforced garrison to the tender mercies of Yamamoto's battle fleet?

Jack Fletcher knows that Halsey would have hurled himself into battle, but he is not a "Bull" Halsey, likely to act before considering all the ramifications; nor can he easily abandon Spruance to an unanswered second strike from Nagumo. It is still midmorning; perhaps, Fletcher thinks, he himself has escaped detection and can get in a blow before the enemy finds him, evening up the score. Fletcher makes the decision to continue to sail west, rather than turn back for Pearl, hoping to narrow the range on Nagumo. A scout plane from the Japanese cruiser *Tone*, on its homeward leg, detects him. Fletcher launches *Yorktown*'s planes when he gets reports of "enemy carriers," hoping perhaps to catch Nagumo recovering his aircraft. America's last hope make their way to the Mobile Force's previous location, but can find only a crippled *Kaga* limping westward, escorted by two destroyers. Despite searching frantically for Nagumo's ships, which have made a sharp turn to the north to recover, they can find no fresh targets. The flight groups from *Yorktown* overwhelm the damaged Japanese carrier, dispatching her and one of her escorts in frustration.

While the American aircrews are pounding *Kaga*, Fletcher's flagship becomes the target of a ferocious attack in turn. Nagumo's other three carriers, having recovered their planes at the prearranged rendezvous to the north, launch their second strike against *Yorktown*, stalked by several floatplanes; she is a smoldering hulk by nightfall. Fletcher's planes are lost when they return to the site, though some of the aircrews who can make it back to all that remains of TF-17 are able to splash nearby. In a single day, *Hornet* had been sunk, *Yorktown* wrecked and scuttled by the same crew who had seen her saved just a few days before, while *Enterprise*, trying to make it home, the fires put out but her flight deck ruined, becomes an easy target for one of Japan's submarines, just as *Lexington* had been at Coral Sea; torpedoed, she sinks near dawn the next day, the fifth of June. With the Japanese navy's surface units closing in for night action to pick off any damaged vessels and American survivors of lost ships and ditched planes bobbing about in the waters near "Point Lucky," could not the "miracle of Midway" have become a massacre? Over the next few days, Japanese destroyers find many survivors, Americans and Japanese, though there is little joy for the prisoners, who find their rescuers interested only in what information they can provide about the defenses of Midway and Hawaii before they are killed. The loss has stripped America's naval air corps of its core of fine pilots and experienced aircrews, while possession of this "ocean battlefield" means many downed Japanese airmen will fly again.

The first consequence of American naval defeat would be the loss of Midway Island itself. Midway Island comes in for the attentions of Nagumo's planes from the Mobile Fleet, who soon reduced the island's airbase to rubble, its aircraft burned or expended in futile efforts to sink fast ships at sea. It is then pummeled by the big guns of the Support Group cruisers and then even the Main Force battleships under Admiral Yamamoto himself, hurling 16- and 18.1-inch shells against the coral. The American garrison, even reinforced as it was, can hardly resist for long unsupported, once Japanese troops go ashore. Yet it proves a bloody affair and a formidable warning for Japan of the dangers inherent in making opposed landings against the U.S. Marines in base-defense mode; the garrison adds "Midway" to the name of "The Alamo," "Wake," and "Bataan" in America's hagiography of last stands.

Nimitz finds himself in our scenario with just a single carrier in the Pacific: *Saratoga*, just in from San Diego. Of course, Halsey wants to steam off directly toward the enemy, "catch 'em gloating," might be the way he would have put it, but Nimitz is aware that the strategic defense he had planned has been ruined by his own impetuosity. He had gone on a hunch—no, a reasoned assessment based on intelligence estimates—but it was a very thin strand that had held it all together. There never seemed to be any consideration of whether the Japanese might have guessed his plans. Most of the fleet had been risked and now it was gone. How could expert strategic intelligence have produced such a catastrophic defeat? How could he have guessed right and still been defeated? He will not learn why until after the war.

The Long War

On the morning after an overwhelming Japanese victory at Midway, what would the strategic situation have been and what alternatives would have presented themselves to the Japanese? Let us consider the possibilities.

The balance of naval power in the Pacific was heavily tilted in Japan's favor, and was likely to remain so for the remainder of the year 1942, and perhaps even the first half of 1943. At the beginning of June 1942, there were only six aircraft carriers in the American fleet; had Nimitz lost three of them at Midway, there was simply no way to make up the numbers in the short term. The remaining three carriers would not be augmented until the end of 1942 when the first of a new generation of *Essex*-class fast carriers was due to arrive. But the schedule for commissioning fleet carriers was six in 1943, seven in 1944, and three in 1945. In other words, assuming no losses, the most frontline carriers America's admirals could hope for was ten by the end of 1943. With U.S. carrier forces nearly an-

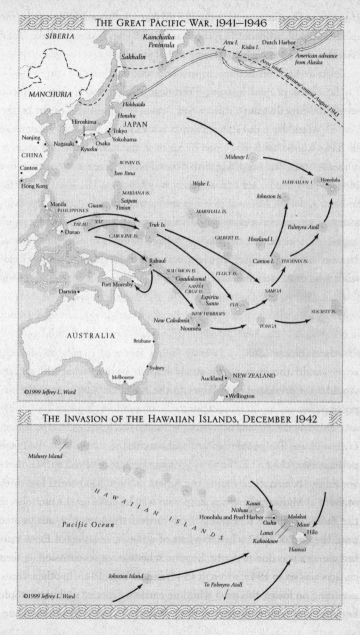

THE GREAT PACIFIC WAR, 1941–1946

SIBERIA

Kamchatka Peninsula

Sakhalin

Attu I.   Kiska I.   Dutch Harbor

American advance from Alaska

Area under Japanese control August 1943

MANCHURIA

Hokkaido

Honshu

JAPAN

Hiroshima

Nanjing   Tokyo

Nagasaki   Osaka   Yokohama

Kyushu

Midway I.

CHINA

BONIN IS.

Iwo Jima

HAWAIIAN I.   Honolulu

Canton

Hong Kong

Wake I.

MARIANA IS.   Saipan   Tinian

Johnston Is.

Manila   Guam

PHILIPPINES

PALAU   YAP

Davao

Truk Is.

MARSHALL IS.

Palmyra Atoll

CAROLINE IS.

GILBERT IS.   Howland I.

Rabaul

Canton I.   PHOENIX IS.

SOLOMON IS.   ELLICE IS.

Guadalcanal

Port Moresby

SANTA CRUZ IS.

Espiritu Santo

SAMOA

Darwin

FIJI

NEW HEBRIDES

SOCIETY IS.

New Caledonia   Noumea   TONGA

AUSTRALIA   Brisbane

Sydney

©1999 Jeffrey L. Ward

Auckland   NEW ZEALAND

Melbourne

Wellington

THE INVASION OF THE HAWAIIAN ISLANDS, DECEMBER 1942

Midway Island

H A W A I I A N   I S L A N D S

Pacific Ocean

Kauai

Niihau

Honolulu and Pearl Harbor

Oahu   Molokai

Maui

Lanai   Hilo

Kahoolawe

Hawaii

Johnston Island   To Palmyra Atoll

©1999 Jeffrey L. Ward

nihilated at the Battle of Midway, the USN must either withdraw the few carriers still afloat from the Atlantic—stripping U.S. convoys there of air coverage and aborting U.S. training and planned offensive operations—or assume a completely defensive posture in the Pacific.

Japan was in a much stronger position. The victorious Nagumo force would hold the initiative if they had come off as well at Midway as the United States did historically. *Shokaku* and *Zuikaku*, the two carriers in the Pearl Harbor raid that were damaged in the Coral Sea battle and required refitting and restaffing with new air units, were ready to rejoin the Mobile Fleet soon after Midway, and two more carriers would join the fleet in mid-1942, so available Japanese strength was likely to remain four or even five fleet carriers for future operations in the coming campaigns, even with refit and repair. Japan's numerical edge in the new measures of naval power, carriers, was secure for some time to come, while Yamamoto retained his battleship advantage—the old arbiter of sea warfare. It was not certain that even the huge number of American lighter warships, including light and escort carriers (eventually to number in the dozens), scheduled to arrive more than a year later, could be used to redress the balance.

Second, Australia was in jeopardy of being completely cut off, at least from the Pacific side, and the American fleet and army air corps were virtually powerless to intervene against Japanese efforts to sever communications between the United States and Australia, at Fiji and then Samoa. The seven million people of Australia would find their land even more isolated than before, as the flow of supplies was pinched and General MacArthur's Southwest Pacific Command threatened to shrivel up even before it could come to life.

Third, the Indian Ocean was the one route still open to Australia, but a lifeline would have to be strung through India and Ceylon, both vulnerable to Japanese attack at many points. Indian nationalism, evidenced by appeals for resistance to British rule and the calls for independence sweeping the subcontinent—while the British army is reeling back before Imperial Japanese army troops in Burma—would surely make India seem less a stable base and more a potential future flash point in June 1942.

At the northern end of the Pacific, an advance up the Aleutians, perhaps even to Dutch Harbor, seems possible, assuming the landings planned for Attu and Kiska carried out with the Midway operation were successful. This move might prove of great importance pending the outcome of the more audacious Japanese plans to come. Dutch Harbor, just off the continental base of the Aleutian chain, is about the same distance from San Francisco as Honolulu (2,034 miles) and was vital to this theater of war, and if contained or perhaps even taken by Japanese troops, would have been defended by miserable cold weather, poor visibility, and heavy seas, placing a formidable barrier in the path of any U.S. alternative to the Central Pacific route to Tokyo.

In the southwestern Pacific, instead of an American "Operation Watchtower" to seize Guadalcanal in August 1942, Japanese advances in the Solomons might proceed nearly unchallenged. They could then threaten Allied outposts in Espíritu Santo, New Caledonia, or perhaps even Fiji and Samoa beyond. Although executed with thin margins for error and scant resources, each move could be supported by Japan's land-based aviation and made at Japan's initiative, and could only be challenged if America itself could somehow get the planes and fuel to the appropriate place to meet them.

Is it beyond the realm of possibility that panic contained after Pearl Harbor might have again swept the West Coast or spread to the corridors of power in Washington, D.C.? Again, a reassessment of the "Germany First" strategy that had become the foundation for the "Rainbow" war plan could well have been considered if the American fleet, the weapon needed to parry the Japanese thrusts, had been broken for a second time at Midway. If it seemed Japan could not be held off until Germany was defeated, what would the impact be on Allied Global Grand Strategy?

As bad as these prospects in the Pacific were, things could get a lot worse for the Americans. What if Hawaii itself was invaded next? Such an operation was not only contemplated but was in the advanced planning stage as the Midway operation was launched; to Yamamoto, at least, the "Eastern Operation" was the logical follow-up to his Aleutians and Midway strikes, hitting at the most significant real estate in the Pacific Ocean.

Hawaii Invasion: Lei's for the Emperor

Almost from the outset of the war, planning for an invasion of Hawaii stirred controversy at the highest level of Japanese military leadership. On January 14, 1942, Rear Admiral Ugaki Matome, chief of staff of the Combined Fleet and Yamamoto's right-hand man, confided in his diary that Japan had to make the attempt "to take Midway, Johnston, and Palmyra after June, send our air strength to those islands, and after these steps are completed, mobilize all available strength to invade Hawaii, while attempting to destroy the enemy fleet in a decisive battle." He knew many would likely oppose his plan, but among the reasons he listed for why it had to be executed were: "What would hurt the United States most is the loss of the fleet and of Hawaii"; "An attempted invasion of Hawaii and a decisive battle near there may seem a reckless plan, but its chance of success is not small"; "As time passes, we would lose the benefit of the war results so far gained. Moreover, the enemy would increase his strength, while we would have to be just waiting for him to come"; and "The destruction of the U.S. fleet would also mean that of the British fleet. So we would be able to do anything we like. Thus, it will be the shortest way to conclude the war." Ugaki noted too that "Time is an important element in war. The period of war should be short. Though a prolonged war is taken for granted, nobody is so foolish as to wish for it himself." Each of these reasons would still have seemed valid after a Japanese Midway.

That Hawaii was the next target for the Imperial Navy after the seizure of Midway is nearly certain. Thanks to the prodigious efforts of John Stephan of the University of Hawaii presented in his book, *Hawaii Under the Rising Sun: Japan's Plans for Conquest After Pearl Harbor,* we have a pretty good idea of what Japanese thinking was in 1941 and 1942 for a Hawaii operation and invasion. The Japanese faced formidable obstacles to success. Certainly a Japanese jump to Pearl Harbor would have been a tremendous gamble, but it would have become a much better wager with the U.S. carriers sent to the bottom and the Hawaiian islands partially isolated by free-ranging Japanese carriers and submarine forces to their east. Having come this far, Yamamoto surely would have made the attempt if he could pry out of the Imperial Army the divisions, aircraft, and supplies needed. Despite the risks, the potential benefits to Japan of a successful seizure of Oahu are hard to exaggerate, so much so that one can even argue that the only way Japan could have hoped to stave off defeat long enough for negotiations may have been with an all-out assault on the islands at the onset of war. But that is another path off our chosen counterfactual road.

Eastern Operation's invasion of Hawaii was planned to unfold over a period of months, in a series of stages, though had the victory at Midway been as complete as suggested in this scenario, calls would have been raised to speed up the timetable. To strike immediately would take advantage of American confusion (not to suggest panic) but it would also invite complete disaster. Oahu, the island where Pearl Harbor was located, could not be taken by storm; its fortifications, garrison, and air bases were formidable and would have to be reduced before any invasion could be attempted. The Japanese sword needed to be kept sharp through time in port and under refit and the carriers' aircraft and aircrews had to be rested and replaced. Yamamoto could not have continued to keep his fleet at sea, flitting from one "triumphant operation" to the next in preparation for a culminating battle for Hawaii, even were he able to find the fuel to do so. Moreover, the Japanese navy would have to secure the full commitment from the army to supply the men and planes needed for the job—not just the few designated before Midway. This would be no small task as they had opposed each of Yamamoto's offensives to this point in the war. But a great Midway victory might have made them enthusiastic supporters, though it seems that few in Japan shared Yamamoto's view that the Americans would be willing to negotiate after Hawaii was in Japanese hands.

With a clear objective, a timetable, and the attention of the commander in chief of the Combined Fleet, Yamamoto Isoroku, the plan most likely to have been attempted posited a strangling of Hawaii from the west and southwest by a careful move against Palmyra Island as the key air link leading on to the South Pacific, a completion of operations in the FS Operation by taking Samoa, and the establishment of Japanese air and sea bases in September. Thus the full-blown invasion of Hawaii might be executed in late 1942, perhaps December. This plan had the advantage of allowing several more carriers to join the fleet and provided for a rapidly accelerated program of converting seaplane tenders into aircraft carriers. Preparations for the Hawaii Campaign were grandiose, but might have been just feasible if America's military forces were crippled at Midway. Like a great scythe sweeping across the southwest and south central Pacific, the first phases of the operation, following the theme of the original Operation FS (Fiji-Samoa) proposed before the Midway invasion would sever the lines of communication and supply that tied Australia to Hawaii and the West Coast of the United States. New Caledonia, Fiji, then Samoa were to be seized (perhaps even Tahiti beyond). Each leap supporting the next. This would be accompanied by landings on Johnston Island and Palmyra Island, another featureless point in the Pacific, leaving the Hawaiian Islands as the only U.S. territory left in the Central Pacific.

American defenses in the Hawaiian Island chain had grown stronger since December 1941, when U.S. Army troops had numbered 40,000 and probably exceeded 65,000 in April 1942. Even larger garrisons were projected for Oahu, home of Honolulu and Pearl Harbor, and for Hawaii, the "Big Island," several hundred miles to the southeast. But these reinforcements would have posed immense problems for American commanders in the coming battle. Hawaii was not the rich island paradise of the travel brochures and prewar navy recruiting posters; provisioning the troops and feeding the civilian population, especially the large concentration of people in Honolulu, would have been a nearly impossible task without easy access to maritime supply. Poor and underdeveloped, except for its pineapple and sugar plantations, the Hawaiian Islands were heavily dependent on imported food, and virtually all the supplies necessary to support the civilian economy, to say nothing of the massive needs of the military forces, had to be imported. Most supplies came from U.S. ports more than 2,000 miles across the Pacific to the northeast. Estimates of Hawaii's food supply on the eve of war were on the order of weeks, rather than months.

The utility of Pearl Harbor and other facilities depended on the local labor force. Moreover, 160,000 of the residents, more than 40 percent of the total population, were what the Japanese at that time called *dôhô*, meaning "compatriots" (a term embracing ethnic Japanese at home and abroad, regardless of their citizenship). It must be said that prewar U.S. Army planning for defense of the islands had rated the loyalty of second-generation Japanese (known as *nisei*) quite high; the Hawaiian Department even recommended recruiting *nisei* soldiers. Despite the Draconian practices employed on the West Coast, very few Japanese Americans or Japanese nationals attracted the attentions of U.S. security authorities—less than 1 percent of Hawaii's population of Japanese descent were interned. Nevertheless, Japanese planners were hoping for a mass rising of "fellow countrymen" when Imperial forces arrived and planned to make good use of a sizable number of Japanese with Hawaiian experience identified in Japan once the islands were conquered for the emperor.

What means had America to contest operations against Hawaii, to supply an expeditionary force there, or to sustain any large-scale operation from the West Coast? Air operations were impossible from the United States against Hawaii—no bomber or transport plane could fly there fully loaded until the B-29 in mid-1944. As we have seen, an overwhelming Japanese victory at Midway would have left no American carriers to contest a Japanese invasion and taking back Hawaii, should it fall to Japan, would have required a massive seaborne operation, on a scale the United States could only mount in late 1943. What a prolonged

Hawaiian campaign might win for Japan must be assessed against what the diversion of force and effort of a greatly outnumbered fleet would have cost the United States. Without a fleet-in-being operating out of "America's Gibraltar," Pearl Harbor, Hawaii Territory's capital, Honolulu, and the island of Oahu were not protected from attack. Its principle defense, besides the coastal guns protecting the harbor, were the planes on Oahu's airfields. Even in the age of air power and the capability of aircraft to strike far out to sea and patrol, keeping the planes aloft depended on supply by sea.

The most likely scenario for the final Japanese assault on the Hawaiian Islands would begin with a strong diversion aimed at Oahu and a carrier-covered landing on Hawaii Island in an effort to secure forward-base facilities at Hilo; rapid construction of airfields to support the bombardment of U.S. Army and Navy installations on Oahu would follow, as the Imperial Navy brought in its bombers and fighters from the south. A furious series of air battles would be fought, and while the Americans could be expected to do well and the Japanese planes and pilots would be operating themselves at the extreme end of a painfully thin line of supply, the Americans, without a fleet-in-being to truly threaten the Japanese, would likely not be able to sustain the struggle indefinitely. Spare parts, ammunition, replacement pilots, to say nothing of fuel and new planes would have to run the gauntlet from the United States and would be most vulnerable as they approached the islands where cargo ships could be intercepted by units of Japan's fleet. If no "rising" had occurred among the Japanese American population, it seems likely that civilian targets on Oahu would be subjected to merciless air attacks and the U.S. fighter force gradually whittled down. There is no doubt that a direct assault on the harbor at Pearl would have been suicidal, and it is likely that the American garrison would have made the northern beaches of Oahu—the most favorable landing sites—quite impregnable to direct assault. But it is possible that elite units of the Imperial Army, such as those used in airborne assaults in Indonesia, could have been employed after the American defenses were hammered by the battleships of Japan once the U.S. air defenses had been suppressed or exhausted. Japan's attacks across the beaches would take terrible casualties in their assaults, but with sufficient fire support from the fleet, they might overwhelm the defenders and force the ignominious surrender of another American Pacific bastion.

Nowhere in the Imperial archives can we find a plan to extend the Imperial sweep further eastward, but, while Japanese fleets or squadrons probably could not operate effectively far beyond Hawaii, occasional raids in force, or lucky cruiser strikes against a few high visibility transports bound for Hawaii in desperate U.S. efforts to reinforce the islands, could have been very bad for American morale. Also, Japanese submarine raids against the West Coast 2,000-odd miles to the northeast—like the shelling of isolated outposts—surely would have heightened tension there and perhaps even have been of some military utility. Hunting packs of Japanese subs, with supply subs as mother ships, or resupply vessels, might have threatened coastal traffic until long-range patrols were established, as they were in the Atlantic. Deploying a few submarines off Panama could disrupt shipping in a major way, even if they could not stay on station long, while a bold raid on the Panama Canal, employing aircraft carried by Japan's largest submersibles, flown on a one-way mission from close in, loaded with high explosives, could have wreaked havoc were they able to seriously damage even one of the locks; again the threat would likely have tied up even more American forces.

1942: Year of Decision

The added confusion of a U.S. catastrophe at Midway and Hawaii could well have forced the Joint Chiefs into even more difficult decisions about priorities between Europe and the Pacific. Around the world that summer of 1942, Allied forces were hard-pressed. On the steppes of Russia, German forces were sweeping toward Stalingrad on the Volga and into the Soviet Union's oil-rich Caucasus region. German's Afrika Corps in North Africa was at the gates of Egypt, while in the Atlantic the U-boat menace was growing ever-more deadly; German submarines had sunk

700,000 tons of Allied shipping in June, and losses would reach their peak of 802,000 tons in November. All claims for resources to meet these threats would have to be balanced by General George C. Marshall and President Franklin D. Roosevelt against Japanese threats to the West Coast. The fragile balance of the Anglo-American accords that gave primacy to Europe and the defeat of Hitler might well remain the stated strategic objective, but the harsh realities of the Pacific Theater could well override many commitments. What would be available for the Soviet Union and how could it be shipped there?

Profound shock, reviving the panic of December 1941, was surely possible throughout America in the aftermath of a Hawaiian debacle. Demands for increased commitment to the defense of the West Coast, leading to diversion of troops, artillery, and vital supplies, including aircraft to coastal defense, would be hard to resist with nothing between Japanese-held Hawaii and California. The few long-range patrol craft available to America at this time could well have led to the great strategic weapon in America's arsenal, the B-17 Flying Fortress heavy bomber, being diverted from a build-up in Britain for a future bombardment campaign against Germany, to coastal defense. Surely, the use of the B-17 in the Philippines and in operations out of Midway's limited airstrips had won no glory to the heavy bomber as a weapon against ships at sea, but what else was there? Calls to create a strategic bombing force based in Britain to attack Germany were less likely to get the support required when anti-ship strikes were still considered a major mission for America's long-range bombers and when the Pacific coast seemed to lie exposed to prowling Japanese forces.

Expansion of industrial production was certain, but a greater sense of immediate vulnerability might well have led to higher manpower calls for military service, with consequent waste in both resources and personnel. Certainly, an aroused America could out-produce the world, but would it do so in time? Could American economic mobilization possibly have been as deliberate as it was had the first great battle of the war ended in a defeat that seemed to make the threat to continental America even greater?

The possibility certainly exists that a 1942 rush to create a more massive U.S. Army, with perhaps more than 100 divisions, would have upset timetables, trashed production schedules, and made a mess of efforts to manage bottlenecks in manpower skills, training, and production. Admiral Ernest King and General Marshall would have been even more hard-pressed to decide priorities between the services were America pushed back on its own coast in the Pacific. While solid realists might have re-asserted control later in the war, time lost certainly would have slowed efforts to bring to bear America's real strength, its mechanical-skill and industrial capacity for the production of quantity, quantity, and more quantity, delivered where most necessary, and everywhere else as well.

Despite the hopes of Yamamoto and perhaps some others in Japan's ruling élites that the capture of Hawaii might provide an opportunity to negotiate a settlement with the United States, this seems far-fetched. There is nothing in the history books to suggest that America would be particularly willing to cooperate with the conquerors of Honolulu. As the resounding words of President Roosevelt to Congress on December 8, 1941, made clear: "No matter how long it may take us to overcome this premeditated invasion, the American people in their righteous might will run through to absolute victory." Long and protracted battle for the islands could have worn down American strength to the point that even with Japan's fleet seriously depleted by the effort, the task of building the entire grand fleet needed to assault and retake the islands might have been judged not worth the time and effort.

It seems to me likely that the Central Pacific Offensive—envisioning the seizure of selected islands and atolls, using each as a base for the next and moving ever closer to Japan—long the dream of America's naval strategists, would have been rendered a relic by Japanese success in Operation MI, Operation AL, and the Eastern Operation culminating in an invasion of Hawaii. Rather than a massive D Day–type invasion against Hawaii, what we might well have seen was the alternative nightmare of Japanese strategic thinkers before the war—a determined United States advance via Alaska.

It is in this strategy that we can best understand Yamamoto's interest in the Aleutian islands at the time of the Midway operation. The only direct route to Japan available under the circumstances foreseen here would be the fog-shrouded, ice-clogged wilderness of the Alaska-Aleutians approach. The Great Circle Route, as it was called, ran from San Francisco to Manila and passed directly through Tokyo. But to make this approach work as a war-winning strategy would require building not just the Alcan Highway, begun in February 1942 to provide a direct overland route to central Alaska, but what we might figuratively call "the Alaska Super-Highway," a string of air bases, naval complexes, transportation nexuses, and depots all the way from western Canada and Seattle, Washington, to Dutch Harbor and beyond. This is the kind of project that America and Canada could handle if the need were determined great enough to complete it—thousands of miles of highway, rendered all-weather with awesome road-borne capacity emerging, supplying short-range leaps through the Aleutians, stretching across the northern Pacific's rim, culminating in Kiska and Attu in the western Aleutians, down through the northern Kurile Islands, wrested from Japan by sea assault covered by the new American Navy that would have been ready in the two years or so this could take.

Whenever one studies the Second World War and American power, one axiom seems to emerge: Whatever America had to build would have been built, drawing on a virtually limitless industrial potential; yet there are at least some flaws in such arguments that might make speculation more than idle. One is that the mobilization of America, begun well before Pearl Harbor and carried on thereafter was not pursued in an environment when ultimate victory in any theater could be doubted. Two American fleets lost in six months—the battle fleet smashed at Pearl Harbor and the carriers lost at Midway—certainly made for no "turning-the-tide" mentality that was historically so important in sustaining American spirit in the still-dark days of 1942. With the Philippines lost, the American flag swept from the western Pacific, the strategic riches of the Dutch

East Indies and Indochina lost to the Allies, the loss of a second fleet at Midway and perhaps the capture of Pearl Harbor by a Japanese invasion, might have shaken that resolve.

Endgame

Would America have lost the war? Not likely, given American economic potential, but winning the war against Japan after a disaster at Midway would have been an even more daunting task. Making up the losses would only have been part of the problem, since with the initiative still in Japanese hands after June 1942, America would still have been on the strategic defensive, forced to allocate resources on the basis in large measure on what the enemy might attempt. This might have drained away enough to prolong the war in Europe, which, as we now know, could have allowed some of the German superweapons to come on-line earlier. The need to match German technical prowess in jet aircraft, and the threat posed by rockets, especially the V-2, might have greatly complicated European Theater operations. For millions languishing in death camps, their fate largely ignored by the Allies, Nazi Germany's "Final Solution," might well have moved even closer to its objective.

A lengthened war could also have meant prolonged Japanese control over East Asia. The captured suffering unspeakable deprivations under Japanese occupation throughout East and Southeast Asia would have seen that horror extended. Japanese mobilization of labor in China and Malaya might well have meant an even more astronomic death toll. In the end, of course, the final toll from a rain of atomic bombs on Japan, when at last the Home Islands were approached is even more terrible to contemplate than the ruin that was suffered in Japan in 1945. This assumes, of course, that speculative "Big Science" projects like Manhattan could have received funding in the face of other crises facing American industry and strategic planners forced to deal with a continued rampage of Japan through 1942.

◆ ELIHU ROSE ◆

THE CASE OF THE MISSING CARRIERS

As the attacking Japanese planes swooped into Pearl Harbor on December 7, 1941, the U.S. Pacific Fleet appeared as sitting ducks. Almost, but not quite. The harbor was chock full of battleships, destroyers, submarines, and any number of auxiliary vessels, but the Pacific Fleet's three aircraft carriers were missing. The gods of war had thus given the U.S. Navy one small gift to assuage its impending humiliation: the *Saratoga* was in overhaul on the West Coast; the *Lexington* was delivering aircraft to Midway; and the *Enterprise* was on a similar mission to Wake.

All lived to fight another day. The *Lexington* was lost at the Coral Sea and the *Saratoga* earned seven Battle Stars in her subsequent career—important though not decisive contributions.

However, it was planes from the *Enterprise*, along with those of the *Yorktown*, that sank four Japanese carriers at Midway, turning the tide of that climactic battle and administering the coup de grace to Japanese hopes of invading Midway and Hawaii as well as aborting plans for operations against Ceylon and Australia. It was the single greatest Japanese naval defeat since Korean ironclads ravaged a Japanese fleet in 1592. As Samuel Eliot Morison observed: "Midway changed the whole course of the Pacific War." In a tantalizing what if, one might speculate upon the outcome of the battle had not the *Enterprise* been out of harm's way on December 7.

◆ *Elihu Rose teaches military history at New York University.*

STEPHEN E. AMBROSE

D DAY FAILS

Atomic Alternatives in Europe

Often, in military history, the dominoes fall where the wind blows them. We have seen that happen with the influence of weather in the preternatural wetness of 1529, the breezes that disrupted the Spanish Armada, and George Washington's fog-aided escape after the Battle of Long Island. But rarely have the whims of weather produced more far-reaching consequences than they did at D Day. June 6, 1944 witnessed not just a genuinely decisive military event, but, in a sense, a political one that determined which ideological path Western Europe would follow in the next half century. What if the Allied invasion of Normandy had been called off or had failed? What if the famous window—a brief break in the storm battering the continent—had not opened, and Dwight D. Eisenhower had withheld the go-ahead or had gone through with the invasion anyway? Would the storm have become for the Germans a force multiplier, giving them the edge that Allied deceptions—which caused Hitler and his generals to divert divisions to other possible invasion sites—had taken away? In this speculation by Stephen E. Ambrose, failure would have resulted in alternatives that ranged from unpleasant to frightening.

✦ *If history is enjoying a resurgence of popularity, one of those chiefly responsible is Professor Ambrose. He has written (at the latest count) twenty books, including multivolume biographies of Dwight D. Eisenhower and Richard M. Nixon, as well as his three most recent bestsellers,* UNDAUNTED COURAGE, *the story of the Lewis and Clark expedition, his two accounts of the end of World War II in* WESTERN EUROPE, D DAY *and* CITIZEN SOLDIERS, *and most recently,* COMRADES.

F or what if history to work, there has to be a real chance that things could have turned out differently because of forces beyond human control—meaning, in most cases, weather. Some parts of weather can be predicted with certainty long in advance—tides and moon conditions—but others, such as wind, waves, and cloud cover can scarcely be guessed much more than twenty-four hours in advance, especially in an area of notoriously volatile weather such as the English Channel.

Overlord—the code name for the Allied invasion of Western Europe—was the most tightly planned offensive of the war. From the beginning, SHAEF (Supreme Headquarters Allied Expeditionary Force) counted on reasonable weather—moderate seas, low winds, scattered cloud cover. Heavy seas, high winds, a zero ceiling would make the assault impossible.

The invasion had originally been scheduled for June 5, 1944. The weather, which had been beautiful for the first three days of June, began to deteriorate. In the channel, a drizzle began to turn into a cold, penetrating rain. The final weather conference was scheduled for 4:00 A.M., June 4. Group Captain J. M. Stagg, whom Dwight D. Eisenhower described as a "dour but canny Scot," made the weather predictions, as he had every day for a month, spending half an hour or more with the SHAEF commander. Stagg had bad news. A low-pressure system was moving in. June 5 would be overcast and stormy. Eisenhower decided to postpone it for at least one day.

In the early hours of June 5, with the wind and rain rattling the windowpanes of the SHAEF headquarters, Stagg made the most famous weather prediction in military history. He thought the storm would ease off later that day, and that by Tuesday, June 6, the weather would be

D DAY: THE WEATHER FACTOR

Twice, weather might have caused an Allied disaster on the beaches of Normandy. A fierce gale let up just in time for the D Day invasion to go forward on June 6, 1944. The next possible day, June 19, brought an even more turbulent tempest, shown here battering the artificial harbor code-named Mulberry.

(Corbis/Bettmann)

acceptable. The rain that was then pouring down would stop before daybreak. There would be thirty-six hours of more or less clear weather. Eisenhower asked for a guarantee; Stagg laughed and said the general knew that was impossible. Then Ike made his decision: "Okay, let's go."

Stagg's prediction was as much hunch as scientific. Though he was only twenty-eight, he had spent several years as a weather forecaster. Other weathermen, from the Royal Navy and the U.S. Navy, for example, disagreed with him—they thought the storm would continue. Stagg wrote in his memoir, *Forecast Overlord*, that even had he had access to modern satellite imagery, he still would have been guessing as much as predicting. A half-century after Overlord, when the BBC has satellites and reporting stations such as Stagg could not imagine, the weather predictions in May or June for twenty-four hours in advance are dead wrong about half the time.

So, what if the storm had continued into June 6? Eisenhower could have called the invasion back, although not easily. Had he done so, he would not only have given away the landing site, but June 19, the next date in which the combination of full moon and low tides was suitable, would witness the worst storm of the year to hit Normandy.

If, on the other hand, he had gone ahead with the invasion, the consequences may have proved disastrous. The landing craft would have been tossed about like toy boats in a bathtub. Men trying to go ashore from any craft that made it to land would have been vomiting, exhausted, suffering all the agonies of seasickness, incapable of fighting. There would have been no air cover and no paratrooper support, as the air drops would have been scattered to hell and gone), no supporting bombardment from the two- and four-engine bombers. The Navy might have been able to fire its big guns, but because of the rolling of the vessels in the waves, accuracy would have been limited. The German defenders, protected from the elements in their bunkers, would have delivered a deadly fire on the hapless Allied infantry.

Eisenhower would have had no choice but to order the follow-up landings canceled. He almost certainly would not have been able to withdraw the men from the initial waves: They would have been killed or captured, as had happened to the raiders at Dieppe in 1942, the war's first major amphibious landing in Europe. At nightfall on June 6, he would have issued his prepared-in-advance statement to the press: "The landings have failed . . ." The Allied fleet would have pulled back to England in disarray, its tail between its legs.

Then what? Eisenhower would have certainly lost his job, and this was something he knew, which was why he had prepared his statement accepting full responsibility for the failure. There was no sense bringing the entire high command down with him. But who could have taken his place? Bernard Montgomery was unacceptable to the Americans, who were making the major contribution. Omar Bradley would have been as tarred by the brush of failure as Eisenhower. George S. Patton, perhaps— he was being readied to take a field command after the landing was established and would not have been implicated in the failure. But Monty would have tried to exercise a veto over Patton's appointment. George C. Marshall, the U.S. Army chief of staff was a possible choice: He had originally hoped to lead the invasion but President Roosevelt felt that he was too valuable in Washington.

The Allied planners, meanwhile, would have been in despair. Despite failure, they still would have had an enormous force at their disposal of land, air, and sea forces. But it had taken more than a year to put the Overlord plan together. There was no alternative plan available. In retrospect, Normandy was the perfect choice; but the planners could not have tried there a second time. Where, then? The Pas de Calais beaches were far better defended than those in Normandy. Le Havre bristled with German guns. Reinforcing the South of France landings (Operation Dragoon) in mid-August would have been the most appealing option, perhaps the only way was to get the forces gathered in Britain into the battle in France. But such a diversion would have created immense logistical problems while leaving the bulk of the Allied army far short of the Rhine, not to mention Berlin. The liberation of southern France was not going to end the war, or even seriously threaten Hitler's empire in northwest Europe. Moreover, with his channel flank secure for the moment, Hitler would risk little in sending reinforcements south—not the case when Operation Dragoon actually took place. Something akin to the stalemate in Italy would have ensued in the Rhone Valley. Still, the south of France seems the most likely alternative.

Failure would have brought immediate political as well as military problems. I would guess that the Churchill government could not have survived—after all, it had bet the kingdom on Overlord. The successor government would have had a mandate—to do what? Prosecute the war more vigorously? Hardly possible. Negotiate with Hitler? Unthinkable. Muddle on and hope for the best? Most likely.

In the United States, meanwhile, Roosevelt—who had also bet the house on Overlord—would have been secure from a no-confidence vote. But he had a presidential election coming up in five months. Without a vigorous display of American military might—and where would that have come from?—he would have lost the election. The Tom Dewey Administration would have had a mandate—to do what? Prosecute the war in the Pacific with more vigor, that's what.

Failure on D Day would not have spared Hitler the problems of a two-front war, because of the Allied forces still intact in Britain, always posing a threat. Still, he would have been free to transfer at least some of his army in France to his Eastern front. Perhaps more important, he could have used the D Day failure to split the strange alliance of West and East. How hard would it have been for Goebbels and the Nazi propaganda machine to convince Stalin that the capitalists were ready to fight to the last Russian? It is not inconceivable that Hitler and Stalin would have groped their way back to 1939, when they were partners, and reinstated the Nazi-Soviet pact. It is also possible that Stalin might have overrun Germany, then France, and the war in Europe would have ended with the Communists in control of the continent. The Red Army would have been on the English Channel. It is hard to imagine a worse outcome.

With the mounting Soviet threat and Operation Dragoon stalled in the South of France, Britain and the United States would have increased the severity of the bombing raids over Germany. A climax would have come late in the summer of 1945, with atomic bombs exploding over German cities. What a finish *that* would have been.

After that, things get extremely murky, as they always do in what if history the farther one goes away from a single event. The vacuum in a Central Europe devastated by atomic bombs would have sucked in armies from the outside—the Red Army from the east and the Allied armies from Britain. Would they have clashed? If so, would the United

States have used a bomb or two against the Soviets? Or would they have cooperated (as they in fact did in 1945), drawing a line through Central Europe?

In the Pacific in the summer of 1945, with the United States expending her atomic arsenal against Germany and Stalin free to transfer some part of his armies from the German to the Japanese front, the Red Army would have invaded the northern Japanese home islands. In this scenario, Japan would have been spared the atomic bombs but subjected to a Communist dictatorship in the northern half of a divided country. This was exactly what Stalin was planning and would have done if the Japanese had not surrendered to the Americans first. Had Stalin gotten into Japan, who knows when, and if, the Russians ever would have left.

That the consequences of a failure on D Day would have been catastrophic is obvious; what they would have been is anyone's guess; what stands out for me is that one of the consequences would *not* have been a Nazi victory. Almost surely, however, one of the consequences would have been a Communist victory in Europe. A Communist Germany, France, Low Countries, and Italy would have meant no NATO and a possibility of a Communist Great Britain. Relations with the Soviet Union would have been impossibly difficult and dangerous. That is a terrible prospect—but it might have happened if the Germans had beaten us on the beaches of Normandy.

THE SOVIET INVASION OF JAPAN

We now know that the Soviet Union, whose armies had raced across Manchuria and down Sakhalin Island in August 1945, intended to invade Hokkaido, the northernmost of the Japanese home islands. That invasion would have taken place two months before Operation Olympic, our invasion of the south island, Kyushu. While Emperor Hirohito's surrender declaration awaited the official signing in Tokyo Bay on September 2, the Soviets continued to gobble up territory and were poised to make a leap to Hokkaido. That amphibious landing would have been an improvised affair, but no matter: Of Cold War confrontations that almost happened but didn't, none is more frightening in its potential for fatal mischief.

It's not just that the Soviets would, in just over two weeks and at minimal cost, have picked up a large share of the Japanese marbles that had taken the Allies almost four years and thousands of lives to gather. If their landing force had established so much as a beach hold on Hokkaido—and American raiders had apparently gone ashore there with little resistance that summer—the Soviets would have had a legitimate claim to the island, a significant (and no doubt troublemaking) role in the formal surrender preparations, and a zone of a partitioned Tokyo. Just think of the Cold War implications of a Berlin in the Pacific. (Looking on the positive side, we could have blockaded the Soviet zone of Tokyo in response to Stalin's blockade of Berlin in 1948, which might have ended that crisis—or created a more general one.) Consider, too, the deadening effect of a Soviet Hokkaido on Japan's reconstruction—or the inhibiting effect that a hostile occupying force on a home island would have had on our decision to intervene in

Korea, using Japan as a base. The chances for future regional and international conflict seem infinite.

We are lucky that the Pacific war ended when it did. If the war had gone on for even a week or two longer, the entire East-West geopolitical situation might have changed irrevocably. In retrospect, it begins to seem that when Harry S Truman warned Stalin to keep away from the Japanese home islands—and the Soviet dictator reluctantly called off the Hokkaido operation at the eleventh hour—our accidental president made one of his most important decisions, one that ranks with his decision to drop the bomb.

If he hadn't, I might not be writing these words today.

❖ *Robert Cowley is the founding editor of* MHQ: The Quarterly Journal of Military History.

DAVID CLAY LARGE

FUNERAL IN BERLIN

The Cold War Turns Hot

F or forty-five years, the divided city of Berlin was at the center of what David
Clay Large calls, "The surreal game known as the Cold War." On a number of occasions, that game could have taken much different forms than it
did, and Large examines the most serious of those scenarios. What if the Germans
and Russians had made a second pact in 1944? Should we have tried to reach Berlin
before the Russians in April 1945? Could we have done so? How real was the threat
of a Soviet invasion of Western Europe in the late 1940s? What would have happened
if we had used force to resist the Berlin blockade in 1948? Or if, on the other hand,
the Allied powers had decided to abandon the city? What were the dangers of making
Germany a "neutral" state, with an independent army, as Stalin proposed in 1952?
What if President Eisenhower had forbidden Francis Gary Powers's fatal U-2 flight?
Or if we had used force to stop the East Germans from building the Berlin Wall?
Could Berlin, Large asks, have become the Sarajevo of World War III?

◈ *David Clay Large is professor of history at Montana State University and the author of such books as* BETWEEN TWO FIRES: EUROPE'S PATH IN THE 1930S, WHERE GHOSTS WALKED: MUNICH'S ROAD TO THE THIRD REICH, *and the forthcoming* BERLIN: THE METROPOLIS IN THE MAKING OF MODERN GERMANY.

As the Cold War dragged on and on, with a kind of ideological permafrost settling over much of the world, many people on both sides of the divide came to perceive the situation as reassuringly "normal," almost as a condition that could not have been otherwise. Believing that no substantial change would come, they imagined that change had never been possible. Yet of course there was nothing immutable about the forty-year standoff we call the Cold War; on a number of occasions it might have evolved very differently than it did, especially in the early phases.

Nowhere were the opportunities for alternative development greater than in Germany, and particularly in Berlin, where the hot war in Europe had ended. Here the wartime partners-turned-adversaries stood toe to toe and tank to tank.

And yet it is quite possible that the surreal game known as the Cold War might never have gotten going at all—or, at the very least, that Germany might not have been its primary arena and most coveted prize. And if Germany had been removed from the game, the nature of the contest would have been very different, as would the relative strengths of the players.

The Allies Take Berlin

Everyone knows that the Nazis made a "nonaggression" pact with the Soviets in August 1939, which allowed the Germans to embark on their aggression against Poland in the following month. Less well known is that Hitler considered making another pact—this one a separate peace—with the Soviets in the fall of 1944. After suffering a series of military reversals beginning with Stalingrad, the Wehrmacht was on the retreat in the

East. Hitler's Japanese allies were urging him to make peace with the Soviets so that he might concentrate all his forces against the United States and Great Britain. The führer had resisted such advice in the past, but now, given the reversal in his military fortunes, he briefly contemplated going back to the negotiating table with his one-time ally. Had he actually sought discussions with Moscow, the Soviets might have been prepared to listen. After all, while formally pledging allegiance to the unconditional surrender doctrine of the Grand Alliance, they had recently promised a group of anti-Hitler officers (the so-called "National Committee for a Free Germany") that Germany could retain its borders of 1937 if the Reich suspended its operations against the USSR.

In the end, of course, Hitler decided that the best way to reverse the tides that were running against him was to launch his ambitious Ardennes offensive in the West. Stalin, smelling German blood, abandoned any further considerations of a separate peace. But what if the Germans and Russians *had* made a second pact in 1944, thereby allowing the Reich to focus all its energies on the West? We cannot know whether Hitler would have been able to bring the Western powers to terms (a similar scenario in 1918 had of course not yielded this result), but the Reich would at least have avoided being invaded from the east as well as from the west. And Russia, for its part, would not have been in a position to exact its pound of German flesh, or, indeed, to gain its foothold in Eastern Europe. Without an Eastern European empire, it is highly doubtful that the Soviets would or could have mounted a challenge to the West in the postwar era at all.

Another chance to avert the Cold War came in spring 1945, as Allied armies overran Germany from west and east. Alliance strategists had earlier agreed that the Red Army would take Berlin, for this seemed dictated by the logistical situation. Moreover, it was planned that Berlin would lie within the Soviet zone of occupation in Germany. But the Western armies had made such rapid progress after crossing the Rhine in March 1945 that a push on to Berlin seemed not only possible but, to some Western military figures, advisable. As is well known, Field Marshall

Montgomery pressed General Eisenhower for permission to lead a "single, full-blooded thrust toward Berlin." Eisenhower rejected this appeal, insisting instead on a broad-front march through Germany that would leave Berlin to the Russians. The British were furious over this decision, contemptuously referring to Eisenhower's deference to Stalin as "Have a Go, Joe," an expression used by London prostitutes seeking custom from American GIs. The Berlin question rose again in mid-April when the American Ninth Army reached the Elbe, only fifty miles from Berlin. The American commander, William Simpson, now pleaded for the chance to take the Nazi capital, which he estimated he could reach in one day. But again Eisenhower said no, not wanting to risk possibly high American casualties for a target he did not consider strategically significant. When he learned of his commander in chief's decision, General George Patton, who had seconded Simpson's plea, was incredulous. "Ike, I don't see how you figure that out. We better take Berlin, and quick—and on to the Oder!" Eisenhower countered that Berlin, with its wrecked infrastructure and hordes of displaced persons, would be more a liability than an asset. "Who would want it?" he asked. To which Patton replied: "I think history will answer that question for you."

For half a century arguments have raged over whether Allied armies could have beaten the Russians to Berlin. The answer is: probably not. For all his cocky bluster, Montgomery was a very cautious and slow-moving general; he was an unlikely candidate to win a race to any goal save a pedestal on which he could prop himself. Simpson was a more energetic leader, but the troops he had led to the Elbe were mere spearheads; the real strength was much farther back. To make the final rush to Berlin, he would have needed large quantities of gasoline, which was in short supply, and he would have had to cross several water barriers, which would have taken time. The Russians, on the other hand, were fifteen miles closer to Berlin than the Americans, and they had a vastly larger force— some 1,250,000 men and 22,000 pieces of artillery. True, it ended up taking the Red Army about two weeks to conquer Berlin from the moment they launched their final offensive, but they would undoubtedly have tried to accelerate their pace had they seen that the Americans were racing for the city.

However, this being an essay on hypothetical scenarios, let us assume for the moment that the Western armies *could have* beaten the Russians to Berlin, or, failing that, at least gotten there at roughly the same time. Would it have made much of a difference? Again, the answer is probably no—unless the changed military situation in Berlin were accompanied by a wholly different geopolitical strategy on the part of the Western powers. Contesting the Red Army's ambition to conquer Berlin would have made sense only if imbedded within a comprehensive determination to reverse the earlier agreements allowing the Soviets spheres of influence in eastern Germany and Eastern Europe. None of the Western leaders, not even Churchill, contemplated such a plan of action in 1945.

Yet this option, or something close to it, was what Patton and Montgomery envisioned and even openly advocated. Once the war against Nazi Germany was over, Patton spoke of "pushing on to Moscow," if need be with help from what remained of the Wehrmacht, while Montgomery called for the immediate establishment of "a flank facing east." In Patton's view, the United States had come to Europe to give the peoples there the right to govern themselves. The Nazis had denied them this right, and now the Soviets were threatening to do so. Thus America's "job" in Europe was not yet done. "We must finish the job now, while we are here and ready," he declared in May 1945, "or [finish it] later under less favorable circumstances."

Patton and Montgomery's scheme was sheer political fantasy in the context of the time, but if the will had been there to attempt such a course (and emphatically it was not), the prospects for its *military* success were by no means nonexistent. At the end of the war in Europe the western parts of the Continent were occupied by the largest coalition army the world had ever seen. The American force stationed in western Germany alone numbered 1.6 million men. The draining war against Japan was about to end and America was about to come into sole possession (at least for a time) of the atomic bomb. The Red Army, while thick on the ground, had been badly beaten up in its final assault on the Reich, and it was so low on food and supplies that it had to live off the land (much to the detriment of its relations with the Germans). A Western military campaign to expel the Red Army from Eastern Europe would obviously have meant more "hot war" in Europe—a hideous concept to just about everybody—but, just as obviously, it would if successful have removed the basis for a subsequent "cold war" waged over divided Germany and Europe.

There was another, rather more modest, alternative open to the Western powers that would have undercut the Soviets' position in Eastern Europe without necessarily pushing them back (again to quote Patton) "to the Asiatic steppes where they belong." The Americans, British, and French might have insisted upon occupying their sectors of Berlin at the same time that the Soviets set up their occupation regime, which was their right, and then demanded genuine Four-Power administration over the entire city, which was also their right. This would have prevented the Soviets from forcing Communist-dominated political institutions on their sector, a tactic that informally divided the city. Without secure control in eastern Berlin, the Soviets' position in the rest of eastern Germany would have been much weaker, which in turn would have weakened their grip on Eastern Europe.

1948: The Soviets Push West or Get Tougher in Berlin

Would Have, Could Have, Should Have. By 1948, the opportunities to avert the Cold War had vanished, for the simple reason that it had already started, and the chance to deny the USSR a power base in Eastern and Central Europe had also been lost. Indeed, the balance of power in the region, at least in terms of conventional military strength, had now shifted dramatically in favor of the Soviets. According to American intelligence estimates (now known to have been exaggerated), the Soviet land army totaled 2.5 million men organized in 175 divisions. Eighty-four were said to be stationed in the Soviet Occupation zone in Germany and in other "satellite" countries. Against this force the West could muster only sixteen divisions stationed in Germany, Austria, the Benelux countries, and France. Because of rapid demobilization and budget cuts, the great American army that had invaded Hitler's Europe was no more. U.S. units on the Continent were undersized, badly equipped, and poorly trained. The forces of America's allies were even worse. Pentagon analysts regarded the Dutch and Belgian troops as practically useless and were also unsure of France, which had a strong Communist Party and extensive colonial commitments. (It was for this reason that the Americans were so anxious to rearm the Germans in the Western zones: *they* at least could be counted on to know how to fight.) It was believed in some quarters that the Russian superiority in conventional forces might allow their armies to cross the Rhine in five days and reach the channel in two weeks. "All the Russians need to reach the Rhine is shoes," said American Under Secretary of State Robert Lovett.

We know now that the Soviets had no plans for an invasion of Western Europe in the first years after the war. Stalin believed that his nation was not yet ready to fight the West. Someday, maybe. But what if the Soviets had not been so patient, or so prudent? What if they had in fact put on their marching shoes and made a dash for the Rhine, or indeed the channel, in 1948? Could they really have made it as easily as some Western analysts feared?

In addition to sturdy shoes, they would have needed antiradiation suits. Given the relative weakness of their conventional defenses, the Western powers were prepared to meet a Russian advance across Central and Western Europe with an immediate deployment of tactical and strategic nuclear weapons. Contingency plans worked out by the service branches of the American military variously envisaged air attacks with atomic weapons on Russian troops and lines of communication, followed by surface counterattacks launched from bridgeheads in Spain and Sicily (the army's option); atomic attacks on the Soviet Union by long-range strategic bombers (the air force proposal); or tactical atomic strikes by carrier-based aircraft on Soviet ground troops (the navy preference). Admiral D. V. Gallery, one of the American defense planners, expressed the hope that tactical atomic attacks on advancing Russian ground troops in Central Europe would obviate the need for an all-out strategic bombardment of the Soviet motherland. "When the Russian armies are stopped short of the Rhine," he wrote, "their leaders and people may see that they had better negotiate a peace or else they will be in for a large-scale atomic blitz. In this case, with their armies halted east of the Rhine, the threat of the blitz might have more effect than the actual blitz itself if their armies were overrunning Europe."

Even if it proved unnecessary to extend the American "atomic blitz" to the Soviet motherland, a tactical nuclear campaign against Russian troops would have yielded horrendous "collateral damage" in Central and Western Europe, the very regions that Washington was hoping to save. Appreciation of this fact fueled "better Red than dead" arguments across Europe, especially in western Germany, where folks began to worry that Washington and its allies intended "to fight World War III to the last German."

Of course, instead of putting on their marching shoes, the Soviets put the squeeze on Berlin, where the West was particularly vulnerable. In response to Western measures aimed at creating a new West German state (which Moscow, still hoping to control all of Germany, resolutely opposed), the Soviets began, in spring 1948, to interfere with Western rail and road traffic between West Berlin and western Germany. The Russians could do this easily because the Western powers had neglected to secure guarantees of unlimited access across the Soviet zone to their sectors in Berlin. Western Allied access was now restricted to three roads, two railroads, a canal, and three air corridors. In June 1948, following the introduction of a new West German currency to Berlin, the Soviets dramatically tightened their squeeze by cutting the land ties between western Germany and West Berlin. Contrary to popular mythology, however, the Soviets did not isolate West Berlin entirely; they continued to allow trade between the western sectors of the city and the Soviet zone, and also the passage of goods and people from East to West Berlin. They left these avenues open largely because their own occupation zone was heavily dependent on trade with West Berlin. Moscow's immediate goal with its somewhat leaky "blockade" was to sabotage the creation of a West German state; down the line Russia hoped that the West would see the folly of keeping garrisons in such a vulnerable place as West Berlin and would simply pull out.

The Soviet initiative produced a sense of crisis in the Western Allied capitals, especially in Washington, which was expected to take the lead in determining an appropriate response. George Kennan, head of the State Department's policy planning staff, recalled: "No one was sure how the Russian move could be countered, or whether it could be countered at all. The situation was dark and full of danger." The situation seemed so dangerous, in fact, that Congress called for an immediate evacuation of American dependents from Berlin, and some politicians advocated military withdrawal as well. Intriguingly, so did General Omar Bradley, the Army chief of staff. Even before the Soviets cut the land ties to West Berlin, Bradley asked General Lucius Clay, American commandant in Berlin, whether it made any sense for the United States to hold its position there at the risk of war : "Will not Russian restrictions be added one by one, which eventually make our position untenable unless we ourselves were prepared to threaten or actually start a war to remove these restrictions?" he asked. And he added: "Here we doubt whether our people are prepared to start a war in order to maintain our position in Berlin and Vienna." Clay, by contrast, believed that the Soviet tactics were simply a bluff to push the West out of Berlin, but if it proved necessary to go to war to "save" Berlin, he was prepared to do so. "If Berlin falls," he warned, "Germany will be next. If we intend to defend Europe against Communism, we should not budge."

As it turned out, the West did not budge from Berlin, but it is worth asking what might have happened had Washington and its allies abandoned the city in 1948, which many then saw as the wisest course. Whether or not holding West Berlin was *militarily* significant in the emerging Cold War, it was certainly *politically* important to do so. By

1948 Western prestige was very much on the line in Berlin, and a pull-back there would have weakened the Allies'—especially the Americans'—leverage throughout Europe and the world. Washington was committed to helping Western Europe recover economically and regain its political confidence, goals that presupposed America's retention of its own high standing. The loss of prestige and clout that would inevitably have accompanied an abandonment of Berlin would have been particularly disastrous for American policy in western Germany, for this would have greatly strengthened the considerable opposition within Germany to the creation of a West German state. Konrad Adenauer, who favored the establishment of a "Bonn Republic" closely tied to the West, would not have been able to prevail without strong American backing. The formal division of Germany in 1949 was unpalatable to many Germans, but without it all of Germany would have been open to continuing destabilization efforts by the Soviets and their German Communist clients. A Germany "up for grabs" would have been far more dangerous than a Germany divided, painful as the division was.

As we know, instead of abandoning Berlin, the Western powers responded to the Soviet blockade by launching a massive airlift that supplied the western sectors of the city with everything from food and coal to candy for the kids (but not, as another myth would have it, with *everything* the Berliners needed to survive). The airlift, however, was not the only option that the West considered to "break" the Soviet blockade. Before the lift was decided upon, General Clay urged a much riskier gambit: the dispatch of an armed convoy from western Germany across the Soviet zone to West Berlin. He asked General Curtis LeMay, commander of the U.S. Air Force in Europe, to provide air support in case the Russians started shooting—an eventuality that LeMay did not expect but believed would provide a fine opportunity for a preemptive strike on all Russian air fields in Germany. "Naturally we knew where they were," he said later. "We had observed the Russian fighters lined up in a nice smooth line on the aprons at every place. If it had happened, I think we could have cleaned them up pretty well, in no time at all."

Of course "it" did not happen, since the convoy idea was quickly dismissed as unworkable. As Bradley cautioned: "The Russians could stop an armed convoy without opening fire one it. Roads could be closed for repair or a bridge could go up just ahead of you and then another bridge behind you and you'd be in a hell of a fix." Had the U.S. military adopted Clay's strategy and stumbled into a "fix," the only way to have gotten out of it, short of surrender, would have been to send larger forces to the rescue, with all the risks of escalation that this would have entailed.

The airlift option that was eventually selected may have made more sense than Clay's convoy, but it was hardly without its own risks. There was considerable concern that the Russians might try to shoot down the Allied planes or obstruct the lift in some other provocative way. Such concerns took on added urgency when, before the full lift was even operational, a Soviet fighter buzzed and then smashed into a British transport plane approaching Gatow airfield in the British sector. Both aircraft crashed, killing the Soviet pilot and fourteen passengers and crew on the British plane. Fortunately there were no more incidents of this kind, and the Soviets never opened fire on any of the airlift planes. They did, however, announce in September 1948 that they would hold air maneuvers over the Berlin area, and this produced a new war scare in Washington because it was interpreted as a possible preliminary to aggressive measures.

Had the Soviets in fact used force against the airlift (which apparently they never seriously considered), war would certainly have erupted, for the United States (and the British) fully intended to answer fire with fire. President Truman reassured Defense Secretary James Forrestal, who was worried that America might back down, that he would order the use of the atomic bomb if push came to shove over Berlin. Coming from the man who had ordered the atomic attacks against Japan in 1945, this promise had some heft to it. B-29 aircraft capable of delivering atomic bombs were duly dispatched to Britain. Reiterating earlier contingency plans, the National Security Council directed that the U.S. military should assume that nuclear weapons would be deployed if war broke out. Had the big trigger indeed been pulled, Berlin, the place from which Hitler had orchestrated World War II, would have become the Sarajevo of World War III. And this new conflict, in turn, might well have managed to become what World War I was supposed to have been but was not: "The War to End All Wars."

In the end, the Soviets lifted the Berlin Blockade not only because of the Allied airlift, but because the West imposed a counterblockade against the USSR. By early spring 1949 the Western measures were effectively disrupting what was left of East-West trade in Central Europe, which was vital to the Soviet economy. If the Russians had been economically stronger—if, so to speak, they had possessed adequate butter to go along with their plentiful guns—they could have imposed a tighter blockade on Berlin and withstood the counterblockade from the West. They could then have put the Allies in a truly desperate situation, since the airlift, even at its peak, had been incapable of simultaneously satisfying West Berlin's total requirements for food, coal, and industrial goods. Even without firing a shot, the Soviets could have forced the Western powers to chose between abandoning their post in Berlin or using their air power to drop bombs instead of bon-bons.

A Dangerous Reunified Germany in 1952

By the early 1950s, the Soviets were obliged to reconcile themselves to the existence of a separate West German state, but there was a real question whether they would tolerate an *armed* West German state operating within the Western alliance structure, which was a major foreign policy goal of the Americans and the Adenauer government in Bonn. Washington had concluded that the most effective way to deter any Soviet expansionist ambitions in Europe was to bolster the West's conventional defenses with the addition of West German troops. At the time this option was raised, many in the Western camp, and in West Germany itself, feared that the very threat of West German rearmament might incite the Soviets to launch a preemptive strike. The Russians, after all, had had some rather intimate experience with German aggression in recent years and were known to dread nothing more than a new *Drang nach Osten* on the part of their old adversaries. Instead of deterring another major war, it was feared, German rearmament might well provoke one.

Such fears seemed all the more credible because the opening of the German rearmament debate coincided with the outbreak of the Korean War, which was widely understood to have been authorized by Moscow, and which many in the West believed might presage a similar fate for Germany, another nation bisected along the Cold War fault line. German newspapers spoke of the Asian crisis as a "test run" for Central Europe. Fearing a "German Korea," West Germans wallowed in apocalyptic fears. Parliamentarians stocked up on cyanide capsules so they could kill themselves rather than fall into enemy hands. Adenauer himself requested two hundred automatic pistols for the defense of his office in case of a Communist attack. Polls showed that over half the West German population believed that if the Communists came over the border, the Western powers would simply abandon the infant Federal Republic.

The West Germans' angst was hardly eased by pronouncements from the new Communist regime in East Germany. The GDR's Stalinist dictator, Walter Ulbricht, declared that Korea proved that "puppet governments" like Adenauer's could not expect to maintain themselves. North Korean leader Kim Il Sung, Ulbricht said, had shown how to reunify Germany, adding: "If the Americans in their imperialist arrogance believe that the Germans have less national consciousness than the Koreans, they have fundamentally deceived themselves."

Ulbricht's threats, of course, were nothing but bluster, but what if he *had* tried to play the role of a German Kim Il Sung? What if his backers, the Soviets, had attempted to rerun the Korean experiment in Germany?

In the first place, Ulbricht would not have had the same advantages as his North Korean counterpart. The East German *Volkspolizei*, which consisted almost exclusively of Wehrmacht veterans, had been built into a military force by the Soviets, but it was not nearly as strong as the North Korean People's Army, which dwarfed the South Korean army in firepower. The Communists' adversary in Europe was considerably more formidable than their target in Korea. Unlike South Korea, West Germany was occupied by three major powers, two of which were geographically close to the region of occupation. The Federal Republic did not yet have an army of its own, but its regional and border police forces would have been a match for the *Volkspolizei*.

To make any significant progress, a Korean-style operation in Germany would have had to involve the Soviets acting not just as backers and suppliers but as active combatants—the role that the Red Chinese took on in Korea after General MacArthur's push to the Yalu River. Had the Soviets thrown their own troops into West Germany in the early 1950s they would have had a harder time of it than in the late 1940s, because since that era the Western powers, especially America, had beefed up their security forces in the region. On the other hand, of course, the Soviets now had a nuclear capacity of their own, having built up a small stockpile of atomic weapons since successfully testing a bomb in 1949. Although they were not yet capable of delivering atomic warheads over long distances, in the event of war their plans called for deployment of tactical atomic weapons on the battlefield and strategic strikes against those targets in the rear that they were capable of reaching. In other words, unlike the Korean War, a "European Korea" would undoubtedly have gone nuclear right from the outset, with the nukes raining in from both sides. Most of Europe would have ended up looking like Berlin in 1945, with the difference that the ruins would have been radioactive.

Stalin, as we now know, had no intention of trying to forcefully re-unify Germany under Communism at the time of the Korean War. But until his dying day, which fortunately came soon, he hoped by political means to wreak havoc in the parts of Germany he did not control. This was the chief motive behind his much-debated diplomatic note of March 1952, in which he proposed to the Western powers the establishment of a reunified and rearmed Germany that would be cleared of all foreign troops and pledged to unconditional neutrality. Stalin never meant for his initiative to be accepted, for he considered a genuinely neutral Germany far too dangerous. For that matter, he believed that even a reunified Germany *allied* to the Soviet Union, but not *controlled* by Moscow, was too dangerous. After all, the Germany that had invaded Russia in 1941 had been Russia's own ally, not an ally of the West. The real target of Stalin's famous note, then, was not the Western powers but West German domestic opinion. The idea was to thwart the development of a West German army and to destabilize the Adenauer government by dangling before the West Germans the tantalizing prospect of reunification in place of West integration. If, with a little diplomatic subterfuge, Stalin could bring down Adenauer and sabotage West German rearmament, this would be a great gain for the Soviet cause.

When Stalin made his "offer" to the Western powers he was assured by one of his diplomats that it would be rejected, which eventually turned out to be the case. But for a brief moment it looked as if the West might actually discuss this proposal, and some Western diplomats thought it had merit.

Let us imagine, therefore, that what Stalin proposed had actually become a reality. Let us imagine that Germany had been reunified not in 1990 but in 1952, and reunified not as a member of NATO but as a "neutral" state with its own independent army. As we know, some Western leaders, most notably Margaret Thatcher and François Mitterand, were not exactly enthusiastic about German reunification in 1990, fearing that the new nation might behave "irresponsibly," might quickly break free of its Western moorings and sail off to some new and terrible adventure. No doubt such fears underestimated the extent to which democratic and peace-loving ideals had taken root in Germany over the past forty years. In the early 1950s, however, there had been precious little time for such values to take root, and a remilitarized Germany without firm Western ties in those days would have been a dangerous vessel indeed, perhaps like the *Bismarck* out for revenge. Stalin worried about a new *Drang nach Osten*, but the *Drang* could have gone in the other direction as well, or in both directions at once, moderation never having been the Germans' strong point. The risk here was not so much of the Cold War turning hot, but of the old hot war reheating. Had this happened, the Cold War antagonists might have been obliged to join forces once again to put out the fires.

Khrushchev in Berlin

As it happened, Stalin's diplomatic gambit was dismissed too soon to have the effect on West German domestic opinion that he had hoped for, and of course Moscow was ultimately unable to prevent Bonn's joining NATO, which occurred in 1955. Even before that point the Soviets, despairing of having much impact in the Federal Republic, had begun focusing on the political and economic consolidation of their own portion of Germany. Yet it proved impossible for the economically strapped USSR to develop its East German satellite into a convincing competitor with West Germany. Over the years East Germany fell further and further behind the West economically, while its political and cultural life remained locked in Stalinist rigidity.

Losing hope for a better life in their own state, East German citizens began decamping by the thousands for the West. The refugees tended to be young, well educated, and highly motivated—the kind of folks that no state can afford to lose.

Trying to stem the flow, the East German government sealed off its border with West Germany in May 1952. Berlin, however, remained an avenue of escape because people could still travel relatively unimpeded from the Soviet sector to West Berlin, and from there it was possible to travel on to West Germany. Tens of thousands more East Germans did just that over the next few years.

In 1958, Nikita Khrushchev decided that the time had come to eliminate West Berlin as a bolt hole for GDR citizens (and as a spy hole for the Western powers). In November of that year he issued an ultimatum: If the Western powers did not agree within six months either to vacate West Berlin, or, as an interim solution, to transform it into a "free city" with no ties to the West, he would sign a treaty with the GDR giving that

CONFRONTATION AT THE BERLIN WALL

In 1961, East German troops in full battle dress stand guard while Communist workmen construct tank traps and reinforce the Berlin Wall. Had the edgy confrontation with the West turned violent, the result might have been World War III.

(Corbis/Bettman—UPI)

state control over all access rights in and out of Berlin. He believed that this threat had credibility because the West was as vulnerable as ever in its isolated outpost. Berlin, Khrushchev liked to say, was the "testicles" of the West, on which he had only to "squeeze" to make his adversaries scream. Moreover, unlike during the first Berlin crisis, Russia now not only had nuclear weapons but the missiles and planes to deliver them to Western cities, including those of the United States. "The leaders of the United States," Khrushchev confidently told his advisors, "are not such idiots as to fight over Berlin."

Khrushchev was wrong about this. American and other Western leaders had no desire to fight over Berlin, but they *were* idiots enough to do so if the issue at stake was their remaining in the city. So if the Soviets themselves had been such idiots as to try once again to squeeze the West out of Berlin, either through a new blockade of their own or one orchestrated by the East Germans, the West would have responded force-fully. Reviving Clay's old convoy idea of 1948, the Pentagon planned to send a platoon-size force across the GDR to Berlin; if the East Germans (or the Soviets) stopped it, a division-size unit would follow. Should even this force run into trouble, an all-out attack would result in which, as Secretary of State John Foster Dulles told Adenauer, "We obviously would not forego the use of nuclear weapons." Indeed, Pentagon strategy called for the United States to use its nukes *first*, to get in its best licks before the Russian rockets flew. The plan also called for extensive use of tactical atomic weapons against enemy targets in Germany. Once again, this would have cause a great deal of collateral damage. Dulles admitted to Adenauer that NATO estimates projected 1.7 million Germans killed and another 3.5 million incapacitated. Even a valiant cold warrior like the German chancellor blanched at the prospect of sacrificing so much to hold the door open in a city he had never liked anyway. "For God's sake, not for Berlin," he gasped.

Hoping for a peaceful resolution to the German crisis, President Eisenhower invited Khrushchev to Camp David in September 1959. The talks were convivial but did not bring much substantial progress; Khrushchev dropped the six-month time frame for a solution to the Berlin crisis, while Ike agreed to a Four-Power summit in Paris in the coming spring on the German problem.

As it turned out, any possible movement at the Paris Summit was scuttled in advance by a momentous event high in the skies over the Soviet Union: the Russians' downing of an American U-2 spy plane on May 1, 1960. Eisenhower had been extremely reluctant to sanction such flights in view of the impending summit, but the CIA had convinced him that one last reconnaissance sortie was necessary to check on Soviet ICBM bases. The Russians were incapable of knocking down a U-2, the CIA promised, and for that very reason they were unlikely to complain publicly about the flights. Alas, the Soviets succeeded not only in bringing down the plane but in capturing the pilot, Francis Gary Powers, who had disobeyed orders to blow up his aircraft and kill himself if he ran into trouble. Failing to extract a public apology from Eisenhower for violating Soviet airspace, Khrushchev walked out of the Paris Summit.

This unhappy turn of events prompts one to ask what might have happened if Eisenhower had acted on his instincts and forbade the U-2 flight. Or, even if the flight had gone ahead as planned, what might have been the result had Powers done what he was supposed to do in the event of trouble, thereby depriving the Soviets of any evidence of American skullduggery?

Here the most likely alternative scenario does not seem very dramatic. Khrushchev had not expected any progress at Paris and was actually looking for a pretext to pull out of the summit. Had he not been able to find another excuse to do so he would have undoubtedly repeated his demands, and perhaps pounded his shoe on the table (which was his want when he got mad), but there is no evidence that Eisenhower was prepared to offer any significant concessions.

The reason Eisenhower was not prepared to dicker on Berlin was that he had come to believe that holding the Western position in the city was symbolically imperative (if militarily difficult). The alternative scenario he conjured up if the West voluntarily gave up Berlin, or was forcibly kicked out, was very dramatic indeed. He saw the old German capital as the first of a proverbial row of dominos, which would inexorably start tumbling if the West abandoned the city. Once Berlin went, Germany would be next, and once Germany fell, all Europe would tumble, and with Europe in Soviet hands, America would be unable to remain a democratic nation. As Eisenhower put it: "If Berlin fell, the U.S. would lose Europe, and if Europe fell into the hands of the Soviet Union and thus added its great industrial plant to the USSR's already great industrial plant, the United States would be reduced to the character of a garrison state if it were to survive at all." In other words, the loss of Berlin meant a fascist America.

Khrushchev hoped to do better with the new American president, John F. Kennedy, who was thought to be skittish on Berlin, which he had barely mentioned in his election campaign. Shortly after being elected,

Kennedy had admitted that of all his foreign policy challenges, Berlin had the greatest potential of forcing a choice between "holocaust and humiliation." The Russian leader knew that fear of Soviet retaliation against Berlin had been a primary motive for Kennedy's failure to save the Bay of Pigs invasion. JFK's cut-and-run approach in that instance convinced Khrushchev that the young American leader would fold even faster if he found his tender parts in a vise over Berlin.

Khrushchev got his chance to squeeze Kennedy hard on this issue during their first face-to-face confrontation at the Vienna Summit in June 1961. That meeting had hardly gotten underway when the Soviet premier began to complain about Washington's "impossible" position on Berlin and Germany. He declared that by staying in Berlin, remilitarizing West Germany, and feeding Bonn's dreams of reunification, America was creating the preconditions for a new world war. Why did not Washington simply accept the fact that Germany was now divided and Berlin a legitimate part of the new East German state? Glaring at Kennedy, he said that he wanted to reach an agreement "with *you*," but if he could not, he would sign a peace treaty with the GDR. Then "all commitments stemming from Germany's surrender will become invalid. This would include all institutions, occupation rights, and access to Berlin, including the corridors."

Before coming to Vienna, Kennedy had been advised by Allan Lightner, the U.S. minister in West Berlin, to tell Khrushchev that the "Soviets should keep their hands off Berlin." This, in effect, is what he proceeded to do. While thanking the chairman for being so "frank," he reminded him that "the discussion here is not only about the legal situation but also about the practical facts, which affect very much our national security." America was in Berlin "not because of someone's sufferance," but because "we fought our way" there. If the United States and its allies were to leave West Berlin, "Europe would be abandoned as well. So when we are talking about West Berlin, we are also talking about Western Europe."

Having expected at least *some* give from Kennedy, Khrushchev became increasingly angry, lecturing him like a schoolchild on the high stakes at play in Berlin. The former Nazi capital, he said, was "the most dangerous place in the world." Upping his ante in metaphors and mixing them prodigiously, he warned that he was determined "to perform an operation on this sore spot, to eliminate this thorn, this ulcer." By signing a peace treaty with East Germany, Moscow would "impede the revanchists in West Germany who want a new war . . ." Slamming his hand on the table, he shouted: "I want peace. But if you want war, that is your problem."

Despite a regimen of amphetamines prescribed by a quack doctor for his Addison's Disease, Kennedy remained calm under the barrage. "It is you, and not I, who wants to force a change," he replied. America would not abandon Berlin. If, as a result, Moscow followed through on its threats and signed a peace treaty with East Germany in December, it would be "a cold winter," he said grimly.

Actually, it might well have been a *hot* winter, for if the East Germans had indeed gotten their treaty and then decided to celebrate it by kicking the Western powers out of Berlin, they would have had a major fight on their hands. Although Kennedy was actually quite ambivalent about Berlin, fuming in private that it seemed "particularly stupid to risk killing a million Americans over an argument about access rights on an Autobahn," he was (like Eisenhower) determined that West Berlin would not be lost on his watch. He would send armed troops down that Autobahn rather than abandon the city to a fate under Communism. There would be no Bay of Pigs on the banks of the Spree.

On the other hand, if a solution could be found in Berlin that did not involve Western abandonment of the city, Kennedy was all for it. He even sympathized with the Soviets' dilemma in Germany—with their frustration at watching their prize client being steadily drained of its best and brightest citizens and thereby becoming a liability rather than an asset to Moscow. "You can't blame Khrushchev for being sore about that," Kennedy admitted.

A "solution" to the Berlin crisis was found on August 13, 1961. In the early morning hours of that day, East German soldiers and police began stringing bales of barbed wire along the sector line between West and East Berlin. Immediately thereafter the wire was replaced by concrete blocks. The Cold War's most famous piece of architecture was taking shape before the eyes of an astonished—and frightened—world. If ever the tensions of prolonged political confrontation were to boil over into open conflict, this seemed to be the most likely moment.

There was in fact considerable pressure on the Western powers to take forceful countermeasures. West Berliners, including West Berlin's dynamic young mayor, Willy Brandt, were demanding action. The Allied garrisons in Berlin, they said, should immediately knock down the horrible wall, with tanks if necessary. Unable to do much about the wall themselves, West Berliners vented their frustration by attacking the Soviet War Memorial in the British sector just to the west of the Brandenburg Gate. The Soviet soldiers guarding the memorial might have been killed had British occupation troops not rushed to their rescue—one of the more ironic twists in that confusing and emotional time.

If the Western Allied garrisons had indeed decided to move against the East German wall builders, as the West Berliners were crying out for them to do, the Soviets were prepared to react forcefully. They had circled Berlin with troops and put their rocket forces on high alert. They hoped that these measures would be sufficient to deter the West from taking any military action, such as attacking the wall or sending troops over the East German border. But if the deterrent did not work, the Soviet forces had orders not just to protect the nascent wall but to crush the Allied garrisons and the entire Western enclave in Berlin. This they certainly could have done, for Western military strength in the city was paltry compared to Soviet might in the area.

The Western powers, however, had no intention of knocking down the Berlin Wall. This structure, after all, did not force them out of Berlin, it merely fenced the East Germans in. President Kennedy, we should remember, had never made any commitments to the entire city of Berlin, only to *West* Berlin. (Later, when he gave his famous speech in the city, he really should have said: *"Ich bin ein* West *Berliner."*) By stabilizing the situation in East Germany, the wall promised to defuse a very explosive situation. Moreover, while it was something of an embarrassment for the West to stand idly by while the wall went up, the thing was a much greater embarrassment for the East Germans and Soviets, who had been forced to put a fence around their "Workers' Paradise" to keep all the workers from running away. (Not that the Communists admitted to this humiliation: they called the wall an "antifascist protective barrier," insisting it was there to protect the security of the GDR.) In short, the West could not have asked for a greater propaganda coup, a more striking symbol of the bankruptcy—economic and moral—of their Communist adversaries. Once the surprise over the wall's erection had subsided, the primary reaction in the Western capitals was a combination of *Schadenfreude* and relief.

Of course, no Western leader could admit to feeling *relieved* over the erection of the Berlin Wall. There had to be some demonstrative handwringing and expressions of solidarity with the people of Berlin. The Western powers all lodged formal complaints with their former Soviet ally. President Kennedy ordered Vice President Lyndon Johnson to fly to West Berlin to reassure the folks that America was still with them. (Johnson at first refused to go, on the grounds that it was too dangerous.) General Clay, much beloved in West Berlin for his tough stand during the 1948/1949 blockade, was pulled out of retirement and dispatched to Berlin as Kennedy's personal representative in the city.

Sending Clay to Berlin turned out to be almost a little *too* demonstrative, for he was determined to show that the United States could still exercise its traditional rights in the city despite the new wall, which in fact he hoped to tear down. When the East Germans started demanding that Americans show passports to enter East Berlin, Clay sent armed jeeps to Checkpoint Charlie to force their way across the border. He followed this up by dispatching ten M-48 tanks to the checkpoint. Alas, the Soviets responded in kind. For several hours the machines stood muzzle to muzzle, with nothing but a flimsy guardrail between them. All the armor was fully loaded, ready to fire. The American commander on the spot admitted that he was worried that a "nervous soldier might acciden-tally discharge his weapon." After seventeen hours, during which rumors abounded that the shooting was about to commence at any moment, but during which the only killing was scored by a pretzel seller who unloaded all his wares to the tankers on both sides, word came from Washington to pull back. Again, the Soviets responded in kind.

Secretary of State Dean Rusk later dismissed this contretemps as "the silly confrontation at Checkpoint Charlie brought on by the macho inclinations of General Clay." The gesture was certainly macho, but hardly without danger. Had an American tank opened fire, either delib-erately or by accident, the Soviets would certainly have fired back, and the wartime partners of yesteryear, who sixteen years before had fa-mously embraced at the Elbe, would have plunged headlong into a slug-out on the Spree, with the chances very good of a much broader conflagration.

We now know that, aside from MAD (the "Mutually Assured De-struction" that a major nuclear exchange was likely to bring), few factors did more to keep the Cold War cold than the erection of the Berlin Wall. After it went up, the level of East-West tension in Europe went down. With the Wall's evolution into a seemingly permanent fixture on the po-litical landscape—not to mention a lucrative tourist attraction and the world's longest art gallery—the primary sites of ideological contention, where the Cold War might yet have turned hot, tended to develop away from Germany and Europe.

ARTHUR WALDRON

CHINA WITHOUT TEARS

If Chiang Kai-shek Hadn't Gambled in 1946

The last what if of this book has to be one of the most poignant. But for the stubborn gamble of one man and bad judgment of another—a genuine American hero—the worst of the Cold War might not have happened. No Korea, no Indochinese War, no Vietnam War, no Cambodia, no crises in the Formosa Strait, no Red Scare in America. More than 100,000 American lives would have been saved, not to mention those of countless Asians. The gambler was the Nationalist leader Chiang Kai-shek—who, at the end of World War II, vowed to eradicate the Communist Chinese presence in Manchuria. Against American advice, he threw in his best troops and in the spring of 1946 seemed on the verge of victory. Suddenly Chiang called a halt, pressured by General George C. Marshall, who was trying to broker peace between the Nationalists and Communists. Chiang's Nationalists *would never regain their momentum, and three years later they would be forced off mainland China. But what if there had been two Chinas, both on the mainland?*

◈   *Arthur Waldron, a specialist in the history of modern China, is a professor of international relations at the University of Pennsylvania and director of Asian studies at the American Enterprise Institute.*

I imagine the Cold War without a "Red China." With its major theater in Central Europe, and that under firm Soviet control, it would probably have been a lot less frightening. Without a Red China supporting him, Kim Il Sung would never have dared invade South Korea. Without a Red China providing active sanctuary, Ho Chi Minh's Communists would never have succeeded in Indochina. Without the division between Communist mainland and anti-Communist Taiwan, the Formosa Strait would never have burst into flame in the 1950s and the 1990s. Without its volatile Asian theater acting as sparkplug, the Cold War would have been far different and far milder.

But is such a possibility even thinkable? It is—because the key event, the Communist conquest of China, would probably never have occurred without the fatal mistake that the nationalist Chinese leader Chiang Kai-shek made in the early summer of 1946.

Late the previous year, after the surrender of Japan, the generalissimo had begun to airlift his best troops into Manchuria, which the Communists had made their stronghold. The Reds resisted, but were no match for the Nationalists' battle-hardened veterans, who moved quickly north, smashing Communist resistance at Sipingjie in May 1946, after a month of fighting. Southern Manchuria was now recovered and the Communists were on the run: On June 6 the Communist commander, Lin Biao, was ordered to prepare the abandonment of Harbin, the security key to the north. But with advanced units already in sight of the city, Chiang Kai-shek halted his attack. It was an error from which he would not recover: He lost his momentum, the Communists had time to regroup and reorganize. His army never reached Harbin. Three years later it was thoroughly beaten and its remnants fled to Taiwan. Chiang had grasped the proverbial defeat from the jaws of victory—with enormous consequences for the rest of Asia felt to this day.

What explains Chiang's action? In two words: American pressure. Chiang's mistake was effectively forced on him by the revered U.S. Army General George C. Marshall, who was then in China on the mission impossible of brokering peace between the Communists and Nationalists. And what of Marshall? He is rightly valued as a soldier and statesman, but in China he was miscast and outmatched. This brave and honorable man walked uncomprehending into the snake pit of Chinese politics. He intended to bring peace, but what he really began was the Cold War in Asia. It was all a terrible surprise.

No one expected the Communists to win in China when Japan abruptly surrendered—reeling under the twin blows of Soviet invasion of Manchuria and U.S. atom bombing of the home islands. When hostilities suddenly ceased, the Communists were mostly holed up in their wartime base at Yanan, far away from the fighting in northern Shaanxi, and in any case lacked heavy military forces. All the foreign powers—the USSR included—recognized Chiang Kai-shek's government at Chongqing as China's sole legitimate authority.

Stalin certainly did not expect the Communists to win. At Yalta he had agreed to secret provisions that gave his forces in Manchuria a privileged administrative and military position and made no reference to Chinese sovereignty in the area. In fact, many people expected Moscow simply to annex the territory, over which Russia and Japan had been struggling since the end of the nineteenth century, and which, in hostile hands, posed a major threat to the Soviet Far Eastern province and the great military port at Vladivostok.

Such reallocation of territory had already been agreed to meet Soviet demands in Europe. Why not in Asia as well? Perhaps the clearest signal came in the wartime best-seller *People on Our Side*, by the fellow-traveling American journalist Edgar Snow. He was almost certainly acting on inside information when he warned his readers to expect Moscow to make just such changes in northeast Asia.

The problem was that the Chinese government would bitterly resist such a solution. Having gone to war with Japan over Manchuria in the first place, it could hardly stand by while the Soviets simply took over Japan's role. So instead of focusing on China proper, where he had problems enough, Chiang Kai-shek and his government turned their attention to the northeast.

Chiang Kai-shek now made his reputation as a soldier in 1925 to 1928 when he recognized a brief window of opportunity in China's north and gambled his southern army on a lightning invasion—the so-called "Northern Expedition," which overthrew the military government in Beijing and established the Republic of China regime at Nanjing. It was a classic *suzhan sujue* operation—"rapidly fought and rapidly decided"—which had long been the preference of Chinese strategists. Assessing the tendencies and propensities of the situation *(shi)* he identified a moment of opportunity *(ji)* and unleashed a strategem *(mou)* designed to use it to win—striking fast, winning a key victory at Wuhan against the north's best, and then snowballing to victory. Chiang was only the second leader ever to conquer China from the south; no mean achievement. His strategy for Manchuria in 1946 rested on the same basic concept.

But Chiang was also controversial and, although Washington was his indispensable ally, he was disliked by many Americans. He spoke not a word of English and was stiff and reserved with foreigners: "Vinegar Joe" Stillwell, the American commander in the China-Burma-India theater, despised him, calling him "the Peanut." Under Chiang's leadership, China had been ruined in a war of futile resistance to Japan—and Chiang was personally blamed for rampant corruption, black marketeering, and violence. The untried Communists looked better to many people, including lots of intelligent and articulate foreigners.

As for the Communists in remote Yanan, strategic opportunity knocked in August 1945 when the Soviet Red Army swept into Manchuria. Strategically, Yanan was nowhere: The Communists had gone there to escape the Nationalist "bandit extermination" campaigns of the 1930s. Its great advantage was proximity to the Mongolian People's Republic, at that time a wholly owned subsidiary of the USSR, effectively under Soviet secret police control—and a final sanctuary should the Nationalists threaten again.

Manchuria was altogether different. Strategically, the territory had always been a key to the control of China proper: the jumping-off place for conquest dynasties, most recently in 1644 when the Manchus, who had given the territory its name, sent their armies through the passes to Beijing and beyond—to establish the great Qing dynasty, which lasted until 1912.

So the decision was easy to move the Communist administration and army into Manchuria behind the Soviet forces. Indeed, the Soviets helped with the move, some of which took place along Soviet-controlled railway lines. But there was a problem. The Soviets paid lip service to the idea that Manchuria was legitimately a part of Nationalist China—and did not recognize the Communists officially at all.

But Red Chinese and Soviets were all Communists—brothers in the international Party—so ways were found to coexist. The Chinese forces were given quarters outside the capital city; they were renamed "local self-defense forces," and their liaison with the Soviets, though good, was "informal." And the Soviets prevented Nationalist forces from entering Manchuria to accept the surrender of the Japanese there.

With the Soviets in control militarily, the Chinese Communists settled down in Manchuria, putting their primary effort into developing a strong civil administrative network. They did not initially concentrate on building up their army. Instead they opened party headquarters in every Manchurian village and town. Probably they expected the Soviet forces to shield them indefinitely.

Meanwhile, the Nationalists—panic stricken about ever getting the Soviets out of Manchuria—embarked on an intensive diplomatic campaign to secure Soviet withdrawal, which eventually succeeded. The stage was set for Chiang Kai-shek's fatal decision.

Suppose Chiang had not contested Soviet and Chinese Communist control of Manchuria? How might Asia have developed? The answer is that something like an East Asian East Germany—a "Chinese Democratic People's Republic"—would almost certainly have emerged in Manchuria, in addition to the Korean Democratic People's Republic that was actually installed in Pyongyang by Soviet troops. But unlike the "People's Republic of China"—that Mao Zedong and his army established in 1949 after a long civil war, this northeastern Red China would have been firmly under Moscow's thumb.

Many Chinese Communist leaders had been educated in the Soviet Union; more still looked to the USSR as the model for China, believing, as Zhou Enlai put it, that "the present of the USSR is the future of China." Even Mao—uneducated, untraveled, and without Soviet connections—instinctively "leaned to one side," toward the USSR, early in the Cold War. So the Chinese Party leadership would almost certainly have settled for—more than that, welcomed—the opportunity to function like Ulbricht's Germans to create a Socialist China under Soviet auspices. They expected as much: That is what their emphasis on administration tells us.

And if Mao had proved intransigent, as Tito did in Yugoslavia? When East European Communists proved difficult, they often disappeared or were "suicided" or otherwise gotten rid of. The same would probably have happened in a Soviet-influenced Chinese client state. Mao's control of the party was by no means absolute. Plenty of Communists hated him. In the early 1950s the USSR evidently supported plots in Manchuria against Beijing. Those failed. But under these circumstances, Moscow would probably have gotten its way. Yugoslavia, after all, was geographically well defended and had its own army—which was never under Soviet control. But Manchuria was almost surrounded by the USSR and Soviet naval and military facilities had been guaranteed even by the Nationalists.

Moreover, the Red China in Manchuria would almost certainly have done well—at least initially. Unlike much of the Chinese heartland, Manchuria was rich: Its land was fertile and not overpopulated; its resources, including coal and steel, were abundant; an extensive industrial plant, built by the Japanese, was already in place; a superb port at Dalian linked it to the maritime world, while the Chinese Eastern railway linked up with the Soviet rail network. Its economy was already developed.

As the Chinese civil war heated up, American advisers to Chiang Kai-shek advised him not to try to take Manchuria. They recognized that it would be a risk to reach too far and might well undermine his good chances of keeping control of China proper. Moscow probably expected the United States to keep Chiang in line on this point and thus assure a non-Communist regime in China proper. Such a situation would push the Communists in Manchuria into Moscow's arms.

Good boundaries make good neighbors. That was clear as World War II ended in Europe, and the Allied and Red Armies advanced up to—but not beyond—agreed lines of demarcation. Local hotheads—whether Communist or anti-Communist—had no luck in embroiling the great powers in conflict. The only dangerous ambiguities were over Berlin—and Yugoslavia, for reasons of its own. Otherwise what could have been a collision of two massive armies proved remarkably quiet.

Had the Asian issues been hashed out as carefully in advance, the same might have happened there. The partition of China into a small Communist and a large non-Communist state could have been agreed by the powers in a way that would have removed from Mao's hands—as from Kim Il Sung's and Ho Chi Minh's—the leverage to bring great power patrons into local disputes. The result would have been a more peaceful Asia.

"You started it!" That was one of the Communist charges leveled as China's civil war escalated into massive fighting between 1945 and 1949—and it had merit. For Chiang's Manchurian expedition was the flare that set the whole country aflame.

At the war's end, Chiang's best troops were in the China-Burma-India theater (CBI). Veterans of the losing and then winning campaigns against the Japanese in the Southeast Asian jungles, they had been reequipped and trained by the Americans in India. They also had some of the brightest and bravest Chinese officers, notably General Sun Lijen, a graduate of the Virginia Military Institute. The New First and New Sixth armies were put into Manchuria: These forces were as tough as well-tempered steel, incomparably stronger than anything the Communists had. Furthermore they had powerful artillery that far outmatched the lightly armed Communist guerrilla forces.

Chiang also had an air force. He shared the Chinese fascination with the most advanced military technology and from the start of the war with Japan had temperamentally favored the airpower visions of General Claire Chennault over the earthbound soldiering urged by Roosevelt's envoy, Stillwell.

So a plan modeled on the "Northern Expedition" of the late 1920s began to take shape in Chiang's mind. The Communists in Manchuria were not expecting war. If the Soviets could be persuaded to withdraw and then the heavy divisions from CBI thrown in, the Nationalist armed force would almost certainly cut through the Communists in Manchuria like the proverbial knife through butter. Meanwhile, airpower could overcome the nemesis of land war in Asia—logistics. Using air transport, Chiang ought to be able to leapfrog his forces behind the Communists and connect and resupply scattered garrisons in the vast territory.

It was a vision not unlike the one that the United States would take to Vietnam two decades later, and initially it seemed to work. The So-viets agreed to withdraw and the Nationalists poured in, first by air, starting in the autumn of 1945. They rolled over all before them. The Communist forces were caught by surprise, unprepared and unequipped for this kind of battle. Up and along the railway line, the Nationalist forces moved north. At Sipingjie, a key junction midway up Manchuria, they fought a month's pitched battle before the Communists cracked: Lin Biao, their commander, threw human wave after human wave against the Nationalist firepower, including 100,000 factory workers from Changchun, a truly desperate throw. By May 18, 40,000 Communists—half their force—were dead and Lin fled to the north.

What followed next is rather like Hitler's famous "Halt Order," which stopped the Wehrmacht as it closed in on the defeated British at

Dunkirk—turning what should have been a decisive German victory into a strategic defeat.

General Marshall was at this point attempting the impossible task of brokering a coalition government between Mao's Communists and Chiang's Nationalists. Nowhere had it been agreed that Chiang would not invade Manchuria. But the Communists at the talks objected vociferously, maintaining that by his surprise attack Chiang had undermined the trust and cooperation necessary for a peaceful resolution. Marshall secured one truce in January but it broke down quickly; now the Communists pressed him to act, for they realized that he—and not their own army—was the only force left that could stop Chiang.

Marshall listened. With all the power of a sole ally, rich and overwhelmingly strong in a ruined world (and in his own mind, some unrealistic ideas), Marshall pressured Chiang to halt his advance—and Chiang did.

When his incredulous commanders begged him to reconsider, telling him that Harbin in Nationalist hands ensured a total victory over Communist military forces in Manchuria, Chiang became very angry. To his supreme commander he said, "You say that taking the city will be easy, but if you knew the reasons why we can't take it, then you would understand why not taking it is not easy at all." Later Chiang would call this the worst mistake he ever made in dealing with the Communists.

Had the Chinese leader refused Marshall's request, one can imagine him actually succeeding in his attempt to deliver a knock-out blow to the Communists and presenting the world with a fait accompli that would have won not only Washington, but Moscow as well, to his side. Or one can imagine his initial triumph going bad, as the Communists reorganized and attacked his extended supply lines. One thing is certain, though: The decision to halt would remove the one chance Chiang had of actually winning the war militarily.

The military momentum of the Nationalist advance was lost. Like Sisyphus, the Nationalist army pushed almost to the top but not quite—and then began to fall back. Suppose, now, that Chiang had not contested

Manchuria. His forces concentrated in China proper would have been much stronger—probably decisively so. Furthermore, his relations with both the Soviet Union and the United States would have been greatly improved. Marshall's fury would then have turned on the Communists if fighting continued in China proper while the Soviets, seeing that Chiang was willing to allow them effective control over the northeast, would probably have cooperated with him to corral the Chinese Red Army and government within the northeast territory.

Mao's forces would have been effectively at the mercy of the Soviet garrisons in Manchuria and as their administration and economy developed, increasingly integrated with Soviet authority and economy in Siberia and the Far East.

Furthermore, this would have been to the liking, if not of Mao himself, who dreamed of ruling all of China, certainly of most of the leadership. Revolution across China would, in any case, not have been ruled out—only postponed until, as the Soviet economists confidently predicted, a global collapse of capitalism dropped the remaining non-Communist states into their lap, like the proverbial ripe fruits.

Such had been Stalin's argument when the French Communist party asked about taking power after the defeat of the Nazis. Wait a few years, he said, relying on the prognostications of his economic gurus. A world crisis is coming. In the meantime, don't unnecessarily stir up the British and the United States.

But of course the gurus were wrong. The global depression that he and others, including many American economists, expected would follow the Second World War as the Great Depression had followed the First, never happened. Instead the free-market economies revived, first slowly, then—as was remarked at the time—miraculously. In Germany came the *Wirtschaftswunder*, or "economic miracle," and in Japan a remarkable climb from the geegaws manufactured in the occupation period to the highest of high tech and high quality production. Hong Kong, a sleepy and underpopulated colonial port adjoining southernmost China, rocketed from abject poverty to relative affluence—until by the end of the century its per capita income surpassed that of Britain, its erstwhile colonial master.

Suppose that Chiang had not invaded Manchuria and that instead a stable partition had taken place. Shanghai—the greatest economic center of East Asia—would have been free to trade in the 1950s, instead of shut tight by both the antiforeign Chinese Communist regime and the Cold War Western embargo. The immense markets and resources, human and material, of the Yangzi valley would have joined in the Asian economic miracle. When China abandoned the worst of Communist economic policy in the 1980s and opened to world trade the results were staggering—double-digit growth rates, massive exports, record-breaking economic boom. It could all have happened twenty years sooner, if the Nationalists had continued to hold China proper.

And that boom would have transformed the strategic equation in China just as it did in Germany and Korea. In Korea the north had traditionally been industrial and the south agricultural, so partition initially favored Pyongyang. But South Korea eventually outstripped the north totally—so that by the 1990s the Communist half was a starving wreck, while the southern was a prosperous democratic state. Likewise the failure of the East German economy and West Germany's success prepared the way for the unification of the two states after 1989.

Manchuria was the Chinese center of heavy industry, of mining, of steelmaking. Initially China proper had nothing to match it. But suppose partition had worked. By 1960 or 1970 the south of China would almost certainly have been surging ahead. Like the industrial resources Communism inherited or created elsewhere, Manchuria would soon have turned into a rusting junkyard under socialist management; just as surely, South China would have become a "dragon economy."

Chiang and the Nationalists would have been more than compensated for their initial sacrifice. By the time the generalissimo died in 1975, his China would have decisively dwarfed the "Red China" in the northeast.

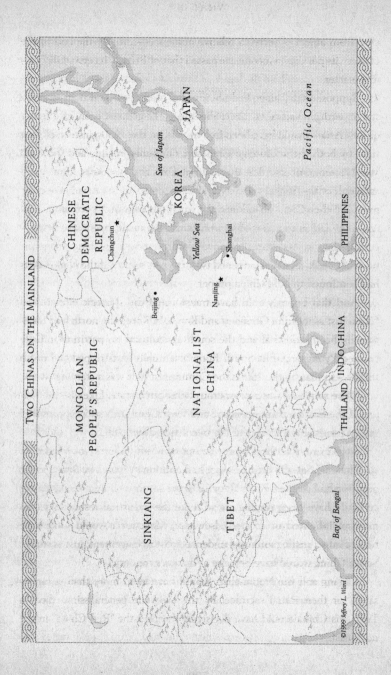

TWO CHINAS ON THE MAINLAND

MONGOLIAN
PEOPLE'S REPUBLIC

CHINESE
DEMOCRATIC
REPUBLIC

Changchun

Beijing

SINKIANG

NATIONALIST
CHINA

Nanjing

Shanghai

TIBET

Yellow Sea

KOREA

Sea of Japan

JAPAN

Pacific Ocean

PHILIPPINES

INDOCHINA

THAILAND

Bay of Bengal

©1999 Jeffrey L. Ward

The pattern of current relations between the small Nationalist-ruled Taiwan and Beijing would have been reversed. The leverage would have been almost entirely in the hands of the non-Communist China proper—as "Red China" became dependent on its prosperous southern neighbor for markets, investment, and technology—and increasingly affected by cross-border radio and television and the greater degree of freedom in the south. Like the German Democratic Republic facing West Germany, the "Democratic People's Republic of China" would have been beleaguered by the 1970s.

But there was no partition. Chiang threw his troops into Manchuria—and almost as soon as that move was made, his dream began to crumble.

The "halt order" was arguably the biggest setback, but other dangers lay just below the surface. Above all it was unrealistic to expect the Communist forces simply to roll over and play dead. Manchuria was their chosen territory, for which they had no choice but to fight—"death ground," as Sun Zi calls it. And fight they did. Tens of thousands of Communists died in the long attritional battle that followed from 1946 to 1948. Lin Biao, the Communist commander, shed rivers of blood to stop the Nationalist advance by putting soldiers in its path.

Lin and the Communists also did what had to be done to improve their forces and match the Nationalists' advantages. Soviet and abandoned Japanese artillery were incorporated into Communist forces; an artillery school was created. As the Communist forces became heavier, the battles became costlier for all. Chiang's troops could no longer count on outclassing their opponents; with antiaircraft artillery directed against Nationalist air transport, the key lines of communication that linked the Nationalist-held cities in Manchuria were cut. Hundreds of thousands of Chiang's best troops were effectively hors de combat. They were tied down, in futile attritional defense of an overextended position, wasting away and unable to concentrate or participate in the active war that would lead to decision.

In Manchuria, the Communists had two critical advantages. First, this was their primary theater—the key, as they well understood. They could concentrate on it—while Chiang had to chase all over the territory of China whenever the Communists launched an attack. Second, the Soviet position in north Manchuria provided active sanctuary for the Communist forces. They could be supplied easily and take refuge when necessary. The Nationalist lines of communication, by air and sea, were by contrast fragile and easily broken.

The Communists drove these advantages home. They stirred up guerrilla insurgency in Shandong to draw off Nationalist forces that could otherwise have gone to Manchuria. They pinned down Nationalist forces all over China in positional defense—and then, as they strengthened their own conventional strength, gradually chewed them up.

The result was like a termite attack on a once-strong building. Appearances were not bad for the Nationalists from 1945 to 1947. Seemingly impressive victories were scored; the appearance of rule existed over most of China's territory. But the military ratios were moving against them. As time passed they were growing weaker and the Communists stronger. In 1948, Manchuria was lost as hundreds of thousands of Nationalist troops, cut off and isolated in dozens of garrisons, had no choice but to surrender. In China proper they could have been the margin of victory. Now the tide turned the other way. In 1949, a powerful series of blows from the now-superior Communist forces brought the whole Nationalist military edifice crashing down.

The shock of the Communist victory in China—the famous "loss of China"—kick-started the McCarthy period, the roughest part of the Cold War in the United States, and it was followed—literally a few months later in June 1950—by the North Korean invasion of South Korea. This crisis was far worse than anything that had happened in Europe and it threw relations with Moscow into deep freeze.

We now know that the astonishing Communist victory in China inspired Kim Il Sung in his blitzkrieg against Seoul. We also know that Stalin and Mao signed off on the Korean invasion, both persuaded that Kim Il Sung might well succeed. Having sat back and done nothing as

China fell, after all, how likely was Washington to do anything when little South Korea was under attack? But a successful partition in China would probably have meant that Kim would never have made his plan. And had he, surely the partition in China would have been a very strong argument against it? The Korean War made the Cold War icy—but without the Manchurian gamble, no such war would ever have been fought.

The defense of Taiwan also drove a wedge between Moscow and Washington. Without a Communist victory in China, this problem would never have existed.

Finally, with an anti-Communist China on its borders, Vietnam would never have gone Communist. Chinese advice and supply, as well as active sanctuary, were critical to the Vietminh victory over the French at Dien Bien Phu. Without a divided Vietnam there would never have been an American role in Vietnam—and the exacerbation of the Cold War that followed. Indeed, the "wars" in the Cold War were almost entirely in Asia, and they grew out of the big Asian Communist victory in China. Asia was the motor that moved the Cold War from crisis to crisis.

A milder Cold War. A bigger and stronger non-Communist world. An earlier and more rapid economic recovery in Asia. A huge Eastern European-style bankruptcy on the USSR's eastern borders, as well as in the Red Chinese state. It all probably adds up, in our counterhistory, to an earlier collapse of Communism and a more decisive end to the Cold War.

Keeping the Red Chinese client state afloat would have drained Moscow's coffers. The Communist regime would have grown weaker. Had Mao been eliminated, a far less charismatic leadership would have been in place, one supported by the Soviets.

By the 1970s, the stage would have been set for "Free China" to absorb "Red China" economically, politically, socially—in every respect, just as dramatically as West Germany swallowed East Germany, and perhaps sooner. What an irony that would have been—for Chiang Kai-shek and his regime would then have achieved their long-standing goal of national unification, precisely as the result of an action—not invading Manchuria—that at the time they thought would have split their country irrevocably.

A QUAGMIRE AVOIDED?

If President Eisenhower had approved Operation Vulture to rescue the encircled French fortress of Dien Bien Phu, the French might have won the battle and the war, averting a second Vietnam War, in which America was mired for a dozen years. Dien Bien Phu was a small mountain outpost in northern Vietnam, on the border with Laos. French forces occupied the town in late 1953 to cut off Vietminh supply lines and to maintain a base against enemy raids. General Giap, the Vietminh military leader, saw this isolated base, close to the borders of China and Laos, as a sitting duck. He proceeded with classic encirclement tactics, surrounding the French with 40,000 men, cutting off all the roads into the base, so that it could only be supplied by air, and bringing up heavy artillery to pound the French lines. Operation Vulture contemplated sending B-29s from bases in Okinawa and the Philippines to carpet bomb Vietminh positions around Dien Bien Phu. In January 1954, the French did appeal to Ike for twenty B-26 bombers and 400 technicians, and he gave them half those numbers. In March, the president agreed to furnish the French with some C-119 Flying Boxcars that could drop napalm and reveal Giap's artillery positions. But when the French asked for two or three atomic bombs, Ike said no. The mantra in Congress was "No more Koreas." Officers in the Pentagon had already formed a betting pool on when the fort would fall. It surrendered on May 7, in one of those decisive defeats that radiates far beyond the military importance to break the will of a nation and force the conclusion of a war. Two months later came a cease-fire and the partition of Vietnam. A decade later came America's turn to fight a war in Vietnam.

◆ *Ted Morgan, who served in the French army, is the author of A COVERT LIFE, a biography of the Communist leader (and later, CIA agent) Jay Lovestone.*

◆ ROBERT L. O'CONNELL ◆

THE END

How quickly we forget. Having passed most of our lives in the shadow of the nuclear standoff and only recently found our way out of the Cold War and into the sunlight, we succumb to sweet oblivion. Who today seriously asks: "What if the sword had dropped?" Should the Cuban Missile Crisis be broached, wise heads stand ready to reassure us that its real lesson was how well deterrence and strategic communication really worked. Perhaps. But they fail to mention another crisis of a similar magnitude—an event in which there was not only no communication, but, in fact, one side barely knew what was happening.

In early November 1983, during a NATO exercise known as Able Archer, American and British monitors were astonished to note a sharp increase in the volume and urgency of Eastern bloc communications, signs indicative of warnings sent of an imminent nuclear attack. It was no mirage. The occupants of the Kremlin were on the edge of believing that the West was about to launch a preemptive nuclear strike.

The delusion went back to the early 1980s, when Vladimir Kryuchkov, then head of the KGB and future leader of the failed coup against Gorbachev, became planning a surprise attack—presumably with their new Pershing II missiles, whose earth-penetrator warheads and short flight times seemed tailor-made for a decapitating first strike. On his advice, the Soviet Union's leadership mobilized their intelligence assets in an antic campaign to find signs of war preparations.

These fears were without substance. The Pershing II's were yet to be deployed and had never been tested at ranges necessary to hit Moscow. This didn't matter to the antique leaders of the Kremlin presiding over a crumbling empire—particularly their chairman Yuri Andropov, graduate of the KGB and a sick man. They responded to their system's mounting troubles with anger and unbridled suspicion.

U.S.-Soviet relations continued to spiral downward. By June 1983, Andropov described them as "marked by confrontation unprecedented in the entire postwar period." Less than two months later, a Russian interceptor deliberately shot down a passenger-laden Korean airliner, supposedly on a spy mission. By November, Andropov was near death, and just who was in charge is open to question. But apparently his colleagues in the Kremlin viewed Able Archer as potentially the last straw.

Days passed and nothing happened. Able Archer wound down and still nothing happened. One by one the Eastern bloc units stood down from their alert. Gradually, it must have dawned on the Soviet leaders that they would live to see 1984. Meanwhile, in the United States, years would pass before there was an understanding of why the East had reacted in such a bizarre fashion. Once again, we had been eyeball to eyeball—only this time one side was hallucinating and the other was dozing. We did make it through, but history had been on cruise control. The war scare of 1983 might have been the end.

✦ *Robert O'Connell is the author of a history of the origin of war, RIDE OF THE SECOND HORSEMAN.*